Applying Critical Thinking to Modern Media

Applying Critical Thinking to Modern Media

EFFECTIVE REASONING ABOUT CLAIMS IN THE NEW MEDIA LANDSCAPE

Lewis Vaughn

New York   Oxford
OXFORD UNIVERSITY PRESS

Oxford University Press is a department of the University of Oxford.
It furthers the University's objective of excellence in research, scholarship,
and education by publishing worldwide. Oxford is a registered trade mark of
Oxford University Press in the UK and certain other countries.

Published in the United States of America by Oxford University Press
198 Madison Avenue, New York, NY 10016, United States of America.

Copyright © 2021 by Oxford University Press.

> For titles covered by Section 112 of the US Higher Education Opportunity Act, please visit www.oup.com/us/he for the latest information about pricing and alternate formats.

All rights reserved. No part of this publication may be reproduced, stored in
a retrieval system, or transmitted, in any form or by any means, without the
prior permission in writing of Oxford University Press, or as expressly permitted
by law, by license, or under terms agreed with the appropriate reproduction
rights organization. Inquiries concerning reproduction outside the scope of the
above should be sent to the Rights Department, Oxford University Press,
at the address above.

You must not circulate this work in any other form
and you must impose this same condition on any acquirer.

Library of Congress Cataloging-in-Publication Data

Names: Vaughn, Lewis, author.
Title: Applying critical thinking to modern media : effective reasoning about claims in the new media / Lewis Vaughn.
Description: New York : Oxford University Press, 2020. | Includes index. | Summary: "This is the only book that teaches critical thinking skills by applying them to the consumption of modern media. The active involvement with this vitally important area enhances student engagement and learning and prepares students to be independent and intelligent consumers of information that they encounter in their daily lives"— Provided by publisher.
Identifiers: LCCN 2020008766 (print) | LCCN 2020008767 (ebook) | ISBN 9780190063405 (paperback) | ISBN 9780190085902 | ISBN 9780190063450 (ebook)
Subjects: LCSH: Critical thinking—Textbooks. | Mass media—Textbooks.
Classification: LCC B809.2 .V39 2020 (print) | LCC B809.2 (ebook) | DDC 160—dc23
LC record available at https://lccn.loc.gov/2020008766
LC ebook record available at https://lccn.loc.gov/2020008767

Printing number: 9 8 7 6 5 4 3 2 1
Printed by LSC Communications, Inc.
United States of America

Brief Contents

Preface xiii

1. Critical Thinking and the Challenges of Modern Media 3
2. Claims, Reasons, and Arguments 27
3. Obstacles to Critical Thinking 65
4. Fake News 91
5. Media Bias 121
6. Manipulation through Fallacies and Rhetoric 147
7. Experts and Evidence 185
8. Science, Nonscience, and the Media 215
9. Advertising: Commercial and Political 283

Appendix A: For Further Reading 304
Appendix B: Answers to Exercises 307
Glossary 311
Notes 316
Index 323

Contents

Preface xiii

CHAPTER 1 **Critical Thinking and the Challenges of Modern Media 3**

1.1 Turning Information into Knowledge 4
   CRITICAL THINKING AND PERSONAL FREEDOM 6
1.2 Hazards of the Infosphere 7
1.3 Post-Truth 12
   FACT AND OPINION 14
1.4 Media Illiteracy 16
   GOING WITH YOUR GUT: I JUST *KNOW*! 18

Review Notes 19
Key Terms 21
Exercises 21
Capstone 24

CHAPTER 2 **Claims, Reasons, and Arguments 27**

2.1 Claims and Reasons 29
   HOW TO WIN EVERY ARGUMENT 30
2.2 Reasons and Arguments 31
2.3 Argument Structure 37
   THE SMART WAY TO ARGUE ONLINE 41
2.4 Argument Patterns 42
   Deductive Arguments 43
   DEDUCTIVE PATTERNS WORTH KNOWING 46
   Enumerative Induction 47

Analogical Induction 48
Inference to the Best Explanation 49
◀── DON'T ARGUE WITH TROLLS 51

2.5 Assessing Long Arguments 52

The Case for Discrimination 53
◀── NO ARGUMENTS, JUST FLUFF 55

Review Notes 57
Key Terms 58
Exercises 58
Capstone 62

CHAPTER 3 Obstacles to Critical Thinking 65

3.1 All Hail the Self 66
◀── IS IT WRONG TO BELIEVE WITHOUT GOOD REASONS? 68

3.2 All Hail My Group 69
◀── RACISM IS GROUP THINKING AT ITS WORST—BUT WHAT IS IT? 72

3.3 The Toughest Mental Obstacles 73
Denying Contrary Evidence 73
Looking for Confirming Evidence 74
Motivated Reasoning 76
Preferring Available Evidence 77

3.4 Your Brain on Social Media 78
Mere Exposure Effect 78
Illusion-of-Truth Effect 79
False Consensus Effect 80
The Dunning-Kruger Effect 80
◀── THE BACKFIRE EFFECT 82

Review Notes 83
Key Terms 84
Exercises 85
Capstone 88

CHAPTER 4 **Fake News 91**

4.1 Taxonomy of Misinformation 94

◁ A FAKE NEWS "MASTERPIECE" 95

4.2 Telling Fake from Real 96

Read Laterally 97

◁ THE ETHICS OF SHARING FAKE NEWS 102

Read Critically 102

Use Google and Wikipedia Carefully 103

◁ DISGUISED, HATEFUL SOURCES 104

Check Your Own Biases 105

◁ TRUSTWORTHY FACT-CHECKERS 105

4.3 Fake Images 106

4.4 Deepfakes 112

Review Notes 114
Key Terms 115
Exercises 116
Capstone 118

CHAPTER 5 **Media Bias 121**

5.1 Objectivity and Bias 122

5.2 Opinion, Analysis, and Advocacy 127

5.3 Liberal and Conservative Bias 130

◁ CAN YOU TELL THE DIFFERENCE BETWEEN FACT AND OPINION? 131

◁ BIAS AND INCONSISTENCY 134

5.4 Commercial Bias 135

Pandering 135

Sensationalism 136

Skewed Focus 136

Chasing Advertising 137

◁ BIAS AND ACCURACY OF SELECTED SOURCES 137

Review Notes 141
Key Terms 142
Exercises 142
Capstone 145

CONTENTS ix

CHAPTER 6 Manipulation through Fallacies and Rhetoric 147

6.1 Fallacies: Irrelevant Premises 149
Genetic Fallacy 149
Composition and Division 150
Appeal to the Person 152
▸ HOW TO RESPOND TO AD HOMINEM ATTACKS 156
Equivocation 157
Appeal to Popularity 157
Appeal to Tradition 158
Appeal to Ignorance 159
▸ CAN YOU PROVE A NEGATIVE? 161
Appeal to Emotion 161
Red Herring 163
Straw Man 164
▸ FALLACIES WITH IRRELEVANT PREMISES 165
Two Wrongs Make a Right 166

6.2 Fallacies: Unacceptable Premises 166
Begging the Question 166
False Dilemma 168
Decision-Point Fallacy 169
Slippery Slope 170
▸ FALLACIES WITH UNACCEPTABLE PREMISES 172
Hasty Generalization 172
Faulty Analogy 173

6.3 Persuaders: Rhetorical Moves 173
▸ WHOSE PANTS ARE ON FIRE? 174
Innuendo 175
Euphemisms and Dysphemisms 175
Stereotyping 176
▸ WHO IS MORE INTOLERANT—LIBERALS OR CONSERVATIVES? 177
Ridicule 178
Rhetorical Definitions 179

Review Notes 180
Key Terms 180
Exercises 181
Capstone 183

CHAPTER 7 Experts and Evidence 185

7.1 Experts and Nonexperts 187
- ARE DOCTORS EXPERTS? 191

7.2 Judging Experts 191
- DO NONEXPERTS KNOW BEST? 194
- FALLACIOUS APPEAL TO (QUESTIONABLE) AUTHORITY 196

7.3 Experts and Personal Experience 196
- Impairment 197
- Expectation 198
- Causal Confusions 199
  - Misidentifying Relevant Factors 199
  - EYEWITNESS TESTIMONY AND WRONGFUL CONVICTIONS 200
  - Mishandling Multiple Factors 200
  - Being Misled by Coincidence 201
  - Confusing Cause with Temporal Order 202
  - Confusing Cause and Effect 204
  - THE DEADLY *POST HOC* FALLACY 204

7.4 Innumeracy and Probability 205
- HIERARCHY OF RELIABILITY 207

Review Notes 208
Key Terms 209
Exercises 210
Capstone 213

CHAPTER 8 Science, Nonscience, and the Media 215

8.1 What Science Is and Is Not 217
- Science Is Not Ideology 218
- Science Is Not Motivated Reasoning 219
- Science Is Not Technology 219
- SEVEN WARNING SIGNS OF BOGUS SCIENCE 220

8.2 How Science Is Done 221
- NONINTERVENTION (POPULATION) STUDIES 226

8.3 Judging Scientific Theories 226
Theories and Consistency 228
Theories and Criteria 228
- Testability 230
- Fruitfulness 231
- Scope 232
- Simplicity 233
- Conservatism 234

◂— WHAT'S WRONG WITH CONSPIRACY THEORIES? 238

8.4 Telling Good Theories from Bad 238
Copernicus versus Ptolemy 241
Evolution versus Creationism 243

◂— CAN WE SEE EVOLUTION? 246

◂— EVOLUTION AND INTELLIGENT DESIGN 248

Climate Change 249

◂— IS IT TOO LATE TO PREVENT CLIMATE CHANGE? 254

◂— IF THE WORLD IS WARMING, WHY ARE SOME WINTERS AND SUMMERS STILL VERY COLD? 259

8.5 How the Media Get Science Wrong 260
Hyping the Science 261
Misunderstanding the Science 263
Is All Health News Wrong? 265

◂— EXPERT REVIEW OF ARTICLE 9: "IS EVERYTHING YOU THINK YOU KNOW ABOUT DEPRESSION WRONG?" 267

8.6 Scientific Opinion Polls 268

◂— HOW SURVEY QUESTIONS GO WRONG 270

◂— MEAN, MEDIAN, AND MODE 272

◂— TRUSTWORTHY SOURCES IN SCIENCE AND MEDICINE 273

Review Notes 273
Key Terms 275
Exercises 275
Capstone 280

CHAPTER 9 Advertising 283

9.1 How Advertising Works 284

9.2 Internet Advertising 286

⬅ OLD SCHOOL ADVERTISING TRICKS 290

9.3 Political Advertising 292

    Falsely Portraying a Democratic Candidate as Anti-ICE 293
    Misleading the Public about a Politician's Voting Record 294
    Telling an Old Lie about Medicare 295
    Paying Women and Children to Cross the U.S. Border? 295
    The Mashup of Two Separate Interviews? 296
    President Trump Loves Nuclear War? 296
    Emma Gonzalez Tears Up the U.S. Constitution? 296

Review Notes 298
Key Terms 298
Exercises 299
Capstone 302

Appendix A: For Further Reading 304

Appendix B: Answers to Exercises 307

Glossary 311

Notes 316

Index 323

Preface

The Information Age was supposed to make us smarter, better informed, more open-minded, more democratic, and more tolerant. It has made available to us vast oceans of information, nearly infinite networks of social connections, and the ability to circulate our thoughts—whether wisdom or gibberish—to everyone on the planet almost instantaneously. But in many ways the technology's powerful advantages have been turned against us, leaving many of us without the skills, knowledge, and habits of mind to use them effectively.

Research has shown (and a lot of teachers have affirmed) that many of today's students—those who were practically born texting friends and surfing the net—lack the skills to understand media messages, use critical thinking to evaluate their truth, check the credibility of their sources, and effectively and responsibly formulate media messages of their own. For example, researchers at the Stanford History Education Group spent a year and a half assessing the ability of middle school, high school, and college students in twelve states to "judge the credibility of information that floods young people's smartphones, tablets, and computers." They concluded that "young people's ability to reason about the information on the internet can be summed up in one word: *bleak*. . . . [W]hen it comes to evaluating information that flows through social media channels, they are easily duped."

Applying Critical Thinking to Modern Media addresses these problems clearly and directly by (1) emphasizing the habits of mind that are prerequisites for making sense of today's media landscape and (2) developing these dispositions by showing students how to apply critical thinking skills to the creation and evaluation of media messages of all kinds.

The habits of mind fostered here include the following:

- Reasonable skepticism—the habit of refusing to accept a claim unless there are legitimate reasons for doing so and resisting the temptation to automatically believe
- Metacognition—the ability to reflect critically on one's own thinking and values

- Overview perspective—the willingness to evaluate claims and ideas in the context of all relevant information and viewpoints
- Openness—the readiness to consider ideas different from one's own and to try to understand opposing views
- Intellectual humility—the tendency to recognize one's own limitations, be aware of the likelihood of error, and suspend judgment until all relevant information is understood
- Responsibility—the recognition that one's beliefs and actions have consequences online and off

The skills that exemplify these attitudes are explained and demonstrated throughout the text, illustrated with real-world examples (from social media, blogs, websites, and old media), and reinforced and tested in chapter exercises and capstone projects. The targets for these skills are many of the most worrisome features of today's media: fake news, filter bubbles, partisan extremism, biased and unreliable sources, post-truth nonsense, pseudoscience, science illiteracy, conspiracy theories, political bias, targeted advertising, propaganda, and more.

Chapter 1: Critical Thinking and the Challenges of Modern Media introduces critical thinking, describes how it works, explains the role it plays in media literacy, and shows how it leads to knowledge, understanding, and personal empowerment. The chapter surveys the many hazards that jut out of today's media terrain: (1) the perils that come from the billions of users themselves (misinformation, propaganda, hoaxes, hype, viral rumors, weaponized lies, conspiracy theories, bad arguments, post-truth thinking, fact-free diatribes, trolling, bullying, and much more); (2) those that arise from the psychological peculiarities of our own minds (confirmation bias, homophily, the Dunning-Kruger effect, etc.); and (3) those that come from the countless ways that internet and AI technology manipulate us and prey on our cognitive weaknesses (filter bubbles, algorithmic control, targeted ads, biased search results, bots and bot networks, sock puppets, etc.).

This chapter also delivers the bad news about students' ability to judge the trustworthiness of online information. Research suggests that their risk of being fooled by the streams of posts, blogs, and sites that they encounter hour by hour is very high. The risk is elevated in every sphere of life where sound judgments and intelligent decisions are essential to success, however that's defined.

Chapter 2: Claims, Reasons, and Arguments introduces the basics of logical argument. It helps students identify and evaluate deductive and inductive arguments, assess the strength of premises and evidence, recognize common argument patterns, evaluate long arguments, and understand the argument/persuasion distinction. It explains and illustrates the essential features of productive arguments online as well as the telltale signs of arguments (and people) that aren't worth the trouble.

Chapter 3: Obstacles to Critical Thinking explains how to identify and minimize the mental obstacles that undermine clear thinking: availability error, motivated reasoning, confirmation bias, prejudice, bias, mere exposure effect, illusion-of-truth effect, false consensus effect, Dunning-Kruger effect, and more.

Chapter 4: Fake News shows how to identify fake news, distinguish between legitimate and illegitimate reasons for accepting a claim, assess the reliability of online information by reading laterally, use Google and Wikipedia judiciously, identify and use trustworthy fact-checkers, and understand the ethical implications of sharing fake news. It provides guidelines for detecting fake images by determining the source, checking for previous uses, looking for incongruities, and being suspicious of images that seem too amazing to be true. The chapter also covers the detection of deepfakes.

Chapter 5: Media Bias explores the problem of bias in news media. It explains what objectivity and bias are in journalism and distinguishes between news, opinion, and analysis. It demonstrates that there are many reasons why accusations of partisan bias *seem* right but are probably wrong, that two of the most common conservative and liberal arguments about news bias are unsound, and that the sweeping accusation that mainstream news outlets consistently lean left or right is harder to prove than many realize.

Chapter 6: Manipulating through Fallacies and Rhetoric shows that propaganda and demagoguery are powerful and dishonest forces in large part because of the fallacies and rhetorical tricks they employ. This chapter—illustrated with many examples from social media—is a lesson in self-defense against a whole range of fallacies and many of the most common rhetorical devices. It details how to detect these ploys and discusses the best strategies for responding to ad hominem attacks online.

Chapter 7: Experts and Evidence explains how to assess the reliability of experts, evidence, and our own judgments based on memory, perception, and reflection. It discusses how to determine who is a true expert, how to avoid the fallacious appeal to authority, when we should suspect bias in an expert, when we should (and should not) trust the evidence of personal experience, and how to avoid misjudgments about coincidences, causes, and probability.

Chapter 8: Science, Nonscience, and the Media addresses major misunderstandings about the nature of science, how it is done, how it relates to ideology and technology, and why its findings are reliable guides to the facts. It explains the scientific method and how theories are tested, offers guidance in how to evaluate science news stories and online science claims, and shows how scientists evaluate evidence for climate change and evolution. The chapter includes critiques of actual media messages purportedly based on scientific research, provides examples of bold online claims that turned out to be false, shows how to use critical thinking to evaluate conspiracy theories, and offers guidelines for determining when scientific evidence does and does not support a claim.

Chapter 9: Advertising: Commercial and Political explains how online targeted advertising works, how advertisers come to know so much about us, and how they use that information to increase the effectiveness of their advertising ploys. It shows how to use critical thinking to avoid being taken in by paid search ads, social media ads, display ads, and native ads. The chapter examines how political video ads can present false or misleading messages through the words they use (lies, half-truths, exaggerations, etc.) and through technical manipulation of the videos themselves. It explains why the most insidious and relentless political ads on the planet may be the ones we see on Facebook. It shows how Facebook ads can micro-target millions of users based on their psychological and behavioral characteristics, hit those users again and again with tailored messages, and run the whole operation indefinitely and below the radar.

All chapters include exercises and capstone projects to test students' ability to critically evaluate actual websites, social media posts, blogs, news stories, articles, advertising, and images.

Ancillaries

The Oxford University Press Ancillary Resource Center (ARC) at oup-arc.com houses an Instructor's Manual with Test Bank and PowerPoint Lecture Outlines for instructor use. Student resources are also available on the ARC and include self-quizzes, flashcards, media activities, and links to helpful material on the internet.

Acknowledgments

Many reviewers have helped make this book better than it would have been otherwise. I thank them for their judicious criticism and thoughtful suggestions:

Maunel P. Arriga, California State University, San Marcos; Larry Atkins, Temple University; Susan Baran, Bryant University; Jennifer Biedendorf,

California State University, Stanislaus; Scott Blackwell, Indian University, Kokomo; Adrienne Cochran, Highline College; Clint Corcoran, High Point University; Michael Doan, Eastern Michigan University; Matt Ferkany, Michigan State University; John Fields, Edgewood College; Gina Firenzi, San Jose State University; Cindy Gruwell, St. Cloud University; Ronald Hirschbein, California State University, Chico; Heidi Kozlowski, San Jose City College; Louis Mancha, Ashland University; Dwayne Mulder, Sonoma State University; Amber Pfannenstiel, Millersville University; Reginald Raymer, University of North Carolina, Charlotte; Greg Rich, Fayetteville State University; Eldar Sarajilic, Borough of Manhattan Community College; Steve Schessler, Cabrillo College; Jeff Share, University of California, Los Angeles; Edward Slowk, Winona State University; Rachel Smydra, Oakland University; Joseph Staub, California State University, Los Angeles; Gordon Stevenson, South Connecticut State University; Karl Stocker, Eastern Connecticut State University; J. Dana Trent, Wake Technical Community College; Michael Tumolo, California State University, Stanislaus; and Jeff Vogel, Saddleback College.

Applying Critical Thinking to Modern Media

Critical Thinking and the Challenges of Modern Media

Chapter Objectives

1.1 Turning Information into Knowledge
- *Distinguish between information and knowledge.*
- *Define* critical thinking, logic, *and* media literacy.
- *Explain how the* cause *of a belief is different from* whether it is worth believing.
- *Appreciate some of the intellectual and practical benefits of critical thinking.*
- *Understand how lack of critical thinking can undermine our personal freedom and our ability to formulate a coherent worldview.*

1.2 Hazards of the Infosphere
- *Define* fake news, confirmation bias, availability error, *and* homophily.
- *Appreciate that a vast amount of information on the internet is suspect, false, misleading, self-serving, and biased, and that much of it is generated by uninformed and unscrupulous people, zealots, trolls, bots, and sock puppets.*
- *Appreciate the insidiousness, prevalence, and danger of the phenomenon of fake news and be aware of its many possible sources, from "fake news factories" to partisan fanatics to your online friends.*
- *Explain how confirmation bias, the availability error, and homophily can lead us into error, confusion, and self-delusion.*
- *Know what filter bubbles are and how they can lock us into opinions and worldviews that are misinformed, one-sided, and bigoted.*

1.3 Post-Truth
- *Define* post-truth *and explain how it is being exemplified in partisan politics, the media, and beliefs and commitments of all kinds.*

(Continued)

Chapter 1 CRITICAL THINKING AND THE CHALLENGES OF MODERN MEDIA

(Continued)

- Understand how tribalism in partisan politics can affect people's attitudes toward those they disagree with.
- Know the difference between fact and opinion.
- Explain how partisan disagreement can often hinge not just on the facts, but on epistemology.

1.4 Media Illiteracy
- Understand the findings of the researchers at the Stanford History Education Group on media literacy.
- Appreciate that spending hours per day online does not necessarily make someone good at evaluating the credibility of information encountered.
- Take seriously the possibility of being duped online by fake news, bogus websites, native ads, deceptive emails, ultra-biased blogs, and countless other sources.

The information age was supposed to be better than the analog Stone Age, back when information meandered through network TV, radio, snail mail, print (newspapers, books, magazines), and word of mouth. Email, Usenet, and the World Wide Web (invented in 1989)—all built on flying zeroes and ones—were supposed to make us smarter, friendlier, better informed, more tolerant, and more open-minded. Digital access was supposed to deliver us from our narrow views of the world, spread democracy, and set our imaginations free.

But the infosphere has fallen short of its promise, despite its obvious contributions to communications, commerce, entertainment, and science. In many ways, the technology's powerful advantages have been turned against us, helping to make our view of the world narrower, darker, and dumber.

We can do better, and critical thinking shows us how.

1.1 Turning Information into Knowledge

Chief among the reasons for using the internet is the pursuit of knowledge—knowledge pertaining to virtually every sphere of life, on every subject, for application in innumerable ways. But the internet delivers not knowledge but *information*. Information is just raw data, assertions or claims of unknown worth and indeterminate truth. **Knowledge** is true belief backed by good reasons—that is, true belief that's supported by sufficient evidence or reasoning. The reasons make the belief more likely to be true. Information becomes knowledge when we process it, examine it, and come to believe for good reasons that it's true.

This process is known as **critical thinking**: *the systematic evaluation or formulation of beliefs or statements by rational standards.* Critical thinking helps us discern the good reasons. Believing a claim without good reasons is arbitrary, a shot in the dark, a guess at what the facts are. Only a tiny percentage of information online qualifies as genuine knowledge.

Critical thinking focuses not on what *causes* a belief, but on *whether it is worth believing*. A belief is worth believing, or accepting, if we have good reasons to believe it. The better the reasons for acceptance, the more likely the belief is to be true. A sociologist might tell you how society has influenced some of your moral choices. A psychologist might describe how your emotions cause you to cling to certain opinions. Your best friend might allege that you have unconsciously absorbed most of your beliefs directly from your parents. But none of these speculations have much to do with the central task of critical thinking. Critical thinking offers us a set of standards embodied in techniques, attitudes, and principles that we can use to assess beliefs and determine if they are worthy of our trust.

Critical thinking, of course, involves **logic**. Logic is the study of good reasoning, or inference, and the rules that govern it. But critical thinking is broader than logic because it involves not only logic but also the truth or falsity of statements, the evaluation of arguments and evidence, the use of analysis and investigation, and the application of many other skills that help us decide what to believe or do.

Ultimately, what critical thinking leads you to is knowledge, understanding, and—if you put these to work—empowerment. In addition, as you're guided by your instructor through this text, you will come to appreciate some other benefits that cannot be fully explored now: Critical thinking enables problem-solving, active learning, and intelligent self-improvement.

Online you are often implored to change not only your beliefs but your entire worldview, the vast web of fundamental ideas that help you make sense of the world, what some people call a philosophy of life. Fortunately, critical thinking applies to your worldview, not just to some of your individual beliefs. We all have a worldview, and most of us want the beliefs that constitute it to be true and coherent (to fit together without internal contradictions). Devising a coherent worldview is the work of a lifetime—and can be done well only with the help of critical thinking.

Our choice whether to apply critical thinking skills is not an all-or-nothing decision. Each of us uses critical thinking to some degree in our lives. We often evaluate reasons for (and against) believing that someone has committed a crime, that an earnest celebrity is deluded, that one candidate in an election is better than another, that a political website is trustworthy, that an online ad is bogus, that the right of free speech on campus should be expanded or restricted, that we should buy a car, that one university is superior to another, that marijuana contains "alien DNA" from outside our solar system, that a pill sold online and endorsed by doctors everywhere can increase your IQ 1000 percent. But the more urgent consideration is not just whether we sometimes use critical thinking, but how well we use it.

We can't deny that digital technology has in many ways been a force for good in society. But we also have to admit that it has had troubling consequences, the most far-reaching being its negative impact on how we think, what we think, and how we interact with others. We can see these effects in social media, news (both traditional and digital), education, politics, entertainment, advertising, and countless other areas of public and private life.

Many of our troubles involving 21st-century media boil down to *us*—to our uneven, slanted, less-than-adequate ability to make sense of media

Critical Thinking and Personal Freedom

In large measure, our lives are defined by our actions and choices, and our actions and choices are guided by our thinking. If we care whether our choices are right and our beliefs true, if we want to rise above blind acceptance and arbitrary choices, we must use the tools provided by critical thinking.

We, of course, always have the option of taking the easy way out. We can simply glom onto whatever beliefs or statements come blowing through cyberspace, adopting viewpoints because they are favored by others or because they make us feel good. But then we forfeit control over our lives and let the wind take us wherever it will, as if we had no more say in the outcome than a leaf in a storm.

A consequence, then, of going with the wind is a loss of personal freedom. If you passively accept beliefs that have been handed to you by your parents, your culture, your teachers, or your newsfeed, then those beliefs are *not really yours*. You just happened to be in a certain place and time when they were handed out. If they are not really yours, and you let them guide your choices and actions, then they—not you—are in charge of your life. Your beliefs are yours only if you critically examine them for yourself to see if they are supported by good reasons.

To examine your beliefs in this way is to examine your life, for your beliefs in large measure define your life. To forgo such scrutiny is to abandon your chance of making your life deliberately and authentically meaningful. The great philosopher Socrates says it best: "The unexamined life is not worth living."

messages and information. Research shows that an alarming number of us would probably fail a fair test of **media literacy**. Media literacy is the ability to access and understand media messages, apply critical thinking to them, and use them responsibly. Without it, in a rapidly transforming digitized world, we likely will misunderstand much, make bad choices, and draw conclusions that will send us down the wrong paths.

Section Query

Consider one of your more important beliefs about politics, religion, or history. Think carefully: What reasons or evidence do you have for accepting the belief as true? Can you honestly say that that you *know* it?

1.2 Hazards of the Infosphere

On the internet our ability to find information on just about anything is nearly limitless. But—as you surely know by now—a massive share of that information is suspect, false, misleading, self-serving, biased, and crazy. A vast trove of it is generated by seriously uninformed people, malicious trolls, unscrupulous organizations, partisan zealots, and bots and sock puppets. (A bot is computer program cleverly pretending to be a person; a sock puppet is a real person assuming fake identities.) According to one estimate, we have 30 trillion unique web pages to rummage through, but the surfeit of sources can often make fact-finding harder, not easier. The volume of data on almost any subject can quickly become overwhelming. Social media, blogs, and websites have made every person a potential publisher who can say almost anything online. But unlike traditional publishers, these writers typically have no one—no fact-checkers, no editors, no peer reviewers—to help ensure factual accuracy and to question their version of the facts. Too many of them are well-meaning but unaware, passionate but vile, interesting but unhinged. New media has given us tools to unify the world through open and respectful discussions about shared values and cultural differences. But too much of cyberspace is fragmented into a multitude of competing voices and factions, each talking past the other, each shouting its own opinions and claiming its own private set of facts. And too often there seems to be not a square inch of common ground anywhere and no reasonable way to bridge the gaps among competing narratives.

One of the symptoms of our digital disorder is the widespread phenomenon of **fake news**—deliberately false or misleading news stories that masquerade as truthful reporting. Fake news (discussed in Chapter 4) has been around for a long time, but thanks to social media, it now spreads faster and more cleverly than ever. It was a force to be reckoned with in the 2016 U.S. presidential election and will continue to deceive, provoke, and harm indefinitely. It is a seemingly unstoppable flood rushing through social media feeds, blogs, and websites. It shows up on sites that look legitimate but aren't. The "news" presented can be completely made up, or it can be so partisan that it says only good things about one political perspective and only bad things about another, or it can be a strange but plausible blend of fact and fiction. (Satirical writings on sites like *The Onion* and *Clickhole* are also sometimes labeled "fake news," but instead of offering deliberate lies and misinformation, they try to present plausible claims and criticisms through humor, irony, and exaggeration.) Fake news can drop into your news feed from almost anywhere, including "fake news factories," internet pranksters and trolls, organizations that seem at first glance to be legitimate but aren't, and news-fabricating teenagers in Macedonia angling for cash. It can also arrive with enthusiastic endorsements from your friends.

Did you know that eating shrimp and taking vitamin C can cause death by arsenic poisoning, that calling a sleeping person's name will cause brain damage, that onions absorb viruses and bacteria from a room, that a morgue employee has been cremated by mistake, and that e-cigarettes cause a horrible disease called "popcorn lung"? The purveyors of fake news have said so, and they have managed to cultivate believers everywhere, even though the claims are false (and absurd). And of course many netizens, whether they believe the lies or not, will reflexively share them, leading others to share them too. Click on Facebook, Twitter, Instagram, or Google, and within minutes or seconds, the fake news can go viral and zoom around the world. Add to the phenomenon of fake news the power of fake followers and fake "likes," all produced easily through fake accounts.

Fake news, however, is neither the biggest nor the most worrying source of falsehoods and confusion online. Modern media is awash with all sorts of intellectual and emotional toxins—propaganda, hoaxes, hype, outrage (fake or otherwise), character assassination, weaponized lies, conspiracy theories, bad arguments, logical fallacies, fact-free diatribes, trolling, bullying, revenge porn, viral rumors, "deepfakes," and much more. (Most of these are covered in the following chapters.)

Like fake news, these sources of misinformation and delusion are made possible largely by two factors: internet technology and the psychological peculiarities of our own minds.

Chief among the many psychological factors that distort our thinking is the well documented cognitive error known as **confirmation bias**—the tendency to look for and recognize only information that confirms our existing views. (This and other psychological errors are detailed in Chapter 3.) We come across a compelling news story that seems to confirm exactly what we already believe. So we skip critical thinking and share the story with our like-minded friends, and soon hundreds of people become believers. But for all we know the story may be fake—and we have no good reason for believing it true or false.

Denying contrary evidence is the cognitive error of refusing to accept or acknowledge evidence that undermines our existing beliefs. When we come across evidence that contradicts our views, we may ignore it, dismiss it out of hand, undervalue it, or interpret it as actually confirming our views.

We commit the **availability error** when we rely on evidence not because it's trustworthy but because it's memorable or striking—that is, psychologically available. In such cases, we put stock in evidence that's surprising, vivid, or shocking—which fake news often is. We see news broadcasts or internet reports about a horrific plane crash and start believing that air travel is far more dangerous than it actually is.

Homophily is the tendency to give more credence to a statement if it comes from our friends. Homophily has a far more powerful effect online than we may realize. P. W. Singer and Emerson T. Brooking make this point in their book *LikeWar: The Weaponization of Social Media*:

> Homophily is an inescapable fact of online life. If you've ever shared a piece of content after seeing it on a friend's newsfeed, you've become part of the process. Most people don't ponder deeply when they click "share." They're just passing on things that they find notable or that might sway others. Yet it shapes them all the same. As users respond positively to certain types of content, the algorithms that drive social media's newsfeeds ensure that they see more of it. As they see more, they share more, affecting all others in their extended network. Like ripples in a pond, each of these small decisions expands outward, altering the flow of information across the entire system.[1]

Internet technology augments our psychological weaknesses in powerful ways that can help generate virtual pandemics of false and misleading content. Social media algorithms curate news and information that you've already indicated you want to see (by your likes and activity). But this kind of curating does not necessarily give you what's true. It's good at finding stories that are likely to go viral, but viral does not mean factual. It often just means fake news.

Social media platforms and search engines collect vast amounts of data on the interests and preferences of their users, and many organizations employ this information to send ads, propaganda, and fake news to precisely targeted audiences. That really compelling story in your news feed may be someone's sly attempt to manipulate or persuade you. Whether the message is political, commercial, or something else, it's engineered to influence you or make money by attracting clicks. Countless web-savvy people have a vested interest in making you believe fake news, bogus sales pitches, and political baloney.

The technology of social networks and search engines jibes perfectly with the human tendency to form exclusive social groups of like-minded people committed to a particular set of strong beliefs. Facebook, Twitter, Tumblr, Snapchat, Reddit, Instagram, and the like make it easy to form such groups, to reinforce each other's beliefs, and to block opposing ideas. Filters built into social media help you see only what you choose to see, only the ideas that you agree with. The result is called personalized feedback loops, or "filter bubbles." Filter bubbles are comfortable, reassuring spaces, but they can have serious downsides. They shore up existing beliefs (whether true or false) and prevent contrary evidence or opposing views from piercing the bubble, often leading to positions that are misinformed, one-sided, bigoted, and hardened to stone. These bastions of opinion can become walled cities and, in extreme cases, asylums. These insular worlds not only encourage uniform opinions but also insist on having their own private set of facts. This Balkanization of factual inquiry obstructs civil discourse—the lifeblood of democracy—and warps the search for truth.

According to Guy Harrison, author of *Think Before You Like*,

> Filter bubbles are personal online zones of customized news, entertainment, and social media posts; tailored search results; targeted ads; and so on that can be so specific and consistent to an individual that the flow of this information places the recipient at a risk of developing a distorted worldview on one or many issues. . . . Algorithms serve up whatever information is deemed most likely to make you happy and content—reality and your personal growth be damned. Remember, social media platforms are hell-bent on keeping you engaged often and for as long as possible. There just isn't a lot of priority given to helping you become well-rounded and worldly.[2]

There now exists internet technology that is even more worrisome. Consider the case of Angee Dixson. She joined Twitter in 2017, tweeting about ninety times a day in defense of President Trump. She railed ferociously against Democrats, the media, late-night comedians, and anyone else who dared to criticize the president. As Singer and Brooking explain,

Three days after Dixson hopped online, a coalition of alt-right groups descended on Charlottesville, Virginia, for what they dubbed the #UniteTheRight rally. As counterprotesters poured into the streets to oppose what became a vivid expression of hate and white nationalism, a far-right terrorist drove his car into the crowd, killing one young woman and wounding three others. When public sentiment turned against President Trump (who claimed "both sides" were to blame for the violence), Dixson furiously leapt to his defense. "Dems and Media Continue to IGNORE BLM [Black Lives Matter] and Antifa [anti-fascist] Violence in Charlottesville," she tweeted, including an image of demonstrators with the caption "DEMOCRAT TERROR." In the days that followed, her tweets grew even more strident, publicizing supposed cases of left-wing terrorism around the country.

But none of the cases were real—and Dixson wasn't either. As Ben Nimmo, a fellow with the Digital Forensic Research Lab at the Atlantic Council, discovered, "Angee Dixson" was actually a bot. . . .

Dixson was one of at least 60,000 Russian accounts in a single "bot-net" (a networked army of bots) that infested Twitter like a cancer, warping and twisting the U.S. political dialogue. This botnet, in turn, belonged to a vast galaxy of fake and automated accounts that lurk in the shadows of Twitter, Facebook, Instagram, and numerous other services. These machine voices exist because they have power—because the nature of social media platforms *gives* them power.[3]

Bots can churn out hundreds of thousands of messages, and these can be quickly retweeted by humans by the tens of thousands. They can operate as "chatbots," carrying on conversations that can be indistinguishable from that of human friends. "Or the bots can be devilishly simple, pushing out the same hashtag again and again," say Singer and Brooking, "which may get them caught but still accomplishes their mission, be it to make a hashtag go viral or to bury an opponent under countermessages."[4] Thus bots can change the course and content of online discussions and make suspect ideas seem suddenly popular and credible.

The way the internet affects its human users makes it hard enough for them to distinguish truth and falsehood. Yet these 4 billion flesh-and-blood netizens have now been joined by a vast number of digital beings, designed to distort and amplify, to confuse and distract. The attention economy may have been built by humans, but it is now ruled by algorithms—some with agendas of their own.[5]

Section Query

How often have you accepted online information as fact, then later discovered that it was fake news? If you have rarely or never had this experience, is it because you usually don't try to verify what you accept as true?

1.3 Post-Truth

In 2016 the Oxford Dictionaries announced that the word of the year was *post-truth*, defined as "relating to or denoting circumstances in which objective facts are less influential in shaping public opinion than appeals to emotion and personal beliefs." The term refers to an attitude toward truth and facts that has always appealed to some people but that began to spread feverishly during the 2016 U.S. presidential election and the debate surrounding Britain's exit from the European Union (Brexit). Observers say that we now seem to be in a post-truth age where asserting obvious falsehoods, denying rigorously confirmed facts, or believing a claim just because it feels good is no longer widely regarded as an egregious error in thinking. The force that channels and magnifies these bouts of unreason is, of course, the media, both new and old.

This is an era when some politicians—both from the left and the right—lie with impunity and maintain the lie even when confronted with evidence to the contrary. It is a time when, in many quarters, feelings outweigh facts, and facts from knowledgeable sources with excellent credentials are called fake news. Some leaders who think with their gut and forgo appeals to reason and evidence are treated as sages. In too many cases, politicians are admired not because they are wise, virtuous, or truthful, but because they say what people want to hear, regardless of the facts. Such uncritical thinking has always plagued society, but now its prevalence and potential for harm seem greater than at in other time in recent memory.

The comedian and pretend journalist Stephen Colbert, the former host of Comedy Central's satirical *The Colbert Report*, has spoofed this blasé attitude toward facts and truth. What political commentators are interested in is not truth, he says, but "truthiness." "Truthiness is sort of what you want to be true, as opposed to what the facts support," he says. "Truthiness is a truth larger than the facts that would comprise it—if you cared about facts, which you don't, if you care about truthiness."[6] Truth is about rational thought; truthiness is for knowing in your heart.

As falsehoods spread, as the number of conflicting voices online increases, and as people lose trust in the facts provided by institutions and traditional media, many give up on truth and doubt everything. Others simply turn to the news sources that offer the narratives that feel emotionally right.

To many in the post-truth age, facts are obstacles that get in the way of preferred subjective beliefs. For them, willful ignorance is the default position. Such blindness is especially strong in politics where people's commitment to their partisan tribe, leader, or cause can be all-consuming. The journalist Amanda Taub describes this kind of outsized fervor:

> Partisan bias now operates more like racism than mere political disagreement, academic research on the subject shows. And this widespread prejudice could have serious consequences for American democracy. . . .
>
> But the fake-news phenomenon is not the result of personal failings. And it is not limited to one end of the political spectrum. Rather, Americans' deep bias against the political party they oppose is so strong that it acts as a kind of partisan prism for facts, refracting a different reality to Republicans than to Democrats.
>
> Partisan refraction has fueled the rise of fake news, according to researchers who study the phenomenon. But the repercussions go far beyond stories shared on Facebook and Reddit, affecting Americans' faith in government—and the government's ability to function. . . .
>
> Today, political parties are no longer just the people who are supposed to govern the way you want. They are a team to support, and a tribe to feel part of. And the public's view of politics is becoming more and more zero-sum: It's about helping their team win, and making the other team lose.[7]

This means that too often, when partisans disagree, they are not really disagreeing about the facts. They are simply showing support for their tribe. They may share fake news not because they believe it, but because they want to strike a blow for their side. They may deny (or affirm) their belief in climate change, not because they really accept or reject the idea, but because they want to show solidarity with their fellow partisans.

The worst scenario is disagreement (whether about facts or tribes) coupled with intense hate, in which the other side is thought to be not just wrong or misinformed, but evil, beyond the pale, irredeemable. And because they are evil, they can be shunned, ignored, or savaged.

In recent research, Democrats and Republicans were asked whether members of the opposing party were "not just worse for politics—they are downright evil." Over 40 percent of those in each party said *yes*. Nearly 60 percent of Republicans and more than 60 percent of Democrats agreed that "the opposing party is a serious threat to the United

States and its people." Around one-fifth of Republicans and Democrats agreed that their political rivals "lack the traits to be considered fully human—they behave like animals." And perhaps most shocking of all, "15 percent of Republicans and 20 percent of Democrats agreed that the country would be better off if large numbers of opposing partisans in the public today 'just died.'"[8]

Such partisan fever widens the gap between opposing sides, prevents intelligent discussion of the issues, puts a stop to any semblance of intelligent disagreement, substitutes invective and dishonest polemics for rational argument, and causes mistakes, misunderstanding, and confusion.

In this caustic fog of political and psychological extremes, the role of critical thinking does not change. Tribal blindness, partisan hate, comforting ignorance—none of these will get you one inch closer to real knowledge, reasonable beliefs, and intelligent action.

In examining the truth of partisan claims, often the issue is not about what is true; it's about *how we know something is true*. It's about what philosophers call *epistemology*, or theory of knowledge, which concerns what we know and how we come to know it. Partisans often differ not just about the facts, but about the criteria for judging whether something is

Fact and Opinion

When we evaluate claims, we often are concerned with making a distinction between facts and opinions. But just what is the difference? We normally use the term *fact* in two senses. First, we may use it to refer to a state of affairs—as in "Examine the evidence and find out the facts." Second, and more commonly, we use *fact* to refer to *true statements*—as in "John smashed the dinnerware—that's a fact." Thus, we say that some claims, or statements, are facts (or factual) and some are not. We use the word *opinion*, however, to refer to a *belief*—as in "It's John's opinion that he did not smash the dinnerware." Some opinions are true, so they are facts. Some opinions are not true, so they are not facts.

Sometimes we may hear somebody say, "That's a matter of opinion." What does this mean? Often it's equivalent to something like "Opinions differ on this issue" or "There are many different opinions on this." But it also frequently means that the issue is not a matter of objective fact but is entirely subjective, a matter of individual taste. Statements expressing matters of opinion in this latter sense are not the kinds of things that people can disagree on, just as two people cannot sensibly disagree about whether they like chocolate ice cream.

In journalism and the news business, "opinion" is used to refer not to this kind of arbitrary subjectivity but to beliefs about objective matters that often cannot be verified entirely through objective evidence. They are explanations, interpretations, judgments, speculations, and the like.

a fact. For Partisan A, for example, a statement is true if (1) her political leader says it is, (2) the statement evokes a satisfying feeling of certainty, (3) it is "confirmed" by her personal experience, and (4) it is acceptable to her friends and dismaying to her adversaries. But to Partisan B, this is all wrong: He thinks a statement is true only if it's affirmed on Fox News or MSNBC or *Breitbart* or *Slate* or any other favored source of news and information.

But what reasons can these partisans give for why we should accept *their* criteria for knowledge and *their* version of the facts? If they say their criteria and facts are just obviously the right ones, they are guilty of begging the question—they are trying to prove their case by assuming the very thing that needs proving. They are basically saying they are right because they are right. But this is to argue in a circle. If they cannot give any non-question-begging reasons for why their views are correct, then their views are unfounded, based not on rational grounds but on an arbitrary preference.

Neither will it do to declare that *every* viewpoint or set of facts is equally true, for that involves us in a logical contradiction. Can it possibly be the case both that a border wall will solve all our immigration problems and that it will not solve all our immigration problems? That gun ownership in the United States is down 32 percent and is not down 32 percent? That Barack Obama was and was not born in Kenya? That Donald Trump did and did not break the law?

What is needed to resolve disagreements and conflicting views is a non-arbitrary, non-question-begging standard for judging the merits of each case. What's needed is the neutral and reliable processes embodied in critical thinking.

But of course all those who, like Partisans A and B, put their faith in a different kind of epistemology will be dubious about the merits of critical thinking. Why should they give up their usual method of discovering the facts to embrace the alleged fact-finding reliability of reason and evidence? The answer must come in clear demonstrations of how in a variety of cases critical thinking is able to reliably ascertain justified beliefs, identify falsehoods, and reduce the likelihood of errors. The main purpose of this text is to provide, in each chapter, such demonstrations.

Section Query

Consider one of your strongly held beliefs about politics or government. Now ask yourself what criteria you used for initially judging the belief to be a fact. Do you now think the criteria reasonable?

1.4 Media Illiteracy

Do today's students—those born with a mouse in their hands, texting a mile a minute, and net surfing as easily as walking—really need lessons in thinking critically online? New research suggests that the answer is *yes*. Researchers at the Stanford History Education Group spent a year and a half assessing the ability of middle school, high school, and college students in twelve states to "judge the credibility of information that floods young people's smartphones, tablets, and computers." Their conclusions are sobering:

> Overall, young people's ability to reason about the information on the Internet can be summed up in one word: *bleak*.
>
> Our "digital natives" may be able to flit between Facebook and Twitter while simultaneously uploading a selfie to Instagram and texting a friend. But when it comes to evaluating information that flows through social media channels, they are easily duped.... [W]e would hope that middle school students could distinguish an ad from a news story. By high school, we would hope that students reading about gun laws would notice that a chart came from a gun owners' political action committee. And ... we would hope college students, who spend hours each day online, would look beyond a .org URL and ask who's behind a site that presents only one side of a contentious issue. But in every case and at every level, we were taken aback by students' lack of preparation.[9]

Students were assessed on a variety of skills, including determining if a tweet is trustworthy, distinguishing between a news article and an opinion column, explaining why a sponsored post may not be reliable, assessing the relative strength of evidence presented in a Facebook exchange, deciding if a website can be trusted, and determining if a partisan site is trustworthy.

In one assessment test, students were shown the home page of Slate.com (see Fig. 1.1) and asked to identify a traditional advertisement, a news story, and a native advertisement (an ad made to look like a news story) and explain the features that distinguish them. The results were mixed:

> More than three-quarters of the students correctly identified the traditional advertisement and the news story. Unfortunately, native advertising proved vexing for the vast majority of students. More than 80 percent of students believed that the native advertisement, identified by the words "sponsored content," was a real news story. Some students even mentioned that it was

sponsored content but still believed that it was a news article. This suggests that many students have no idea what "sponsored content" means.[10]

In another test, students were shown a post from a photo-sharing site featuring a picture of odd-looking flowers (Fig. 1.2) and a caption saying that the flowers are an example of "nuclear birth defects" related to the nuclear disaster at Japan's Fukushima Daiichi Nuclear Power Plant. Students were asked, "Does this post provide strong evidence about the conditions near the Fukushima Daiichi Power Plant? Explain your reasoning."

"Successful students" maintained that the photo "does not provide strong evidence about conditions near the nuclear power plant," and they questioned the source of the post. Less than 20 percent of students gave this "successful" response.

On the other hand, nearly 40 percent of students argued that the post provided strong evidence because it presented pictorial evidence about conditions near the power plant. A quarter of the students argued that the post did not provide strong evidence, but only because it showed flowers and not other plants or animals that may have been affected by the nuclear radiation.[11]

If this research reflects accurately the level of media literacy of

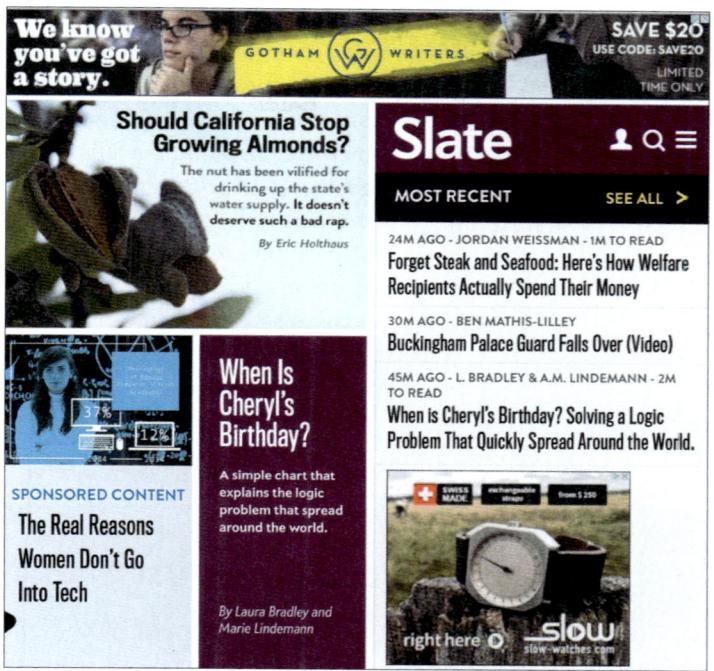

Fig. 1.1   Sample home page of Slate.com used in the Stanford History Education Group's media literacy tests.

Fig. 1.2   Photo allegedly showing evidence of "nuclear birth defects" related to the nuclear disaster at Japan's Fukushima Daiichi Nuclear Power Plant.

most students, then millions of them are at high risk for being duped online by fake news, bogus websites, native ads, deceptive emails, ultra-partisan blogs, and more. And this risk is elevated not only in politics, but also in every other subject under the sun, including many important and controversial ones: climate change, immigration, health care, hate speech, mass shootings, racism, sexual harassment and assault, and gun ownership. Personal life choices—everything from which toothpaste to buy to what career to pursue—can also be undone by questionable information or advice gleaned online and off.

In large measure, our lives are defined by our actions and choices, and our actions and choices are guided by our thinking—so our

Going with Your Gut: I Just *Know*!

Can your "gut" help you find credible information online? Suppose you make a claim that you have neither evidence nor argument to back up, and someone asks, "How do you know?" And you say, "I just know," or "My gut (or intuition) tells me it's true." In such situations, do you really know—do you really possess knowledge? Many epistemologists (philosophers who study knowledge) would argue that you do not, unless your ordinary means of acquiring knowledge (reason and observation) have validated the reliability of your intuition or gut. Nevertheless many people believe that their gut is a reliable way of knowing. Here's a famous case of "gut knowing" that has been criticized by several authors, including the philosopher Stephen Law:

> Notoriously, during George W. Bush's presidency, Bush's gut became the oracle of the state. Bush was distrustful of book learning and those with established expertise in a given area. When he made the decision to invade Iraq, and was subsequently confronted by a skeptical audience, Bush said that ultimately, he just *knew in his gut* that invading was the right thing to do....
>
> The invasion went ahead. A few months later, Senator Joe Biden told Bush of his growing worries about the aftermath. In response, Bush again appealed to the reliability of his "instincts...."
>
> How did Bush suppose his gut was able to steer the ship of state? He supposed it was functioning as a sort of God-sensing faculty. Bush believed that by means of his gut he could sense what God wanted of him.... Those who, like George W. Bush, place a simple trusting faith in their gut, or wherever else they think their sensus divinitatis is located, are being irresponsible and foolish.[12]

Assuming this account of George Bush's thinking is accurate, do you think he really *knew* that invading Iraq was the right thing to do? If so, how does this kind of intuitive knowing work? Exactly how is knowledge gained this way? If not, where do you think Bush's error lies? What is wrong with "knowing in your gut"?

thinking had better be good. In no area of life is this fact more relevant than in the beguiling, perilous, inescapable world of 21st-century media. If we care whether our beliefs are true, if we want to rise above blind acceptance and arbitrary choices, if we want a reliable defense against nonsense, we have no choice but to use the tools provided by critical thinking.

Section Query

How well do you think you would do on a test of media literacy like the one used by the researchers at the Stanford History Education Group? If the researchers had shown you the home page of Slate.com (Fig. 1.1), would you have been able to successfully identify a traditional advertisement, a news story, and a native advertisement—and explain their essential differences?

REVIEW NOTES

1.1 TURNING INFORMATION INTO KNOWLEDGE

- Information is just raw data, assertions or claims of unknown worth and indeterminate truth. **Knowledge** is true belief backed by good reasons—that is, true belief that's supported by sufficient evidence or reasoning. Information becomes knowledge when we process it, examine it, and come to believe for good reasons that it's true.

- **Critical thinking** is *the systematic evaluation or formulation of beliefs or statements by rational standards.* Critical thinking helps us discern the good reasons. Believing a claim without good reasons is arbitrary, a guess at what the facts are. Only a tiny percentage of information online qualifies as genuine knowledge.

- **Logic** is the study of good reasoning, or inference, and the rules that govern it.

- Critical thinking focuses not on what *causes* a belief, but on *whether it is worth believing.* A belief is worth believing, or accepting, if we have good reasons to believe it. Critical thinking offers us a set of standards embodied in techniques, attitudes, and principles that we can use to assess beliefs and determine if they are worthy of our trust. Critical thinking leads you to knowledge, understanding, and empowerment. It enables problem-solving, active learning, and intelligent self-improvement.

- Many of our troubles involving 21st-century media boil down to us—to our less-than-adequate ability to make sense of media messages and information. Research shows that an alarming number of us would probably fail a fair test of **media literacy**. Media literacy is the ability to access and understand media messages, apply critical thinking to them, and use them responsibly.

1.2 HAZARDS OF THE INFOSPHERE

- A massive share of online information is suspect, self-serving, false, misleading, and biased. Social media, blogs, and websites have made every person a potential publisher who can say almost anything online. But unlike traditional publishers, these writers typically have

- no one—no fact-checkers, no editors, no peer reviewers—to help ensure factual accuracy and to question their version of the facts.

- One of the symptoms of our digital disorder is the widespread phenomenon of **fake news**—deliberately false or misleading news stories that masquerade as truthful reporting. Fake news can drop into your news feed from almost anywhere, including "fake news factories," internet pranksters and trolls, sites that look legitimate but aren't, and well-meaning friends.

- Our acceptance of misinformation and delusion online is encouraged by the psychological peculiarities of our own minds. Chief among the many psychological factors that distort our thinking is the cognitive error known as **confirmation bias**—the tendency to look for and recognize only information that confirms our existing views. **Denying contrary evidence** is the cognitive error of refusing to accept or acknowledge evidence that undermines our existing beliefs. We commit the **availability error** when we rely on evidence not because it's trustworthy but because it's memorable or striking—that is, psychologically available. **Homophily** is the tendency to give more credence to a statement if it comes from our friends.

- Internet technology augments our psychological weaknesses in powerful ways. Social media algorithms curate news and information that you've already indicated you want to see (by your likes and activity). Social media platforms and search engines collect vast amounts of data on the interests and preferences of their users, and many organizations employ this information to send ads, propaganda, and fake news to precisely targeted audiences.

- The technology of social networks and search engines jibes perfectly with the human tendency to form exclusive social groups of like-minded people committed to a particular set of strong beliefs. Facebook, Twitter, Tumblr, Snapchat, Reddit, and the like make it easy to form such groups, to reinforce each other's beliefs, and to block opposing ideas. Filters built into social media help you see only what you choose to see, only the ideas that you agree with. The result is called personalized feedback loops, or "filter bubbles."

1.3 POST-TRUTH

- Observers say that we now seem to be in a post-truth age where asserting obvious falsehoods, denying rigorously confirmed facts, or believing a claim just because it feels good is no longer widely regarded as an egregious error in thinking. The force that channels and magnifies these bouts of unreason is, of course, the media, both new and old.

- To many in the post-truth age, facts are obstacles that get in the way of preferred subjective beliefs. For them, willful ignorance is the default position. Such blindness is especially strong in politics where people's commitment to their partisan tribe, leader, or cause can be all-consuming.

- Too often, when partisans disagree, they are not really disagreeing about the facts. They are simply showing support for their tribe. They may share fake news not because they believe it, but because they want to strike a blow for their side. The worst scenario is disagreement coupled with intense hate, in which the other side is thought to be not just wrong or misinformed, but evil, beyond the pale, irredeemable.

- In examining the truth of partisan claims, often the issue is not about what is true; it's about *how we know something is true*. Partisans often differ not just about the facts, but about the criteria for judging whether something is a fact. What is needed to resolve disagreements and conflicting views is a non-arbitrary, non-question-begging standard for judging the merits of each case. What's needed is the neutral and reliable processes embodied in critical thinking.

1.4 MEDIA ILLITERACY

- Researchers at the Stanford History Education Group assessed the ability of middle school, high school, and college students to "judge the credibility of information that floods young people's smartphones, tablets, and computers." Their conclusion: "Overall, young people's ability to reason about the information on the Internet can be summed up in one word: *bleak*."

- If this research reflects accurately the level of media literacy of most students, then millions of them are at high risk for being duped online by fake news, bogus websites, native ads, deceptive emails, ultra-partisan blogs, and more. This risk is elevated not only in politics, but also in every sphere of life where sound judgments and intelligent decisions are essential to success, however that's defined.

KEY TERMS

availability error
confirmation bias
critical thinking
denying contrary evidence
fake news
homophily
knowledge
logic
media literacy

EXERCISES

Exercises marked with an asterisk (*) have answers in "Answers to Exercises" (Appendix B).

Exercise 1.1

1. What is the difference between knowledge and information?
*2. What is critical thinking, and what does it have to do with converting information to knowledge?
3. What is the difference between what causes a belief and whether that belief is worth believing?
4. What does critical thinking have to do with our personal freedom?
5. What is fake news? What are its most common sources online?
*6. What is confirmation bias?
7. What is the availability error?
*8. What is homophily?
9. What are filter bubbles? What psychological or technological factors help form them?
10. What is post-truth, as defined by Oxford Dictionaries?
11. What is the difference between fact and opinion?
12. What is media literacy?
*13. What are some of the serious downsides of filter bubbles?

Exercise 1.2

1. Review the following tweet and answer this question: "Why might this post not be a reliable source about conservatives' opinions on social network censorship?" List any sources used to make your decision.

Fig. 1.3 Ben Shapiro Facebook post.

2. Examine this sponsored post and explain why its implicit claim about results from supplements might not be reliable.

Fig. 1.4 Screen grab of sponsored post.

3. Research online to determine if this social media post is true—that BuzzFeed News ran a news story claiming that white people should have their guns taken away. List any sources used in your research.

Fig. 1.5 Screen grab of Buzzfeed tweet.

4. Research the partisan site OccupyDemocrats.com to determine if it is trustworthy. Compare your findings to those of the reliable fact-checker Snopes.com.

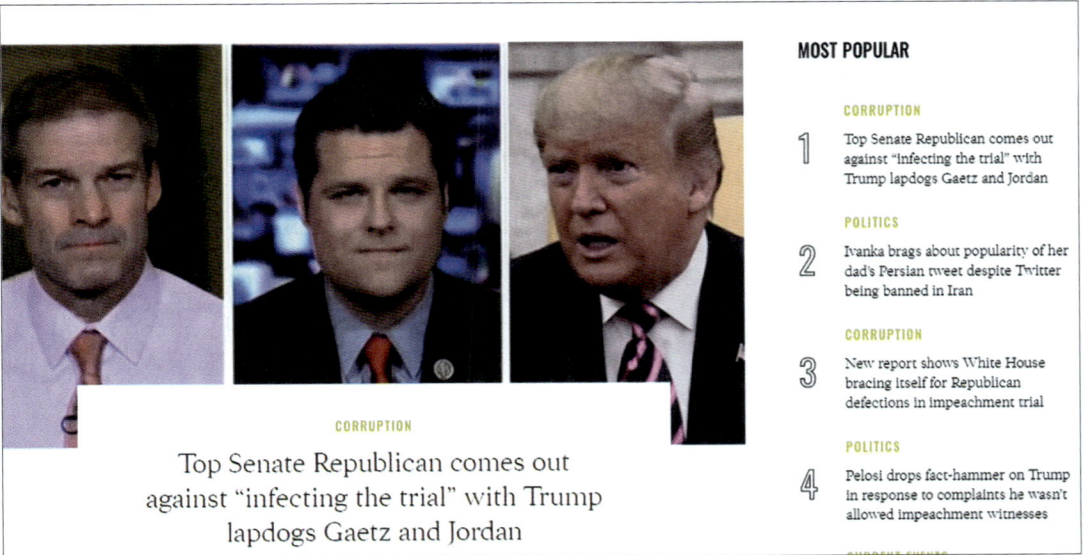

Fig. 1.6 Screen grab of the site's home page.

5. Is it true, as suggested in this Twitter post, that a photo of a Marine saluting the U.S. flag violated Twitter's rules?

Fig. 1.7 Screen grab of tweet from James Woods.

CAPSTONE

Claims that seem plausible may not be; those that seem implausible may be true. Only critical thinking and reliable sources can help you tell which is which. To test your ability to judge plausibility, rate the following online claims as either Probably True or Probably False. Check the accuracy of your answers by consulting Appendix B, Chapter 1. Then grade your performance using this scale: 8 to 10 correct answers, good; 6 to 7 correct, fair; 1 to 5 correct, poor.

1. In 2019, the Walt Disney Co. acquired the pornographic video website Pornhub.
2. The U.S. president Thomas Jefferson once said, "The government will one day be corrupt and filled with liars, and the people will flock to the one that tells the truth."
3. You shouldn't consume aerated drinks such as Coca Cola after eating mangos because the two combined can form a poison that can cause instant death.

4. Women blink nearly twice as often as men.
5. Police in Houston, Texas, arrested a man who killed and ate more than 30 people.
6. Oxygen is the most common element in Earth's crust.
7. In May 2019, a human traffic jam was partially to blame for the deaths of several climbers on Mount Everest.
8. The Food and Drug Administration announced that vaccines cause autism.
9. Shark teeth are as hard as steel.
10. California schools will soon teach kindergartners that there are 15 genders.

Claims, Reasons, and Arguments

Chapter Objectives

2.1 Claims and Reasons
- *Define* statement *and distinguish between statements and nonstatements.*
- *Understand the distinction between Arguing 1 and Arguing 2.*
- *Explain Sinnott-Armstrong's approach to winning arguments.*

2.2 Reasons and Arguments
- *Define* argument, premise, conclusion, *and* explanation.
- *Know how to use indicator words to help pinpoint premises and conclusions.*
- *Be able to identify arguments in various contexts and distinguish between arguments and superfluous material, arguments and explanations, and premises and conclusions.*

2.3 Argument Structure
- *Distinguish between* deductive *and* inductive *arguments.*
- *Understand the terms* valid, invalid, *and* sound.
- *Understand the terms* strong, weak, *and* cogent.
- *Appreciate the basic guidelines for arguing intelligently online.*

2.4 Argument Patterns
- *Memorize and be able to recognize the argument patterns known as* modus ponens, modus tollens, hypothetical syllogism, denying the antecedent, affirming the consequent, *and* disjunctive syllogism.
- *Know what enumerative induction is and how it's used.*
- *Understand the two ways in which an enumerative induction can fail to be strong.*
- *Understand the error known as hasty generalization and know how to avoid it.*
- *Understand what inference to the best explanation is and how it differs from other kinds of induction.*
- *Understand the importance of using criteria to judge the adequacy of theories.*

2.5 Assessing Long Arguments
- *Understand the challenges involved in assessing long arguments.*
- *Be able to follow the three-step procedure for assessing long arguments.*

Online, there is arguing, and then there is arguing. Or, to be more precise, there is Arguing 1 and Arguing 2. Arguing 2 is arguing in the usual sense of arguing—not as the offering of well-supported statements, but as a pointless back-and-forth of unsupported assertions, or as a tense attack and counterattack of words, which at its worst degrades into accusations, name-calling, ridicule, insults, and rage. This is the bailiwick of trolls, baiters, harassers, bullies, narcissists, sadists, and other toxic players. It is the domain of those who naively believe they prove a proposition simply by boldly stating it. Or by screaming it in ALL CAPS. Arguing 2 has very little to do with critical thinking or logical argument and everything to do with satisfying the needs of the perpetrators—needs to be noticed, to feel powerful and in control, to feel better about themselves, to be entertained, to strike a blow for their side. Generally, people who argue this way cannot be reasoned with, and in arguing with them, you usually learn nothing. Nobody wins in Arguing 2, and cyberspace is filled from end to end with this kind of fake arguing.

Arguing 1 is arguing in the critical thinking sense. It is logical argument. It involves making a statement and trying to show that the statement is true by offering reasons and evidence to support it. Arguing 1 is about establishing what is and is not reasonable to believe. This is the kind of arguing that prevails among serious thinkers of all stripes, all political persuasions, and all levels of education. When such people argue, they strive for an objective perspective, commit to following reason and evidence wherever they may lead, try to understand and respect opposing views, and reject arguing that is personal, abusive, intolerant, or dishonest. The aim is understanding. Winning, conquering, impressing, or troubling the waters is beside the point. This is how critical thinkers have been pursuing knowledge in every field for at least two millennia. Arguing 1 does happen online; it takes place most often in serious and thoughtful blogs, websites, e-journals, and comment streams.

Every day online, people try to make you believe something, hoping that if you believe, you will act—you will support, join, comply, follow, love, hate, buy. Your beliefs—whatever their origin—can guide you to both failure and success, ignorance and understanding, paralysis and empowerment. Some of your beliefs truly inform you, and some blind you. Some are true; some are not. But the question is, *which ones are which?* This kind of question—a question about the *quality* of your beliefs—is the fundamental concern of critical thinking. And the real work of critical thinking gets done mainly through Arguing 1, through logical argument aimed at justified true belief.

2.1 Claims and Reasons

Critical thinking is a rational, systematic process that we apply to beliefs of all kinds. As we use the term here, *belief* is just another word for statement, or claim. A **statement** is an assertion that something is or is not the case. The following are statements:

- A triangle has three sides.
- I am cold.
- You are a liar.
- You are not a liar.
- I see blue spots before my eyes.
- 7 + 5 = 12
- You should avoid trolls at all costs.
- The best explanation for his behavior is that he was in a trance.

So statements, or claims, are the kinds of things that are either true or false. They assert that some state of affairs is or is not actual. You may know that a specific statement is true, or you may not. There may be no way to find out at the time if the statement is true or false. There may be no one who believes the statement. But it would be a statement nonetheless.

Some sentences, though, do *not* express statements:

- Does a triangle have three sides?
- Is God all-powerful?
- Turn that music off.
- Stop telling lies.
- Hey, dude.
- Holy crap!

The first two sentences are questions. The second two are commands or requests. The fifth sentence is a greeting. The sixth one is an exclamation. None asserts that something is or is not the case.

When you're engaged in critical thinking, you're mostly either evaluating statements or formulating them. In both cases your primary task is to figure out how strongly to believe them. The strength of your belief should depend on the quality of the reasons in favor of the statements. Statements backed by good reasons are worthy of strong acceptance. Statements that fall short of this standard deserve weaker acceptance.

How to Win Every Argument

The eminent philosopher Walter Sinnott-Armstrong says that too many people think arguments are fights or competitions (what we have called Arguing 2). But such verbal wrestling matches, he says, will not help you win in any way that really matters. As he sees it,

> If you see a conversation as a fight or competition, you can win by cheating as long as you don't get caught. You will be happy to convince people with bad arguments. You don't mind interrupting them. You can call their views crazy, stupid, silly or ridiculous, or you can joke about how ignorant they are, how short they are or how small their hands are. None of these tricks will help you understand them, their positions or the issues that divide you, but they can help you win—in one way.

But things will turn out better, he says, if you engage in argument in the critical thinking sense (Arguing 1):

> Suppose you give a reasonable argument: that full-time workers should not have to live in poverty. Then I counter with another reasonable argument: that a higher minimum wage will force businesses to employ less people for less time. Now we can understand each other's positions and recognize our shared values, since we both care about needy workers.
>
> What if, in the end, you convince me that we should increase the minimum wage because there are ways to do so without creating unemployment or underemployment? Who won? You ended up in exactly the position where you started, so you did not "win" anything, except perhaps some minor fleeting joy at beating me. On the other side, I gained a lot: more accurate beliefs, stronger evidence and deeper understanding of the issues, of you and of myself. If what I wanted was truth, reason and understanding, then I got what I wanted. In that way, I won. Instead of resenting you for beating me, I should thank you for helping me. That positive reaction undermines the common view of arguments as fights or competitions, while enhancing our personal relationships.[1]

Sometimes you may not be able to assign any substantial weight at all to the reasons for or against a statement. There simply may not be enough evidence to rationally decide. Generally when that happens, good critical thinkers don't arbitrarily choose to accept or reject a statement; they suspend judgment until there is enough evidence to make an intelligent decision.

 ### Section Query

Do you believe—or have you ever believed—that if you offer a clear statement of your belief, you have given an argument? Have you encountered posts on social media in which the writer seems to assume that a statement equals an argument?

2.2 Reasons and Arguments

Reasons provide support for a statement. That is, they provide us with grounds for believing that a statement is true. Reasons are themselves expressed as statements. So a statement expressing a reason or reasons is used to show that another statement is true or likely to be true. This combination of statements—a statement (or statements) supposedly providing reasons for accepting another statement—is known as an **argument**. Arguments are the most important tool we have for evaluating the truth of statements (our own and those of others) and for formulating statements that are worthy of acceptance. And this goes for the millions of arguments and statements we run into online. The fact is that most of the statements we encounter every day, especially those on the internet, are unsupported—they come with no reasons at all for believing them.

So *argument* refers to the assertion of reasons in support of a statement. The statements (reasons) given in support of another statement are called the **premises**. The statement that the premises are intended to support is called the **conclusion**. With these terms, we can define an argument as "a statement or statements (the premises) supposedly providing reasons for accepting another statement (the conclusion)."

Here are some simple arguments:

1. Because banning assault rifles violates a constitutional right, the U.S. government should not ban assault rifles.
2. CNET says that people should invest heavily in stocks. Therefore, investing in stocks is a smart move.
3. When Judy drives her car, she's always late. Since she's driving her car now, she will be late.
4. Listen, any movie with clowns in it cannot be a good movie. Last night's movie had at least a dozen clowns in it. Consequently, it was awful.
5. The war on terrorism must include a massive military strike on nation X because without this intervention, terrorists cannot be defeated. They will always be able to find safe haven and support in the X regime. Even if terrorists are scattered around the world, support from nation X will increase their chances of surviving and launching new attacks.
6. No one should buy a beer brewed in Canada. Old Guzzler beer is brewed in Canada, so no one should buy it.

Here are the same arguments with the parts easily identified:

1. [Premise] Because banning assault rifles violates a constitutional right, [Conclusion] the U.S. government should not ban assault rifles.
2. [Premise] CNET says that people should invest heavily in stocks. [Conclusion] Therefore, investing in stocks is a smart move.
3. [Premise] When Judy drives her car, she's always late. [Premise] Since she's driving her car now, [Conclusion] she will be late.
4. [Premise] Any movie with clowns in it cannot be a good movie. [Premise] Last night's movie had at least a dozen clowns in it. [Conclusion] Consequently it was awful.
5. [Premise] Without a military intervention in nation X, terrorists cannot be defeated. [Premise] They will always be able to find safe haven and support in the X regime. [Premise] Even if terrorists are scattered around the world, support from nation X will increase their chances of surviving and launching new attacks. [Conclusion] The war on terrorism must include a massive military strike on nation X.
6. [Premise] No one should buy a beer brewed in Canada. [Premise] Old Guzzler beer is brewed in Canada. [Conclusion] So no one should buy it.

What all these arguments have in common is that reasons (the premises) are offered to support or prove a claim (the conclusion). This logical link between premises and conclusion is what distinguishes arguments from all other kinds of discourse. This process of reasoning from a premise or premises to a conclusion based on those premises is called **inference**. Being able to identify arguments, to pick them out of a block of nonargumentative prose if need be, is an important skill on which many other critical thinking skills are based.

Now consider this passage:

> The cost of the new XJ fighter plane is $650 million. The cost of three AR21 fighter bombers is $1.2 billion. The administration intends to fund such projects.

Is there an argument here? No. This passage consists of several claims, but no reasons are presented to support any particular claim (conclusion), including the last sentence. This passage can be turned into an argument, though, with some minor editing:

> The GAO says that any weapon that costs more than $50 million apiece will actually impair our military readiness. The cost of the new XJ fighter plane is

$650 million dollars. The cost of three AR21 fighter bombers is $1.2 billion. We should never impair our readiness. Therefore, the administration should cancel both these projects.

Now we have an argument because reasons are given for accepting a conclusion.

Here's another passage:

Allisha went to the bank to get a more recent bank statement of her checking account. The teller told her that the balance was $1725. Allisha was stunned that it was so low. She called her brother to see if he had been playing one of his twisted pranks. He wasn't. Finally, she concluded that she had been a victim of bank fraud.

Where is the conclusion? Where are the reasons? There are none. This is a little narrative hung on some descriptive claims. But it's not an argument. It could be turned into an argument if, say, some of the claims were restated as reasons for the conclusion that bank fraud had been committed.

Now check this passage:

It is easy to mock Rush Limbaugh's gushing over Trump's maternity and child-care plan as some sort of political masterstroke. One can just as easily imagine today's Rush Limbaugh rationalizing Nixon's announcement of across-the-board wage-and-price controls as an act of genius, and liberals had already killed the free economy, and Republican price controls are better than Democratic price controls, and we're all Keynesians now anyway, and blah, blah, blah. But for all of Limbaugh's cynicism, there is something to learn. [*National Review*]

Again, we have assertions, but no argument.

Being able to distinguish between passages that do and do not contain arguments is a very basic skill—and an extremely important one, especially online. Many people think that if they have clearly stated their beliefs on a subject, they have presented an argument. But a mere declaration of beliefs is not an argument. Here is an example from Twitter:

I choose these words carefully because I mean them sincerely: Guns are disgusting, despicable creations of human engineering, and ownership of them is creepy and disturbing.

This is not an argument. It proves nothing. It's merely an assertion of beliefs. Often such assertions of opinion are just a jumble of unsupported claims. Search high and low and you will not find an argument anywhere. A writer or speaker of these claims gives the readers or listeners no grounds for believing the claims.

Here's another example of verbiage sans argument:

> Offense is taken, not given. I can take offense at whatever I want, and so can you. That doesn't mean you can prevent people from saying what they want to say. As long as they don't physically assault you, it is not a crime. People who think "hate speech" should be banned are kidding themselves. Yes, that includes forms of cyberbullying, including rape and death threats. How is it that Twitter can tolerate death threats to Donald Trump, but will ban you if you do the same to Anita Sarkeesian?

This Reddit post looks like it's warming up to make an argument, but it's not an argument yet.

Sometimes people also confuse **explanations** with arguments. An argument gives us reasons for believing *that something is the case*—that a claim is true or probably true. An explanation, though, tells us *why or how something is the case*. Arguments have something to prove; explanations do not. Ponder this pair of statements:

1. Adam obviously stole the money, for three people saw him do it.
2. Adam stole the money because he needed it to buy food.

Statement 1 is an argument. Statement 2 is an explanation. Statement 1 tries to show that something is the case—that Adam stole the money. And the reason offered in support of this statement is that three people saw him do it. Statement 2 does not try to prove that something is the case (that Adam stole the money). Instead, it attempts to explain why something is the case (why Adam stole the money). Statement 2 takes for granted that Adam stole the money and then tries to explain why he did it.

It's not always easy to recognize an argument, to locate both premises and conclusion, but there are a few tricks that can make the job more manageable. For one, there are **indicator words** that frequently accompany arguments and signal that a premise or conclusion is present. For example, in argument 1, cited earlier in this chapter, the indicator word *because* tips us off to the presence of the premise "Because banning assault rifles violates a constitutional right." In argument 2, *therefore* points to the conclusion "Therefore, investing in stocks is a smart move."

Here are some common premise indicators:

because	due to the fact that	inasmuch as
in view of the fact	being that	as indicated by
given that	since	for
seeing that	assuming that	the reason being
as	for the reason that	

And here are some common conclusion indicators:

therefore	it follows that	it must be that
thus	we can conclude that	as a result
which implies that	so	which means that
consequently	hence	ergo

Using indicator words to spot premises and conclusions, however, is not foolproof. They're just good clues. You will find that some of the words just listed are used when no argument is present. For example,

- I am here *because* you asked me to come.
- I haven't seen you *since* Woodstock.
- He was *so* sleepy he fell off his chair.

Note also that arguments can be put forth without the use of *any* indicator words:

> We must take steps to protect ourselves from criminals. We can't rely on the government— law enforcement is already stretched thin. The police can't be everywhere at once, and they usually get involved only after a crime has been committed.

As you may have noticed, the basic structure of arguments can have several simple variations. For one thing, arguments can have any number of premises. Arguments 1 and 2 have one premise. Arguments 3, 4, and 6, two premises; argument 5, three premises. In extended arguments that often appear in blogs, essays, editorials, reports, and other works, there can be many more premises. Also, the conclusion of an argument may not always appear after the premises. As in argument 5, the conclusion may be presented first.

Another wrinkle: Some arguments have unstated, or implicit, premises, and a few even have unstated conclusions. For example,

> Any judge who supports capital punishment for juvenile offenders is an enemy of the Bill of Rights. Judge Simpson is definitely an enemy of the Bill of Rights.

The conclusion of this argument is "Judge Simpson is definitely an enemy of the Bill of Rights," and the only premise is the first statement. But there seems to be a leap of logic from the premise to the conclusion. Something is missing. The conclusion follows logically only if we insert an additional premise to bridge the gap, something like this:

> Any judge who supports capital punishment for juvenile offenders is an enemy of the Bill of Rights. Judge Simpson supports capital punishment for juvenile offenders. Therefore, Judge Simpson is definitely an enemy of the Bill of Rights.

Now we can see both the stated premise as well as the one left unmentioned, and we can conduct a complete evaluation.

When you're evaluating an argument, you should always bring any implicit premises out into the open. Finding the implicit premise makes evaluation easier. It also helps you avoid falling into a logical trap. Often premises that are left unstated are dubious or false. You should never let questionable premises slide by unnoticed.

Sometimes the parts of an argument are not so much implicit or unstated as unclear. For example,

> If we just paint all white people with the same racist brush, then it becomes about their race not their actions. This is what racists do. While I believe your intentions are good, others will use those same arguments to define other races for ill purpose.

This post may be clearer when read in the context of its larger thread, but as a stand-alone argument, its conclusion and premises are less than explicit. Paraphrasing it can make it easier to evaluate:

> We should not accuse all white people of racism. To do so is to judge them by the color of their skin, which is itself racism. Racists think this way, judging people by the color of their skin instead of by their actions.

Probably the best advice for anyone trying to uncover or dissect arguments is this: *Find the conclusion first.* Once you know what claim someone is trying to prove, isolating the premises becomes much easier. Ask yourself, "What claim is this writer or speaker trying to persuade me to believe?" If the writer or speaker is not trying to convince you of anything, there is no argument to examine.

Finally, a fundamental distinction in critical thinking is this: Persuading people to agree with you is *not the same thing* as presenting them with a good argument. You can influence people's opinions by using words to appeal to their ego, gullibility, bigotry, greed, anger, prejudice, and more. You just have to use emotional language, psychological ploys, semantic or syntactic tricks, and outright lies. But having done so, you would not have demonstrated that *any* belief is true or warranted. You would not have shown that a claim is *worthy of acceptance*. This latter task is a matter of logic and argument. The machinations of raw persuasion are not.

Certainly the presentation of a good argument (in the critical thinking sense) can sometimes be psychologically compelling. And there are times when persuasion through psychological or emotional appeals is appropriate, even necessary. You just have to keep these two functions straight in your mind.

Section Query

The last time you debated someone online or in person, did you use logical arguments (premises supporting a conclusion)? If not, why not?

2.3 Argument Structure

The point of *devising* an argument is to try to show that a statement, or claim, is worthy of acceptance. The point of *evaluating* an argument is to see whether this task has been successful—whether the argument shows that the statement (the conclusion) really is worthy of acceptance. When the argument shows that the statement is worthy of acceptance, we say that the argument is *good*. When the argument fails to show that the statement is worthy of acceptance, we say that the argument is *bad*. There are different ways, however, that an argument can be good or bad. There are different ways because there are different types of arguments.

Arguments come in two forms—**deductive** and **inductive**. A deductive argument is intended to provide logically *conclusive* support for its conclusion. An inductive argument is intended to provide *probable*—not conclusive—support for its conclusion.

A deductive argument that succeeds in providing such decisive logical support is said to be **valid**; a deductive argument that fails to provide such support is said to be **invalid**. A deductively valid argument is such that if its premises are true, its conclusion *must* be true. That is, if the premises are true, there is *no way* that the conclusion can be false. In logic, *valid* is not a synonym for *true*. A deductively valid argument simply has the kind of logical structure that *guarantees* the truth of the conclusion *if* the premises are true. *Logical structure* refers not to the content of an argument but to its construction, the way the premises and conclusion fit together. Because of the guarantee of truth in the conclusion, deductively valid arguments are said to be *truth-preserving*.

Here's a simple deductively valid argument:

> *All dogs have fleas.*
> *Bowser is a dog.*
> *So Bowser has fleas.*

And here's a golden oldie:

> *All men are mortal.*
> *Socrates is a man.*
> *Therefore, Socrates is mortal.*

And here is one in regular paragraph form:

> [Premise] If abortion is the taking of a human life, then it's murder. [Premise] It is the taking of a human life. [Conclusion] So it necessarily follows that abortion is murder.

In each of these arguments, if the premises are true, the conclusion must be absolutely, positively true. It is impossible for the premises to be true and the conclusions false. The conclusion *logically follows* from the premises. And the order of the premises makes no difference.

A deductively *invalid* version of these arguments might look like this:

> *All dogs are mammals.*
> *All cows are mammals.*
> *Therefore, all dogs are cows.*

> *If Socrates has horns, he is mortal.*
> *Socrates is mortal.*
> *Therefore, Socrates has horns.*

In each of these, the conclusion does *not* logically follow from the premises. Each is an attempt at a deductively valid argument, but the attempt fails. And, again, this would be the case regardless of the order of the premises.

An inductive argument that succeeds in providing very probable—but not conclusive—logical support for its conclusion is said to be **strong**. An inductive argument that fails to provide such support is said to be **weak**. An inductively strong argument is such that if its premises are true, its conclusion is *very likely* to be true. The structure of an inductively strong argument cannot guarantee that the conclusion is true if the premises are true—but the conclusion can be rendered very probable and worthy of acceptance. (Here again, the structure and content of an argument are distinct elements.) Because the truth of the conclusion cannot be guaranteed by the truth of the premises, inductive arguments are not truth-preserving.

Let's turn our first two deductively valid arguments into inductively strong arguments:

Ninety-five percent of dogs have fleas.
Therefore, Bowser, my dog, very likely has fleas.

Ninety-eight percent of humans are mortal.
Socrates is human.
Therefore, Socrates is very likely to be mortal.

Notice that in the first argument, it's entirely possible for the premise to be true and the conclusion false. After all, if only 95 percent of dogs have fleas, there is no guarantee that Bowser has fleas. Yet the premise, if true, makes the conclusion very probably true. Likewise, in the second argument it is possible that even if 98 percent of humans are mortal and Socrates is human, the conclusion that Socrates is mortal could be false. But the premises, if true, make it very likely that the conclusion is true.

Here are three more inductive arguments about some everyday concerns:

Almost every computer I've purchased at an online store has been a dud.
Therefore, the next computer I purchase at the same online store will likely be a dud.

Maria's car broke down yesterday.
When it broke down, it made the same noise and spewed the same stinky exhaust that it always does when it breaks down.
Maria's car breaks down a lot.

Her mechanic, who does excellent work, always says the same thing: The problem is the carburetor.

Therefore, Maria's car trouble yesterday was probably due to a carburetor problem.

Twenty toddlers out of the twenty-one at the day-care center have a cold.

Therefore, this toddler (Johnny) very probably has a cold.

Logical validity or logical strength is an essential characteristic of good arguments. But there is more to good arguments than having the proper structure. Good arguments also have *true premises*. A good argument is one that has the proper structure—*and* true premises. Take a look at this argument:

All pigs can fly.

Vaughn is a pig.

Therefore, Vaughn can fly.

The premises of this argument are false—but the conclusion follows logically from those premises. It's a deductively valid argument with all the parts in the right place—even though the premises are false. But it is not a good argument. A good argument must have true premises, and this argument doesn't. A deductively valid argument that has true premises is said to be **sound**. A sound argument is a good argument, which gives you good reasons for accepting its conclusion.

Note, however, that deductively valid arguments can have true or false premises and true or false conclusions. Specifically, deductively valid arguments can have false premises and a false conclusion, false premises and a true conclusion, and true premises and a true conclusion. A valid argument, though, cannot have true premises and a false conclusion—that's impossible. See for yourself:

False Premises, False Conclusion

All dogs have flippers.

All cats are dogs.

Therefore, all cats have flippers.

False Premises, True Conclusion

My dog Bowser is a cat.

All cats bark.

Therefore, Bowser barks.

True Premises, True Conclusion

Bowser is a dog.

All dogs are mammals.

Therefore, Bowser is a mammal.

The Smart Way to Argue Online

Suppose you go online intending to engage in some serious, honest, productive debate on an important issue. You want to do Arguing 1, and you want to avoid Arguing 2, the usual pointless, snarky, muddled back-and-forth that wastes people's time and brings out the worst in them. How do you do that? Here's how:

- Begin by avoiding people you suspect are interested only in scoring points, grandstanding, letting off steam, or trying to get a rise out of you. If halfway through the conversation you discover they are not interested in rational argument, say goodbye and leave. Gravitate toward forums where respectful, intelligent discussions are the norm.
- Keep the focus on the argument. Critique the argument's form or the truth of the premises, *not* the person. Making the debate personal sidetracks the debate, injects emotion into it, and adds nothing relevant.
- Try to understand the other person's point of view and what motivates it. By doing so you increase your chances of winning the argument, learning something you didn't know, and calming the discussion through your show of empathy. Appreciating your opponent's objections can help make your own argument stronger and demonstrate that you are serious and fair-minded.
- Show your opponent moral respect. Give her a fair hearing. Don't assume the worst about her motives, values, or background. Don't stereotype her based solely on her political leanings or affiliations. Avoid snarky comments, sarcasm, name-calling, and insults.
- Stay on point; don't veer off into irrelevant side issues or nitpicking. Pointing out your opponent's bad grammar and spelling errors does not advance your argument one bit and will likely put an end to any chance of rational discussion.
- Rein in your emotions. If you get angry, agitated, or exasperated, you won't be able to think as clearly as you should, you may start hurling insults instead of solid arguments, and your opponent will probably respond in kind.
- Know what you're talking about. Suppose you begin arguing with someone for a position, only to discover that you are ignorant of the facts. But you keep insisting that you're right, because you're too embarrassed to admit you know nothing about the topic. This situation is a colossal waste of time. It's better to know the facts before you jump into the fray. Research the topic ahead of time, noting the arguments for and against the position in question.
- Think twice before trying to engage in a serious argument on Twitter. Twitter's short character limit makes conversations about complex issues and long arguments difficult or pointless. And the back-and-forth becomes even more unwieldy when a half dozen people chime in to add their two cents.

A good inductive argument must also have true premises. For example,

Scientific studies show that 99 percent of dogs have three eyes.
So it's likely that the next dog I see will have three eyes.

This is an inductively strong argument, but it's not a good argument because its premise is false. When inductively strong arguments have true premises, they are said to be **cogent**. Good inductive arguments are cogent. Bad inductive arguments are not cogent.

You may have noticed another important difference between deductive and inductive arguments. The kind of support that a deductive argument can give a conclusion is *absolute*. Either the conclusion is shown to be true or not. There is no sliding scale of truth or falsity. The support that an inductive argument can provide a conclusion, however, can vary from weak to extremely strong.

Both deductive and inductive arguments can be manipulated in various ways to yield new insights. For example, let's say that you have formulated a valid deductive argument, and you know that the conclusion is false. From these facts you can infer that at least one of the premises is false. Using this tack, you can demonstrate that a premise is false because in a valid argument it leads to an absurd conclusion. Or let's say that you've fashioned a valid argument, and you know that your premises are true. Then you can infer that the conclusion must be true—even if it's contrary to your expectations. Or maybe you put forth a strong inductive argument, and you know that the premises are questionable. Then you know that the conclusion also can't be trusted.

Section Query

What can you conclude from an argument with solid logic but at least one false premise?

2.4 Argument Patterns

Very often, when you examine an argument, you will see right away whether the conclusion follows from the premises. At other times, you may have to think about the argument's structure for a while. But in many cases, you will need some help in sizing up the argument—the kind of help offered in the following pages.

Deductive Arguments

Fortunately, deductive arguments often occur in certain classic patterns. The forms, or structures, of the arguments show up again and again. Being familiar with these patterns can help you quickly determine whether an argument is valid.

Look at this argument:

ARGUMENT 1

If stealing harms people, then it is morally wrong.
Stealing does harm people.
Therefore, stealing is morally wrong.

The structure of this argument can be symbolized like this:

If p, then q.
p.
Therefore, q.

This kind of argument is known as a *conditional* (also, *hypothetical*). A conditional argument contains at least one conditional, or if-then, premise (If p, then q). The first half of a conditional premise (the *if* part) is called the *antecedent*. The second half (the *then* part) is known as the *consequent*. It happens that argument 1 is a conditional argument in a classic pattern called *modus ponens* (or *affirming the antecedent*). In *modus ponens*, the second premise affirms the antecedent of the first premise. Any argument using this pattern or form is *always* valid. So if you come across an argument in this pattern, you will know that it is valid—no matter what the statements say.

Another classic conditional pattern is called *modus tollens*, or denying the consequent:

ARGUMENT 2

If the cat is on the mat, then she is asleep.
But she is not asleep.
Therefore, she is not on the mat.

ARGUMENT 3

If the mind is identical to the brain, then damaging the brain will damage the mind.
But damaging the brain will not damage the mind.
Therefore, the mind is not identical to the brain.

Modus tollens, then, is symbolized like this:

> If p, then q.
> Not q.
> Therefore, not p.

Any argument having this form is valid.

Here's a slightly more involved conditional form known as *hypothetical syllogism*:

ARGUMENT 4

> If the cat is on the mat, then she is asleep.
> If she is asleep, then she is dreaming.
> Therefore, if the cat is on the mat, then she is dreaming.

The hypothetical syllogism is symbolized like this:

> If p, then q.
> If q, then r.
> Therefore, if p, then r.

Any argument having this form is valid.

And here is a powerful, valid form that has been used to devastating effect at least since Socrates. It's known as *reductio ad absurdum* (reduction to absurdity). The idea behind it is that if the contradictory (negation) of a statement leads to an absurdity or falsehood, then the negation of the statement is false and the statement itself must be true. You must accept the statement because denying it gets you into logical trouble. So if you want to demonstrate that a statement is true (or false), you assume the statement's negation and show that it leads to an absurd or false statement. Here's the form of this type of argument:

> p.
> If p then q.
> Not q.
> Therefore, not p.

In plain English, this says: Let's suppose that p is true. If p is true, then q must be true. But there's no way that q can be true. (Or, q being true is absurd.) So it must not be the case that *p* is true. Here is an example:

> Suppose that water cannot freeze.
> If water cannot freeze, then ice cannot exist.
> But obviously ice does exist.
> Therefore, water can freeze.

There are also common forms that are *not* valid. This one is known as *denying the antecedent*:

ARGUMENT 5
> If the cat is on the mat, then she is asleep.
> She is not on the mat.
> Therefore, she is not asleep.

Denying the antecedent is symbolized like this:

> If p, then q.
> Not p.
> Therefore, not q.

Finally, there is this invalid form, called *affirming the consequent*:

ARGUMENT 6
> If the cat is on the mat, then she is asleep.
> She is asleep.
> Therefore, she is on the mat.

Affirming the consequent is symbolized like this:

> If p, then q.
> q.
> Therefore, p.

The best way to use these argument forms to evaluate deductive arguments is to memorize them so you can more easily identify examples of the forms when you encounter them. Then you need only match the form of the deductive argument you are evaluating with one of these classic forms. If the argument matches one of the valid forms, it is valid; if one of the invalid forms, it is invalid.

Inductive arguments also have distinctive forms, and being familiar with the forms can help you evaluate the arguments. Let's look at three common forms of inductive arguments.

Deductive Patterns Worth Knowing

Valid Forms

AFFIRMING THE ANTECEDENT (*Modus Ponens*)

Example:

If Spot barks, a burglar is in the house.
Spot is barking.
Therefore, a burglar is in the house.

If p, then q.
p.
Therefore, q.

DENYING THE CONSEQUENT (*Modus Tollens*)

Example:

If it's raining, the park is closed.
The park is not closed.
Therefore, it's not raining.

If p, then q.
Not q.
Therefore, not p.

HYPOTHETICAL SYLLOGISM

Example:

If Ajax steals the money, he will go to jail.
If Ajax goes to jail, his family will suffer.
Therefore, if Ajax steals the money, his family will suffer.

If p, then q.
If q, then r.
Therefore, if p, then r.

DISJUNCTIVE SYLLOGISM

Example:

Either we light the fire or we will freeze.
We will not light the fire.
Therefore, we will freeze.

Either p or q.
Not p.
Therefore, q.

Invalid Forms

AFFIRMING THE CONSEQUENT

Example:

If the cat is on the mat, she is asleep.
She is asleep.
Therefore, she is on the mat.

If p, then q.
q.
Therefore, p.

DENYING THE ANTECEDENT

Example:

If the cat is on the mat, she is asleep.
She is not on the mat.
Therefore, she is not asleep.

If p, then q.
Not p.
Therefore, not q.

Enumerative Induction

In *enumerative induction*, we arrive at a generalization about an entire group of things after observing just some members of the group. (Thus enumerative induction represents the basic logic behind opinion polls.) Here are some typical enumerative inductive arguments:

ARGUMENT 7

Every cell phone I have bought from the computer store is defective.

Therefore, all cell phones sold at the computer store are probably defective.

ARGUMENT 8

All the hawks in this wildlife sanctuary that I have observed have had red tails.

Therefore, all the hawks in this sanctuary probably have red tails.

ARGUMENT 9

Sixty percent of the Bostonians I have interviewed in various parts of the city are pro-choice.

Therefore, 60 percent of all Bostonians are probably pro-choice.

As you can see, enumerative induction has this form:

X percent of the observed members of group *A* have property *P*.

Therefore, X percent of all members of group *A* probably have property *P*.

The observed members of the group are simply a sample of the entire group. So based on what we know about this sample, we can generalize to all the members. But how do we know whether such an argument is strong? Everything depends on the sample. If the sample is large enough and representative enough, we can safely assume that our generalization drawn from the sample is probably an accurate reflection of the whole group of members. A sample is representative of an entire group only if each member of the group has an equal chance of being included in the sample. In general, the larger the sample, the greater the probability that it accurately reflects the nature of the group as a whole. Often common sense tells us when a sample is too small. Reasoning from a sample that's too small results in a *hasty generalization* (discussed in the next chapter).

We do not know how many cell phones from the computer store are in the sample mentioned in argument 7. But if the number is several dozen and the cell phones were bought over a period of weeks or months, the sample is probably sufficiently large and representative. If so, the argument is strong. Likewise, in argument 8 we don't know the size of the sample or how it was obtained. But if the sample was taken from all the likely spots in the sanctuary where hawks live, and if several hawks were observed in each location, the sample is probably adequate—and the argument is strong. In argument 9, if the sample consists of a handful of Bostonians interviewed on a few street corners, the sample is definitely inadequate and the argument is weak. But if the sample consists of several hundred people, and if every member of the whole group has an equal chance of being included in the sample, then the sample would be good enough to allow us to accurately generalize about the whole population. Typically, selecting such a sample of a large population is done by professional polling organizations.

Analogical Induction

In the argument form known as *analogical induction* (or *argument by analogy*), we reason in this fashion: Two or more things are similar in several ways; therefore, they are probably similar in one further way.

ARGUMENT 10

Humans can walk upright, use simple tools, learn new skills, and devise deductive arguments.

Chimpanzees can walk upright, use simple tools, and learn new skills.

Therefore, chimpanzees can probably devise deductive arguments.

This argument says that because chimpanzees are similar to humans in several respects, they probably are similar to humans in one further respect.

Here's an argument by analogy that has become a classic in philosophy:

ARGUMENT 11

A watch is a complex mechanism with many parts that seem arranged to achieve a specific purpose—a purpose chosen by the watch's designer. In similar fashion, the universe is a complex mechanism with many parts that seem arranged to achieve a specific purpose. Therefore, the universe must also have a designer.

We can represent the form of an argument by analogy in this way:

> X has properties $P1$, $P2$, $P3$, plus the property $P4$.
> Y has properties $P1$, $P2$, and $P3$.
> Therefore, Y probably has property $P4$.

The strength of an analogical induction depends on the relevant similarities between the two things compared. The more relevant similarities there are, the greater the probability that the conclusion is true. In argument 10, several similarities are noted. But there are some unmentioned dissimilarities. The brain of a chimpanzee is smaller and more primitive than that of a human, a difference that probably inhibits higher intellectual functions such as logical argument. Argument 10, then, is weak. A common response to argument 11 is that the argument is weak because although the universe resembles a watch in some ways, in other ways it does not resemble a watch. Specifically, the universe also resembles a living thing.

Inference to the Best Explanation

The third type of inductive argument is known as *inference to the best explanation*, a kind of reasoning that we all use daily and that is at the heart of scientific investigations (Chapter 8). Recall that an argument gives us reasons for believing *that* something is the case. An *explanation*, on the other hand, states *how* or *why* something is the case. It attempts to clarify or elucidate, not offer proof. For example,

1. Megan definitely understood the material, for she could answer every question on the test.
2. Megan understood the material because she has a good memory.

Sentence 1 is an argument. The conclusion is "Megan definitely understood the material," and the reason (premise) given for believing that the conclusion is true is "for she could answer every question on the test." Sentence 2, however, is an explanation. It does not try to present reasons for believing something; it has nothing to prove. Instead, it tries to show why something is the way it is (why Megan understood the material). Sentence 2 assumes that Megan understood the material and then tries to explain why. Such explanations play a crucial role in inference to the best explanation.

In this type of inductive argument, we begin with premises about a phenomenon or state of affairs to be explained. Then we reason from those premises to an explanation for that state of affairs. We try to produce not just any old explanation but the best explanation among several possibilities. The best explanation is the one most likely to be true. The conclusion of the argument is that the preferred explanation is indeed probably true. For example,

ARGUMENT 12

Tariq flunked his philosophy course. The best explanation for his failure is that he didn't read the material. Therefore, he probably didn't read the material.

ARGUMENT 13

Ladies and gentlemen of the jury, the defendant was found with the murder weapon in his hand, blood on his clothes, and the victim's wallet in his pocket. We have an eyewitness putting the defendant at the scene of the crime. The best explanation for all these facts is that the defendant committed the murder. There can be very little doubt—he's guilty.

Here's the form of inference to the best explanation:

Phenomenon Q.
E provides the best explanation for Q.
Therefore, it is probable that E is true.

In any argument of this pattern, if the explanation given is really the best, then the argument is inductively strong. If the explanation is not the best, the argument is inductively weak. If the premises of the strong argument are true, then the argument is cogent. If the argument is cogent, then we have good reason to believe that the conclusion is true.

The biggest challenge in using inference to the best explanation is determining which explanation is the best. Sometimes this feat is easy. If our car has a flat tire, we may quickly uncover the best explanation for such a state of affairs. If we see a nail sticking out of the flat, and there is no obvious evidence of tampering or of any other extraordinary cause (that is, there are no good alternative explanations), we may safely conclude that the best explanation is that a nail punctured the tire.

In more complicated situations, we may need to do what scientists do to evaluate explanations, or theories—use special criteria to sort through the possibilities. Scientists call these standards the criteria of adequacy. Despite this fancy name, these criteria are basically just common sense, standards that you have probably used yourself.

Don't Argue with Trolls

You have already encountered internet trolls—people who specialize in posts that are deliberately insulting, disturbing, threatening, inflammatory, or otherwise disruptive. "There are multiple explanations for troll behavior," says journalist and social media expert Guy P. Harrison.

> Some of them are just standard-issue jerks, offline as well as online, nothing too complicated about it. They probably never quite figured out how basic socializing works and may not even appreciate how cruel and inappropriate they are. . . .
>
> Then there are the trolls who lead dual lives. Socially competent and pleasant enough out on the streets but monstrous inside a computer, these Jekyll-and-Hydes behave as if they are playing a first-person shooter game but with real people taking fire. Social media, for all the wonderful things it allows, is also a vast wilderness in which angry cowards feel empowered because they can provoke, harass, and threaten people at will with impunity.
>
> I reviewed numerous expert opinions on how best to handle trolls. There are many recommendations—counter their lies with facts; use humor to disarm them; report them to site moderators; be nice to win their hearts, and so on—but I believe one defensive tactic outperforms all others by far. It's called silence. A tried-and-true method of dealing with trolls is to hit back with nothing more than cold, hard silence. Just ignore them. Don't react, don't reply, don't engage. The old saying, "Don't feed the trolls," is a good one. When you explode, scream back in all-caps, and trade threat for threat, you give them the win. Deny trolls the reaction they seek.[2]

One of these criteria is called *conservatism*. This criterion says that, all things being equal, the best explanation or theory is the one that fits best with what is already known or established. For example, if a Facebook friend of yours says—in all seriousness—that she can fly to the moon without using any kind of rocket or spaceship, you probably wouldn't believe her (and might even think she needed psychiatric help). Your reasons for doubting her would probably rest on the criterion of conservatism—that what she says conflicts with everything science knows about space flight, human anatomy, aerodynamics, laws of nature, and much more. It is logically possible that she really can fly to the moon, but her claim's lack of conservatism (the fact that it conflicts with so much of what we already know about the world) casts serious doubt on it.

Here is another useful criterion for judging the worth of explanations: *simplicity*. Other things being equal, the best explanation is the one that is the simplest—that is, the one that rests on the fewest assumptions. The theory making the fewest assumptions is less likely to be false because there are fewer ways for it to go wrong. In the example about the flat tire, one possible (but strange) explanation is that space aliens punctured the tire. You probably wouldn't put much credence in this explanation because you would have to assume too many unknown entities and processes—namely, space aliens who have come from who knows where using who knows what methods to move about and puncture your tires. The nail-in-the-tire theory is much simpler (it assumes no unknown entities or processes) and therefore much more likely to be true.

We will examine conspiracy theories, or explanations, in Chapter 8. For now, just note that the criterion of simplicity is usually the knock-out punch against such conspiratorial explanations.

When you are carefully reading an argument (whether in an essay or some other context), you will be just as interested in whether the premises are true as in whether the conclusion follows from the premises. If the writer is conscientious, he or she will try to ensure that each premise is either well supported or in no need of support (because the premise is obvious or agreed to by all parties). The needed support will come from the citing of examples, statistics, research, expert opinion, and other kinds of evidence or reasons. This arrangement means that each premise of the primary argument may be a conclusion supported in turn by premises citing evidence or reasons. In any case, you as the reader will have to carefully evaluate the truth of all premises and the support behind them.

When you are trying to write a good argument, the story will be much the same. You will want to provide good reasons to your readers for accepting the premises, for you understand that simply explaining your premises is not enough. You will have to provide support for each premise requiring it and ensure that the support is adequate and reliable.

Section Query

Which patterns of argument do you encounter most online? What proportion of those arguments do you think are actually sound or cogent?

2.5 Assessing Long Arguments

Some arguments are embedded in extended passages, persuasive essays, long reports, even whole books. When you have to evaluate a very long passage, you're almost always faced with three obstacles:

1. Only a small portion of the prose may contain statements that serve as the premises and conclusion. (The rest is background information, reiterations of ideas, descriptions, examples, illustrations, asides, irrelevancies, and more.)

2. The premises or conclusion may be implicit.
3. Many longer works purporting to be filled with arguments contain very few arguments or none at all. (It's common for many books—even bestsellers—to pretend to make a case for something but to be devoid of genuine arguments.)

Fortunately, you can usually overcome these impediments if you're willing to put in some extra effort. The following is a three-step procedure that can help.

Step 1. Study the text until you thoroughly understand it. You can't locate the conclusion or premises until you know what you're looking for—and that requires having a clear idea of what the author is driving at. Don't attempt to find the conclusion or premises until you "get it." This understanding entails having an overview of a great deal of text, a bird's-eye view of the whole work.

Step 2. Find the conclusion. When you evaluate extended arguments your first task, as in shorter writings, is to find the conclusion. There may be several main conclusions or one primary conclusion with several subconclusions. Or the conclusion may be nowhere explicitly stated but embodied in metaphorical language or implied by large tracts of prose. In any case, your job is to come up with a single conclusion statement for each conclusion—even if you have to paraphrase large sections of text to do it.

Step 3. Identify the premises. Like the hunt for a conclusion, unearthing the premises may involve condensing large sections of text into manageable form—namely, single premise statements. To do this you need to disregard extraneous material and keep your eye on the "big picture." Just as in shorter arguments, premises in longer pieces may be implicit. At this stage you shouldn't try to incorporate the details of evidence into the premises, though you must take them into account to fully understand the argument.

Let's see how this procedure works on the following selection:

The Case for Discrimination

Edgardo Cureg was about to catch a Continental Airlines flight home on New Year's Eve when he ran into a former professor of his. Cureg lent the professor his cell phone and, once on board, went to the professor's seat to retrieve it. Another passenger saw the two "brown-skinned men" (Cureg is of Filipino descent, the professor Sri Lankan) conferring and became alarmed that they, and another man, were "behaving suspiciously." The three men were taken off the plane and forced to get later flights. The incident is now the subject of a lawsuit by the ACLU.

Several features of Cureg's story are worth noting. First, he was treated unfairly, in that he was embarrassed and inconvenienced because he was wrongly suspected of being a terrorist. Second, he was not treated unfairly, because he was not wrongly suspected. A fellow passenger, taking account of his apparent ethnicity, his sex and age, and his behavior, could reasonably come to the conclusion that he was suspicious. Third, passengers' anxieties, and their inclination to take security matters into their own hands, increase when they have good reason to worry that the authorities are not taking all reasonable steps to look into suspicious characters themselves. . . .

Racial profiling of passengers at check-in is not a panacea. John Walker Lindh could have a ticket; a weapon could be planted on an unwitting 73-year-old nun. But profiling is a way of allocating sufficiently the resources devoted to security. A security system has to, yes, discriminate—among levels of threat. (*National Review*, July 1, 2002)

In this example, the author has given us a break by alluding to the conclusion in the title: Discrimination by racial profiling is a justified security measure. Notice that this conclusion is not explicitly stated in the text but is implied by various remarks, including "A security system has to, yes, discriminate." Given this conclusion, we can see that the entire first paragraph is background information—specifically, an example of racial profiling. The first premise is implicit. We glean it from the comments in the second paragraph: Racial profiling is a reasonable response in light of our legitimate concerns about security. The second premise is explicit: Profiling is a way of allocating sufficiently the resources devoted to security.

Laid out in neat order, this argument looks like this:

(1) *Racial profiling is a reasonable response in light of our legitimate concerns about security.*

(2) *Profiling is a way of allocating sufficiently the resources devoted to security.*

(3) *Therefore, discrimination by racial profiling is a justified security measure.*

A fact that can further complicate the argument structure of a long passage is that complex arguments can sometimes be made up of simpler arguments (subarguments). For example, the conclusion of a simple

No Arguments, Just Fluff

Once you get really good at spotting arguments in a variety of contexts, you may be shocked to see that a massive amount of persuasive writing contains no arguments at all. Apparently many people—including some very good writers—think that if they clearly express their opinions, then they have given an argument. You could look at this state of affairs as evidence that people are irrational—or you could view it as a timesaver: No need to waste your time on a bunch of unsupported opinions.

Unsupported opinions are everywhere, but they seem to permeate political writing, posts on social media, and anything that's labeled "spiritual." Sometimes opinions are so weakly supported that they're almost indistinguishable from completely unsupported ones. Here's a taste:

> My family and friends have season tickets for the Buffalo Bandits. The disrespect that is shown to America by this team is appalling, particularly in this time of war. As both the Canadian and American national anthems are sung before each game, members of the team are hopping around, tugging at their uniforms, talking and carrying on amongst themselves. The players can't even wait for the national anthem to finish before they run off to their respective field positions. Whether one is for or against the war is irrelevant. Have some respect for America and what it stands for. (Letter to the editor, *Buffalo News* website)

No argument here, just indignation.

> So after a decade of progress, we have our smog problem back (as if it ever left). Another problem overlooked? Couldn't be because of all the giant behemoths (SUVs) on the road, could it? Nah. Or letting all the trucks from south of the border into our country without safety and smog inspections could it? Nah. It couldn't be because the government you think? Nah. (Letter to the editor, *Daily News* [Los Angeles] website)

No argument here either.

argument can serve as a premise in another simple argument, with the resulting chain of arguments constituting a larger complex argument. Such a chain can be long. The complex argument can also be a mix of both deductive and inductive arguments. Fortunately, all you need to successfully analyze these complex arguments is mastery of the elementary skills discussed earlier.

Let's take a look at another long passage:

Contemporary debates about torture usually concern its use in getting information from suspects (often suspected terrorists) regarding future attacks, the identity of the suspects' associates, the operations of terrorist cells, and the like. How effective torture is for this purpose is in dispute, mostly because of a lack of scientific evidence on the question. We are left with a lot of anecdotal accounts, some of which suggest that torture works, and some that it doesn't. People who are tortured often lie, saying anything that will make the torturers stop. On the other hand, in a few instances torture seems to have gleaned from the tortured some intelligence that helped thwart a terrorist attack.

Is torture sometimes the right thing to do? The answer is yes: in rare situations torture is indeed justified. Sometimes torturing a terrorist is the only way to prevent the deaths of hundreds or thousands of people. Consider: In Washington, D.C. a terrorist has planted a bomb set to detonate soon and kill a half million people. FBI agents capture him and realize that the only way to disarm the bomb in time is for the terrorist to tell them where it is, and the only way to get him to talk is to torture him. Is it morally permissible then to stick needles under his fingernails or waterboard him? The consequences of not torturing the terrorist would be a thousand times worse than torturing him. And according to many plausible moral theories, the action resulting in the best consequences for all concerned is the morally correct action. When we weigh the temporary agony of a terrorist against the deaths of thousands of innocents, the ethical answer seems obvious.

The length of this passage might suggest to you that the argument within it is long and tangled. But that's not the case here. The conclusion is this: In rare situations torture is morally justified. The first paragraph just provides background information; the second contains two premises. A paraphrase of the first premise would go something like this: In a ticking-bomb scenario, the consequences of not torturing a terrorist would be far worse than those of torturing him. The second premise says that the morally right action is the one that results in the best consequences for all concerned.

The argument then looks like this:

(1) *In a ticking-bomb scenario, the consequences of not torturing a terrorist would be far worse than those of torturing him.*
(2) *The morally right action is the one that results in the best consequences for all concerned.*
(3) *Therefore, in rare situations torture is morally justified.*

The best way to learn how to assess long passages is to practice, which you can do in the following exercises. Be forewarned, however, that this skill depends heavily on your ability to understand the passage in question. If you do grasp the author's purpose, then you can more easily paraphrase the premises and conclusion and uncover implicit statements. You will also be better at telling extraneous stuff from the real meat of the argument.

Section Query

What is your best guess: What proportion of the books, blogs, and long posts that you read contain arguments?

REVIEW NOTES

2.1 CLAIMS AND REASONS

- Arguing 2 is arguing in the usual sense of arguing—not as the offering of well-supported statements, but as a pointless back-and-forth of unsupported assertions, or as a tense attack and counterattack of words, which at its worst degrades into accusations, name-calling, ridicule, insults, and rage. Arguing 1 is arguing in the critical thinking sense. It is logical argument. It involves making a statement and trying to show that the statement is true by offering reasons and evidence to support it. Arguing 1 is about establishing what is and is not reasonable to believe.

- A **statement** is an assertion that something is or is not the case. When you're engaged in critical thinking, you are mostly either evaluating a statement or trying to formulate one. In both cases your primary task is to figure out how strongly to believe the statement (based on how likely it is to be true). The strength of your belief will depend on the strength of the reasons in favor of the statement.

- Sinnott-Armstrong says that truly productive arguing is not a fight or a competition (Arguing 2). It's a respectful exchange of reasons for belief that can lead to better understanding (Arguing 1).

2.2 REASONS AND ARGUMENTS

- In critical thinking an argument is not a feud but a set of statements that supposedly provide reasons for accepting another statement. The statements given in support of another statement are called the **premises**. The statement that the premises are used to support is called the **conclusion**. An **argument** then is a group of statements in which some of them (the premises) are intended to support another of them (the conclusion).

- Being able to identify arguments is an important skill on which many other critical thinking skills are based. The task is made easier by indicator words that frequently accompany arguments and signal that a premise or conclusion is present. Premise indicators include *for*, *since*, and *because*. Conclusion indicators include *so*, *therefore*, and *thus*.

- Arguments almost never appear neatly labeled for identification. They usually come imbedded in a lot of statements that are not part of the arguments. Arguments can be complex and lengthy. Your main challenge is to identify the conclusion and premises without getting lost in all the other verbiage.

2.3 ARGUMENT STRUCTURE

- Arguments come in two forms: deductive and inductive. A **deductive argument** is intended to provide logically conclusive support for a conclusion; an **inductive** one, probable support for a conclusion. Deductive arguments can be valid or **invalid**; inductive arguments, strong or weak. A **valid argument** with true premises is said to be **sound**. A **strong argument** with true premises is said to be **cogent**.

- To argue productively and intelligently online, gravitate toward forums where respectful, intelligent discussions are the norm; keep the focus on the argument; critique the argument's form or the truth of the premises, not the person;

show your opponent moral respect; stay on point, don't veer off into irrelevant side issues or nitpicking; and rein in your emotions.

2.4 ARGUMENT PATTERNS

- Arguments can come in certain common patterns, or forms. Two valid forms that you will often run into are *modus ponens* (affirming the antecedent) and *modus tollens* (denying the consequent). Two common invalid forms are denying the antecedent and affirming the consequent.
- An inductive argument is intended to provide only probable support for its conclusion, being considered strong if it succeeds in providing such support and **weak** if it does not.
- Inductive arguments come in several forms, including enumerative and analogical. In enumerative induction, we argue from premises about some members of a group to a generalization about the entire group.
- An enumerative induction can fail to be strong by having a sample that's too small or not representative. When we draw a conclusion about a target group based on an inadequate sample size, we're said to commit the error of hasty generalization.
- In analogical induction, or argument by analogy, we reason that since two or more things are similar in several respects, they must be similar in some further respect.
- In **inference** to the best **explanation**, we reason from premises about a state of affairs to an explanation for that state of affairs. We use the criteria of adequacy to judge the plausibility of a theory in relation to competing theories. The best theory is the one that meets the criteria of adequacy better than any of its competitors.

2.5 ASSESSING LONG ARGUMENTS

- Assessing very long arguments can be challenging because they may contain lots of verbiage but few or no arguments, and many premises can be implicit. Evaluating long arguments, though, requires the same basic steps as assessing short ones: (1) Ensure that you understand the argument, (2) locate the conclusion, and (3) find the premises.

KEY TERMS

argument
cogent argument
conclusion
deductive argument
explanation
inductive argument
inference
invalid argument
premise
sound argument
statement
strong argument
valid argument
weak argument

EXERCISES

Exercises marked with an asterisk (*) have answers in "Answers to Exercises" (Appendix B).

Exercise 2.1

1. What is a deductive argument?
2. What is an inductive argument?
3. Are inductive arguments truth-preserving? Why or why not?

*4. The terms *valid* and *invalid* apply to what types of arguments?

5. What kind of guarantee does a deductive argument provide when it is valid?

6. Can an inductive argument guarantee the truth of the conclusion if the premises are true? Why or why not?

7. What is the difference between an inductively strong argument and an inductively weak one?

*8. What is the term for valid arguments that have true premises?

9. What is the term for strong arguments that have true premises?

10. Can a valid argument have false premises and a false conclusion? False premises and a true conclusion?

11. What logical conclusion can you draw about an argument that is valid but has a false conclusion?

*12. Is it possible for a valid argument to have true premises and a false conclusion?

13. In what way are conclusions of deductive arguments absolute?

Exercise 2.2

For each of the following passages, determine if there is an argument present. If so, identify the premises and the conclusion.

1. "We live in an incredibly over-reactionary society where the mindless forces of victim demagoguery have unfortunately joined with the child-worship industry. It is obviously tragic that a few twisted kids perpetuated such carnage there in Columbine." (Letter to the editor, Salon.com)

2. "'War doesn't solve problems; it creates them,' said an Oct. 8 letter about Iraq. World War II solved problems called Nazi Germany and militaristic Japan and created alliances with the nations we crushed. . . . The Persian Gulf war solved the problem of the Iraqi invasion of Kuwait. The Civil War solved the problem of slavery. These wars created a better world. War, or the threat of it is the only way to defeat evil enemies who are a threat to us. There is no reasoning with them. There can be no peace with them. . . . [S]o it's either us or them. What creates true peace is victory." (Letter to the editor, *New York Times*)

3. When conservative John Wately last spoke on this campus, he was shouted down by several people in the audience who do not approve of his politics. He tried to continue but finally had to give up and walk away. That was unfortunate, but he's not the only one. This kind of treatment has also happened to other unpopular guest speakers. How easily the students at this university forget that free speech is guaranteed by the Bill of Rights. University regulations also support free speech for all students, faculty, and visitors and strictly forbid the harassment of speakers. And this country was founded on the idea that citizens have the right to freely express their views—even when those views are unpopular.

4. "[Francis Bacon] is the father of experimental philosophy. . . . In a word, there was not a man who had any idea of experimental philosophy before Chancellor Bacon; and of an infinity of experiments which have been made since his time, there is hardly a single one which has not been pointed out in his book. He had even made a good number of them himself." (Voltaire, *On Bacon and Newton*)

Exercise 2.3

For each of the following arguments, indicate whether it is valid or invalid, strong or weak.

1. Joe says that the food in the restaurant is first-rate. So it's first-rate.
2. Social welfare is by definition a handout to people who have not worked for it. But giving people money that they have not earned through labor is not helping anyone. It follows then that social welfare does not help anyone.
*3. If CNN reports that war has started in Syria, then war has started in Syria. CNN has reported exactly that. War must have started.
4. Any sitcom that tries to imitate *The Big Bang Theory* is probably a piece of trash. All of this season's sitcoms try to ape *The Big Bang Theory*. They've gotta be trash.
5. Either you're lying or you're not telling the whole story. You're obviously not lying, so you're just relating part of the story.
*6. Either your thinking is logical or it is emotional. It's obviously not logical. It's emotional.
7. A recent Gallup poll says that 80 percent of Americans believe in the existence of heaven, but only 40 percent say they believe in hell. People are just too willing to engage in wishful thinking.
8. Many young black men have been shot dead by white police officers. Black people have often been harassed by white policemen. From these facts we can conclude that the recent tragic shooting in Chicago of a black teen by a white police officer was a case of first-degree murder.
9. "We say that a person behaves in a given way because he possesses a philosophy, but we infer the philosophy from the behavior and therefore cannot use it in any satisfactory way as an explanation, at least until it is in turn explained." (B. F. Skinner, *Beyond Freedom and Dignity*)
10. You flunked the last three tests. You didn't show up for the last eight classes. And you haven't written any of the essays. Looks like you don't know the material.
*11. Bachelors are unmarried. George is a bachelor. He has never taken a wife.
12. Bachelors are unmarried, and George acts like he's not married. He's a bachelor for sure.
13. If Alicia is alone on a trip, she will be afraid. She's alone on the latest trip. She is afraid.
14. If the universe had a beginning, then it was caused to begin. We know that the universe did have a beginning in the form of the Big Bang. So it was caused to come into existence. If it was caused to come into existence, that cause must have been God. God caused the universe to come into existence.
*15. If the United States is willing to wage war in the Middle East, it can only be because it wants the oil supplies in the region. Obviously the United States is willing to go to war there. The United States wants that oil.
16. "Someone must have been telling lies about Joseph K., for without having done anything wrong he was arrested one fine morning." (Franz Kafka, *The Trial*)
17. Anyone willing to take the lives of innocent people for a cause is a terrorist. Many Christians, Jews, and Muslims have taken innocent lives in the name of their religious cause. Many Christians, Jews, and Muslims have been terrorists.
18. If he comes back, it's probably because he wants money. There he is. He wants money.
19. If you're 18, you're eligible to vote. But you're only 17. You're not eligible to vote.
*20. I like geometry. My geometry teacher likes me. Therefore I will pass my geometry course with flying colors.

EXERCISES

Exercise 2.4

For each of the following tweets, determine whether it is an argument. If so, restate it in clearer form if necessary and supply any missing premises. Indicate whether the argument is good (whether the premises are true and the logic is solid).

1.

    David Chan @DavidCh95421096 · 2/21/19
    Never abolish our 2nd amendment, we need it more than ever today. Look at all the European countries that banned guns, all overran by Muslim immigrants, people living in fear.

    Fig. 2.1 Screen grab of tweet from David Chan.

2.

    Lee Camp [Redacted] @LeeCamp

    It's not a refugee's fault that you don't have a living wage. It's not women, it's not PoC, and it's not immigrants. It's the capitalists who Trump enriches on a daily basis - the .1% who love it when we spend energy hating immigrants instead of them.

    Fig. 2.2 Screen grab of tweet from Lee Camp.

3.

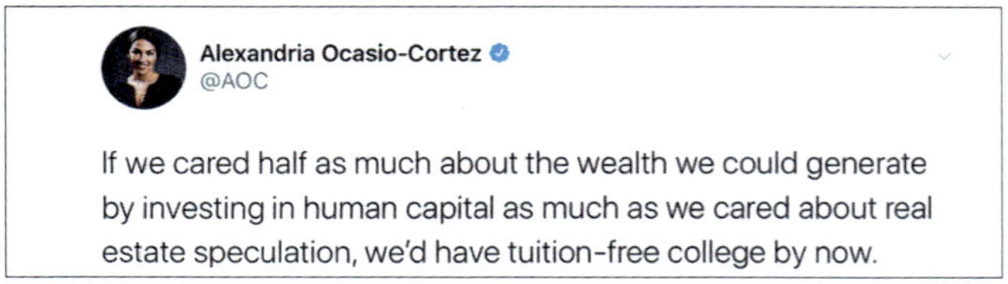

    Alexandria Ocasio-Cortez @AOC

    If we cared half as much about the wealth we could generate by investing in human capital as much as we cared about real estate speculation, we'd have tuition-free college by now.

    Fig. 2.3 Screen grab of tweet from Alexandria Ocasio-Cortez.

4.

    Denial Bot 6000 @denybot6000

    The weatherman cannot accurately predict the weather tomorrow. How can they predict climate change?
    #ClimateChange #GlobalWarming

    Fig. 2.4 Screen grab of tweet from Denial Bot 6000.

5.

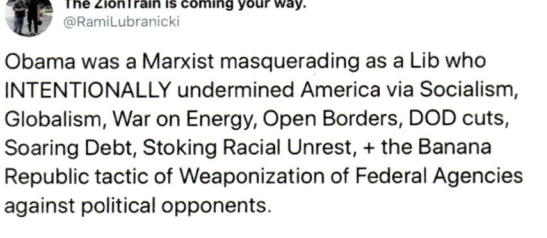

Fig. 2.5 Screen grab of tweet.

6.

Fig. 2.6 Screen grab of tweet from the *Atlantic*.

CAPSTONE

For each of the following passages, determine whether it contains an argument. If so, identify the premises and conclusion and determine if the argument is good—whether it is sound or cogent. If it is not, identify the problem (faulty logic or false premises).

1. Drone Strikes Overseas

   Drone strikes make the United States safer by decimating terrorist networks across the world. Drone attacks in Pakistan, Afghanistan, Yemen, and Somalia have killed upwards of 3,500 militants, including dozens of high-level commanders implicated in organizing plots against the United States. According to President Obama, "dozens of highly skilled al Qaeda commanders, trainers, bomb makers and operatives have been taken off the battlefield. Plots have been disrupted that would have targeted international aviation, US transit systems, European cities, and our troops in Afghanistan. Simply put, these strikes have saved lives." David Rohde, a former New York Times reporter held hostage by the Taliban in Pakistan for several months in 2009, called the drones a "terrifying presence" for militants. On Nov. 1, 2013 drone strikes killed Pakistani Taliban leader Hakimullah Mehsud. (ProCon.org, "Drone Strikes Abroad")

2. Gun Violence

Re "Man Kills at Least 12 in Virginia Beach Rampage"

In Virginia Beach, a "law-abiding" citizen with legally purchased guns and no history of felonies went on a murderous rampage. It is reported that the shooter had recently become belligerent in his workplace.

The gun industry has churned out guns for millions of "law-abiding" citizens. However, at the point of sale, there is no way to know if the purchaser has a hair-trigger temper, anger management issues or poor impulse control, or is seething with resentments.

The motive of the Virginia Beach shooter may never be known. But why make it so easy to buy a gun? Yes, he had a Second Amendment right to buy a gun for personal protection. But each of the 12 victims also had a right to life. (Letter to the editor, *New York Times*, June 3, 2019)

3. Mandatory National Service

Mandatory national service would foster unity and bring people from diverse backgrounds together. The partisan divide in the United States has never been greater: Pew Research tracked an increase in partisan differences from 15 percentage points in 1994 to 36 points in 2017. Dan Glickman, JD, former US congressman from Kansas, believes that mandatory service would be a solution to our "current dysfunction" because "National service, be it in the military, Peace Corps, or other public or private sector opportunities, breaks down the barriers of race, class, income, geography, and even language. Young adults are granted the opportunity to see their peers and fellow Americans as a member of their team."

Around 30 countries have compulsory military service. Switzerland, which has four official languages and three major ethnic groups, bridges its divides with a mandatory national service program. The European nation is identified as one of the happiest countries in the world by the United Nations.

Gene Yaw, JD, state senator in Pennsylvania, recommends a two-year universal public service requirement to promote civility and understanding of what it means to be an American: "We cannot generate enthusiasm for our way of life when less than 2% of our population has put forth any effort for our country." (ProCon.org, "Should the United States Have Mandatory National Service?," April 25, 2019)

Obstacles to Critical Thinking

Chapter Objectives

3.1 All Hail the Self
- *Know the forms that self-interested thinking can take.*
- *Be aware that self-centered thinking can prevent careful evaluation of claims, limit critical inquiry, and lead you to suppress or ignore evidence.*
- *Know that you can learn how to detect and overcome self-interested thinking by watching out when things get very personal, being alert to ways that critical thinking can be undermined, and ensuring that nothing has been left out.*

3.2 All Hail My Group
- *Appreciate how group thinking can distort critical thinking.*
- *Understand the meaning and be able to cite examples of* peer pressure, appeal to popularity, appeal to common practice, *and* stereotyping.

3.3 The Toughest Mental Obstacles
- *Appreciate why we need to counteract the human tendency to resist contrary evidence.*
- *Become sensitive to the possibility of confirmation bias.*
- *Be aware of how motivated reasoning can seriously distort our thinking, and understand how we can avoid the trap.*

3.4 Your Brain on Social Media
- *Appreciate how our thinking can be affected and undermined by the mere exposure effect, the illusion-of-truth effect, and the false consensus effect.*
- *Be alert to the Dunning-Kruger effect in ourselves and others, and understand how we can become more sensitive to this common human failing.*

Critical thinking does not happen in a vacuum, but in an "environment" that's often hostile to it. It takes place in the real world in the minds of real people who almost always have thoughts, feelings, experiences, and cognitive tendencies that, given half a chance, would sabotage critical reasoning at every turn. The sparkling palace of our mind is grand—except for the demons chained in the basement.

Recall our definition of critical thinking: *the systematic evaluation or formulation of beliefs, or statements, by rational standards.* This means, of course, that several factors must be present for the process of critical thinking to be fully realized. If the process fails to be systematic, or falls short of being a true evaluation or formulation, or ignores rational standards, critical thinking can't happen. Because we are fallible, there are a thousand ways that this failure of reason could come about. And there is no cure for our fallibility.

We should expect, then, that thinking critically will often be difficult and even unpleasant (as painful truths sometimes are), and indeed it is. But there are ways to (1) detect errors in our thinking (even subtle ones), (2) restrain the attitudes and feelings that can distort our reasoning, and (3) achieve a level of objectivity that makes critical thinking possible.

Doing all this—and doing it consistently—requires *awareness*, *practice*, and *motivation*. If we are to think critically, we must be *aware* of not only what good critical thinking involves but also what sloppy thinking entails. Then we must *practice* avoiding the pitfalls and using the skills and techniques that critical thinking requires. And we must be *motivated* to do all of this, for it is unlikely that we will use critical thinking very much if we can't appreciate its value and therefore have little motivation to make the extra effort.

The most common impediments to critical thinking are psychological, arising from our fears, attitudes, motivations, desires, and cognitive dispositions. Long before the information age, these factors were skewing judgment, twisting reason, and leading smart people into dead-ends of bad judgment. But many of them now seem tailor-made for sabotaging our thinking online, especially on social media.

3.1 All Hail the Self

As humans we spend a great deal of time protecting, maintaining, and comforting our own mental life, our own *selves*—a perfectly natural urge that does no harm until we push our self-serving efforts too far. How far is too far? From the standpoint of critical thinking, we have taken things too far when we accept claims for no good reason—when our thinking is no longer systematic and rational. In the service of our almighty selves, we distort our judgment and raise our risk of error, which is ironically a risk to ourselves.

Self-interested thinking takes several forms. We may decide to accept a claim *solely on the grounds that it advances, or coincides with, our interests*. You may think, "I believe the city should lower the sales tax for convenience stores because I own a convenience store," or, "I am against all forms of gun control because I am a hunter," or, "This university should not raise tuition because I am a student, and I don't want to pay more tuition." There is nothing inherently wrong with accepting a claim that furthers your own interests. The problem arises when you accept a claim as true *solely because* it furthers your interests. Self-interest alone simply cannot establish the truth of a claim. To base your beliefs on self-interest alone is to abandon critical thinking.

The influence of self on your thinking can take another form. You may be tempted to accept claims *for no other reason than that they help you save face*. We all like to think of ourselves as excelling in various ways. We may believe that we are above average in intelligence, integrity, talent, compassion, physical beauty, sexual prowess, athletic ability, and much more. But we not only like to think such things about ourselves, we want others to think the same about us. The rub comes, however, when we accept or defend claims just to cover up the cracks in our image. You make a mistake, and so you blame it on someone or something else. You behave badly, and you try to justify your behavior. You make a judgment or observation that turns out to be wrong, and you're too embarrassed or proud to admit it.

The consequences of self-centered thinking can be, well, self-destructive. In the realm of critical thinking, this devotion to yourself can prevent careful evaluation of claims, limit critical inquiry, blind you to the facts, provoke self-deception, engender rationalizations, lead you to suppress or ignore evidence, and beget wishful thinking. And these mistakes can decrease your chances of success (however you define success) and hamper your personal growth, maturity, and self-awareness. Such egocentrism can also leave you wide open to propaganda and manipulation by people who appeal to your personal desires and prejudices. How easy would it be for people to control your choices and thoughts if they told you exactly what you wanted to hear?

Other people (especially those who know you fairly well) may be amused or puzzled by your stubborn adherence to claims that obviously conflict with the evidence. Or they may think it odd that you cling to ideas or behaviors that you loudly condemn in others.

When examining a claim or making a choice, how can you overcome the excessive influence of your own needs? Sometimes you can do it only

Is It Wrong to Believe without Good Reasons?

Some philosophers have asserted that it is morally wrong to believe a proposition without justification or evidence. One of these is the famous biologist Thomas Henry Huxley. Another is mathematician W. K. Clifford (1845–1879). This is how Clifford states his view:

> It is wrong always, everywhere, and for anyone, to believe anything upon insufficient evidence. If a man, holding a belief which he was taught in childhood or persuaded of afterwards, keeps down and pushes away any doubts which arise about it in his mind . . . and regards as impious those questions which cannot easily be asked without disturbing it—the life of that man is one long sin against mankind.[1]

Clifford thinks that belief without evidence is immoral because our actions are guided by our beliefs, and if our beliefs are unfounded, our actions (including morally relevant actions) are likely to be imprudent.

with great effort, and sometimes the task is much easier, especially if you remember these three guidelines:

- Watch out when things get very personal.
- Be alert to ways that critical thinking can be undermined.
- Ensure that nothing has been left out.

You are most likely to let your self-interest get in the way of clear thinking when you have a big personal stake in the conclusions you reach. You may be deeply committed to a particular view, dogma, political party, political leader, or partisan principle; or you may want desperately for a particular claim to be false or unjustified; or you may be devoted not to particular claims but to *any* claims that contradict those of someone you dislike. Such zeal can wreck any attempt at careful, fair evaluation of a claim.

The 20th-century philosopher Bertrand Russell asserts that the passionate holding of an opinion is a sure sign of a lack of reasons to support the opinion:

> When there are rational grounds for an opinion, people are content to set them forth and wait for them to operate. In such cases, people do not hold their opinions with passion; they hold them calmly, and set forth their reasons quietly. The opinions that are held with passion are always those for which no good ground exists; indeed the passion is the measure of the holder's lack of rational conviction.[2]

The dead giveaway that you are skewing your thinking is a surge of strong emotions. If your evaluation or defense of a position evokes anger, passion, or fear, your thinking could be prejudiced or clouded. It is possible, of course, to be emotionally engaged in an issue and still think critically and carefully. But most of the time, getting worked up over a claim or conclusion is reason enough to suspect that your thinking is not as clear as it should be.

The rule of thumb is this: If you sense a rush of emotions when you deal with a particular issue, stop. Think about what's happening and why. Then continue at a slower pace and with greater attention to the basics of critical reasoning, double-checking to ensure that you are not ignoring or suppressing evidence or getting sloppy in your evaluations.

None of this should lead you to think that emotions have no place in clear thinking. Our emotions are an essential part of us, and they are important. They can alert us to danger, make us sensitive to injustice, enable empathy for others, and lead us to better informed moral judgments. A problem comes not when we appeal to emotions in our arguments, but when we appeal to *nothing but* emotions. That is, we try to persuade someone of a conclusion solely by arousing his or her feelings—guilt, anger, pity, fear, compassion—rather than presenting relevant reasons. Substituting strong emotions for solid reasons is an elementary mistake in reasoning—and too often a prelude to regrettable actions.

If you understand the techniques and principles of critical thinking, and you have practiced applying them in a variety of situations, you are more likely than not to detect your own one-sided self-centered thinking when it occurs. An alarm should go off in your head: "Warning—faulty reasoning." When your alarm sounds, double-check your thinking, look for lapses in arguments and claims, and weed them out.

Section Query

Think back to a discussion or debate you've had (either with yourself or someone else) in which you became upset. Consider carefully: Why were you upset? Was it because you had no good reasons to support your position?

3.2 All Hail My Group

In the old television series *Star Trek: The Next Generation*, the crew of the starship *Enterprise* encounters an unusual threat: the Borg. The Borg is a collective of individual minds that have been stripped of individuality and merged into a single group-mind with evil intentions. Much of the Borg storyline (which spans several episodes) is about the dignity and importance of individualism, as opposed to the conformism of the

Borg hive. The thought of losing one's self in the monolithic Borg is presented as a profound tragedy—a theme that strikes a chord with humans. Individualism, independence, and freedom of thought are what we want, what we must have.

Or so we say. Despite our apparent longings, we humans spend a great deal of our time trying to conform to, or be part of, groups. We want to belong, we want the safety and comfort of numbers, we want the approval of our beloved tribe. All of which is perfectly normal. We are, after all, social creatures. Conformist tendencies are a fact of life. But trouble appears when our conformism hampers—or obliterates—critical thinking.

We all belong to multiple groups—family, employees, gender, race, church, club, professional society, political party, partisan discussion group, you name it—and we can be susceptible to pressure from all of them. Much of the time, there is intense pressure to fit into groups and to adopt ideas, attitudes, and goals endorsed by them. Sometimes the influence of the group is subtle but strong and can occur in the most casual, "unofficial" gatherings. The claims and positions adopted by the group can be implicit, never spoken, but well understood. The political blog, the group of Christians or Muslims or Jews who happen to meet on the bus, the collection of peers who support the same political cause—all these can exert a noticeable influence on personal beliefs.

Guy Harrison uses the traditional term "groupthink" to denote group pressure. Groupthink, he says, is

> the common and dangerous tendency to fall in line and agree, even when we should know better. . . . Groupthink can be a problem for social media users because platforms like Facebook and Twitter cater to it so well. For example, many Facebook users build a coalition of family members, real-world friends, coworkers, and online acquaintances. How many Facebook users post any and all opinions without any thought given to possible negative reactions from others? I suggest most don't. Within the mostly closed world of a particular Facebook community, groupthink can be a powerful and near-constant presence. What if all or at least a majority of someone's Facebook friends, post, share, and "like" a report about a dubious herbal concoction said to cure AIDS, diabetes, eczema, and low self-esteem? There is a good chance that this person will either join in by also giving the news story a "like" or react to it with silence, which itself can be a form of agreement and conformity. If groupthink comes into play, as it so often does, the least likely response from most people in these situations is to challenge it. For all of the talk about trolls and flame wars, most people go along to get along.[3]

Group pressure to accept a statement or act in a certain way has several overlapping subtypes (some of which we'll cover in more detail in later chapters). When the pressure to conform comes from your peers, it's called—surprise—**peer pressure**. When the pressure comes from the mere popularity of a belief, it's known as—believe it or not—an **appeal to popularity (or appeal to the masses)**. When the pressure comes from what groups of people do or how they behave, it's called an **appeal to common practice**. In all cases, the lapse in critical thinking comes from the use of group pressure *alone* to try to support a claim.

There's another kind of group influence that we have all fallen prey to: the pressure that comes from *presuming* that our own group is the best, the right one, the chosen one, and that all other groups are, well, not as good. You can see this kind of ethnocentrism in religions, race relations, political parties, generations, social classes, and many other groups. The assumption that your group is better than others is at the heart of **prejudice**, a negative or adverse belief about others without sufficient reasons. It is dislike or intolerance based on no good evidence.

This we-are-better pressure may be the most powerful of all. We all have certain beliefs not because we have thought critically about them but because our parents raised us to believe them or because the conceptual push and pull of our social or political group has instilled them in us. That is, we may believe what we believe—and assume that our beliefs are better than anyone else's—merely because we were born into a family or society that maintains such views. We may be a Catholic or a Democrat or a racist primarily because we were born into a Catholic or Democratic or racist family or society. Like the influence of the self, this endemic pressure can lead to wishful thinking, rationalization, self-deception, and—worst of all—violence. Group thinking of this kind can also easily generate narrow-mindedness, resistance to change, and **stereotyping** (classifying individuals into groups according to oversimplified or prejudiced attitudes or opinions).

But as comfortable as our inherited beliefs are, when we accept them without good reason, we risk error, failure, and delusion. And as we discussed in Chapter 1, if we have certain beliefs solely because they were given to us, they are not really our beliefs. The sign of a maturing intellect is having the will and the courage to examine and gradually prune beliefs that are groundless.

Sometimes partisan group commitment can go from mere affiliation with a political party to partisan *tribalism*, which operates more like racism than political difference. In extreme cases, partisans no longer assert what they take to be true, but rather make partisan noises just to show support for their tribe or tribal leader.

For critical thinkers, the only way to counter the outsize influence of the group is to achieve an impartial stance and *proportion your belief to the strength of reasons*. Both actions take courage, dedication, and practice.

After thinking critically about claims favored by groups, you may find that the claims are actually on solid ground, and you really do have

Racism Is Group Thinking at Its Worst—But What Is It?

No serious observer of contemporary society believes that racism no longer exists, and it seems clear that racism in the United States is far more prevalent and insidious today than most people realize. But according to some race scholars, the label of "racism" or "racist" may often be misapplied.

Racism begins with the belief that races exist and can be differentiated by significant moral, intellectual, or cultural characteristics. This supposition of readily identifiable racial differences, however, is not in itself racism, no more than simply identifying someone's race is racism. According to philosopher and race scholar Lawrence Blum, what transforms this assumption about race into racism is the addition of the belief that (1) some races are inferior to others in important respects or (2) some races deserve distain, hatred, or hostility. Blum calls these two factors *inferiorization* and *antipathy*:

> Inferiorization is linked to historical racist doctrine and racist social systems. Slavery, segregation, imperialism, apartheid, and Nazism all treated certain groups as inferior to other groups. . . .
>
> Though race-based antipathy is less related to the original concept of "racism," today the term unequivocally encompasses racial bigotry, hostility, and hatred. Indeed, the racial bigot is many people's paradigm image of a "racist." . . .
>
> Historical systems of racism did of course inevitably involve racial antipathy as well as inferiorization. Hatred of Jews was central to Nazi philosophy; and it is impossible to understand American racism without seeing hostility to blacks and Native Americans as integral to the nexus of attitudes and emotions that shored up slavery and segregation.[4]

But if inferiorization and antipathy are the heart of racism, then many actions, attitudes, institutions, and people that are being called racist don't deserve the label. As Blum says,

> Some feel that the word [racist] is thrown around so much that anything involving "race" that someone does not like is liable to castigation as "racist." . . . A local newspaper called certain blacks "racist" for criticizing other blacks who supported a white over a black candidate for mayor. A white girl in Virginia said that it was "racist" for an African American teacher in her school to wear African attire. . . . Merely mentioning someone's race (or racial designation), using the word "Oriental" for Asians without recognizing its origins and its capacity for insult, or socializing only with members of one's own racial group are called "racist." . . .
>
> Not every instance of racial conflict, insensitivity, discomfort, miscommunication, exclusion, injustice, or ignorance should be called "racist." Not all *racial* incidents are *racist* incidents. We need a more varied and nuanced moral vocabulary for talking about the domain of race. . . . All forms of racial ills should elicit concern from responsible individuals. If someone displays racial insensitivity, but not racism, people should be able to see that for what it is.[5]

good reason to accept them. Or you may find that there is no good reason for believing them, and so you don't accept them. Either way, critical thinking will give you a clearer view of the group and yourself.

Section Query

Go online and find one example in which partisan group commitment seems to have gone from mere affiliation to partisan tribalism.

3.3 The Toughest Mental Obstacles

Possibly the most common psychological impediments to critical thinking—and the hardest to overcome—are the following, most of them mentioned in Chapter 1. They are hindrances that affect humans in every endeavor, from personal judgments to high-stakes decision making in business, government, politics, social networks, and even scientific research.

To define them, we need a correct understanding of the concept of **evidence**. In its most general sense, *evidence is something that makes a statement more likely to be true*. It does not mean "something that I feel or perceive is true." Evidence that there's a tree in the quad is your unimpaired, clear perception of such a tree (and your confidence that there is no reason to doubt your perception). Evidence that most Republicans (or most Democrats) drink alcohol is a scientific opinion survey (done by a reputable, unbiased polling organization) showing the alcohol drinking habits of those groups. Evidence that a measles vaccine does not cause autism in young children is a growing body of scientific research showing no connection between autism and a measles vaccine (and the discrediting and non-replication of a study that once tied those two together). The mere fact that you strongly believe a statement, or have a friend who strongly believes it, or have read Twitter posts by people swearing that it's true, or hear from your favorite YouTube personality that it's so—*such things do not, by themselves, constitute evidence*. They do not, by themselves, make a statement more likely to be true. They may, however, give you good reason to start looking for evidence.

Denying Contrary Evidence

An all-too-human tendency is to try to deny or resist evidence that flies in the face of our cherished beliefs. We may deny evidence, or ignore it, or reinterpret it so it fits better with our prejudices. **Denying contrary evidence** may be psychologically comforting (for a while, anyway), but it thwarts any search for knowledge and stunts our understanding.

It's shockingly easy to find examples of the blatant denial of evidence. Scientific research and commonsense experience show that the practice permeates all walks of life. A political activist may refuse to consider evidence that conflicts with his party's principles. A scientist may be so committed to her theory that she refuses to take seriously any data that undermine it. An administrator of a grand program may insist that it is a huge success despite all evidence to the contrary.

Often our resistance to contrary evidence takes a subtle form. If we encounter evidence against our views, we frequently don't reject it outright. We simply apply more critical scrutiny to it than we would to evidence in favor of our views, or we seek out additional confirming information, or we find a way to interpret the data so it doesn't conflict with our expectations.

In one study, proponents and opponents of the death penalty were presented with evidence concerning whether capital punishment deterred crime. Both those opposed to and those in favor of capital punishment were given two types of evidence: (1) some that supported the practice and (2) some that discredited it. Psychologist Thomas Gilovich describes the outcome of the study:

> The results of this experiment were striking. The participants considered the study that provided evidence consistent with their prior beliefs—regardless of what type of study that was—to be a well-conducted piece of research that provided important evidence concerning the effectiveness of capital punishment. In contrast, they uncovered numerous flaws in the research that contradicted their initial beliefs. . . . Rather than ignoring outright the evidence at variance with their expectations, the participants cognitively transformed it into evidence that was considered relatively uninformative and could be assigned little weight.[6]

There is no cure for our tendency to resist opposing evidence. The only available remedy is to *make a conscious effort to look for opposing evidence*. Don't consider your evaluation of a statement or argument finished until you've carefully considered *all the relevant reasons*. Ask yourself, "What is the evidence or reasons against this statement?" This approach is at the heart of science. A basic principle of scientific work is not to accept a favored theory until competing (alternative) theories are thoroughly examined.

Looking for Confirming Evidence

We often not only resist conflicting evidence, but also seek out and use only confirming evidence—a phenomenon known as **confirmation bias**.

When we go out of our way to find only confirming evidence, we can end up accepting a claim that's not true, seeing relationships that aren't there, and finding confirmation that isn't genuine.

In scientific research on confirmation bias, when subjects are asked to assess a claim, they often look for confirming evidence only, even though disconfirming evidence may be just as revealing. For example, in one study, a group of subjects was asked to assess whether practicing before a tennis match was linked to winning the match; another group, whether practicing before a match was linked to losing the match. All the subjects were asked to select the kind of evidence (regarding practice and winning or losing matches) that they thought would be the most helpful in answering the relevant question. Not surprisingly, the subjects deciding whether pregame practicing was linked to winning focused on how many times players practiced and then won the match. And subjects assessing whether practicing was associated with losing focused on how many times players practiced and then lost the match.

Sometimes we look for confirming evidence even when disconfirming evidence is more telling. For example, take this claim: All swans are white. You can easily find confirming instances; white swans are plentiful and ubiquitous. But even your seeing thousands of white swans will not conclusively confirm that all swans are white because there may be swans in places where you haven't looked. But all you have to do is find one black swan to conclusively show that the claim is false. (People used to believe that the claim was absolutely true—until black swans were discovered in Australia.) In such cases, confirmation bias can lead us way off course.

The pull of confirmation bias is insidious and potent. It is an incredibly strong tendency to cherry-pick evidence while we think we're being perfectly fair and reasonable. It makes false statements seem not only true, but irrefutable. It gives the deluded social media gadfly, who touts the reality of the nonexistent and the obvious evil of everyone in the opposing party, supreme confidence in the truth of the absurd and incredible.

Confirmation bias is one of the reasons that trying to carry on a coherent logical argument on social media can be so beat-your-head-against-the-wall frustrating. According to Tom Nichols, author of *The Death of Expertise*,

> Confirmation bias makes attempts at reasoned argument exhausting because it produces arguments and theories that are *nonfalsifiable*. It is the nature of confirmation bias itself to dismiss all contradictory evidence as irrelevant, and so *my* evidence is always the rule, *your* evidence is always a mistake or an exception.[7]

The moral of this story is that when we evaluate claims, we should look for disconfirming as well as confirming evidence. Doing so requires a conscious effort to consider not only the information that supports what we want to believe but also the information that conflicts with it. We have to seek out disconfirming evidence just as we keep an eye out for confirming evidence—an approach that goes against our cognitive grain. We naturally gravitate to people and policies we agree with, to the books that support our views, to the magazines and newspapers that echo our political outlook. Acquiring a broader, smarter, more critical perspective takes effort—and guts.

Motivated Reasoning

Suppose before beginning your investigation into a crime, before knowing anything about it, you decide what conclusion you will reach: Alex murdered Alice with an ax. So you glom onto evidence that Alex knew Alice, that they attended the same college, that they disliked each other, and that Alex owned an ax. And you disregard evidence that points in the opposite direction—evidence like phone records showing Alex and Alice 200 miles apart at the time of the crime, and testimony of her friends that her boyfriend, not Alex, threatened to kill her. How likely is it that your investigation will uncover the truth?

Not very. Yet research shows that this is the kind of thinking we all engage in far more often than we would like to admit, especially when we want to protect or promote our cherished political or personal beliefs. It's called **motivated reasoning**—reasoning for the purpose of supporting a predetermined conclusion, not to uncover the truth. It's confirmation bias in overdrive. It's a way of piling up evidence that agrees with our preferred conclusion and of downplaying, ignoring, or devaluing evidence that supports the contrary view. We set out to prove our point, not to determine whether the point is justified.

Online, motivated reasoning has been the modus operandi of those who want to prove to themselves and others that the Apollo moon landing never happened, that climate change is a hoax, that evolution is a fraud, that Barack Obama was not born in the United States, and that the Holocaust didn't happen. Through motivated reasoning, even very smart people can build, without realizing it, a very complex and impressive case for a claim that is complete rubbish. And the internet, with its vast stores of information easily accessible to anyone, is all the motivated reasoner needs to make the case overwhelming and irresistible—and dead wrong.

On social media, many people spend hours expounding on their one-sided arguments without once examining opposing views (except perhaps to try to trash them), or trying to understand the larger picture that could put issues and evidence in context, or examining contrary evidence impartially without indulging in knee-jerk rejection.

Defeating motivated reasoning is hard (and harder still to debate someone arguing in this way). But experts have offered some advice on how to avoid the trap:

- Be reasonably skeptical of *all* sources—but especially of those that support your beliefs.
- Be wary of your assessments of the credibility of sources that contradict your beliefs. Ask: Is this source *really* irrelevant, weak, or suspect—or is that my bias talking?
- Give opposing views a chance. Examine them carefully before deciding their worth. Do not dismiss them out of hand.
- Break out of the filter bubble. Seek out alternative views, read sources that you often disagree with, don't surround yourself with people who always agree with you.

Preferring Available Evidence

Another common mistake in evaluating evidence is the **availability error**. We commit this blunder when we rely on evidence not because it's trustworthy but because it's memorable or striking—that is, psychologically available. In such cases, we put stock in evidence that's psychologically impressive or persuasive, not necessarily logically acceptable. You fall for the availability error if you vote to convict a murder suspect because he looks menacing, not because the evidence points to his guilt; or if you decide that a Honda Civic is an unsafe vehicle because you saw one get smashed in a highway accident; or if, just because you watched a TV news report about a mugging in your city, you believe that the risk of being mugged is extremely high.

Being taken in by the availability error can lead to some serious misjudgments about the risks involved in various situations. Some people (are you one of them?) believe that air travel is more dangerous than many other modes of transportation, so they shun travel by airplane in favor of the automobile. Their conclusion is based on nothing more than a few vivid media reports of tragic plane crashes. But research shows that per mile traveled, flying is far safer than automobile travel. Your chances of dying in a plane crash in 2001 were 1 in 310,560, but the odds of your dying in a car accident were only 1 in 19,075. The fact is, there are plenty of less vivid and less memorable (that is, psychologically unavailable) things that are much more dangerous than air travel: falling down stairs, drowning, choking, and accidental poisoning.

The availability error is very likely at work in many controversies regarding environmental hazards. Because the alleged hazard and its effects can be easily and vividly imagined and the scientific data on the issue are not so concrete or memorable, the imagined danger can provoke a public scare even though the fear is completely unwarranted. Brain cancer from the use of cell phones and childhood leukemia from living near power lines—both these putative hazards have provoked fear and public demands for action. But scientific studies have shown these concerns to be groundless. Many environmental hazards are real, of course. But concluding that they exist solely on the basis of scary thoughts is to commit the availability error.

If we're in the habit of basing our judgments on evidence that's merely psychologically available, we will frequently commit the error known as *hasty generalization*. We're guilty of hasty generalization when we draw a conclusion about a whole group based on an inadequate sample of the group. We fall into this trap when we assert something like this: "Honda Civics are pieces of junk. I owned one for three months, and it gave me nothing but trouble." Our experience with a car is immediate and personal, so for many of us it can be a short step from this psychologically available evidence to a very hasty conclusion. If we give in to the availability error and stick to our guns about lousy Civics in the face of good evidence to the contrary (say, automobile-reliability research done by the Consumer's Union or similar organizations), we should get an F in critical thinking.

 **Section Query**

In online debates on serious issues, what would constitute an intelligent, productive response to clear-cut cases of motivated reasoning?

3.4 Your Brain on Social Media

As we've seen, homophily—the increased likelihood of believing a claim if it comes from your friends—is a widespread intellectual hazard on social media. But there are other cognitive biases that are just as prevalent and just as beguiling when given free rein in the information free-for-all found on Twitter, Facebook, Instagram, Snapchat, and all the rest.

Mere Exposure Effect

What if all the garbage we encounter online—all the lies, come-ons, fake news, misinformation, trivia, and rants—could affect our thinking without our conscious awareness, even after we dismiss what we read as so much bunk? The bad news is that this is a real phenomenon that happens often. It's called the **mere exposure effect**, the idea that just being exposed repeatedly to words or images (even without registering them consciously) can induce a favorable or comfortable feeling toward them, whether or not there is any good reason for doing so. This means you could end up liking or feeling positive toward a viral meme or nonsensical theory without knowing why. The element that makes the mere exposure effect work is familiarity with the thing exposed. Here's the famous psychologist and winner of the Nobel Prize in economics Daniel Kahneman discussing research on the mere exposure effect:

> A demonstration [of the effect] conducted in the student newspapers of the University of Michigan and of Michigan State University is one of my favorite experiments. For a period of some weeks, an ad-like box appeared on the front page of the paper, which contained one of the Turkish (or Turkish-sounding) words: *kadirga, saricik, biwonjni, nansoma,* and *iktitaf*. The frequency with which the words were repeated varied: one of the words was shown only once, the others appeared on two, five, ten, or twenty-five separate occasions....
>
> When the mysterious series of ads ended, the investigators sent questionnaires to the university communities, asking for impressions of whether each of the words "means something 'good' or something 'bad.'" The results were spectacular: the words that were presented more frequently were rated much more favorably than the words that had been shown only once or twice. The finding has been confirmed in many experiments, using Chinese ideographs, faces, and randomly shaped polygons.[8]

Perhaps the most disturbing aspect of the mere exposure effect is that it works without our conscious awareness. As Kahneman says, "It occurs even when the repeated words or pictures are shown so quickly that the observers never become aware of having seen them. They still end up liking the words or pictures that were presented more frequently."[9]

Illusion-of-Truth Effect

If there's one constant on social media it's repetition: the same lies, ads, rants, bad arguments, and fervid affirmations hitting you again and again, day after day. Research reveals that these repeat performances can be more than just annoying. They can alter your perception of what is true. This is called the **illusion-of-truth effect**, a phenomenon in which you come to believe that a false claim is actually true simply because it is familiar. In a typical study of the effect, scientists showed people statements without any indication of whether they were true or not. Then days later, the researchers showed them the statements again mixed in with new statements. When asked to assess the statements' truth, the people judged the original statements as truer than the new ones—just because the earlier statements felt familiar. They had seen them before. But, of course, familiarity is no guarantee of truth.

The worrisome part is that the illusory truth effect can happen even when we know better—that is, even when we have the opportunity to draw upon our store of knowledge. Too often, people don't apply what they know, and they allow familiarity to decide for them. Lies repeated are many times taken as truth—simply because they are repeated. Repetition and familiarity should cue our skepticism and remind us to look closer.

False Consensus Effect

Social media is the best incubator ever devised for what psychologists call **false consensus effect**, the tendency to overestimate the degree to which other people share our opinions, attitudes, and preferences. We like to think that most people agree with us (on a single issue or all issues), believe what we believe, have the same values, and look at the world the same way we do. We especially want to believe that attractive and respected people have the same beliefs we do. Thinking that many others agree with us gives us confidence that we are right, reasonable, smart, worthy, or sane. Our views aren't eccentric or beyond the pale; they are part of the consensus.

The problem is that we are often wrong about how widely our beliefs and attitudes are shared by others. We might say "everyone knows this" or "most people believe this," but there's a good chance that our estimates of how many concur are a huge exaggeration. There is little doubt that false consensus effect contributed to people's shocked reactions to the results of the 2016 U.S. presidential election. Filter bubbles and social media communities of course generate internal consensus, but this internal agreement leads members to think that the consensus also exists outside the groups.

One disconcerting consequence of the false consensus effect is that it can make us pigheaded. If we have the unwarranted conviction that our beliefs are shared by most people (or by most people who matter to us), then we are likely to hold them with much greater confidence or passion and be less likely to give them up when confronted with solid evidence and reasoning to the contrary.

The Dunning-Kruger Effect

This scenario happens online every day: The least informed person in a discussion decides to educate everyone else on the topic, confidently lecturing on the fine points and presuming to correct people's "obvious" misconceptions, never doubting for a minute his own grasp of the facts and his own superior understanding, while gushing forth a lot of bad information, misjudgments, and non sequiturs. The problem here (other than the obnoxiousness of the gusher) is not just that he is ignorant, but that he doesn't know how ignorant he is. This is the **Dunning-Kruger effect**, the phenomenon of being ignorant of how ignorant we are. Tom Nichols puts it this way:

> Dunning-Kruger Effect, in sum, means that the dumber you are, the more confident you are that you're not actually dumb. Dunning and Kruger [the researchers who originally studied the phenomenon] more gently label such people as "unskilled" or "incompetent." But that doesn't change their central finding: "Not only do they reach erroneous conclusions and make unfortunate choices, but their incompetence robs them of the ability to realize it."[10]

The Dunning-Kruger effect, unfortunately, is not just speculation. It's a fact about a common human failing. In an article titled "Confident Idiots," David Dunning says of the relevant research,

> This isn't just an armchair theory. A whole battery of studies conducted by myself and others have confirmed that people who don't know much about a given set of cognitive, technical, or social skills tend to grossly overestimate their prowess and performance, whether it's grammar, emotional intelligence, logical reasoning, firearm care and safety, debating, or financial knowledge. College students who hand in exams that will earn them Ds and Fs tend to think their efforts will be worthy of far higher grades; low-performing chess players, bridge players, and medical students, and elderly people applying for a renewed driver's license, similarly overestimate their competence by a long shot.[11]

The Dunning-Kruger effect is made worse by the tendency of many to believe that because they know a little something about a subject, they are experts, and because they have read a book or a few internet pages on a topic, they are as much an expert as any PhD. Nichols declares that

> the pernicious idea that "everyone can be an expert" is . . . dangerous. It's true in a relative sense that almost anyone with particular skills can develop specialized knowledge to which others, in most circumstances, must defer. Trouble, however, rears its head when people start to believe that knowing a little bit about something means "expertise." It's a thin line between the hobbyist who knows a lot about warships from reading *Jane's Fight Ships* and an actual expert on the capabilities of the world's naval vessels, but that line exists.

Knowing things is not the same as understanding them. Comprehension is not the same thing as analysis. Expertise is not a parlor game played with factoids.[12]

So how can we avoid the Dunning-Kruger trap? Here's Guy Harrison's advice:

Having the mere awareness and understanding that all people—yourself included—struggle to accurately assess competency levels can inspire the crucial and necessary pause, that moment of reflection before speaking, writing, clicking, liking, or swiping. Prior to declaring the "obvious answer" to gun violence, racism, sexism, or poverty—and then digging in to defend it—we must recall that confidence is not the same thing as knowledge. The Dunning-Kruger effect explains much of the loud, proud folly you find on social media.[13]

The Backfire Effect

A few years ago, scientific research seemed to suggest an alarming possibility—that facts were ineffective in helping people overcome their own mistaken beliefs. The idea was that when given accurate information that contradicts their inaccurate views (especially political ones), people will experience a *backfire effect* in which the corrections lead them not only to persist in their errors but to cling to them even more strongly.

But new studies suggest that the backfire effect is a far weaker phenomenon than at first supposed. People do fall prey to confirmation bias and motivated reasoning, but in general facts and evidence do not cause them to double down on the misinformation. As science writer Steven Novella says,

To be clear, people generally still engage in motivated reasoning when emotions are at stake. There is clear evidence that people filter the information they seek, notice, accept, and remember. Ideology also predicts how much people will respond to factual correction.

The backfire effect, however, is very specific. This occurs when people not only reject factual correction, but create counterarguments against the correction that move them further in the direction of the incorrect belief. It's probably time for us to drop this from our narrative, or at least deemphasize it and put a huge asterisk next to any mention of it. . . .

So if people do not respond to ideologically inconvenient facts by forming counterarguments and moving away from them (again—that is the backfire effect) then what do they do? The authors [of recent research] discuss a competing hypothesis, that people are fundamentally intellectually lazy. In fact, forming counterarguments is a lot of mental work that people will tend to avoid. It is much easier to just ignore the new facts.

Further there is evidence that to some extent people not only ignore facts, they may think that facts are not important. They may conclude that the specific fact they are being presented is not relevant to their ideological belief. Or they may believe that facts in general are not important.

What that generally means is that they dismiss facts as being biased and subjective. You have your facts, but I have my facts, and everyone is entitled to their opinion—meaning they get to choose which facts to believe.[14]

Section Query

Can you think of an example in which a public figure has seemed to fall prey to the Dunning-Kruger effect—that is, an instance in which they seemed not to know what they don't know?

REVIEW NOTES

3.1 ALL HAIL THE SELF

- From the standpoint of critical thinking, we have taken self-centered thinking too far when we accept claims for no good reason. In the service of our almighty selves, we distort our judgment and raise our risk of error, which is ironically a risk to ourselves.

- Self-interested thinking takes several forms. We may decide to accept a claim *solely on the grounds that it advances, or coincides with, our interests*. Or we may be tempted to accept claims *for no other reason than that they help us save face*.

- To overcome the excessive influence of your own needs, watch out when things get very personal, be alert to ways that critical thinking can be undermined, and ensure that nothing has been left out.

3.2 ALL HAIL MY GROUP

- Group pressure to accept a statement or act in a certain way has several overlapping subtypes. When the pressure to conform comes from your peers, it's called **peer pressure**. When the pressure comes from the mere popularity of a belief, it's known as an **appeal to popularity**. When the pressure comes from what groups of people do or how they behave, it's called an **appeal to common practice**. In all cases, the lapse in critical thinking comes from the use of group pressure alone to try to support a claim.

- The assumption that your group is better than others is at the heart of **prejudice**, a negative or adverse belief about others without sufficient reasons. It is dislike or intolerance based on no good evidence.

- We all have certain beliefs not because we have thought critically about them but because our parents raised us to believe them or because the conceptual push and pull of our social or political group has instilled them in us. That is, we may believe what we believe—and assume that our beliefs are better than anyone else's—merely because we were born into a family or society that maintains such views. This endemic pressure can lead to wishful thinking, rationalization, self-deception, and—worst of all—violence. Group thinking of this kind can also easily generate narrow-mindedness, resistance to change, and **stereotyping** (classifying individuals into groups according to oversimplified or prejudiced attitudes or opinions).

- For critical thinkers, the only way to counter the outsize influence of the group is to achieve an impartial stance and proportion your belief to the strength of reasons. Both actions take courage, dedication, and practice.

3.3 THE TOUGHEST MENTAL OBSTACLES

- In its most general sense, **evidence** is something that makes a statement more likely to be true. It does not mean "something that I feel or perceive is true." The mere fact that you strongly believe a statement, or have a friend who strongly believes it, or have read Twitter posts by people swearing that it's true, or hear from your favorite radio or TV personality that it's so—such things do not, by themselves, constitute evidence.

- An all-too-human tendency is to try to deny or resist evidence that flies in the face of our cherished beliefs. We may deny evidence, or ignore it, or reinterpret it so it fits better with our prejudices. **Denying contrary evidence** may be psychologically comforting (for a while, anyway), but it thwarts any search for knowledge and stunts our understanding.

- We often not only resist conflicting evidence, but also seek out and use only confirming evidence—a phenomenon known as **confirmation bias**. When we go out of our way to find only confirming evidence, we can end up accepting a claim that's not true, seeing relationships that aren't there, and finding confirmation that isn't genuine.

- **Motivated reasoning** is reasoning for the purpose of supporting a predetermined conclusion, not to uncover the truth. It's confirmation bias in overdrive. It's a way of piling up evidence that agrees with our preferred conclusion and of downplaying, ignoring, or devaluing evidence that supports the contrary view. We set out to prove our point, not to determine whether the point is justified.

- We commit the **availability error** when we rely on evidence not because it's trustworthy but because it's memorable or striking—that is, psychologically available. In such cases, we put stock in evidence that's psychologically impressive or persuasive, not necessarily logically acceptable.

3.4 YOUR BRAIN ON SOCIAL MEDIA

- The **mere exposure effect** is the idea that just being exposed repeatedly to words or images (even without registering them consciously) can induce a favorable or comfortable feeling toward them, whether or not there is any good reason for doing so.

- The **illusion-of-truth effect** is a phenomenon in which you come to believe that a false claim is actually true simply because it is familiar. But, of course, familiarity is no guarantee of truth. The worrisome part is that the illusory truth effect can happen even when we know better—that is, even when we have the opportunity to draw upon our store of knowledge.

- The **false consensus effect** is the tendency to overestimate the degree to which other people share our opinions, attitudes, and preferences. We like to think that most people agree with us (on a single issue or all issues), believe what we believe, have the same values, and look at the world the same way we do. The problem is that we are often wrong about how widely our beliefs and attitudes are shared by others.

- The **Dunning-Kruger effect** is the phenomenon of being ignorant of how ignorant we are. The Dunning-Kruger effect is made worse by the tendency of many to believe that because they know a little something about a subject, they are experts, and because they have read a book or a few internet pages on a topic, they are as much an expert as any PhD.

KEY TERMS

appeal to common practice
appeal to popularity (or appeal to the masses)
availability error
confirmation bias
Dunning-Kruger effect
denying contrary evidence
evidence
false consensus effect
illusion-of-truth effect
mere exposure effect
motivated reasoning
peer pressure
prejudice
stereotyping

EXERCISES

Exercises marked with an asterisk (*) have answers in "Answers to Exercises" (Appendix B).

Exercise 3.1

1. What is confirmation bias?
2. What is the availability error?
*3. What is motivated reasoning?
4. What did W. K. Clifford say about the morality of believing claims?
5. What is stereotyping?
*6. From the standpoint of critical thinking, what event signals that we have allowed our bias in favor of ourselves to go too far?
7. According to the text, what effect can our urge to save face have on our thinking?
8. What is the mere exposure effect?
9. What is the illusion-of-truth effect?
10. When are you most likely to let your self-interest get in the way of clear thinking?
*11. How might the influence of a group that you belong to affect your attempts to think critically?
12. According to the text, what may be the most powerful group pressure of all?
13. What is the appeal to popularity?
*14. What is the Dunning-Kruger effect?
15. According to Blum, what is racism?
16. What is evidence?

Exercise 3.2

For each of the following passages, indicate whether it contains examples of self-interested thinking, face-saving, or group pressure. Some of these are really tough.

*1. MARY: Animals have the same rights as humans.

   JENNA: What makes you think that?

   MARY: I love animals, and there are so many that are treated horribly all over the world. It's heartbreaking.

2. JONATHAN: My essay is better than Julio's.

   BETTY: Why do you think yours is better than all the others? Do you agree that the content and writing of all the essays are similar?

   JONATHAN: Well, yes.

   BETTY: Do you agree that all the other benchmarks of quality are nearly identical?

   JONATHAN: Yes, but mine is still better.

3. Dear friends, as your state senator I will continue my tireless work on your behalf. I will continue to use my considerable talents to make this district even better. I will continue to let my integrity be the guide for all my actions.

*4. We cannot allow those people to move into this neighborhood. They're not like us.

5. I oppose women becoming members of this club. If I endorsed their claims, every friend I've got in the club would turn his back on me.

6. His statements about the West Bank are all false, of course. He's an Israeli.

*7. Christianity is superior to all other religions. I was raised Christian, and all my relatives are Christians. This is the only religion I've known, and the only one I need.

8. I'm due for tenure next year, so I am in favor of continuing the tradition of tenure at this university.

9. The United States is the greatest nation on the face of the earth. I don't know anything about other countries, and I don't want to know.

*10. If Joan is appointed to the committee, I am guaranteed to have a job for the rest of my life. I wholeheartedly favor Joan's appointment.

11. Free speech should not extend to pornographers. Right now they are allowed to espouse their smut on the Internet and many other places. That's just not how I was raised.

Exercise 3.3

Read each of the following claims. Then select from the list any statements that, if true, would constitute good reasons for accepting the claim. Be careful: In some questions, none of the choices is correct.

*1. John: The newspaper account of the charges of pedophilia lodged against Father J. Miller, a Catholic priest in our town, should never have been printed.
   a. The charges are false.
   b. John is a Catholic.
   c. Important evidence that would exonerate Father Miller was not mentioned in the newspaper account.
   d. The town is predominantly Catholic.

2. Alice: The speed limit on I-95 should be 70 mph.
   a. Raising the speed limit to 70 mph would result in faster and safer traffic.
   b. The state commission on highways did a study showing that I-95 should have a limit of 70 mph.
   c. Alice travels I-95 every day and needs to drive 70 mph to get to work on time.
   d. Alice drives I-95 every day.

*3. Janette: Women are less violent and less emotional than men.
   a. A study from Harvard shows that women are less violent and less emotional than men.
   b. Janette is a woman.
   c. Janette is a member of a group of women who are fighting for the rights of women.
   d. Janette and all her friends are women.

4. Brie: People should buy stock in IBM, an action that will push the price per share higher.
   a. Brie owns a large proportion of IBM stock.
   b. Brie is chair of the board at IBM.
   c. The stock market is weak.
   d. Brie has a large family to support.

5. Colonel Stockton: The United States should attack the terrorists in Iran, even at the risk of a full-scale war with Arab states.
   a. The terrorists have humiliated Colonel Stockton's forces.
   b. The terrorists have humiliated the United States.
   c. Colonel Stockton is loyal to his troops, all of whom want to attack the terrorists in Iran.
   d. Attacking the terrorists in Iran would cause no casualties and would result in world peace.

*6. Morgan: Capital punishment is always wrong.
   a. All of Morgan's friends agree that capital punishment is wrong.
   b. If Morgan favored capital punishment, her friends would abandon her.

c. Morgan is president of the Anti–Capital Punishment League.

d. Morgan has already made her views known and cannot change her mind without seeming to be inconsistent.

7. Angelo: Marijuana should be legalized.

a. All of Angelo's friends smoke marijuana.

b. Legalizing marijuana would reduce the consumption of marijuana and save lives, money, and resources.

c. Angelo has already said on television that marijuana should be legalized.

d. Angelo likes to smoke marijuana.

Exercise 3.4

Read each of the following passages. Indicate whether it contains examples of the kind of group pressure that encourages people to conform (peer pressure or appeal to popularity) or the type that urges people to think that one's own group is better than others. For each example of group pressure, specify the possible negative consequences. A couple of these are very difficult to classify.

*1. Ortega is deeply religious, attending church regularly and trying to abide by church law and the Scriptures. He has never considered any other path. He believes that laws should be passed that forbid people to shop on Sunday and that designate Easter as a national holiday.

2. John goes to a prestigious college where many students use illegal drugs. Nearly everyone in John's frat house uses them. So far, he hasn't tried any, but his frat brothers frequently ask if he wants some. And he has noticed that he is rarely invited to any frat parties.

*3. A northeastern college has invited a famous writer to be a guest speaker in the campus-wide distinguished speaker series. She is an accomplished poet and essayist. She is also a Marxist and favors more socialism in the United States. During her speech she is shouted down by a small group of conservative students and faculty.

4. Yang Lei is a conservative columnist for one of the best conservative journals in the country. But she yearns for greener pastures— namely, a regular column for a weekly newsmagazine. She gets her dream job, though the magazine does have liberal leanings. The first few columns she writes for the magazine are a shock to her friends. Politically they are middle-of-the-road or even suspiciously liberal.

5. Alex is a fourth-grade teacher at a suburban elementary school in Tennessee. He is liked by students and teachers alike, and he has superior teaching skills. He is also a homosexual. When a group of fundamentalist Christians learn that Alex is gay, they pressure the school board to fire him.

6. Sylvia writes a column for the university newspaper. In her last installment, she argues that in a time of national crisis, the U.S. Justice Department should have the power to arrest and detain literally anyone suspected of terrorism. Her arguments are well supported and presented with a tone of tolerance for those who disagree with her. And most students do disagree—vehemently. Hundreds of letters to the editor arrive at the newspaper, each one denouncing Sylvia and calling her a fascist and a few names that could not be published. In Sylvia's next column, she apologizes for her

statements, says that she made serious errors, and declares that her statements should be viewed as hypothetical.

*7. Advertisement: When you make the best car in the world, everyone wants it. Audi XK2. A car in demand.

Exercise 3.5

For each of the following claims, decide whether you agree or disagree with it. If you agree with it, indicate what evidence would persuade you to reject the statement. If you disagree with it, indicate what evidence would persuade you to accept the statement. In each case, ask yourself whether you would really change your mind if presented with the evidence you suggested.

1. Affirmative action should be abolished at all state colleges.
2. Same-sex marriage should be legally recognized in all fifty states.
*3. An alien spacecraft crashed in Roswell, New Mexico, in 1947.
4. Earth is only 10,000 years old.
5. There is life on Mars.
6. Some people can twist their heads around on their necks a complete 360 degrees.
7. On Tuesday, a new computer virus will shut down every network and every PC in the world.
*8. Meditation and controlled breathing can shrink cancerous tumors.
9. All swans are white.
10. "Corporate welfare"—tax breaks and other special considerations for businesses—should be discontinued.

CAPSTONE

Consider this classic experiment conducted at Stanford years ago, one of many that has confirmed the power of confirmation bias:

> For this experiment, researchers rounded up a group of students who had opposing opinions about capital punishment. Half the students were in favor of it and thought that it deterred crime; the other half were against it and thought that it had no effect on crime.
> The students were asked to respond to two studies. One provided data in support of the deterrence argument, and the other provided data that called it into question. Both studies—you guessed it—were made up, and had been designed to present what were, objectively speaking, equally compelling statistics. The students who had originally supported capital punishment rated the pro-deterrence data highly credible and the anti-deterrence data unconvincing; the students who'd originally opposed capital punishment did the reverse. At the end of the experiment, the

students were asked once again about their views. Those who'd started out pro-capital punishment were now even more in favor of it; those who'd opposed it were even more hostile.[15]

Answer honestly: If you had been a student in this experiment, would your judgment have been any more rational? Are your evaluations of evidence pertaining to political issues generally less biased and more reasonable than this?

Fake News

Chapter Objectives

4.1 Taxonomy of Misinformation
- *Be able to distinguish between* lies, propaganda, opinions, hoaxes, *and* satire.
- *Explain how Cameron Harris created a "masterpiece" of fake news.*

4.2 Telling Fake from Real
- *Distinguish between legitimate and illegitimate reasons for accepting a claim.*
- *Know how to assess the reliability of online information by reading laterally, reading critically, using Google and Wikipedia carefully, and checking your own biases.*

4.3 Fake Images
- *Understand that when people encounter images online, (1) they tend to believe photos and videos, too easily thinking that what they see is the whole, undistorted, simple truth, and (2) they are not good at recognizing when images have been changed or doctored.*
- *Know that we can detect many of the fakes ourselves by determining the source, checking for previous uses, looking for incongruities (like shadows that aren't where they should be or cloned regions of the image), and being suspicious of images that seem too amazing to be true.*

4.4 Deepfakes
- *Know what deepfakes are and how they can fool people into believing falsehoods.*
- *Know how to investigate a deepfake by reading laterally—looking beyond the video to try to determine where it came from.*

Chapter 4 FAKE NEWS

As noted in Chapter 1, **fake news** is deliberately false or misleading news stories that masquerade as truthful reporting. In modern media, the term has been used as a warning about misinformation, as an accusation against adversaries, and as an incantation that's supposed to make objective truth disappear. Liberals have used it to accuse conservatives of promoting misinformation and half-truths, while conservatives have wielded it to charge liberals with trying to unfairly discredit views on the right. Some conservatives have claimed that fact-checking, which has often resulted in a charge of fake news against them, is a left-wing conspiracy, and some liberals have argued that conservatives undermine legitimate journalism by falsely labeling real news as fake. We can see these crosscurrents of skepticism in two extreme modes of thinking: the acceptance of claims coming only from one's own partisan tribe, or the rejection of all claims from all other partisan tribes. As one observer puts it,

> Fake news, and the proliferation of raw opinion that passes for news, is creating confusion, punching holes in what is true, causing a kind of funhouse effect that leaves the reader doubting everything, including real news.
>
> That has pushed up the political temperature and increased polarization. No longer burdened with wrestling with the possibility that they might be wrong, people on the right and the left have become more entrenched in their positions, experts say. In interviews, people said they felt more empowered, more attached to their own side and less inclined to listen to the other. Polarization is fun, like cheering a goal for the home team.[1]

Yet the fact remains: Fake news, whether real or imagined, whether soothing or vexing, is bad for intelligent discourse, bad for the pursuit of knowledge, bad for sane politics, and bad for democracy. Critical thinking, whether pleasing or upsetting, offers a necessary corrective.

Much of the fake news we see is LOL funny or ridiculous, but a great deal of it is harmful, destructive, and dangerous. Fake news has sown distrust among people, pushed political conflict to the boiling point, exaggerated disagreements and social conflicts, and incited confrontation and violence by proclaiming the reality of imaginary events. Conspiracy theorists and their accomplices have, in the aftermath of mass shootings and other tragedies, posted fake news designed to incite fear, suspicion, and hate. Even before the flames are extinguished and the victims are counted, conspiracy theories fly around the internet to blame the innocent, point fingers randomly, or declare that the innocent victims were really actors.

The most unsettling recent example of the damage that fake news can do to a democracy is the 2016 fake news attack orchestrated by the

Russian government. According to the Center for Information Technology and Society at UC Santa Barbara,

> During and after the 2016 election, Russian agents created social media accounts to spread fake news that stirred protests and favored presidential candidate Donald Trump while discrediting candidate Hillary Clinton and her associates. They paid Facebook for advertisements that appeared on that site to spread fake news and turn Americans against one another. The U.S. Congressional Intelligence committees responsible for investigating fake news have released 3,500 of these advertisements to the public.
>
> Ads focused on controversial social issues such as race, the Black Lives Matter movement, the 2nd Amendment, immigration, and other issues. The Russians even went so far as to instigate protests and counter protests about a given issue, literally having Americans fight one another . . . Facebook messages . . . created "events" out of thin air, in an effort to get people to believe them, show up, and make trouble.[2]

Fake news has also harmed innocent people by falsely accusing them of immoral or criminal acts, arousing unjustified anger or hatred against them, and causing them to be the targets of relentless trolling. The classic example of fake news leading to harassment and violence is the "Pizzagate" incident. In 2016 a 29-year-old North Carolina man carrying three guns showed up at a Washington DC pizzeria and fired off a military-style assault rifle, frightening employees and customers who ran terrified out of the restaurant. Why did he do such a thing? He read some fake news. He saw a tweet from a white supremacist account claiming, falsely, that the restaurant housed a child sex-trafficking ring tied somehow to Democratic presidential candidate Hillary Clinton. So he went to the pizzeria to rescue the enslaved children. But there were none. He was arrested, convicted, and sentenced to four years in prison and three years of probation. Before the shooting, the false tweet had been appearing in other news feeds, prompting many people to harass those who worked at the pizzeria.

Such dramatic episodes overshadow the countless bomblets of familiar fake news that are quietly and potentially hazardous. For example, there are myriad websites, emails, and blogs that promote "miracle" cures and novel treatments for both minor and serious diseases. Typically the products are unproven, disproven, or seriously harmful. Just as bad are online campaigns against medical treatments proven through rigorous research to work.

Research on fake news shows that it spreads much faster and farther through social media than true stories can. Why? Researchers speculate that that false stories win the race partly because they are political, anger-provoking, surprising, strange, or sensational. This fact fits with the old witticism (often attributed to Mark Twain but actually traced back to Jonathan Swift in 1710) that a lie can travel halfway around the world before the truth can put on its boots. And of course, thanks to digital technology, lies really can travel halfway around the world in a blink.

4.1 Taxonomy of Misinformation

Fake news overlaps, or is distinct from, other kinds of messages and misinformation:

lies Because fake news involves *deliberate* deception, it is a lie—a falsehood intended to deceive. But false statements that arise because of mistakes, errors, or misunderstandings are not lies and do not constitute fake news.

propaganda Propaganda is deliberately biased or misleading information designed to promote a political cause or point of view. Propaganda and fake news are distinct, but the latter can be used in the former. In contemporary public relations work and political lobbying, propaganda is a common tool.

opinions Writing that expresses opinions or advocates change (advocacy journalism) is not fake news unless there is a deliberate attempt to deceive. The same goes for inept reporting and sloppy writing. The information may be false, unclear, or controversial, but that alone does not make it fake news.

bias Biased reporting is not necessarily fake news, but it can easily become fake news with the addition of intentional deception. A writer who cherry-picks facts to support her arguments, ignores contrary evidence, and mischaracterizes her opponents' views may or may not be churning out fake news (because she may not be trying to deliberately deceive), but she is, at the very least, practicing bad journalism and dishonest reporting. (See more about media bias in Chapter 5.)

hoaxes A hoax is a lie intentionally fabricated to appear truthful and to gain an advantage (financial or otherwise) or to provoke a reaction. Many hoaxes propagated through the media are rightly considered fake news, but others are better known as financial or health scams, computer virus hoaxes, urban legends, email hoaxes, and art-world hoaxes.

A Fake News "Masterpiece"

How is fake news created? According to experts, it can be shockingly easy. A case in point is Cameron Harris, who in the days leading up to the 2016 election, concocted in fifteen minutes a fake news story that zoomed around the web, paid him a lot of cash, and fooled thousands of breathless, pro-Trump readers.

At the time, candidate Donald Trump was alleging a rigged election, so Harris decided to riff off that. According to the *New York Times*,

> Mr. Harris started by crafting the headline: "BREAKING: 'Tens of thousands' of fraudulent Clinton votes found in Ohio warehouse." It made sense, he figured, to locate this shocking discovery in the very city and state where Mr. Trump had highlighted his "rigged" meme.[3]

To flesh out the story, Harris invented a Trump-supporting electrical worker who accidentally discovered boxes of fake ballots marked for Clinton and ready to be mixed with the genuine ballots. Harris attached a photo he pulled off the web showing a man in work clothes standing next to boxes labeled "Ballot Box." He told readers exactly what to think about this scene: "What [the man] found could allegedly be evidence of a massive operation designed to deliver Clinton the crucial swing state."[4]

Harris launched the story on a site he created called Christian Times Newspaper and promoted it with a few Facebook pages. The response was overwhelming: The ballot box story was shared with six million people and drew comments from many of them who were absolutely sure that Hillary Clinton was going to steal the election from Donald Trump and who were happy to finally have proof. Harris said that his part-time endeavor paid him about $1000 an hour in ad revenue, for a total of $22,000 during the election campaign. Less successful were

Fig. 4.1 Cameron Harris's fake news story featured on his invented site, Christian Times Newspaper.

his fake Clinton stories—including "NYPD Looking to Press Charges Against Bill Clinton for Underage Sex Ring," "Hillary Clinton Files for Divorce in New York Courts," and "Hillary Clinton Blames Racism for Cincinnati Gorilla's Death."

According to the *Times*, Harris concluded "that people wanted to be fed evidence, however implausible, to support their beliefs."[5]

satire Satirical news is intended to be funny or outrageous and is definitely fake—but is not necessarily fake news. It is often mistaken for real news, even though websites and stories are frequently identified plainly (or not so plainly) as satirical. In the world of satirical reporting, President Trump has sold California to Mexico, the pope has declared all religions true-fiction and satire, and the Clinton Foundation has smuggled refugees. The distinction between satire and intentional misinformation is often lost on readers. (Satire sites include *The Onion*, *Daily World Update*, *The Daily Mire*, *Clickhole*, and many others.)

Section Query

When was the last time you were duped by fake news? How could you have avoided being fooled?

4.2 Telling Fake from Real

If you've already concluded that fake news is so widespread and insidious that there's nothing much you can do to protect yourself from it, your conclusion is premature. Many internet-savvy people who have thought a lot about the problem say there is indeed an effective defense against fake news, and it is—you guessed it—critical thinking. But although applying the tools of critical thinking to media fallacies and fictions is crucial, something even more important is required, something without which critical thinking is not possible: an attitude of ***reasonable skepticism***.

This attitude entails that we give up the habit of automatically accepting claims in the media, that we reject the questionable assumption that most of what's said online is true, that we stop taking the word of online sources on faith. Above all, reasonable skepticism means that we *do not believe a claim unless there are legitimate reasons for doing so*. Legitimate reasons are those that increase the likelihood of a claim being true. Such reasons come from reliable evidence, trustworthy sources, and critical reasoning. The problem is that we too often reach for illegitimate reasons, those that are *irrelevant* to the truth of a claim. Here are some illegitimate reasons for accepting or rejecting claims from a media source:

- My group (political faction, fans of politician X or pundit Y, online community, etc.) trusts this source. (So I will too.)
- This source contradicts my beliefs. (If I disagree with it, it must be fake news.)

- An opposing group rejects this source. (So I will accept it because I hate the opposing group.)
- This source reinforces what I'd like to believe. (So I will believe it without question.)
- I reject any claim that comes from sources I don't like. (Because nothing they say can be right.)
- I feel strongly that the claims made by this source are true; therefore they are true. (Because my feelings alone can certify claims.)
- I have faith in my leader, and he or she hates this source. (So I will hate it too, because I believe whatever he or she says.)
- Believing this claim or source makes me feel good. (And feeling good is what matters.)
- I let my intuition or gut tell me whether to trust a source. (It saves time and energy.)

There are times when it's perfectly rational to believe a claim just because a source says it's true. But that attitude is appropriate only when you have previously verified the reliability of the source by checking for legitimate reasons supporting the source's claims.

Maybe you're already a skeptic: You mistrust *all sources* in the mainstream media. Perhaps you're right to do so. Or not. In any case, the crucial question to ask is, again, What are the legitimate reasons for your view? Just saying that the mainstream media is untrustworthy does not relieve you of the duty to apply critical thinking to the claim.

When critically evaluating media (mainstream or otherwise) for trustworthiness, there is no way around the hard work of checking for good reasons to believe or disbelieve. And there is no denying that doing this often takes tremendous courage. Remember, *a good critical thinker is prepared to believe almost anything—given enough good reasons.*

So in overcoming the menace of fake news, cultivating a reasonable skepticism is essential. Fortunately even in the Wild West of the infosphere, there are also helpful strategies we can employ to discern what's real, what's fake, and what's worth our time.

Read Laterally

When professional fact-checkers want to know whether a website is a reliable source of information, they read *laterally*—they leave the site after a quick look and see what other sources have to say about the person or organization behind the site. They don't just read *vertically*—they don't stay within the site and let themselves be distracted by features that are not sure indicators of reliability (like the site's layout, design, and authoritative-sounding

Chapter 4 FAKE NEWS

names). Thus good fact-checkers are more likely than others to reach accurate conclusions about a site's reliability and to do so quicker.

That's the upshot of recent research that examined how 10 historians, 25 Stanford undergraduates, and 10 professional fact-checkers evaluated digital information.[6] The study looked at how these participants evaluated the credibility of online sources covering six different social and political issues. For one of these issues, participants were asked to evaluate articles about bullying on the websites of the American Academy of Pediatrics ("the Academy") and the American College of Pediatricians ("the College").

Despite the similar names, the organizations differed dramatically in their goals and in their reliability. According to the researchers,

> The Academy, established in 1932, is the largest professional organization of pediatricians in the world, with 64,000 members and a paid staff of 450. The Academy publishes *Pediatrics*, the field's flagship journal, and offers

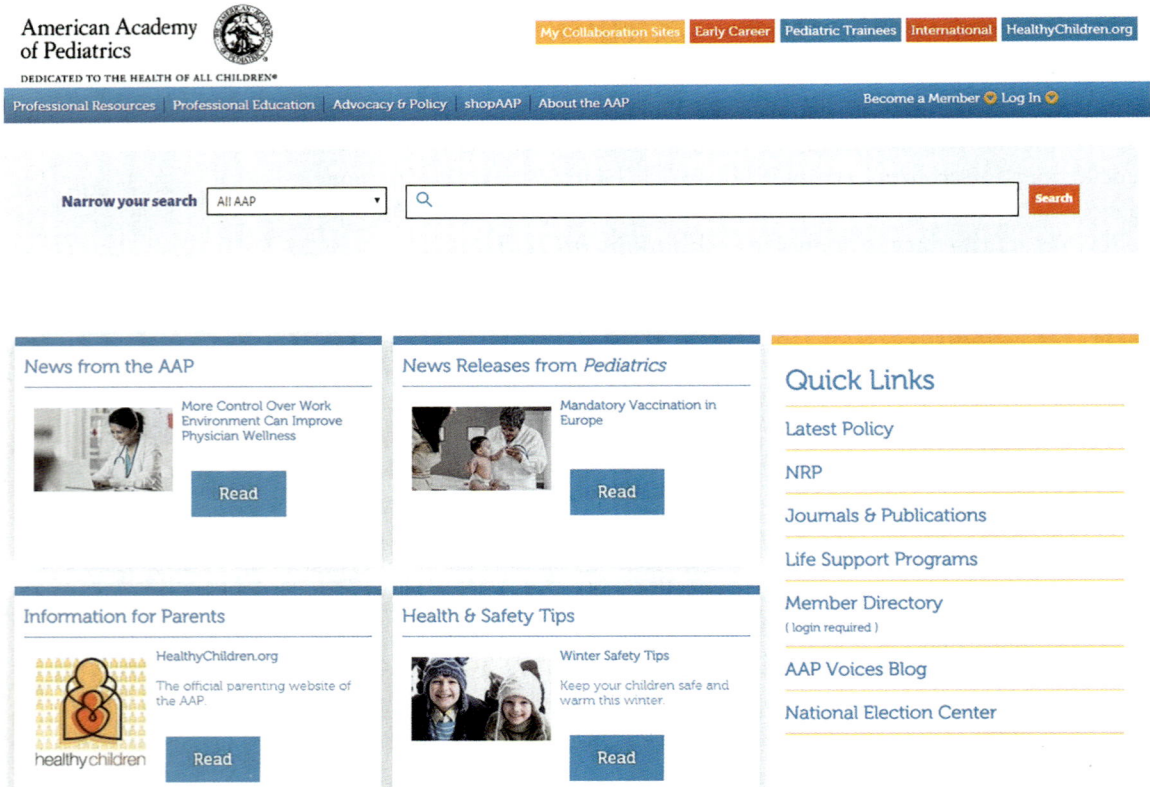

Fig. 4.2 Website for the American Academy of Pediatrics.

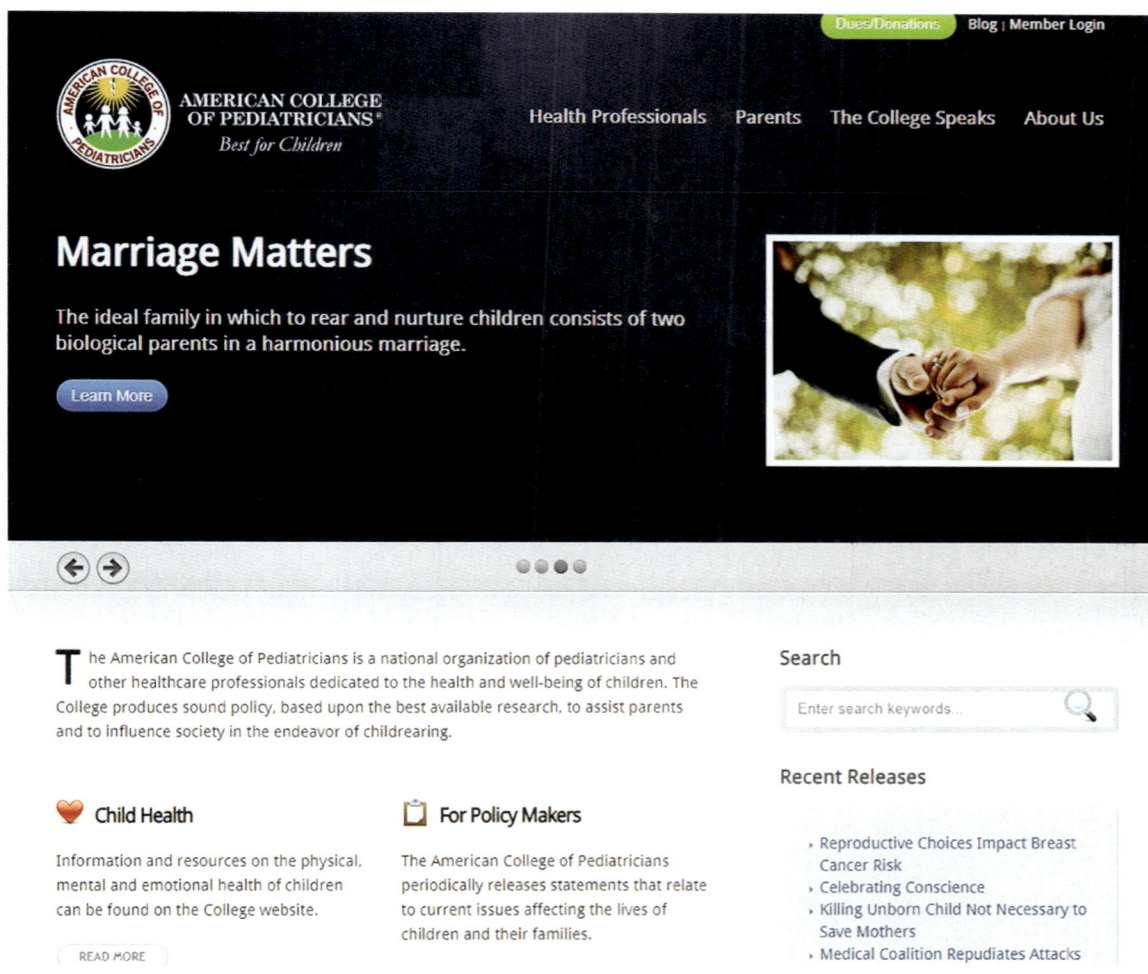

Fig. 4.3 Website for the American College of Pediatricians.

continuing education on everything from Sudden Infant Death Syndrome to the importance of wearing bicycle helmets during adolescence.

By comparison, the College is a splinter group that in 2002 broke from its parent organization over the issue of adoption by same-sex couples. It is estimated to have between 200–500 members, one full-time employee, and publishes no journal. The group has come under withering criticism for its virulently anti-gay stance, its advocacy of "reparative therapy" (currently outlawed for minors in nine U.S. states), and incendiary posts (one advocates adding P for pedophile to the acronym LGBT, since pedophilia is "intrinsically woven into their agenda") (American College of Pediatricians, 2015). The Southern Poverty Law Center has labeled the College a hate group that is "deceptively named" and acts to "vilify gay people." The College's portrayal of research findings on LGBT youth has provoked the ire of the nation's leading scientists, including Francis Collins, the former director of National Institutes of Health, who wrote that "the American College of Pediatricians pulled language out of context from a book I wrote . . . to support an ideology that can cause unnecessary anguish and encourage prejudice. The information they present is misleading and incorrect."[7]

Participants were asked which website was most reliable, and their answers differed in surprising ways:

Every fact checker unreservedly viewed the Academy's site as the more reliable; historians often equivocated, expressing the belief that both sites were reliable; and students overwhelmingly judged the College's site the more reliable.[8]

The fact-checkers reached accurate conclusions about each website's credibility because they looked beyond the confines of the website. They did lateral reading. For example, one fact-checker (Checker C)

spent a mere eight seconds on the College's landing page before going elsewhere. "The first thing I would do is see if I can find anything on the organization," he said as he typed the organization's name into Google. He clicked on Wikipedia's entry about the College and read that it is a "socially conservative association of pediatricians . . . founded in 2002 . . . as a protest against the [American Academy's] support for adoption by gay couples." Wikipedia's entry linked to sources including a Boston Globe story ("Beliefs drive research agenda of new think tanks," Kranish, 2005), a report from the Southern Poverty Law Center ("American College of Pediatricians Defames Gays and Lesbians in the Name of Protecting Children," Lenz, 2012), and a brief from the American Civil Liberties Union ("Misinformation from Doctors . . . Out to Hurt Students?," Coleman, 2010). . . .
  Rendered in under two minutes, Checker C's conclusion was not only an accurate evaluation of the bullying article but also of the rest of the College's website, which presents an anti-gay stance throughout.[9]

Most of the historians did not read laterally, relying instead on the more superficial and less telling features of the site. They were impressed by the College's name and logo, the site's pleasing aesthetics, the layout of the information, and the "scientific" appearance signaled by abstracts, footnotes, and degrees after authors' names.

Most of the students did not read laterally either, and 60 percent of them thought the College's site was the more reliable one. The researchers cite this typical response:

> Student 19, who planned to major in either ancient Greek or bioengineering, based her evaluation almost exclusively on features like the organization's name ("sounds pretty legitimate"); the site's layout, which included bullet points ("nice to understand quickly") and section headings ("that's really smart"); and the absence of banner ads ("makes you focus on the article"). Largely on the basis of graphic design, she concluded that the College's page was the more reliable of the two: "What struck me was how [the College's site] was laid out." Student 19's approach was representative of how the majority of students conducted their evaluations.[10]

So by reading laterally, you can quickly do at least three things:

(1) determine who is really behind the information you're seeing,
(2) uncover the purpose or motivation behind the information (is it to sell you something, persuade you to support a cause, push political views, report the news, or entertain you?), and
(3) find out how credible the source of the information is.

Reading laterally is about comparing sources, and that's especially important in debates about political or social questions. Consulting a variety of sources helps you put the information in proper perspective, uncover errors and bias, pinpoint consensus and disagreement among experts, and find out where the preponderance of evidence points. Certainly your hunt for sources should be carefully planned and limited, but examining too few of them can lead to views that are one-sided, incomplete, and wrong.

How can you tell if the news you're getting is incomplete, if there's important news or facts you're not seeing? You can't, unless you check alternative news sources for any missing stories. Reading a variety of newspapers, newsmagazines, blogs, websites, and journals of opinion is the best way to ensure that you're getting the big picture.

A useful aid in comparing perspectives is the website AllSides.com. Using reasonable criteria, it rates the political biases of hundreds of media outlets and writers and then, for particular news stories, provides articles that cover those stories from multiple political perspectives, ranging from left to center to right. Another reliable site that also covers multiple perspectives on controversial issues is ProCon.org.

The Ethics of Sharing Fake News

Like many of our actions and choices, how we handle fake news—whether we create it, disseminate it, or change our lives because of it—has moral implications. For example, since fake news is a lie (an intentionally told falsehood), communicating it is morally problematic. A common argument in ethics goes like this: A lie is wrong because it violates or undermines people's autonomy, their rational capacity for self-governance or self-determination, their ability to direct their own lives and choose for themselves. When we lie to people, we violate their autonomy by interfering with or thwarting their ability to choose their own paths and make their own judgments.

Autonomy involves the capacity to make personal choices, but choices cannot be considered entirely autonomous unless they are fully informed. When we make decisions in ignorance—without relevant information or blinded by misinformation—our autonomy is diminished just as surely as if someone physically manipulated us.

If this is correct, then concocting fake news or sharing it after receiving it is, in most cases, morally wrong. (This judgment, of course, would not apply to jokes, satire, and any other obviously unserious content.) This means that when the fake news we share causes harm (by, for example, provoking violence, harassment, or emotional distress), we would bear some responsibility for that harm. If we share it only with friends, we still may not be off the hook because they may also share it—and who knows where the sharing will end? Sharing information that we *know* is fake news is worse than sharing it when we are not sure, but most ethicists would probably condemn both actions.

Read Critically

Ultimately, the credibility of websites, social media, and other sources of information comes down to the truth of the claims. Critical thinking tells us that it is reasonable to

(1) accept claims that are supported independently by reliable authorities, evidence, or other claims that you know to be true;

(2) accept claims that are adequately supported by the source itself through citations to other credible sources (experts, research, reports, etc.) or through references to supporting facts;

(3) reject claims when there is good reason for believing them false; and

(4) suspend judgment on claims that you are unsure of, for it is unreasonable to accept a claim without good reasons, and the only cure for uncertainty about a source's claims is further research and reflection.

The key questions to ask:

- *Are the claims plausible?* Do the claims make sense on their face? Did ICE (U.S. Immigration and Customs Enforcement) throw a pregnant woman over a border wall so she wouldn't have her baby on U.S. soil, as reported by the satirical site *The Onion*? Definitely not plausible. The feat would be almost physically impossible, and it is reported by a satirical website famous for just such wacky stories. (See the Snopes.com debunking of this claim.) If a post or website announces that a UFO landed on the White House lawn yesterday, you would be right to doubt the claim because, among other things, such outrageous assertions are common on the internet, no UFO claims have ever been proven, no major news organization has ever reported an actual UFO landing, and scientists and competent investigators have never authenticated even one UFO case, and so on. If a claim doesn't seem plausible to you, don't believe it, unless you have verified it.

- *What is the support for the claims?* Check if they are supported by references to trustworthy websites or news organizations, scientific research, legitimate experts, or polls by reputable organizations. See if the arguments are solid—that is, whether the supporting premises are true and the conclusions follow logically from the premises (Chapter 2). If photos are offered as evidence, check them out: Do a reverse-image search on images.google.com or TinEye.com (more on this later).

- *Have reliable fact-checking organizations examined the claims?* Viral stories are often fact-checked by at least one of the top fact-checkers—including Snopes.com, FactCheck.org, PolitiFact.com, TruthOrFiction.com, Hoax-Slayer.com, and *Washington Post's* Fact Checker. (See the box "Trustworthy Fact-Checkers.")

Use Google and Wikipedia Carefully

Skilled researchers use Google and Wikipedia—but they do so sensibly. When you type questions or keywords into Google, the first sources listed will almost certainly be sponsored sources—ads—which are likely to be biased or misleading. Other results at the top of the list will be chosen by Google's algorithms or by others who want their websites listed first. Thus the first results will not necessarily be reliable or relevant.

But Google can still be a useful research tool if you know how to employ it. Try these tips:

- Search with Google Scholar (scholar.google.com). It will retrieve links only to trustworthy scholarly journals, papers, and books.

- Narrow your searches to domains most likely to yield reliable information—that is, to domains ending in ".edu" (educational sites), ".gov" (official governmental agencies at national, state, and local levels), and ".org" (nonprofit and for-profit entities including schools and communities).

- To better zero in on your topic and to avoid getting a lot of extraneous hits, use quotation marks around words that should be searched as a unit:

  Type: "John Carson" novelist Chicago

  Instead of: John Carson novelist Chicago

- Search *inside* specific websites with the syntax "site:"—for example, to find an article in *USA Today* on refugees, type "site:usatoday.com refugees."

- Search for websites similar to one you're interested in with the syntax "related:"—for example, type: "related:artvoice.com.my" to find websites similar to Artvoice.com.

Wikipedia articles are user-created and thus considered by scholars and journalists to be not as consistently accurate or dependable as reference works from well-known, reputable publishers. This is why citing a Wikipedia article as a source in an academic paper is so often frowned on. Nevertheless, Wikipedia is a very useful place to *start* a research project. The extensive lists of resources at the end of articles can point you to huge

Disguised, Hateful Sources

In 2019, a Snopes.com investigation revealed that a network of extreme anti-Islam Facebook pages, supposedly coming from diverse demographic groups, were actually the work of a single individual. These findings showed how easy it can be to promote misinformation and repugnant views and make them appear to have broad public support. As Snopes reports,

These pages claim that Islam is "not a religion," that Muslims are violent and duplicitous, and that Islamic refugee resettlement is "cultural destruction and subjugation." Just hours after the April 2019 Notre Dame spire collapsed in a catastrophic fire, this network went into overdrive sowing doubt about the possible role Muslims had in its collapse. Multiple pages within this network have stated that their purpose is "message boosting & targeting." . . .

These pages, however, are steeped in fantastical notions of "globalist" conspiracies linking Islam, Socialism, and multi-billionaire philanthropist and Democratic Party supporter George Soros to the decline of Western civilization. Some of these pages also claim that survivors of the Parkland High School massacre in the U.S., for instance, are on a Soros-funded "Leftist-Islamist payroll." . . .

Though the actual authorship of the posts within these pages is opaque, their titles imply diverse representation from a broad swath of American demographic groups, including "Jews & Christians for America" and "Blacks for Trump." In reality, however, the pages in this network are all connected to evangelical activist Kelly Monroe Kullberg. But she is neither black nor Jewish, and her views appear to represent an extreme subset of the broader evangelical movement in America.[11]

troves of authoritative books, essays, reference materials, experts, and websites. Starting at these resource lists, you can follow where your research leads, checking out the reliability and suitability of the resources as you go.

Check Your Own Biases

As you know by now, confirmation bias—the tendency to seek out and trust only information that confirms our existing beliefs—is a common human weakness. It is rampant in all media and in public and private life. (It seems to reign supreme in politics.) But when we go out of our way to

Trustworthy Fact-Checkers

Fact-checking websites rate the reliability of sources and the truth of claims, but who rates the trustworthiness of the fact-checkers? Fortunately the best, most reliable fact-checker organizations share certain characteristics that we can readily identify: (1) They are nonpartisan, and their funding is fully disclosed, (2) they explain their fact-checking methodology and disclose their sources, (3) they use nonpartisan and primary sources whenever possible and are appropriately skeptical of strongly biased information, (4) they employ neutral wording and minimize appeals to emotions, stereotypes, and logical fallacies, (5) they avoid partisan considerations in selecting topics to cover, (6) they promptly correct errors after publication, and (7) they have a solid track record in accurate reporting. Here are five top sites that meet all or almost all of these criteria.*

Snopes.com—One of the oldest and possibly the most trusted of fact-checking sites. For years it has been rendering definitive verdicts on urban legends, rumors, myths, and fake news. Factual accuracy: high.
PolitiFact.com—The best site for checking the accuracy of political claims. Won the Pulitzer Prize. Factual accuracy: high.
FactCheck.org—Like Politifact, this site strives to decrease deception and misinformation in American politics. Checks the accuracy of political statements in speeches, TV ads, news releases, interviews, and more. Factual accuracy: very high.
TruthOrFiction.com—Similar to Snopes, this site fact-checks urban legends, myths, internet rumors, and other questionable claims but typically focuses on recurring stories rather than on those arising from current events. Factual accuracy: very high.
Hoax-Slayer.com—A reliable site that mainly debunks internet hoaxes, especially those that crop up on Facebook. Factual accuracy: very high.

Other recommended sites: Fact Checker at the *Washington Post*, AP Fact Check (*https://www.apnews.com/APFactCheck*), NPR Fact Check (*npr.org*), the Sunlight Foundation (*sunlightfoundation.com*), the Poynter Institute (*poynter.org*), *AllSides.com*, *FlackCheck.org*, and *OpenSecrets.org*.

The source for these judgments is MediaBiasFactCheck.com, the authoritative rater of bias and accuracy in traditional and online news sources. MediaBiasFactCheck.com itself meets all seven criteria noted earlier. Some recommended fact-checkers such as Snopes.com and FactCheck.org are also signatories to the International Fact-Checking Network (IFCN) code of principles (https://www.poynter.org/ifcn-fact-checkers-code-of-principles/).

find only confirming evidence, we can end up accepting a claim that's not true, seeing relationships that aren't there, and finding confirmation that isn't genuine.

The best cure is to look for *disconfirming as well as confirming evidence*. We naturally gravitate to people and policies we agree with, to the books that support our views, to the magazines and newspapers that echo our political outlook. Acquiring a broader, smarter, more critical perspective takes effort and courage.

 **Section Query**

Do you think you have a moral obligation *not* to share news that you know is probably fake (and that may be taken seriously by your recipient)? Why or why not?

4.3 Fake Images

Modern fake images—created, altered, or miscaptioned—have been around for at least 180 years. Myths were made and delusions were affirmed through all sorts of photographic shenanigans—like the ghostly "spirit photos," the Cottingley Fairy photos made by two girls using cutouts from a book, and the infamous staged photo of the Loch Ness monster. Fake photos helped brutal regimes pretend that political enemies never existed; conveniently erasing the offending faces was easy. And now we are amused and often duped by images (photos and videos) of sharks swimming down a flooded street after a hurricane, Albert Einstein riding a bicycle in Nevada as a nuclear bomb detonates in the background, ducks in Germany waiting for a green light before crossing the street, a zebra walking along 56th Street in New York, a gorilla knitting.

But as digital technology and AI leap forward, we are not just entertained. We are seeing and believing things that never happened and don't exist, being urged toward belief, outrage, or action by digitally created lies. We see footage of Muslims celebrating the Paris terrorist attack—but it's fake. We see a viral photo of Russian president Vladimir Putin at the G-20 summit surrounded by other world leaders—but it's fake. We see a photo of Trump supporters wearing shirts that display the words "Make America White Again"—but it's fake. We see an image of an NFL player burning an American flag—but it's fake. And then we learn some *real* truth: Fake news and images have led to real violence and real deaths in Myanmar, Nigeria, Sri Lanka, and India.

Two obstacles to critical thinking are at work here. First, people tend to believe photos and videos, too easily thinking that what they see is the whole, undistorted, simple truth. But this assumption has always been dubious, and now in the post-Photoshop AI world, it seems downright foolish. Second, experts point out that people are not good at recognizing when images have been changed or doctored.

As you might guess, the first step in countering these factors is applying reasonable skepticism—unlearning the habit of automatically accepting a photo or video at face value. This means we should not believe that an image is what it purports to be unless there are good reasons for doing so. Good reasons include (1) the image comes from, or is corroborated by, a trusted source, and (2) you have information about the image's creation or context that lends it credibility.

Some examples might help. Consider the following images, with commentary from a reliable fake-photo debunker, Snopes.com. (For additional image debunking, see the previous list of recommended fact-checkers, as well as @PicPedant, @hoaxeye, Hoaxoffame, and @FakeAstropix.)

Fig. 4.4   The alleged "Haiku Bird."

Is the "Haiku Bird" (Fig. 4.4) a Real Creature? Photographs purportedly showing a "haiku bird" have been circulating on social media for a number of years. In April 2019, interest in this enigmatic four-legged bird was renewed in part by a post from the "Universal Nature" Twitter account.

These images are often attached to the claim that this animal is native to Nepal, and a viral video about the "haiku bird" that racked up more than one million views claimed that this "mysterious animal" was the "lord parvathi devi's pet," that it eats bananas, and that it was immortal.

Alas, these photographs do not document the existence of a four-legged, banana-eating, immortal pet of a deity. Photographs of this "haiku bird" actually show a posable art doll created by Deviant Artist CMWyvern.[12]

Does This Photograph (Fig. 4.5) Show a Girl Forced Into Child Marriage by Muslims? Among the many

Fig. 4.5   A girl being sold into sexual slavery?

vexing problems with which the world continues to grapple is the issue of child marriage, a matter that predominantly affects girls in less developed countries. As the United Nations Population Fund (UNFPA) notes, 20 percent of girls worldwide are married before reaching the age of 18, and in some parts of the globe the rate is twice as high.

Unfortunately, social media platforms are full of inaccurate postings on the subject from persons who are not seeking to raise awareness of the child marriage issue, but simply to demonize other religions and cultures. [This photo] is one such example of this phenomenon. . . .

However, the blonde girl pictured here was not being sold into sexual slavery as a child bride by Muslims (or anyone else), and no credible reports (outside of the inflammatory meme itself) suggested she was a Christian who had seen her "father beheaded and her mother raped."

The image used in the meme originated with a (no longer available) video from 2013 that captured a 7-year-old girl participating in a Quran recital competition, as noted in a *Morocco World News* article.[13]

Does This Photograph (Fig. 4.6) Show a Migrant Caravan Member Urinating on the U.S. Flag? A caravan of asylum seekers heading toward the United States border from Guatemala in the fall of 2018 was seized on as a campaign issue by many politicians heading into the 2018 U.S. midterm elections. As with most hot-button political issues, internet trolls quickly spread hoaxes and unfounded rumors maligning the caravan group.

On 2 November 2018, a social media user shared a photograph to the "Bill O'Reilly Fans" Facebook group that supposedly depicted a scene in which "migrants in the Guatemalan Caravan stand on, and then urinate on, U.S. flag before throwing it in the trash can."

But the image depicted none of those claimed aspects: It was several years old (not recent), was taken in the United States (not along the caravan), and didn't capture anyone urinating on a flag.

This photograph was snapped in April 2016 at the University of Wisconsin-Milwaukee before a campaign appearance there by then-candidate Donald Trump, and it shows a protester standing (not urinating) on a U.S. flag.[14]

Fig. 4.6   Migrants urinating on the American flag?

4.3 FAKE IMAGES

Does This Photograph (Fig. 4.7) Show John McCain with Osama bin Laden? As a number of politicians, world leaders, and Arizonans mourned the passing of U.S. Senator John McCain on 25 August 2018, a certain sect of social media users redoubled their efforts to tarnish the legacy of the late lawmaker. An image purportedly showing McCain and Senator Lindsey Graham of South Carolina posing for a photograph with terrorist mastermind Osama bin Laden was widely spread on conspiracy forums and social media sites:

Fig. 4.7 Did Senator John McCain pose with Osama bin Laden?

A video posted to YouTube with a hashtag referencing #Qanon—an unfounded right-wing conspiracy theory which frequently employs doctored photographs, unconnected coincidences, and illogical conclusions to claim that the investigation into Russian interference in U.S. elections is sham run by the "deep state"—claimed that the photograph showed McCain, Graham, and bin Laden posing after a "deep state fundraiser."

This image, however, does not capture Graham and McCain posing with bin Laden, and it is not evidence of any sort of secret underhanded dealing. The original, undoctored photograph was taken in July 2013 and recorded the U.S. senators meeting with Hamid Karzai, the former president of Afghanistan.[15]

Does This Image (Fig. 4.8) Show a Peaceful Meeting of a Lion and a Zebra at a Watering Hole? Lions and zebras generally don't coexist completely peacefully in the wild. Photographs and videos of these animals together in the plains of Africa frequently depict stalking, hunting, chasing, fighting, and, of course, eating behaviors. That's probably why an image purportedly showing a lion and zebra sharing a moment of peace together at a watering hole is frequently shared with comments such as "unbelievable but true!"

This image has been shared with a variety of captions over the years, such

Fig. 4.8 Lions and zebras are now drinking-hole pals?

Fig. 4.9 A border patrol agent taking an immigrant child by gunpoint?

as "It's not eating time," "Alex and Marty" (a reference to the animated zebra-lion friendship in the movie *Madagascar*), "National Geographic: Behind the Scenes," and "Morning Sam" (a reference to an old cartoon in which Ralph E. Wolf and Sam Sheepdog put their feud on hold when they clock out of work for the day).

This picture however, is not an accurate representation of a lion and a zebra enjoying a moment at a watering hole. This image was digitally created for a 2010 advertisement for Traveler's Insurance.[16]

Does This Photograph (Fig. 4.9) Show Border Agents Forcibly Separating Children From Families? In June 2018, a number of genuine photographs showing children who have been forcibly separated from their families at the border of the United States and Mexico stirred up considerable outrage online. As these images made their way around the Internet, a few fakes were slipped into the mix.

For example, [this] image was shared as if it showed a Border Patrol agent acting on orders to forcibly separate an immigrant child from his family in 2018.

This is actually an infamous Pulitzer Prize-winning photograph that was captured on 22 April 2000, nearly two decades earlier, by the Associated Press's Alan Diaz.

Elián González was five years old in November 1999, when he was found three miles off the coast of Ft. Lauderdale, Florida by a group of fishermen. His mother had drowned with eleven other people while trying to cross the ocean to the United States from Cuba to seek political asylum, and Elián was placed into the custody of his uncle, Lazaro González, in Miami. . . .

This photograph shows the dramatic moment that federal agents seized Elián González from his Miami relatives at gunpoint in order to return the child to his father in Cuba.[17]

With today's advanced technology, creating extremely sophisticated fake images and videos—those that seem to most people indistinguishable from the real thing—has become far easier. Often it takes a photo forensics specialist to separate the fake from the real. But there are also ways that we can detect many of the fakes ourselves:

Determine the source. Where did the image come from? Who posted it? Such questions are not always easy to answer, but knowing the source of an image can give you important clues about its credibility. A photo posted by a known internet hoaxer or conspiracy theorist cannot be trusted—at least not without further investigation.

Check for previous uses. Fake images seem to never die; they often recirculate, appearing again and again, sometimes with modifications or misleading captions. There's a good chance that the more jaw-dropping ones have already been debunked by the photo sleuths just mentioned. You can find out if this is the case and if an image has appeared previously by conducting a *reverse-image search*. Reverse-image search engines offered by Google (images.google.com) and TinEye (tineye.com) can take an image URL or filename that you supply and comb through massive databases of images to see if the image has been used before. You might find that a recent photo purportedly showing hundreds of thousands of Iranians marching for democracy is actually a photo of a protest in Bahrain in 2011. Or that a photo of a bear chasing a cyclist down a mountain road is actually a doctored version of a 2014 photo of a bear running on a mountain road alone.

Be wary of the incredible. As is the case with outrageous claims, photos that seem too amazing to be true, probably aren't. Real horses can't fly, babies can't bench-press a thousand pounds, polar bears don't ride mass transit in Russia, and space aliens don't eat hamburgers at McDonald's. Be cautious when confronted with the incredible.

Look for incongruities. If something in a photo doesn't look right, be suspicious. Check for (1) shadows that aren't where they should be (given the light source), (2) cloned (repeated) regions of the image, like repeated faces in a crowd or several identical swaths of foliage, (3) broken or disjointed lines, like a doorframe that doesn't meet the floor, (4) a situation where *everything* is in focus (both foreground and background), the sign of a composite image, and (5) a lack of lines or pores on faces.

Section Query

Have you ever been fooled by a fake photo or video? How could you have avoided being taken in?

4.4 Deepfakes

Deepfakes are counterfeit videos that have been manipulated with artificial intelligence (AI) to show people doing things they never actually did or saying things they never actually said. They are created from real images that are transformed digitally into something significantly different but more or less believable. As the AI technology known as machine learning advances and as computers continue to run faster and smarter, deepfakes become easier to create—and harder to detect.

In a now famous deepfake, we see former president Obama saying things that he never said. He speaks in his familiar voice with his lips synced perfectly with his words. He intones that "Killmonger was right," insults President Trump and Ben Carson, and ends with "Stay woke, bitches." The voice is actually that of comedian and filmmaker Jordan Peele, and the lip-syncing is courtesy of machine learning.

Fig. 4.10   YouTube deepfake of President Obama. (Published by BuzzFeed, April 17, 2018; https://www.youtube.com/watch?v=cQ54GDm1eL0.)

One of the easier deepfake ruses is face swapping—like putting Steven Buscemi's face on Jennifer Lawrence's body during her Golden Globe speech, or Nicolas Cage's face on Elvis Presley's body as Presley sings and gyrates, or the faces of countless celebrities on the bodies of pornographic actors. More sophisticated deepfakes have popped up too—like the notorious video of Facebook CEO Mark Zuckerberg boasting about his "total control of billions of people's stolen data."

The quality and realism of deepfakes will likely improve immeasurably over a very short time. As one report says,

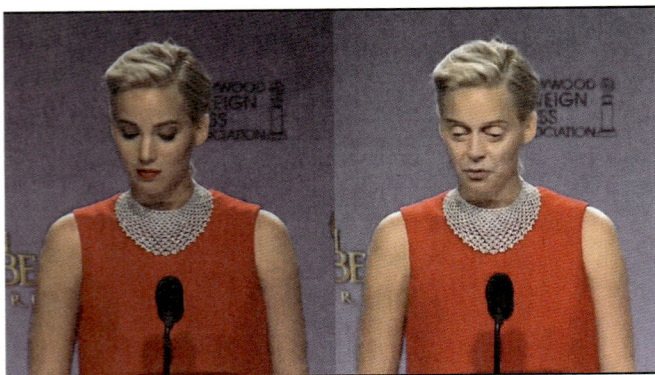

Fig. 4.11   Deepfake of Steven Buscemi's face on Jennifer Lawrence's body during her Golden Globe speech. (From VillainGuy/YouTube; https://www.msn.com/en-us/news/good-news/deepfakes-explained-how-doctored-videos-are-tricking-us/vp-BBWkndK.)

Off-the-shelf video-editing and artificial intelligence software has made it easier than ever to create so-called deepfakes. . . . And if left unchecked, the phenomenon could supercharge fake news of the sort that pervaded Facebook and other online sites during the 2016 campaign, which spread false rumors that Hillary Clinton was dying of Parkinson's disease or that Pope Francis had endorsed Donald Trump. Eventually, the widespread existence of deepfakes could even make some people dismiss legitimate videos as fabricated—in yet another blow to public faith in objective reality.[18]

As the technology leaps forward, concerns about its potential abuses have spread among experts, journalists, and policymakers. A business and technology writer for *Business Day* says,

Fig. 4.12 Deepfake of Mark Zuckerberg. Originally uploaded to Instagram. (https://www.washingtonpost.com/nation/2019/06/12/mark-zuckerberg-deepfake-facebook-instagram-nancy-pelosi/?noredirect=on&utm_term=.211653a084b8.)

Deepfakes are one of the newest forms of digital media manipulation, and one of the most obviously mischief-prone. It's not hard to imagine this technology's being used to smear politicians, create counterfeit revenge porn or frame people for crimes. Lawmakers have already begun to worry about how deepfakes could be used for political sabotage and propaganda. . . .

Online misinformation, no matter how sleekly produced, spreads through a familiar process once it enters our social distribution channels. The hoax gets 50,000 shares, and the debunking an hour later gets 200. The carnival barker gets an algorithmic boost on services like Facebook and YouTube, while the expert screams into the void.

There's no reason to believe that deepfake videos will operate any differently. People will share them when they're ideologically convenient and dismiss them when they're not. The dupes who fall for satirical stories from The Onion will be fooled by deepfakes, and the scrupulous people who care about the truth will find ways to detect and debunk them.[19]

Computer scientist Hany Farid at Dartmouth College, like many other experts, is very aware of the possible dangers:

I am worried about the weaponization [of AI] and I'm worried about how it's impacting us as a society. So, we are working as hard as possible to detect these things. . . .

The nightmare situation is that there's a video of President Trump saying, "I have launched nuclear weapons against North Korea." And somebody hacks his Twitter account, and that goes viral, and, in 30 seconds, we have global nuclear meltdown.

Do I think it's likely? No. But it's not a zero probability, and that should scare the bejesus out of you, right? Because the fact that that is not impossible is really worrisome.[20]

Deepfakes are quickly becoming indistinguishable from the real thing, except by experts who can use AI to detect the AI-created fakes. So what can we—the nonexperts who want the straight story and don't like being fooled—do?

We can do what good fact-checkers do: *Read laterally.* Look beyond the video to try to determine where the video came from. Ask, Who uploaded or posted it? Who created it (or claims to have created it)? Did it come from a reputable source? Or from some guy on Instagram or Facebook you know nothing about? Have reputable publications or reliable fact-checkers examined it?

If you can find no information about the video's source, be suspicious. Very suspicious.

Section Query

Suppose you come across a deepfake that shows a politician you loathe saying or doing something despicable. Be honest: Would you automatically accept the video as real, just because you don't like him or her?

REVIEW NOTES

4.1 TAXONOMY OF MISINFORMATION

- **Fake news** overlaps, or is distinct from, other kinds of messages and misinformation—lies, propaganda, opinions, bias, hoaxes, and satire.
- Cameron Harris, in the days leading up to the 2016 election, easily concocted a fake news story that flew around the web, paid him a lot of cash, and fooled thousands of breathless, pro-Trump readers.

4.2 TELLING FAKE FROM REAL

- Although applying the tools of critical thinking to media fallacies and fictions is crucial,

- something even more important is required, something without which critical thinking is not possible: an attitude of **reasonable skepticism**. Reasonable skepticism means that we *do not believe a claim unless there are legitimate reasons for doing so*. Legitimate reasons are those that increase the likelihood of a claim being true. Such reasons come from reliable evidence, trustworthy sources, and critical reasoning.
- Strategies we can employ to distinguish fake from real include reading laterally, reading critically, using Google and Wikipedia carefully, and checking our own biases.
- It is reasonable to (1) accept claims that are supported independently by reliable authorities, evidence, or other claims that you know to be true; (2) accept claims that are adequately supported by the source itself through citations to other credible sources; (3) reject claims when there is good reason for believing them false; and (4) suspend judgment on claims that you are unsure of.
- The best, most reliable fact-checker organizations share certain characteristics that we can readily identify: (1) They are nonpartisan, and their funding is fully disclosed, (2) they explain their fact-checking methodology and disclose their sources, (3) they use nonpartisan and primary sources whenever possible and are appropriately skeptical of strongly biased information, (4) they employ neutral wording and minimize appeals to emotions, stereotypes, and logical fallacies, (5) they avoid partisan considerations in selecting topics to cover, (6) they promptly correct errors after publication, and (7) they have a solid track record in accurate reporting.
- Highly recommended fact-checkers include Snopes.com, PolitiFact.com, FactCheck.org, Hoax-Slayer.com, Fact Checker at the *Washington Post*, and AP Fact Check.

4.3 FAKE IMAGES

- Two obstacles to detecting fake images are (1) people tend to believe photos and videos, too easily thinking that what they see is the whole, undistorted, simple truth and (2) people are not good at recognizing when images have been changed or doctored.
- We can detect many fake images ourselves by checking for previous uses, looking for incongruities (like shadows that aren't where they should be or cloned regions of the image), and being suspicious of images that seem too amazing to be true.

4.4 DEEPFAKES

- **Deepfakes** are counterfeit videos that have been manipulated with artificial intelligence (AI) to show people doing things they never actually did and saying things they never actually said.
- The best way—often the only way—to investigate a deepfake is by reading laterally—looking beyond the video to try to determine where it came from.

KEY TERMS

deepfake   fake news   reasonable skepticism

EXERCISES

Exercise 4.1

1. How has fake news adversely affected legitimate news, news consumers, and the idea of objective truth?
2. What is the Pizzagate incident? What does it suggest about the possible real-world consequences of fake news?
3. How are lies different from merely false statements?
4. Is biased reporting the same thing as fake news? Why or why not?
5. What is reasonable skepticism?
6. What are legitimate reasons for believing that a claim is true?
7. What are three illegitimate reasons for accepting or rejecting claims from a media source?
8. What are three questions to ask to help you determine the reliability of an online source?
9. Do you agree that it's unethical to share fake news? Why or why not?
10. In assessing the accuracy of a news story, why is it important to consult other sources?
11. When is Google most useful as a research tool?
12. What is the best way to use Wikipedia?
13. What are deepfakes? What is the best way for a nonexpert to investigate them?
14. What is lateral reading?
15. What does critical thinking tell us about reading critically?

Exercise 4.2

1. Consider the fake news "masterpiece" (created by Cameron Harris) mentioned earlier in this chapter. If you were seeing this news item for the first time, how would you go about checking its trustworthiness? Describe each step in the process.
2. Examine this website, determine whether it is trustworthy, and give reasons for your judgment.
3. Go to PolitiFact.com to fact-check the following tweet by filmmaker and liberal commentator Michael Moore: "Ammo used in AR-15/M-16 is banned by Geneva Convention. It enters the body, spins & explodes. Show the crime scene photos and the NRA is over."

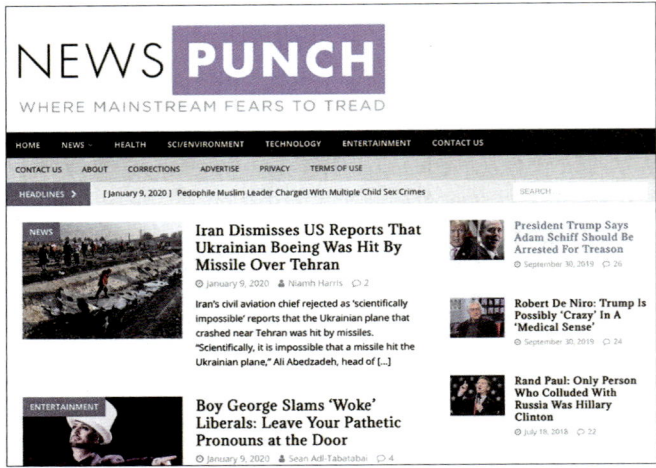

Fig. 4.13   Home page for News Punch.

Exercise 4.3

Research each of the following stories to determine if it is fake. Give detailed reasons for your verdict.

1.

   Fig. 4.14 "Pope Francis says gun owners 'can't call themselves Christians.'"

2.

   Fig. 4.15 Fake or Real? "BREAKING: 3 Liberal Celebrities Arrested for Conspiracy to Assassinate President Trump."

Exercise 4.4

I. Answer the following questions after reading the report by FactCheck.org assessing whether the polio vaccine in the 1950s and 1960s caused people to develop cancer: "Did the Polio Vaccine Cause Cancer?" (https://www.factcheck.org/2018/04/did-the-polio-vaccine-cause-cancer/).

   1. What is FactCheck.org's verdict on the vaccine-cancer claim?
   2. What sources does FactCheck.org use to discover the facts?
   3. How confident are you that FactCheck.org has arrived at the correct answer? Give reasons for your answer.

II. Answer the following questions after reading the report by Snopes.com assessing whether "... 700-Plus Undocumented People, Including Sex Offenders, [Were] Caught in El Paso Overnight" (https://www.snopes.com/fact-check/700-arrests-el-paso-border/).

   1. What exactly did Snopes.com discover about this claim? For example, were there really 700-plus migrants involved? Were there sex offenders in this group? If so, how many? Did most of the migrants present themselves peacefully while seeking asylum? What was the makeup of the 700—were they mostly families, juveniles, adult men? Why were they seeking asylum?
   2. Where did the initial media report about the migrants appear? Were there discrepancies between this report and the later fully researched report done by Snopes? If so, what were the differences?
   3. What sources did Snopes.com use to confirm the facts?
   4. How could the initial report have been used for political purposes?

CAPSTONE

1. Curate your own personal news feed, one that keeps you informed but contains as little fake news and bad information as possible. Make sure it includes the following:

   - Highly rated newspapers, magazines, and websites with diverse perspectives (e.g., the *Economist*, World News, *Chicago Tribune*, Politico, *Commentary* magazine, the *New York Times*, *National Affairs* magazine, *National Journal*, Washington Blade, the *Washington Post*, *U.S. News and World Report*, *Barron's*, *Fortune* magazine)
   - Several top fact-checkers (e.g., FactCheck.org, PolitiFact.com, Snopes.com, TruthOrFiction.com, Hoax-Slayer.com, and *Washington Post*'s Fact Checker)
   - News agencies (AP, UPI, Reuters, AFP)
   - Credible reference sites, both general and more specialized (e.g., Encyclopedia Britannica, Refseek, Google Scholar, Google Books, Science.gov, WorldWideScience, Infotopia, and PubMed Central)

2. How easy is it to create fake news? To find out, try creating some of your own. Write a newspaper or magazine article or blog post that features news that is a combination of fake and real. Make it as convincing as possible. You may include photos or video clips, invented quotes, or fake statistics. Then ask other students if they can tell what's made up and what's real. (And, of course, *do not* add your fake-news creation to the fake news that's already infesting cyberspace.)

Media Bias

Chapter Objectives

5.1 Objectivity and Bias
- *Understand that objectivity in journalism is ensuring that the story exhibits no explicit or implicit preference for one set of values over another.*
- *Understand that bias is a distorted and unfair perspective caused by the values of the writer or editor. A biased news story contains a distorted and unfair presentation of facts, and the distortion and unfairness is caused by the writer's or editor's values, not merely by error or oversight.*
- *Be aware that (1) a partisan reporter does not necessarily produce biased stories (she may control her bias while writing and reporting), (2) a nonpartisan reporter may produce biased stories, and (3) a story defending a partisan view is biased only if it contains distortions caused by the reporter's values.*

5.2 Opinion, Analysis, Advocacy
- *Learn the differences between* news, opinion, *and* analysis.
- *Know that opinions in the news business are expressions of views that cannot be verified in the same way that news can.*
- *Understand that news becomes biased when it introduces inaccuracies and unfairness caused by the writer's values.*
- *Opinions can be biased, but when they are well supported by evidence, they can be free of distortions.*

5.3 Liberal and Conservative Bias
- *Be aware of reasons why accusations of partisan bias seem right but are probably wrong.*
- *Understand the factors that are known to affect media coverage of candidates and election outcomes.*
- *Recognize the two common conservative and liberal arguments about news bias and how they are unsound.*

5.4 Commercial Bias
- *Be aware that commercial bias in news organizations arises from their financial and institutional interests.*
- *Recognize two key forms of commercial bias: pandering involves (slanting the news merely to increase rather than inform the audience) and sensationalism (covering events to rouse emotions and distract from more important issues).*

We seem to be of two minds about what we want from the news media. On one hand, we like news that echoes our beliefs, reinforces our prejudices, and validates our membership in a union of like-minded believers. On the other hand, we want (or say we want) the objective truth, the real news unslanted and unobscured by partisan bias, unwarped and undiluted by commercial and financial interests. The former is a detour into self-interest, and the challenge is to contend with our own biases as we wrestle with reality. The latter is a concern about the biases and objectivity of others, about the view of the world constructed for us by purveyors of news. So understanding what media bias really is, how it affects us, and what we can and should do about it is a taller order than many might think. Let's see what progress we can make.

5.1 Objectivity and Bias

As news consumers, we expect responsible journalists to be truthful, or at least to strive to be. And most of them do aim at truthfulness, as they understand this value. Truthfulness in the news, however, is not a straightforward concept; it contains several elements, some of which are not widely understood. Truth-telling involves, among other things, *accuracy, completeness, objectivity*, and *lack of bias*. Accuracy entails faithfulness to the evidence. Stephen Klaidman and Tom L. Beauchamp, who have written about the ethics of journalism, say, "To be as accurate as possible requires reporting as facts only information for which there is good and sufficient evidence, and no reasonable doubt about the preponderance of the evidence."[1] Incompleteness refers to leaving out important parts of a story (context, for example) and thereby distorting the presentation of the facts. A story can also be rendered incomplete by telling it from only one perspective when several perspectives are needed to fully understand it. As Klaidman and Beauchamp say,

> If we view the concept of completeness as a continuum with "no truth" at one end and "the whole truth" as the other, the threshold standard that journalists should satisfy is *substantial completeness*, the point at which a reasonable reader's requirements for information are satisfied.... By providing substantially complete coverage, we mean that . . . a news organization would, over the course of its coverage, publish enough information to satisfy the needs of an intelligent nonspecialist who wants to evaluate the situation.[2]

For over a century, journalists have thought of objectivity as their defining aspiration, the journalistic standard that separates their work from the work of the world's marketers, hacks, partisans, and propagandists. But the traditional concept of objectivity has proven itself problematic. For a long time, journalists thought objectivity demanded reporting that had as little input from them as possible, a journalism of "just the facts," without the intrusion of the journalist's opinions, judgments, explanations, and interpretations. But this objective "view from nowhere" is impossible to achieve. There is a way the world is—an objective reality—but journalists, like the rest of humanity, are forced to view it from where they are and who they are, influenced by their emotions, evaluations, reasons, and personal prejudices. The nothing-but-the-facts approach, says award-winning journalist John McManus, has caused the profession nothing but trouble:

> First, [the traditional concept of] objectivity conveys false assurance that journalists see the world as it is—without any biases of their own....
>
> Second, objectivity creates the misperception that news media "reflect" the world like a mirror. In actuality, a few fallible humans assemble a partial description of a tiny percentage of current events with carefully selected, words, sounds, and images.... Even the very best reporting is an incomplete and rough first draft of history....
>
> Third,... even journalists who have sworn allegiance to objectivity can't agree on its definition....
>
> Fourth, objectivity encourages reliance on official sources, even when reporters believe they are being spun or deceived. That's because it's much easier to report and defend the accuracy of *quotes* from designated authorities than to seek and defend the best version of the *truth* a journalist can obtain.[3]

Fortunately, journalists have adopted a more reasonable notion of objectivity. Klaidman and Beauchamp explain:

> To present a story objectively entails writing and organizing the material so as not to express or suggest a preference for one set of values over another (even though, of course, there are reasons for covering the story that are themselves evaluative judgments of what is newsworthy).[4]

So objectivity is about fairness, which involves a particular kind of balance:

> Fairness does not always entail giving equal weight to the views of those on either side of an issue; some views might be absurd, uninformed, framed and calculated to political ends, and so on. If the preponderance of thoroughly assembled evidence overwhelmingly supports the conclusion that the earth

is an oblate spheroid, this view deserves more weight than the tenuously supported opinion that the earth is flat. . . . Balance entails more than a mechanistic measuring of words so that each partisan position is given an equal number of inches, minutes, or representation.[5]

Also, some partisan views may be more complicated or nuanced than others and thus may require more explanation or analysis. So a news story that pays more attention to one side in a dispute than another is not necessarily violating the principle of objectivity.

Objectivity in journalism, then, is ensuring that the story exhibits no explicit or implicit preference for one set of values over another.

Bias is a charge often leveled at the news media, sometimes by readers and viewers who are confused about what bias is. Conservatives see liberal bias, liberals see conservative bias, and some see bias in any expression of opinion whatsoever. The dictionary meaning of *bias* is "an inclination or prejudice for or against a person or group." But a better definition relating to journalism and the media is this: **bias**—a distorted and unfair perspective caused by the values of the writer or editor. A biased news story contains a distorted and unfair presentation of facts, *and* the distortion and unfairness is caused by the writer's or editor's values, not merely by error or oversight. A news story inadvertently containing factual errors is not necessarily biased. But note: (1) A partisan reporter does not necessarily produce biased stories (she may control her bias while writing and reporting), (2) a nonpartisan reporter may produce biased stories, and (3) a story defending a partisan view is biased only if it contains distortions caused by the reporter's values.[6]

Bias can manifest itself in the selection of information contained in a news story, or in the selection of topics that a site or publication chooses to cover or not cover. By omitting unflattering or incriminating information about a presidential candidate, for example, a story can paint a picture of the candidate that is inaccurate and one-sided. By including these negative facts and downplaying positive ones, the opposite picture can emerge. Many news sites have been guilty of bias not because they publish inaccurate information, but because when they write about a partisan group they don't like, they include only stories that make the group look bad and ignore the stories that do the opposite. The work of the bias-monitoring group Media Bias/Fact Check (MBFC), at mediabiasfactcheck.com, shows that many news sites report the facts accurately but still exhibit a strong bias due to the misleading and unfair selection of stories they cover.

This caution about introducing bias through selection of information also applies to selection of sources. It's easy to spin an essay or post in a particular direction by quoting or citing only the sources that agree with your view of things, or using better-quality sources to support your side, or supporting only your view with sources and omitting sources for the opposing side.

A very potent kind of news bias occurs when a story is presented without the context from which the reported events arose. W. James Potter, author of *Media Literacy*, explains the problem:

> Context is what helps audiences understand the meaning of the event in the news stories. For example, a story could report that Mr. Jones was arrested for murder this morning. That fact can convey very different meanings if we vary the context. Let's say that the journalist put in some historical context that Mr. Jones had murdered several people a decade ago, was caught and convicted, served time in prison, but was recently let go because of a ruling of an inexperienced and liberal judge. In contrast, let's say that Mr. Jones, one of the candidates running for mayor, was arrested despite the fact that police had in custody another man who possessed the probable murder weapon and who had confessed. The fact of the arrest takes on a very different meaning within different contexts.[7]

Probably the most obvious indicators of bias are rhetorical—specifically, the use of emotional and evaluative words to skew the audience's view. This skewing is achieved mainly by manipulating the connotation of words. *Denotation* refers to the literal or primary meaning of words (sometimes called the dictionary meaning), but *connotation* is the feelings and attitudes associated with words, associations beyond the literal meanings of a term. People use connotations to put an argument or view in a negative or positive light, one that may be misleading or partisan and not justified by any evidence or argument.

For example, some people might call a politician with strong views "resolute" and "principled," while others might call the same politician "stubborn" and "pigheaded." The connotations change, and the emotional associations change with them. A capable business executive might be characterized as "self-confident" and "decisive" by some and "bossy" and "overbearing" by others. An American president may be called "strong and decisive" by his supporters but "cruel and impulsive" by his political opponents. In debates about abortion, those who oppose abortion may refer to their position as "pro-life" or "pro-child"; those opposed to this view may call it "anti-choice" or even "anti-woman." In disputes about guns, those who want to restrict gun ownership may label their position "anti-assault weapon"; those opposed to this position may call it "anti-self-defense."

Consider this faux news report about the aftermath of a mass shooting:

> After the October 5 shooting of ten students at Logan High School in Ames, Iowa, *anti-gun forces went on the attack against the Second Amendment* and demanded more restrictions on the *right to own guns* and to protect one's *family against criminals*. Editorials in the *New York Times* and the *Washington Post* played up the loss of life at the school, without mentioning the *many lives saved by armed shopkeepers and homeowners who have successfully defended themselves against murderous thieves and intruders*. Yesterday at the school, a *left-wing mob threw* insults at the NRA and at members of Congress who *believe in constitutional rights*.

The connotations of the italicized words in this passage paint gun regulation supporters in a uniformly negative (and distorted) way—as unreasonable, aggressive, callous, and extremist. A more neutral version might go like this:

> After the October 5 shooting of ten students at Logan High School in Ames, Iowa, advocates of gun restrictions criticized the unrestricted private ownership of guns and called for some reasonable regulations to help reduce the risk of gun of violence. Editorials in the *New York Times* and the *Washington Post* decried the loss of life at the school and urged the passage of new legislation that would deny gun ownership and possession to the psychologically impaired and to people convicted of violent crimes and violations of protection orders. The columnists argued that such legislation would save lives. Yesterday at the school, about a hundred people gathered to peacefully protest current gun policies. They denounced the NRA and criticized members of Congress who regularly vote against gun regulation.

Evaluative terms are words that imply value judgments about something. Of course the connotations of words do this, but other value-laden words do too, and they can easily convey bias. Consider this headline: "President sends Congress $4.4 trillion budget that features *excessively high* deficits." The value-laden term here is *excessively high*. The headline may be biased—but only if the deficits cannot be realistically described in such a troubling way. And look at this headline: "*Erratic* president of Philippines *starves* population by preventing imports of food." The evaluative words *erratic* and *starving* convey the message that the Philippine president is mentally unstable and that the people are in the midst of an extreme humanitarian crisis. If these alarming words don't accurately describe the situation—if the president is actually just *unpredictable* and the people are simply *dissatisfied* with the kind of food available to them—then this headline is unacceptably biased.

So not all evaluative language indicates bias. Suppose a journalist writes a news piece about a large oil spill in the Gulf of Mexico, and to describe the situation she uses the evaluative (and prejudicial) words "disaster," "horrific," "terrified," "infuriatingly," "disheartening," "disregard," and "recklessness." Are such adjectives proof of bias in the report? Look:

> Today in the Gulf of Mexico, in an oil rig accident that has become a greater commercial and environmental *disaster* than the Deepwater Horizon spill in 2011, the Sunsea Point oil rig exploded into flames, killing three rig workers, and spilling thousands of barrels of crude oil into the Gulf. The fire itself was *horrific*, forcing over one hundred workers to abandon the rig. Several ships arrived quickly on the scene to help evacuate the *terrified* survivors, but rescue ships from Sunsea, which should have come immediately, were seen later *infuriatingly* idle on shore. Documents show a *disheartening* history of safety violations and preventable accidents in Sunsea's history. Survivors from the rig blamed the deaths on Sunsea for its *disregard* of the safety of its employees. They did not seem surprised that Sunsea's *recklessness* had finally led to a tragedy.

This is a damning news report that describes the actions of the oil company critically and unfavorably. But is there bias here? Evaluative words introduce bias only when they create a distorted and unfair account. The question is whether there is good evidence to support the evaluative assessments. In the Sunsea case, does it seem there are good reasons to believe that the spill is more accurately described as a "disaster" than merely as an "accident"? Does the evidence suggest that Sunsea's history of safety violations really is "disheartening" and that the company really is "reckless"? If the answer to such questions is *yes*, then the evaluative language does not constitute bias. In that case, *omitting* the language might be a distortion.

Section Query

How much biased language (connotations, evaluative terms) is present in the sources of news you read most?

5.2 Opinion, Analysis, and Advocacy

According to a recent Pew Research Center study, people are bad at telling the difference between news and opinion—a finding that may help explain why news stories are so often *incorrectly* accused of bias (and fake news).[8] The idea behind the accusations is that the presence of an opinion in a piece of writing is a sure sign of bias. But this assumption is false.

Most major news organizations try to make a distinction between *news*, *opinion*, and *analysis*. In general, news is an account of events or situations that can be verified through objective evidence. Oil spills, traffic accidents, deaths, hurricanes, speeches, discoveries, jury verdicts, interviews—these and an infinite number of other happenings are considered news. **Opinions**, in the news business, are expressions of views that often cannot be verified entirely in this way—they are explanations, interpretations, judgments, speculations, and the like. In newspapers, magazines, and other publications, opinion articles are frequently labeled as such or as "editorial," "op-ed," or "commentary." "Analysis" (or news analysis) is a kind of opinion writing consisting of examinations, interpretations, or explanations of news events. It includes facts plus opinions about those facts. Journalists and editors strive to maintain these distinctions even though the difference between news and opinion is not always clear-cut. Sometimes, for example, the best way to make news understandable is to include some clarifying or interpretive opinion.

News becomes biased (in the sense used here) when it introduces inaccuracies and unfairness caused by the writer's values. Opinions can be biased for the same reason, but they need not be. When opinions are well supported by evidence, they can be free of distortions and actually enhance the audience's understanding and awareness of complex social and political issues. Consider this passage from an opinion piece by Paul Krugman, a Nobel Prize–winning economist and a columnist for the *New York Times*:

> In one way, Donald Trump's attack on our foreign trade partners resembles his attack on immigrants.... In another way, however, the trade crisis is quite different from the humanitarian crisis at the border. Children ripped from their parents and put in cages can't retaliate. Furious foreign governments, many of them U.S. allies that feel betrayed, can and will.
>
> But all indications are that Trump and his advisers still don't get it. They remain blithely ignorant about what they're getting into.
>
> Back in March, as the U.S. was imposing tariffs on steel and aluminum imports—and yes, justifying its actions against Canada (!) on the grounds of national security—Peter Navarro, the White House trade czar, was asked about possible retaliation. "I don't believe any country will retaliate," he declared, basing his claim on the supposed upper hand America has because we import more than we export.

On Sunday, Canada—a country that, by the way, imports about as much from us as it exports in return—announced retaliatory tariffs against $12.6 billion of U.S. products.[9]

In this article, Krugman's point of departure is the news about President Trump's levying of tariffs against America's trading partners (Canada, the European Union, and China). His opinion is that the administration doesn't know what it's doing, and the country will suffer because of this ignorance. He speaks as an expert in economics and international affairs, analyzing the situation, offering commentary, and explaining how the tariffs run counter to international trade realities and the country's best interests. The point here is not that Krugman's opinions are correct, but that they are backed by authoritative support and are free of obvious distortions. This is what we should expect from any good journalistic reporting and blogging. This kind of respectable journalism can be found on both the political left and right.

Nowadays opinion writing is called "advocacy journalism," especially if it vigorously advocates for a cause or advances an agenda. You can find it on blogs, websites, cable TV, social media, and talk radio. It ranges in quality from the professional, literate, and insightful to the over-the-top biased, daft, and barely readable. (Krugman's piece is an example of the higher quality kind of advocacy journalism.) Larry Atkins, the author of *Skewed: A Critical Thinker's Guide to Media Bias*, notes the positive benefits of this form:

> Advocacy journalism has a long tradition and has served many purposes. Its goal is to inform people and give them information in a manner that attempts to convince the receiver of a certain viewpoint. It can validate people's views and give them information and talking points; it can shed light on issues that are not getting much attention and can educate the public to the fact that the issue needs to be addressed. The journalist takes a side on an issue, has a specific point of view, and then argues as persuasively as possible to justify it. Reporters, bloggers, and others who engage in advocacy journalism use journalistic techniques and their specific medium—be it writing, radio, or audiovisual—as a method of advancing their cause or belief. These journalists often start with a certain premise or objective and then use their reporting skills to support that premise.[10]

But Atkins points out that advocacy journalism also has downsides:

> Over the past fifteen years, as newspaper circulation has declined, more and more people are turning to advocacy journalism via websites, talk radio, cable

TV, and blogs to get their news. These outlets are often entertaining, provocative, and thought provoking. The problem is that many of these news sources, especially those run by just one person or a handful of people, are biased, have an agenda, don't have the resources or time to do much fact-checking, aren't heavily or carefully edited, and aren't held accountable when they get their facts wrong. . . .

Sometimes advocacy journalism is used to promote a narrative even if the facts don't fit. The host's bias can be shown through tone, choice of stories, opinions, and the way he or she interviews guests. . . . There is also a tendency to demonize the other side.[11]

Consider this bit of advocacy writing:

Previous immigration policies were a fraud. They were based on the idea that the U.S. had no illegal immigration problem whatsoever. That was a ridiculous notion then and an absurd myth now, circulated by mindless liberals and know-nothing trolls. Everyone with a brain and a modest knowledge of current events knows that illegal immigrants were pouring across the border by the millions, and they still are. Illegal immigrants should get in line and wait their turn like everyone else. The U.S.-Mexican border should be sealed by ICE, and 99 percent of those applying for citizenship should be rejected.

This looks like a typical blog or Facebook opinion, and it is characteristically unsupported and unfair. No evidence is cited for its assertions; there is only an appeal to popularity ("Everyone . . . knows"), a logical fallacy. It puts forth false statements and makes false assumptions. Taken together, these errors help to paint an inaccurate, and therefore unfair, picture of both immigrants and immigration policy. This post is strongly biased; it is bad advocacy journalism.

Section Query

How good are you at distinguishing fact from opinion? Take the Pew Research Center test and find out.

5.3 Liberal and Conservative Bias

The question of partisan media bias is a hot one, with the public seeing bias everywhere in the news, conservatives and liberals trying to prove bias by citing seemingly clear-cut cases, and many commentators simply assuming widespread media bias based on the flimsiest evidence. But

Can You Tell the Difference between Fact and Opinion?

The Pew Research Center tested 5,035 U.S. adults on their ability to "recognize as factual—something that's capable of being proved or disproved by objective evidence—or as an opinion that reflects the beliefs and values of whoever expressed it."

The study found that

> a majority of Americans correctly identified at least three of the five statements in each set [two sets in all]. But this result is only a little better than random guesses. Far fewer Americans got all five correct, and roughly a quarter got most or all wrong. Even more revealing is that certain Americans do far better at parsing through this content than others. Those with high political awareness, those who are very digitally savvy and those who place high levels of trust in the news media are better able than others to accurately identify news-related statements as factual or opinion.

In the study, test subjects were asked to choose between the following:

A factual statement regardless of whether it was accurate or inaccurate. In other words, they were to choose this classification if they thought that the statement could be proved or disproved based on objective evidence.

and

An opinion statement, regardless of whether they agreed with the statement or not. In other words, they were to choose this classification if they thought that it was based on the values and beliefs of the journalist or the source making the statement, and could not definitively be proved or disproved based on objective evidence.

Take the test yourself. Following are the ten statements; decide which ones are factual statements and which ones are opinion statements. (Answers are at the end.)

1. Abortion should be legal in most cases.
2. Immigrants who are in the U.S. illegally are a very big problem for the country today.
3. Health care costs per person in the U.S. are the highest in the developed world.
4. President Barack Obama was born in the United States.
5. Government is almost always wasteful and inefficient.
6. Immigrants who are in the U.S. illegally have some rights under the Constitution.
7. ISIS lost a significant portion of its territory in Iraq and Syria in 2017.
8. Spending on Social Security, Medicare, and Medicaid make up the largest portion of the U.S. federal budget.
9. Democracy is the greatest form of government.
10. Increasing the federal minimum wage to $15 an hour is essential for the health of the U.S. economy.

1. Opinion, 2. Opinion, 3. Factual, 4. Factual, 5. Opinion, 6. Factual, 7. Factual, 8. Factual, 9. Opinion, 10. Opinion.

From Amy Mitchell, Jeffrey Gottfried, Michael Barthel, and Nami Sumida, "Distinguishing between Factual and Opinion Statements in the News," Pew Research Center, June 18, 2018, https://www.journalism.org/2018/06/18/distinguishing-between-factual-and-opinion-statements-in-the-news/; "Quiz: How Well Can You Tell Factual from Opinion Statements?," Pew Research Center, survey of 5,035 U.S. adults between February 22 and March 8, 2018, http://www.pewresearch.org/quiz/news-statements-quiz/ (accessed July 24, 2019).

decades of research on the question show that charging the media with overall bias and making the charge stick is harder than most people think. Adam J. Schiffer, author of *Evaluating Media Bias*, sums up some of the relevant research:

> Political-science and mass communication scholars have spent forty years characterizing the degree of tilt in the mainstream US news media, with varying levels of quantitative sophistication and attention to crucial theoretical and definitional quandaries. The most defensible read of the literature is that the popular claim of an overall, systematic leftward tilt is unsupported.[12]

And there are many reasons why accusations of partisan bias based on less rigorous grounds may *seem* right but are probably wrong:

> Bias charges succumb to many pathologies. Among the most common are that the charge attacks journalists or owners rather than their product, the charger fails to specify a standard, the standard is ideologically loaded and thus is more of a partisan talking point than a valid media criticism, the charger expects balance between unbalanced phenomena, an alleged imbalance can be explained by factors other than media bias, the charger cherry-picks confirming evidence and ignores disconfirming content, or a charger with a vested interest in a particular conclusion makes a subjective assessment of news slant. Consumers of news criticism should also be on the lookout for blatantly dishonest argumentation such as misrepresentation of the accused content. Though rare, even the mainstream bias-watchdog organizations will occasionally stoop to this level.[13]

One of the obstacles to proving a systematic partisan bias in news coverage is what Schiffer calls "reality." In elections, there are factors besides journalistic favoritism that are known to affect election outcomes and to increase negative or positive news coverage of a candidate. These "reality" factors can undermine charges of partisan bias against the news media. Schiffer says such elements played a big role in coverage of the 2008 presidential election:

> The "reality" of presidential elections is largely set by a handful of underlying conditions that are comparable across time. These conditions include the economy and whatever factors are baked into presidential approval—war and peace, scandals, legislative success, and so forth. The fall campaign itself, with all of its twists and turns, does matter at the margins, but not nearly as much as most casual observers assume. In fact, as long as both candidates

run competent campaigns, the fall events serve less as persuasion than as a way to bring voters to where we already knew they would be....

In addition, news-relevant reality slanted even further against Republicans than the summer forecasting models could measure. President Bush's Gallup approval rating was, by historical standards, atrocious. He bottomed out at 25 percent during three of the four polls taken in October 2008. His high for the whole year was 34 percent in January, and he mostly wallowed in the high 20s during the crucial campaign months. And then, of course, the economy crashed. The Great Recession began with a string of bank failures and ended up tanking the stock market and dragging GDP growth deep into negative territory by the election quarter.

The campaign-related factors in the election only exacerbated the imbalance. Obama was the first major-party nominee of a minority ethnicity, a fact that surely would have garnered attention regardless of party. He also parlayed his youth, charisma, and a tech-savvy staff into generating enthusiasm, particularly among young voters, that was unprecedented in recent campaigns. It is tough to cover those factors, particularly in the horse-race style that dominates election news, without the measurable tone slanting in his favor.[14]

Conservatives sometimes argue this way: Surveys consistently show that most American journalists are liberals; thus, the media has a liberal slant, for liberal journalists cannot help but insert their worldview into their work. Liberals make a parallel argument: Large conglomerates own all large national news organizations, and their heads (who are often conservatives) are thought to skew media coverage toward conservative positions that benefit the corporations financially and economically; therefore, the news media has an overall conservative bias.

But neither bias argument is sound. From the fact that many reporters have liberal beliefs, it does not follow that their reporting is liberal. Their biases may be restrained by professional ethics, audience expectations, conscientious editors, or owners loathe to offend large segments of their readership. Establishing that liberal reporters' personal beliefs lead to liberal reporting requires direct empirical evidence. In the same vein, from the fact that major news organizations have conservative leaders and tend toward conservative economic views of the world, it does not follow that the reporting coming out of those organizations is conservative. Such a claim requires supporting evidence.

It's not difficult to find particular instances of biased reporting in ostensibly neutral media organizations ("ostensibly neutral media organizations" does not include blatantly partisan outlets like Fox News and MSNBC). A critical examination of a report's claims, assumptions, tone, and evidence will tell you whether it is biased and to what degree. But the sweeping accusation that mainstream news outlets consistently lean left or right is harder to prove, though not impossible.

Bias and Inconsistency

In case you didn't know already, because of strong bias, public figures often make pronouncements that are logically inconsistent (as well as moronic, offensive, and mystifying). Worse, the rest of the world may swallow the contradictory statements without noticing anything amiss. For example,

- If a TV pundit finds that his favorite politician has been having an extramarital affair, he declares the episode a "personal matter" that should not be publicly discussed. But if a politician he loathes is guilty of the same indiscretion, he declares it an outrage and can't stop talking about it on the air.
- In support of a vice presidential candidate whose only executive experience is a term as mayor of a small town, a radio talk show host insists that such experience is perfect preparation for being vice president. But she asserts that another vice presidential candidate whom she opposes and who has almost identical credentials is unsuitable for the office—because he doesn't have enough executive experience.
- Commentators criticize a woman televangelist for making sexist remarks about another woman—but they use the same sexist language to deride the televangelist.

Such contradictions abound in the public square and often go unnoticed by the media. A few astute commentators, though, are happy to point out such addled thinking. No matter who is guilty of it, this brand of inconsistency shows that bias is hard at work, undercutting clear thinking. And when we inconsistently apply a rule or standard of judgment, the rule or standard itself is called into question.

If we take an extramarital affair or blatant sexism seriously only when it suits our rhetorical aims, do we really believe these issues are important? How can we detect this problem in ourselves? We can manage it only through careful reflection on the logic of what we say. One trick is what can be called the *"turned tables" test*. If you criticize someone or something you dislike for violating some standard, ask yourself: Would I judge someone or something I like in the same way for the same reasons? Logic demands that you treat equals equally.

Try this: Think of the strongest criticism you could make about the behavior of the political leader you respect the least. Now suppose your favorite political leader is guilty of the same behavior. Would you be willing to criticize him or her just as strongly?

 **Section Query**

Have you ever detected blatant political bias in a major news outlet? If so, was your judgment fair—or was it the result of cherry-picking instances from the articles to fit your prior expectation of bias?

5.4 Commercial Bias

Partisan bias is a challenge to media integrity, but there is another kind of bias that can have an even greater, more distorting, influence on the news. It's called **commercial bias**, and it has been worrying thoughtful observers and scholars of news organizations for decades—and seems to be worrying them now more than ever. According to Schiffer,

> the obsession with partisan bias distracts critics and citizens from the more serious failures of political news. While the media aren't literally trying to kill us, they sometimes inflict serious injury on informed citizenship through a litany of routines, biases, and shortcomings that leave news consumers ill equipped to navigate contemporary politics. To name only a few, news coverage of politics focuses on the strategic game and the personalities at the center of political conflicts rather than the underlying policy issues, it presents events as isolated episodes rather than in any meaningful socio-economic-political context, it fails to adjudicate the veracity of politically loaded factual questions, and it privileges events that are dramatic, scandalous, simple, novel, timely, and emotional over more important events that do not meet those criteria. In short, the press is a mess, and not because of partisan slant.[15]

These almost invisible biases arise from a central fact about the news: News organizations are caught between serving the information needs of free societies and serving their own financial and institutional needs. Or, as John McManus says,

> Information-providers often face a conflict between their self-interest and the public interest.... Particularly for profit-seeking institutions, their short-term self-interest *conflicts more than coincides* with the purpose of socially responsible journalism. Most corporations seek to maximize profit rather than maximizing public understanding of those current issues and events with the greatest impact on the community served.[16]

Commercial bias can take several forms, including pandering, sensationalism, skewed focus, and chasing advertising.

Pandering

This bias involves slanting the news merely to increase the size of the audience rather than to enhance readers' understanding or appreciation of an issue. A well-documented example of **pandering** is the lack of critical scrutiny by many news organizations (including the *New York Times* and Fox News) of the Bush administration's rationale for going to war in Iraq in 2003. By not covering the issue critically, they avoided appearing unpatriotic, which would have decreased their audience.[17]

Sensationalism

Sensationalism in news is the covering or hyping of events (often trivial) to rouse emotions that distract from more important subjects or issues. (Fake news, on the other hand, hypes both events and non-events.) Prime examples of sensationalism include titillating stories about scandals involving powerful people (especially political leaders); celebrity outrages, divorces, and murders; famous mysteries (like the disappearance of Malaysia Airlines Flight 370); "miracle" survival tales; health scares (like Ebola); and shocking crimes ("Whole Family Found Dead"). And of course any story can be sensationalized through an exaggerated or overdramatized telling. Online, hyping news events is as common as air, and the breathless "reports" are not called clickbait for nothing.

Skewed Focus

This bias distorts news coverage with a misleading perspective. Many news outlets give more weight and attention to certain kinds of stories regardless of how important the stories are to the well-being of society. This usually means that the news is dominated by stories about crimes, disasters, scandals, violence, or bizarre or unusual events; by reports that can be made into a dramatic tale; or by content that is simple or novel. These biases can lead to fear of nonexistent threats, distrust of institutions, and cynicism toward fellow citizens or society as a whole.

Schiffer offers an example of how this type of skewed reporting may have had a widespread negative effect on people's lives:

> In one of the more peculiar puzzles of contemporary American life, citizens became more afraid of violent crime during the 1990s and 2000s, even as the crime rate dropped. Gallup often asks whether there is "more crime in the U.S. than there was a year ago," and in all but two years between 1989 and 2011, a majority of respondents said "yes"—typically by margins of more than fifty points over "no." Meanwhile, the violent crime rate fell during nearly all of those years, until it was less than half of its 1980s levels. It is not a stretch to posit a prominent role for violence-obsessed

local television news in explaining this disconnect. Indeed, a multimethod study by three communication scholars provided compelling evidence that fear of crime is correlated with heavy local-news viewership, irrespective of local crime rates.[18]

Chasing Advertising

News organizations depend on advertising for most or all of their revenue, yet their professed duty is to keep advertising and news separate and to prevent the former from biasing the latter. Still the influence of advertising on editorial content is often substantial. McManus explains:

> By far the most common type of advertiser influence, however, is even more subtle: editors choose story topics and assign "beats" not based on citizens' information needs but in order to attract demographic groups advertisers hope to reach with their messages. The news is structured for the benefit of advertisers.
>
> This subordination of public interest to advertisers' interests leads to two abuses. First, sponsored topics—those that advertisers believe will channel attention to their ads—may get more attention than they deserve. Think of whole sections of the newspaper devoted to automobiles, real estate, food, entertainment, and travel. But topics that don't sell *products* . . . get less attention than they merit. The second abuse is that those members of the community with the best "customer potential" for advertisers will have stories addressed to their interests. Those citizens less able or less inclined to buy will be less likely to have their information needs served.[19]

Bias and Accuracy of Selected Sources

The website Media Bias/Fact Check (mediabiasfactcheck.com) is a reputable fact-checker and trusted judge of political bias in over 2,400 magazines, newspapers, television shows, and websites. It rates bias as reflected in a source's selection of stories, biased wording, and slanted headlines, and it determines whether a source reports factually and backs up claims with well sourced evidence.

MBFC grades political bias on a scale:

◀ Extreme Left—Left—Left Center—Least Biased—Right Center—Right—Extreme Right ▶

Factual reporting is rated from VERY LOW to VERY HIGH.

The following list shows ratings and comments for a selection of sources. Notice that bias is rated separately from factual reporting, for even very biased sources can report the facts accurately, and relatively unbiased sources can do a poor job of factual reporting.

LEFT BIAS

CNN

"CNN has a left bias in story selection that often favors the left while being critical of the right. ... CNN typically utilizes loaded emotional words in sensational headlines such as this: 'Trump pounces on Justice Department report findings.' CNN usually sources its news properly through credible reporters/journalists and through hyperlinking to credible media sources. However, CNN has failed numerous fact checks from Politifact. It should be noted that these fact checks were almost exclusively from guests on their numerous talk shows and not from the reporting of actual news, which tends to be factual." Factual Reporting: **Mixed**.

DAILY KOS

"Daily Kos is an outlet for Political Blogging. It functions as a discussion forum and group blog for a variety of netroots activists whose efforts are primarily directed toward influencing and strengthening progressive policies and candidates." Factual Reporting: **Mixed**.

TALKING POINTS MEMO

"Talking Points Memo (or TPM) is a liberal web-based political journalism website created and run by Josh Marshall, a journalist, liberal blogger and historian. ... TPM has liberal bias in story selection and produces some very credible journalism." Factual Reporting: **High**.

LEFT CENTER

NEW YORK TIMES

"Overall, we rate the New York Times Left-Center biased based on word and story selection that favors the left, but highly factual and considered one of the most reliable sources for information due to proper sourcing and well respected journalists/editors." Factual Reporting: **High**.

ABC NEWS

"ABC News is what some call a mainstream media source. They typically publish/report factual news that uses moderately loaded words in headlines such as this: 'At Montana rally, President Trump praises Greg Gianforte for body-slamming reporter.' Story selection tends to favor the left through both wording and bias by omission where they under report some news stories that are favorable to the right. ABC always sources their information to credible sources that are either low biased or high for factual reporting." Factual Reporting: **High**.

USA TODAY

"In review, USA Today publishes stories with emotionally loaded headlines such as 'President Trump's 2017 performance review, from Putin with love.' USA Today also publishes opposite view articles such as 'Democrats, it's time for you to dump Hillary Clinton.' ... Overall, we rate USA Today Left-Center Biased based on editorial positions that slightly favor the left and factually high due to proper sourcing." Factual Reporting: **High**.

LEAST BIASED

THE ECONOMIST

"The Economist takes an editorial stance of classical and economic liberalism that supports free trade, globalization, open immigration, and social liberalism. There is minimal use of loaded language in both headlines and articles. ... In fact, most articles are well written with very low emotional bias. Economically, The Economist leans right, but they also support such initiatives as a carbon tax and environmental protectionism, which are not right-wing positions. Editorially, The Economist endorses both Republicans and Democrats in the United States. ... Overall, we rate The Economist Least Biased based on balanced reporting and High for factual reporting due to a clean fact check record." Factual Reporting: **High**.

POLITICO

"Editorially, Politico provides a balance of opinions as evidenced by the criticism they have received from both sides. Further, their news articles tend to be balanced through covering both sides and counterpoints to the story they are reporting on. A factual search reveals they have not failed a fact check. Overall, we rate Politico Least Biased based on balanced coverage of news stories." Factual Reporting: **High**.

PROCON.ORG

"ProCon.org is a non-profit charitable organization headquartered in Santa Monica, California in the United States. It operates the ProCon.org website, an online resource for research on controversial issues. . . . [I]ts stated mission is 'Promoting critical thinking, education, and informed citizenship by presenting controversial issues in a straightforward, nonpartisan, primarily pro-con format.'. . . Every issue is perfectly sourced and balanced. Overall, this is a least biased resource that is high in factual reporting." Factual Reporting: **High**.

REUTERS

"Overall, we rate Reuters Least Biased based on objective reporting and Very High for factual reporting due to proper sourcing of information with minimal bias." Factual Reporting: **Very High**.

UNITED PRESS INTERNATIONAL (UPI)

"United Press International (UPI) is an international news agency whose newswires, photo, news film, and audio services provided news material to thousands of newspapers, magazines and radio and television stations during the 20th century. UPI is similar to Reuters and the AP, but on a smaller scale today. Provides low biased news content that is factual." Factual Reporting: **High**.

RIGHT CENTER

NEW YORK POST

"The New York Post tends to publish stories utilizing sensationalized headlines with emotionally loaded wording. . . . The New York Post also republishes news from other sources such as the least biased Associated Press. In general, more stories favor the right, but the NY Post does not shy away from reporting negative coverage of the right, if it is a big story. They also tend to source their information properly, however many times the headline misleadingly exaggerates the actual story they are reporting. . . . A factual search reveals several failed checks. . . . Overall we rate the New York Post on the far end of Right-Center Biased due to story selection that typically favors the Right and Mixed (borderline questionable) for factual reporting based on several failed fact checks." Reporting: **Mixed**.

REAL CLEAR POLITICS

"Most of the news content on Real Clear Politics is aggregated from other sources such as: Washington Post, New York Post, Salon, Fox News, The Federalist and National Review. Several of the sources used by Real Clear Politics are listed as Mixed factual due to failed fact checks. In reviewing original Real Clear Politics articles, there is a right leaning bias in wording and story selection. . . . Overall, we rate RCP as Right-Center biased based on source selection that leans right and Mixed for factual reporting due to use of multiple sources who have failed fact checks." Factual Reporting: **Mixed**.

RIGHT BIAS

FOX NEWS

"Fox News publishes stories with emotionally loaded headlines such as 'They Wanted It to Blow Up: Limbaugh Says Success of Trump-Kim Summit Caught Media Off Guard' and 'Tucker: 2016 Russia Collusion "Witch Hunt" Now Extends to Jill Stein.' When it comes to sourcing they typically utilize pro-Trump pundits such as Rush Limbaugh who has a very poor record with fact checkers, as well as credible sources such as the Wall Street Journal. Fox News is also known to publish right wing conspiracy theories, although after being sued they retracted the story. Fox News has also been deemed the least accurate cable news source according to Politifact." Factual Reporting: **Mixed**.

COMMENTARY

"Commentary is a monthly American magazine on religion, Judaism, and politics, as well as social and cultural issues. Besides its strong coverage of cultural issues, Commentary provided a strong voice for the anti-Stalinist left. Norman Podhoretz the founder, originally a liberal Democrat turned neoconservative, moved the magazine to the right and toward the Republican Party in the 1970s and 1980s. Well sourced information with a right-wing bias in wording and story selection." Factual Reporting: **High**.

EXTREME RIGHT (QUESTIONABLE SOURCE)

DRUDGE REPORT

"The Drudge Report is a politically conservative American news aggregation website run by Matt Drudge. The site consists mainly of links to stories from the United States and international mainstream media about politics, entertainment, and current events; it also has links to many columnists. . . . Almost all news stories favor the right and link to right leaning sources. Frequently, the Drudge Report links to conspiracy sources such as ZeroHedge and Infowars as well as Questionable sources, with very poor fact check records, such as Breitbart, WND and the Gateway Pundit. Drudge Report also publishes columns from right-wing journalists who have poor track records with factual information. . . . The Drudge Report has also promoted numerous debunked conspiracy theories. . . . A factual search reveals a very poor track record with fact checkers. . . . Overall, we rate the Drudge Report Right Biased and Questionable due to promotion of propaganda and conspiracy theories, as well as for publishing fake news and the use of highly questionable sources." Factual Reporting: **Questionable**.

EXTREME LEFT (QUESTIONABLE SOURCE)

LIBERAL SPEAK

"Liberal Speak is a news and opinion website with an extreme left wing bias in reporting. All articles favor the left and discredit the right through the use of loaded emotional words in the headlines and content of articles. There is rarely presentation of both sides of a story and sourcing typically comes from left wing or other questionable sources such as Real Time Politics or propaganda sites such as the Palmer Report. Liberal Speak does make an effort to use proper credible sources, but ultimately they cannot be taken seriously when sourcing questionable sources who have failed many fact checks. Overall, this is an extreme left biased website that uses sensational headlines and is poorly sourced." Factual Reporting: **Questionable**.

Source: Media Bias/Fact Check (mediabiasfactcheck.com) (accessed March 25, 2019).

 **Section Query**

Would you trust a news source that you knew was guilty of flagrant pandering and sensationalism? Why or why not?

REVIEW NOTES

5.1 OBJECTIVITY AND BIAS

- *Accuracy* entails faithfulness to the evidence, and *incompleteness* refers to leaving out important parts of a story and thereby distorting the presentation of the facts.
- **Objectivity** in journalism is ensuring that the story exhibits no explicit or implicit preference for one set of values over another.
- **Bias** is a distorted and unfair perspective caused by the values of the writer or editor. A biased news story contains a distorted and unfair presentation of facts, *and* the distortion and unfairness is caused by the writer's or editor's values, not merely by error or oversight.
- A partisan reporter does not necessarily produce biased stories (she may control her bias while writing and reporting), a nonpartisan reporter may produce biased stories, and a story defending a partisan view is biased only if it contains distortions caused by the reporter's values.
- Evaluative terms can be used to express judgments about something, but not all evaluative language expresses bias.

5.2 OPINION, ANALYSIS, ADVOCACY

- *News* is an account of events or situations that can be verified through objective evidence. **Opinions**, in the news business, are expressions of views that often cannot be verified entirely in this way—they are explanations, interpretations, judgments, speculations, and the like. In newspapers, magazines, and other publications, opinion articles are frequently labeled as such or as "editorial," "op-ed," or "commentary." "Analysis" (or news analysis) is a kind of opinion writing consisting of examinations, interpretations, or explanations of news events.
- News becomes biased when it introduces inaccuracies and unfairness caused by the writer's values. Opinions can be biased for the same reason, but they need not be. When opinions are well supported by evidence, they can be free of distortions and actually enhance the audience's understanding and awareness of complex social and political issues.
- Opinion writing is sometimes called "advocacy journalism," especially if it vigorously advocates for a cause or advances an agenda. You can find it on blogs, websites, cable TV, social media, and talk radio, and it ranges in quality from the professional, literate, and insightful to the over-the-top biased, daft, and barely readable.

5.3 LIBERAL AND CONSERVATIVE BIAS

- There are many reasons why accusations of partisan bias *seem* right but are probably wrong. In elections, there are factors besides journalistic favoritism that are known to affect election outcomes and to increase negative or positive news coverage of a candidate.
- Two common conservative and liberal arguments about news bias are unsound. Conservatives argue that surveys consistently show that most American journalists are liberals; thus, the media has a liberal slant, for liberal journalists cannot help but insert their worldview into their work. Liberals argue that large conglomerates own all large national news organizations, and their heads (who are often conservatives) are thought to skew media coverage toward conservative positions that benefit the corporations financially and economically; therefore, the news media has an overall conservative bias.
- It's not difficult to find particular instances of biased reporting in ostensibly neutral media organizations. A critical examination of a report's claims, assumptions, tone, and

evidence will tell you whether it is biased and to what degree. But the sweeping accusation that mainstream news outlets consistently lean left or right is harder to prove, though not impossible.

5.4 COMMERCIAL BIAS

- **Commercial bias** in news organizations arises from their financial and institutional interests, and these almost invisible biases arise because news organizations are caught between serving the information needs of free societies and serving their own financial and institutional needs.
- Commercial bias can take several forms. **Pandering** involves slanting the news merely to increase the size of the audience rather than to enhance readers' understanding or appreciation of an issue, and **sensationalism** is the covering or hyping of events to rouse emotions that distract from more important subjects or issues.

KEY TERMS

bias
commercial bias

objectivity
opinion

pandering
sensationalism

EXERCISES

Exercise 5.1

1. What is objectivity in journalism? What is bias?
2. What are the ways that bias can be manifested in news stories?
3. What is connotation? How can the connotations of words introduce bias into a news story? Do connotations and evaluative language always introduce bias?
4. In journalism, what is the difference between news and opinion?
5. According to Pew Research, what is the difference between factual statements and opinion statements?
6. What are the factors that might lead someone to think that a news report is biased when in fact it is not?
7. What is commercial bias? What are some of the ways that commercial bias influences the presentation of the news?
8. What is pandering? What is sensationalism?
9. Does research support the idea that there is an overall, systematic leftward tilt in mainstream news media?
10. Is the mere expression of opinion in a news piece a sure sign of bias? Why or why not? What makes an expression of opinion biased?

Exercise 5.2

Examine the following excerpts from opinions published online and (1) identify any word connotations and other evaluative terms, (2) indicate whether the wording introduces bias, and (3) determine whether the opinions expressed are supported by evidence.

1.

One thing no liberal will ever turn down is the opportunity to get a standing ovation for accusing *someone else* of racism.

    Democrats have placed their opening bid in the immigration talks on Trump's 10-yard line—a hilariously unbalanced "compromise" that is worse than their original proposal. Now, they are battering him with accusations of racism to force him into an amnesty deal that he was specifically elected to prevent.

    Forced to choose, soccer moms are going with MSNBC—and, hey, if that means we'll still have Rosa to clean the house, well, that's OK, too!

    Liberals have gotten a free ride for too long on using phony claims of "racism" to promote policies that hurt black people but help themselves. It's like spoiling a kid; by the time he's 15, it's impossible to get him to clean his room.

    The virtue signalers have been out in force lately, putting in museum-quality performances ever since receiving an unsubstantiated report about Trump's alleged "s---hole countries" comment in a private meeting.

Ann Coulter, "The Left's Dirty Little Secret—Cleaned by Rosa!," January 17, 2018, http://www.anncoulter.com/columns/2018-01-17.html.

2.

Rush Limbaugh is coming for your children. Not in the flesh, thank God. But on his radio show last Thursday, the right's favorite gasbag announced that, after a two-decade hiatus, he is returning to the publishing world, this time with a history lesson for the grade-school set.

    The title of his forthcoming book is *Rush Revere and the Brave Pilgrims: Time Travel Adventures with Exceptional Americans*. As befitting an author of such extraordinary narcissism, the book's hero is "a fearless middle-school history teacher named Rush Revere, who travels back in time and experiences American history as it happens," and the book's cover features the colonial-themed caricature of Limbaugh that also serves as the logo of his patriot-themed brand of iced tea.

Michelle Cottle, "Rush Limbaugh Has No Business Teaching History to Our Kids," Daily Beast, September 10, 2013, https://www.thedailybeast.com/rush-limbaugh-has-no-business-teaching-history-to-our-kids.

3.

The great myth of many is that the left cares about people, that the compassion in American politics is almost exclusively found in the Democrat Party.

    It's the exact opposite. Look at the people that vote for 'em. They're all angry. They're all miserable. They all feel left out in one way. They all need therapy. They're all constantly enraged. And you know why? Because nothing the Democrat Party ever promises 'em happens. Their lives do not get better. They've allowed themselves to become victims, thereby waiting for everybody else to do something for them because they've been convinced they can't do anything on their own because they're a victim, the deck's stacked against them.

    So they're waiting for the Democrat Party, they're waiting for the Democrats and the American left to make things better. How do they define that? Making things better is punishing their enemies, not really making things better for them. I defy anybody, other than the wealthy Hollywood tech sector and the Wall Street sector, [to] go out and find your average radical leftist Democrat voter, and you will not find a happy person. And you will not find a person satisfied with what the Democrat Party has done to improve life for those people.

Rush Limbaugh, transcript, April 5, 2018, rushlimbaugh.com, https://www.rushlimbaugh.com/daily/2018/04/05/myth-liberals-care-people/.

4.

TRUMP MUST BE IMPEACHED. We can NOT wait until November of 2020 for that to happen. We simply won't make it til then. The country we know as the United States of America will not be the same after three more years of Trump. You know it and I know it. Turning the TV off and trying to avoid the daily insanity won't make him go away.

Donald J. Trump has proven himself to be completely unfit for office, a threat to our country and an imminent danger to this world. He is also not well. He is a malignant narcissist and an active sociopath. Because he holds the codes to, on his own, launch nuclear weapons, he is a singular threat to humanity.

Michael Moore, michaelmoore.com, https://michaelmoore.com/impeach/ (accessed July 23, 2018).

5.

Almost every day brings news of awful crimes, but some are so heinous, so horrendous and malicious, that they dwarf all else. One of those rare events took place on July 17, when Malaysian Airlines MH17 was shot down in Eastern Ukraine, killing 298 people.

The Guardian of Virtue in the White House denounced it as an "outrage of unspeakable proportions," which happened "because of Russian support." His UN Ambassador thundered that "when 298 civilians are killed" in the "horrific downing" of a civilian plane, "we must stop at nothing to determine who is responsible and to bring them to justice." She also called on Putin to end his shameful efforts to evade his very clear responsibility.

True, the "irritating little man" with the "ratlike face" (Timothy Garton Ash) had called for an independent investigation, but that could only have been because of sanctions from the one country courageous enough to impose them, the United States, while Europeans cower in fear.

Noam Chomsky, "Outrage," August 14, 2014, https://chomsky.info/20140814/.

6.

By all accounts, the flooding that has inundated Iowa—along with much of the Midwest—has been devastating. So naturally, when Rep. Steve King traveled to Iowa this week, he offered words of comfort and promises of assistance.

Nah. After all, this is noted white supremacist and hatemonger Steve King. Instead, he opted to insult the New Orleans victims of Hurricane Katrina, claiming that some unnamed FEMA official—perhaps created in King's fevered brain after an evening of perusing Stormfront—told King, "We go to a place like New Orleans and everybody's looking around saying, who's gonna help me, who's gonna help me?"

And then, of course, this anonymous—imaginary?—FEMA official allegedly went on to praise Iowans because they help themselves "rather than waiting for outside assistance." Because of course those overwhelmingly white Iowans are busy "helping each other" and pulling themselves up by those old bootstraps, unlike, say, those predominantly black New Orleanians, who are just sitting around waiting for a handout. Subtle, Steve. Jackass.

Barbara Morrill, "Not Breaking News: White Supremacist Steve King Can't Stop Himself from Being a Racist Pig," Daily Kos, March 22, 2019, https://www.dailykos.com/stories/2019/3/22/1844045/-Not-breaking-news-White-supremacist-Steve-King-can-t-stop-himself-from-being-a-racist-pig.

CAPSTONE

From the box "Bias and Accuracy of Selected Sources" (or from the website mediabiasfactcheck.com itself), choose a news source and review its latest online reporting. Write a paragraph answering these questions: Do you agree with MBFC's judgment about the source's bias? Do you agree with the rating for factual accuracy? Give reasons for your answers.

Manipulation through Fallacies and Rhetoric

Chapter Objectives

6.1 Fallacies: Irrelevant Premises
- *Distinguish between fallacies that have irrelevant premises and those that have unacceptable premises.*
- *Remember that (1) just because an argument is fallacious, that doesn't necessarily mean its conclusion is false, and (2) it's generally not a good idea to dismiss an opponent outright by declaring that he or she has just used a fallacy.*
- *Know that fallacies with irrelevant premises include the genetic fallacy, composition and division, appeal to the person, equivocation, appeal to popularity, appeal to tradition, appeal to ignorance, appeal to emotion, red herring, straw man, and two wrongs make a right.*

6.2 Fallacies: Unacceptable Premises
- *Know that fallacies with unacceptable premises include begging the question, false dilemma, decision-point fallacy, slippery slope, hasty generalization, and faulty analogy.*

6.3 Persuaders: Rhetorical Moves
- *Understand that rhetoric presents us with techniques for influencing through emotion while proving nothing through reason.*
- *Know that rhetorical devices include innuendo, euphemisms and dysphemisms, stereotyping, ridicule, and rhetorical definitions.*

As we have seen, modern media is a world-changer, a connector of people and machines, a potential force for good—and a tangle of misinformation, deceit, fakery, foolishness, and unreason. The worst parts of today's media are deliberately and intensely manipulative, calculated to control what you think about issues, policies, and people. And probably the two most potent and dangerous strains of manipulation are propaganda and demagoguery.

Propaganda is deliberately biased or misleading information designed to promote a political cause or point of view. Like advertising, publicity, and promotion, its aim is to sell you something, but it is decidedly political and far more insidious and forceful. Propaganda wars have been waged for decades by virtually every country on the planet, and now cyber propaganda campaigns on social media are a fact of life, undermining and promoting political ideas and candidates through the dissemination of memes, hashtags, and non-stop messaging.

Demagoguery refers to the actions of political leaders who seek support by appealing to the desires and **prejudices** of ordinary people rather than by using rational argument. According to one commentator, demagoguery is characterized by authoritarianism (restriction of political liberties), sanctions against those thought not to be part of the preferred group, a commitment to "traditional" social norms (often defined arbitrarily), ready acceptance of claims deemed to be "The truth" despite contradictory or nonexistent evidence, and the belief that some people are better than others, not because of their character or behavior but because of their identity as part of a group.[1] In recent history, Donald Trump has often been accused of being a demagogue, but so has Barack Obama, Rush Limbaugh, Louis Farrakhan, Rachel Maddow, and many others.

Propaganda and demagoguery are powerful, dishonest forces allied against all who want to know what's really going on in the world. They are powerful and dishonest in large part because of the fallacies and rhetorical tricks they employ.

Fallacies are certain types of defective (fallacious) arguments that recur so frequently that they have names (given to them, in many cases, by ancient philosophers or medieval scholars) and are usually gathered into critical thinking texts so students can become aware of them.

Fallacies are often beguiling; they can *seem* plausible. Time and again they are *psychologically* persuasive, though *logically* impotent. The primary motivation for studying fallacies, then, is to be able to detect them so you're not taken in by them.

We can divide fallacies into two broad categories: (1) those that have irrelevant premises and (2) those that have unacceptable premises.[2] Irrelevant premises have no bearing on the truth of the conclusion. An argument may seem to offer reasons for accepting the conclusion, but the "reasons" have nothing to do with the conclusion. Unacceptable premises are relevant to the conclusion but are nonetheless dubious in some way. An argument may have premises that pertain to the conclusion, but they do not adequately support it. Premises can be unacceptable because they are as dubious as the claim they're intended to support, because the evidence they offer is too weak to adequately support the conclusion, or because they're otherwise so defective that they provide no support at all.

Alas, critical thinking is undone by more than just fallacies. It is easily weakened or wrecked by subtler means—by **rhetoric**, the use of nonargumentative, emotive words and phrases to persuade or influence an audience. Arguments try to persuade through logic and reasons, but rhetoric tries to persuade primarily through the artful use of emotion-laden language. Fallacies at least have the semblance of arguments, but rhetorical devices are nonargument persuaders. There's nothing inherently wrong with using rhetoric. Its use can become worrisome, though, when there's an attempt to persuade or coerce through rhetoric alone.

In this chapter we examine numerous fallacies of both types as well as some of the more popular rhetorical ploys. Once again, the key to immunizing yourself against manipulation by fallacies or rhetoric is practice in identifying the species and subspecies when you see them.

6.1 Fallacies: Irrelevant Premises

Two important reminders about fallacies: (1) Just because an argument is fallacious, that doesn't necessarily mean its conclusion is false. A fallacious argument doesn't offer any support to its conclusion, but the conclusion itself might be true or false. (2) Online it's generally not a good idea to dismiss an opponent outright by declaring that he or she has just used a fallacy. Assuming the argumentative exchange is worth your time, the better strategy is to (respectfully) explain why the fallacious argument cannot prove what it purports to prove. (Also, yelling "fallacy!" online can be considered rude, like pointing to a stranger's message T-shirt and saying "dumb.")

Genetic Fallacy

The term **genetic fallacy** has both a general and specific meaning. In the general sense—that is, when it applies to arguments that a claim is true or false solely because of its origin or history—it refers to both nonhuman and abstract origins (such as a group of people, organizations, or a piece of writing) as well as to particular individuals (such as John Smith). But to avoid confusion, it's best to restrict *genetic fallacy* to nonhuman and abstract origins and history, and to use the terms *appeal to the person* or *ad hominem* (discussed later) to refer to individual persons.

When we are guilty of the genetic fallacy, we fail to distinguish the *content* of an idea or claim from its *source*. Generally, an idea or claim is not bogus just because it comes from an unpopular or detested source, and it is not golden just because its source is popular or well-liked. What matters is the merits of the idea or claim itself—which usually comes down to the goodness of the argument that backs it or the quality of the evidence in its favor.

For example,

> *The editorial board of the* New York Times *says that Donald Trump's border "solutions" will just make things worse. Is there any merit at all in the board's arguments? I'll save you some time: Of course not! It's the New York Times.*
>
> *What could he possibly know about social justice in America? He's a white, cisgender, heterosexual male.*
>
> *You can safely dismiss that alternative energy plan. It's the brainchild of a liberal think tank in Washington.*
>
> *We should reject that proposal for solving the current Social Security mess. It comes straight from the Republican Party.*
>
> *Russell's idea about tax hikes for the middle class came to him in a dream, so it must be bunk.*

These arguments fail because they reject a claim based solely on where it comes from, not on its merits. In most cases, the source of an idea is irrelevant to its truth. Good ideas can come from questionable sources. Bad ideas can come from impeccable sources.

Composition and Division

The fallacy of **composition** is arguing that what is true of the parts must be true of the whole. The error here is thinking that the characteristics of the parts are somehow transferred to the whole, something that is not always the case. Likewise, the error is committed whenever we assume that what's true of one member of a group is true of the group as a whole. For example,

> *The atoms that make up the human body are invisible. Therefore, the human body is invisible.*
>
> *Each member of the club is productive and effective. So the club will be productive and effective.*

> *Each note in the song sounds great. Therefore, the whole song will sound great.*
>
> *Every part of this motorcycle is lightweight; therefore, the whole motorcycle is lightweight.*

Sometimes, of course, the parts do share the same characteristics as the whole. We may safely conclude that since all the parts of the house are made of wood, the house itself is made of wood. We commit the fallacy of composition, though, when we assume that a particular case must be like this.

The fallacy of composition often shows up in statistical arguments. Consider this:

> *The average small investor puts $2,000 into the stock market every year. The average large investor puts $100,000 into stocks each year. Therefore, the group of large investors as a whole invests more money in the stock market than the small-investor group does.*

Just because the average small investor invests less than the average large investor does not mean that small investors as a group invest less than large investors as a group. After all, there may be many more small investors than large investors.

The flip side of the fallacy of composition is the fallacy of **division**—arguing that what is true of the whole must be true of the parts. The fallacy is also committed when we assume that what is true of a group is true of individuals in the group.

> *This machine is heavy. Therefore, all the parts of this machine are heavy.*
>
> *Since the committee is a powerful force in Washington politics, each member of the committee is a powerful force in Washington politics.*
>
> *University students study every conceivable subject. So that particular university student over there also studies every conceivable subject.*

These arguments are fallacious because they assume that characteristics of the whole must transfer to the parts or that traits of the group must be the same as traits of individuals in the group.

Like the fallacy of composition, the fallacy of division is frequently used in statistical arguments:

> *The average SAT test score of seniors [as a group] is higher than the average SAT score of sophomores. Therefore, this senior's test score must be higher than the score of that sophomore.*

Just because the average score for seniors is higher than the average score for sophomores doesn't mean that any individual senior must have a higher score than any sophomore. The scores of individuals, which make up the average, may vary greatly.

Appeal to the Person

The fallacy of **appeal to the person** (or **ad hominem**, meaning "to the man") is rejecting a claim by criticizing the person who makes it rather than the claim itself. It is probably the most widespread train wreck of reasoning in American politics. For example,

> You can't believe anything Rep. Morris says about welfare reform. He's a bleeding-heart liberal.

> Jones has argued for a ban on government-sanctioned prayer in schools and at school-sponsored events. But he's a rabid atheist without morals of any kind. Anything he has to say on the issue is bound to be a perversion of the truth.

> My opponent—"sexual harasser" David Springer—is always spouting off about the evils of sexual predators and workplace harassment. But he's the last person on Earth we should listen to on this topic.

President Donald Trump may be one of Twitter's most prolific users of ad hominem ploys:

Donald J. Trump
@realDonaldTrump

Crooked Hillary Clinton is the worst (and biggest) loser of all time. She just can't stop, which is so good for the Republican Party. Hillary, get on with your life and give it another try in three years!

Fig. 6.1   Screen grab of tweet from Donald J. Trump.

Donald J. Trump
@realDonaldTrump

Wacky @NYTimesDowd, who hardly knows me, makes up things that I never said for her boring interviews and column. A neurotic dope!

Fig. 6.2   Screen grab of tweet from Donald J. Trump.

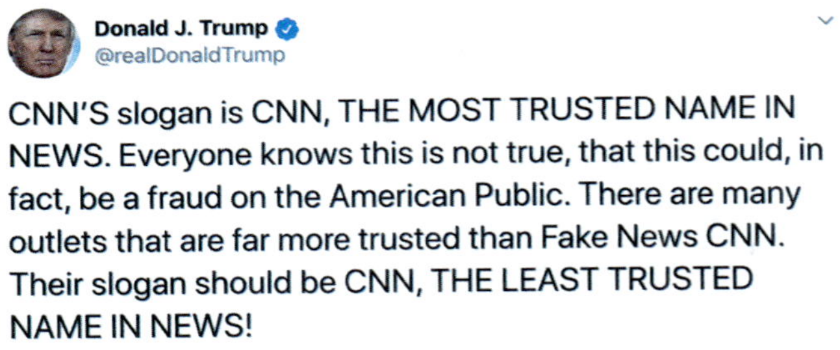

Donald J. Trump ✓
@realDonaldTrump

CNN'S slogan is CNN, THE MOST TRUSTED NAME IN NEWS. Everyone knows this is not true, that this could, in fact, be a fraud on the American Public. There are many outlets that are far more trusted than Fake News CNN. Their slogan should be CNN, THE LEAST TRUSTED NAME IN NEWS!

Fig. 6.3 Screen grab of tweet from Donald J. Trump.

But the president is by no means alone:

"Elizabeth Warren: The world's most famous fake Indian spent her year tossing off socialist boilerplate, positioning herself for 2020 and pretending to be very offended when Trump called her Pocahontas, thus guaranteeing that she will be called that "racist" term 14 kajillion times over the next 4 years." (John Hawkins, Townhall, January 2018)

"I would say the biggest handicap we have right now is some nutcases in or country that don't believe in global warming. I think they are going to change their position because of pressure from individuals, because the evidence of the ravages of global warming is already there." (Jimmy Carter)

"They [Tea Party Republicans] are political terrorists, and like all terrorists, including those who use bombs, their number one goal—their only goal—is to blow things up. [Senators Ted] Cruz, [Rand] Paul and Mike Lee are on a mission to destroy, shut down the American government, destroy Obamacare, drive the country into default, destroy the U.S. credit rating. Terrorists with one purpose: to bring down not just this administration, but, let's face it, the American government." (Chris Matthews, "Hardball," 2013)

"There is nothing about this skinhead lesbian that impresses me and there is nothing that she has to say unless you're a frothing at the mouth moonbat." (Leslie Gibson, Maine politician, referring to a Marjory Stoneman Douglas High School shooting survivor and antigun activist, in a deleted tweet, 2018)

Such arguments are fallacious because they attempt to discredit a claim or point of view by appealing to something that's almost always irrelevant to it: a person's character, motives, or personal circumstances. Claims must be judged on their own merits; they are not guilty by association. We are never justified in rejecting a claim because of a person's faults unless we can show how a person's faults translate into faults in the claim—and this is almost never the case. Even when a person's character is relevant to the truth of claims (as when we must consider the merits of testimonial evidence), we are not justified in believing a claim false just because the person's character is dubious. If the person's character is dubious, we are left with no reason to think the claim either true *or* false.

The fallacy of appeal to the person comes in several varieties. One is the personal attack, often simply consisting of insults. The gist is familiar enough: Reject X's claims, ideas, or theories because X is a radical, reactionary, extremist, right-winger, left-winger, fool, bonehead, moron, nutbar, or scum of the earth. Whatever psychological impact such terms of abuse may have, logically they carry no weight at all.

Another form of this fallacy emphasizes not a person's character but his or her circumstances. Here someone making a claim is accused of inconsistency—specifically, of maintaining a view that is inconsistent with his or her previous views or social or political commitments.

> *Edgar asserts that evolution is true, but he's an ordained minister in a fundamentalist church that has taken a firm stand against evolution. So he can't accept this theory; he must reject it.*
>
> *Madison says she's opposed to abortion, but you can't take her seriously. Her view goes against everything her party stands for.*

These arguments are fallacious if they're implying that a claim must be true (or false) just because it's inconsistent with some aspect of the claimant's circumstances. The circumstances are irrelevant to the truth of the claim.

When such arguments are put forth as charges of hypocrisy, we get another ad hominem fallacy known as **tu quoque** (or "you're another"). The fallacious reasoning goes like this: Ellen claims that X, but Ellen doesn't practice/live by/condone X herself—so X is false. Look:

> *Alice, the town liberal, tells us that we shouldn't drive SUVs because the cars use too much gas and are bad for the environment. But she drives an SUV herself. What a hypocrite! I think we can safely reject her stupid pronouncements.*

But whether someone is hypocritical regarding their claims can have no bearing on the truth of those claims. We may, of course, condemn someone for hypocrisy, but we logically cannot use that hypocrisy as a justification for rejecting her views. Her views must stand or fall on their own merits.

A version of the *tu quoque* fallacy that often pops up in the media is **whataboutism**, the reversing of an accusation by arguing that an opponent is guilty of an equally bad or worse offense. When Individual A is accused of an offense, she asks "what about" her opponent who she says is guilty of an offense that's just as bad or worse than the one she's accused of. During the Cold War, whataboutism was a favorite ploy of the Soviet Union, which would typically respond to criticisms of its human rights violations by pointing to the U.S. treatment of black people in southern states. In recent American politics, the technique's most famous practitioner has been, again, President Donald Trump.

...What about all of the Clinton ties to Russia, including Podesta Company, Uranium deal, Russian Reset, big dollar speeches etc.

Fig. 6.4 Screen grab of tweet from Donald J. Trump.

So many people are asking why isn't the A.G. or Special Council looking at the many Hillary Clinton or Comey crimes. 33,000 e-mails deleted?

Fig. 6.5 Screen grab of tweet from Donald J. Trump.

What about all of the contact with the Clinton campaign and the Russians? Also, is it true that the DNC would not let the FBI in to look?

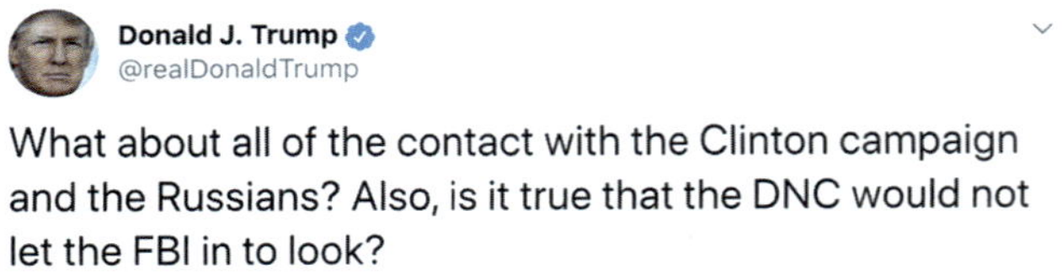

Fig. 6.6 Screen grab of tweet from Donald J. Trump.

Like other ad hominem arguments, whataboutism of course establishes nothing.

In another variation of circumstantial ad hominem reasoning, someone might deduce that a claim is false because the person making it, given his or her circumstances, would be expected to make it. For example,

> *Wilson claims that the political system in Cuba is exemplary. But he has to say that. He's a card-carrying communist. So forget what he says.*

But whether Wilson is a communist, and whether he would be expected or required to have certain views because of his connection to communism, is irrelevant to the truth of his claim.

Finally, we have the ad hominem tactic known as "poisoning the well." In this one, someone argues like this: X has no regard for the truth or has nonrational motives for espousing a claim, so nothing that X says should be believed—including the claim in question. The idea is that just as you can't get safe water out of a poisoned well, you can't get reliable claims out of a discredited claimant. This tack is fallacious because the fact that someone might have dubious reasons for making a claim does not show that the claim is false, nor does it mean that everything that comes out of the "poisoned well" can be automatically dismissed.

How to Respond to Ad Hominem Attacks

You can't swim in the uncertain waters of social media without someone reacting to your well-wrought argument by offering dazzling ad hominem retorts like "You're an idiot" or "I looked up 'moron' in the dictionary and your picture was there." Or maybe the response to your argument is a little less insulting but still ad hominem. How do you counter such unreason? Here are some options to consider, from the philosophy and science website Effectiviology (effectiviology.com):

- **Point out the irrelevance of the ad hominem attack.** You can do this by pointing out that the personal attack has nothing to do with the argument at hand, and by calling out your opponent on their use of this fallacy. It's best to not become defensive when doing this, and if necessary, you should go on the offense and ask your opponent to justify *why* their personal attack on you is relevant to the discussion.
- **Respond to the attack.** In some cases, you might want to fully address the ad hominem attack, even if it's not directly relevant to the discussion at hand. This is a reasonable course of action when the attack has to do with factors such as your motives, which might be relevant to the discussion somehow, but it's generally not recommended in cases when the attack is strictly personal or abusive, and has nothing to do with the discussion.
- **Ignore the attack.** You can choose to keep the discussion going, while refusing to engage with the personal attack that your opponent made. This can work in some cases, and especially when ignoring the personal attacks makes you appear more credible, by showing that you refuse to stoop to your opponent's level. However, in some cases this isn't a viable option, and especially when you feel that not responding will imply that you agree with whatever was said against you, even if it's not relevant to the discussion.
- **Acknowledge the attack and move on.** This is similar to ignoring the ad hominem attack, except that you first acknowledge the attack in order to show that you don't care about it, before moving on with the discussion. This doesn't necessarily mean that you have to agree with the attack; rather, it means that you have to show that you're aware of it, which might look better than ignoring it entirely. To do this, you can use language such as "I get it that *you think* that I'm X, but that doesn't have anything to do with what we're discussing here, so I'm not going to address it."

Keep in mind that in some cases, you can choose to counterattack with personal attacks of your own when your opponent uses an ad hominem attack against you. However, this means that you are resorting to logically fallacious arguments, so think carefully before you choose to do this.[3]

Equivocation

The fallacy of **equivocation** is the use of a word in two different senses in an argument. For example,

> *The end of everything is its perfection.*
> *The end of life is death.*
> *Therefore, death is the perfection of life.*
>
> *Only man is rational.*
> *No woman is a man.*
> *Therefore, no woman is rational.*
>
> *Laws can only be created by law-givers.*
> *There are many laws of nature.*
> *Therefore, there must be a Law-Giver, namely, God.*

In the first argument, *end* is used in two different senses. In the first premise it means purpose, but in the second it means termination. Because of this flip-flop in meanings, the conclusion doesn't follow from the premises—but it looks as if it should.

In the second argument, *man* is the equivocal term. In the first premise it means humankind, but in the second, male. So the conclusion doesn't follow, making it appear that a sound argument has banished women's rationality.

In the third argument, *laws* is used in two senses—rules of human behavior in the first premise, regularities of nature (as in "law of gravity") in the second. Consequently, the conclusion trying to establish the existence of God doesn't follow.

The fallacy of equivocation occurs whenever a word has one meaning in one premise and another meaning in another premise or the conclusion. This switch of senses always invalidates the argument.

Appeal to Popularity

The fallacy of the **appeal to popularity (or appeal to the masses)**, mentioned in Chapter 3, is arguing that a claim must be true merely because a substantial number of people believe it. The basic pattern of this fallacy is "Everyone (or almost everyone, most people, many people) believes X, so X must be true." For example,

> *Most people approve of the government's new security measures, even though innocent people's privacy is sometimes violated. So the measures must be okay.*

> *Of course the war is justified. Everyone believes that it's justified.*
>
> *The vast majority of Americans believe that there's a supreme being, so how could you doubt it?*

These arguments are fallacious because they assume that a proposition is true merely because a great number of people believe it. But as far as the truth of a claim is concerned, what many people believe is irrelevant. Many people used to believe that certain women were witches and should be burned, that slavery was perfectly acceptable, that Earth was the center of the universe, and that bleeding and purging were cures for just about every ill. Large groups of people are no more infallible than an individual is. Their belief in a proposition, by itself, is no indication of truth.

What many other people believe, however, can be an indication of truth if they are experts or have expert knowledge in the issue at hand. If almost all farmers say that the fall harvest will be abundant, ordinarily we should believe them.

In the era of social media, the bandwagon fallacy takes on an ominous meaning. On Twitter, Google, Facebook, and other platforms, the popularity of claims, ideas, and opinions can be pushed to the limit in a matter of hours. Someone says online that global warming is a hoax, that a massacre of school students never happened, that children should not be vaccinated against measles, that the pope is a child molester—and suddenly bandwagons full of believers boost the claims' popularity, a popularity quantified and pumped by Twitter "likes" and retweets, Google's hyperlinks and keywords, and Facebook's "likes" and sharing. But a billion likes and retweets cannot prove the truth or falsity of any claim, no more than an opinion poll can establish scientific facts or validate moral decisions.

Appeal to Tradition

The **appeal to tradition** is arguing that a claim must be true just because it's part of a tradition. For example,

> *Acupuncture has been used for a thousand years in China. It must work.*
>
> *Of course publishing pornography is wrong. In this community there's a tradition of condemning it that goes back a hundred years.*

Such appeals are fallacious because tradition, like popular consensus, can be wrong. Remember that an established tradition barred women from voting, stripped African Americans of their civil rights, promoted the vengeful policy of "an eye for an eye," and sanctioned the sacrifice of innocents to the gods.

Be careful, though. Automatically rejecting a claim because it is traditional is not reasonable either. The point is that a tradition should be neither accepted nor rejected without good reason. Knee-jerk acceptance of tradition is as bad as knee-jerk rejection.

Appeal to Ignorance

The **appeal to ignorance** is arguing that a lack of evidence proves something. In one type of this fallacy, the problem arises by thinking that a claim must be true because it hasn't been shown to be false. For example,

> *No one has shown that ghosts aren't real, so they must be real.*
>
> *It's clear that God exists because science hasn't proved that he doesn't exist.*
>
> *You can't disprove my theory that JFK was killed by LBJ. Therefore, my theory is correct.*

The problem here is that a lack of evidence is supposed to prove something—but it can't. A lack of evidence alone can neither prove nor disprove a proposition. A lack of evidence simply reveals our ignorance about something.

In another variation of this fallacy, the breakdown in logic comes when you argue that a claim must be false because it hasn't been proved to be true. Look at these:

> *No one has shown that ghosts are real, so they must not exist.*
>
> *It's clear that God doesn't exist because science hasn't proved that he does.*
>
> *You can't prove your theory that JFK was killed by LBJ. Therefore, your theory is false.*

Again, the moral is: Lack of evidence proves nothing. It does not give us a reason for believing a claim.

But what if our moral is wrong? If we could prove something with a lack of evidence, we could prove almost anything. You can't prove that invisible men aren't having a keg party on Mars—does this mean that it's true that invisible men are having a keg party on Mars? You can't prove that Socrates belched at his famous trial—does this prove that he didn't belch?

There are cases, however, that may seem like appeals to ignorance but actually are not. Sometimes when we carefully search for something, and such a thorough search is likely to uncover it if there is anything to uncover, the failure to find what we're looking for can show that it probably isn't there. A botanist, for example, may scan a forest looking for a rare plant but not find it even though she looks in all the likely places. In this case, her lack of evidence—her not finding the plant after a thorough search—may be good evidence that the plant doesn't exist in that environment. This conclusion would not rest on ignorance, but on the knowledge that in these circumstances any thorough search would probably reveal the sought-after object if it was there at all.

This kind of inductive reasoning is widespread in science. Drugs, for example, are tested for toxicity on rodents or other animals before the drugs are given to humans. If after extensive testing no toxic effects are observed in the animals (which are supposed to be relevantly similar to humans), the lack of toxicity is considered evidence that the drug will probably not cause toxic effects in humans. Likewise, in the realm of extraordinary claims, some scientists regard the failure to find the Loch Ness monster or Bigfoot after decades of searching to be evidence that these creatures do not exist.

Appeals to ignorance involve the notion of **burden of proof**. Burden of proof is the weight of evidence or argument required by one side in a debate or disagreement (in the critical thinking sense). Problems arise when the burden of proof is placed on the wrong side. For example, if Louise declares that "no one has shown that gremlins aren't real, so they must be real," she implicitly puts the burden of proof on those who don't agree with her. She's asserting, in effect, "I say that gremlins are real, and it's up to you to prove I'm wrong." Or, "I'm entitled to believe that gremlins are real unless you prove that they're not." But as we saw earlier, this line is just an appeal to ignorance, and the burden of proof for showing that gremlins are real rests with *her*—not with those who don't share her belief. If her claim is unsupported, you need not accept it. If you take the bait and try to prove that gremlins don't exist, you are accepting a burden of proof that should fall on Louise's shoulders, not yours.

Note that in a case like this, when the claim is improbable or extraordinary, and no evidence for it is offered, it would even be reasonable to presume that it is false. For example, if someone claims without evidence that an alien spacecraft has landed on the White House lawn (the kind of claim that probably appears somewhere on social media every day of the week), you would not be guilty of the fallacious appeal to ignorance if you asserted that the claim is probably false.

Usually, the burden of proof rests on the side that makes a positive claim—an assertion that something exists or is the case, rather than that something does not exist or is not the case. So in general, if a person (the claimant) makes an unsupported positive claim, he or she must provide evidence for it if the claim is to be accepted. If you doubt the claim, you are under no obligation to prove it wrong. You need not—and should not—accept it without good reasons (which the claimant should provide). Of course, you also should not reject the claim without good reasons. If the claimant does provide you with reasons for accepting the claim, you

> ### Can You Prove a Negative?
>
> As you might imagine, appeals to ignorance can result in strange (and frustrating) conversations.
>
> ALICE: Unicorns exist!
> YOU: Oh, yeah, can you prove they exist?
> ALICE: Can you prove they don't?
>
> Alice's appeal to ignorance, of course, does not prove that unicorns exist. (The proper response to her unsupported claim is to point out that the claim is unsupported and that you therefore have been offered no good reason to believe it.) Moreover, her demand for proof that unicorns don't exist is unfair because she is asking you to do the impossible. She is asking you to *prove a universal negative*—a claim that nothing of a certain kind exists. To prove that unicorns do not exist, you would have to search throughout all space and time. But no one can do that. So her request is unreasonable.
>
> It is possible, however, to prove a more limited negative claim, such as "There are no baseballs on this table." Some limited negative claims are very difficult to prove, but not impossible—such as "There are no Chevrolet trucks in this state."

can either accept them or reject them. If you reject them, you are obligated to explain the reasons for your rejection.

Appeal to Emotion

The fallacy of the **appeal to emotion** is the use of emotions as premises in an argument. That is, it consists of trying to persuade someone of a conclusion solely by arousing his or her feelings rather than presenting relevant reasons. When you use this fallacy, you appeal to people's guilt, anger, pity, fear, compassion, resentment, pride—but not to good reasons that could give logical support to your case. Take a look:

> *You should hire me for this network analyst position. I'm the best person for the job. If I don't get a job soon, my wife will leave me and I won't have enough money to pay for my mother's heart operation. Come on, give me a break.*
>
> *Political ad: If school music programs are cut as part of the new district budget, we will save money—and lose our children to a world without music, a landscape without song. Let the children sing. Vote no on Proposition 13.*

As arguments, these passages are fallacious, not because they appeal to strong emotions, but because they appeal to almost *nothing but* strong emotions. They urge us to accept a conclusion but offer no good reasons for doing so. We may feel compassion for the job hunter and his mother, but those feelings have no bearing on whether he is truly the best person for the job. We may recoil from the idea of children in a stark, tuneless world, but that overblown image and the emotions it evokes in us provide no logical support for the conclusion.

Good writers often combine arguments with emotional persuasion in the same piece of writing, and no fallacy need enter the picture. A strong argument is presented, and it's reinforced by strong feelings. Consider this piece of persuasive prose:

> I am a mother though my child is dead. He did not die of an incurable disease, of a virus beyond the ken of medical science. He was not taken from me by a foreign enemy while defending his country. No, he was needlessly slaughtered on the highway. A drunk driver ran broadside into his motorcycle. My son was shot fifty feet through the air by the collision and hit the blacktop at forty-five miles per hour.
>
> My son's assassin is not yet out of high school and yet that boy was able to walk into a liquor store and purchase two six packs of beer, most of which he drank that evening. This boy does not have the mental capability to graduate from high school in the prescribed time (he was held back in his senior year), and yet the law has given him the right to purchase alcohol and decide for himself what is appropriate behavior with regard to alcoholic consumption. I do not trust most of my adult friends to make such mature judgments. How can anyone trust the eighteen-year-old?
>
> The law must change. Statistics have shown that states which have a minimum drinking age of twenty-one years also have significantly fewer automobile accidents caused by drunken teenagers. I lost my son, but why do any of the rest of us have to suffer as I have? Please, support legislation to increase the drinking age to twenty-one.[4]

This passage evokes sympathy and indignation—but also gives an argument using statistics to support a conclusion about the need for new legislation.

As you would expect, appeals to emotion come in different forms, some of which are identified by name:

> **Appeal to pity:** The attempt to persuade people to accept a conclusion by evoking their pity, compassion, or empathy. Example: *I should get this merit scholarship. I'm homeless and penniless, so the money would be put to good use.*
>
> **Apple polishing:** The attempt to persuade people to accept a conclusion by flattering them. Example: *I know you'll vote for me in the upcoming election because you have the true American spirit and the genuine wisdom that comes from faith and hard work.*
>
> **Scare tactics:** The attempt to persuade people to accept a conclusion by scaring them. Example: *Unless we defeat Proposition 13, the homosexual agenda will be taught in our schools, and more kids will want to become gay.*

Argument from outrage: The attempt to influence people to accept a claim by getting them intensely angry at a particular situation. Example: *We need to stop the flow of immigrants into this country right now! Do you want an illegal immigrant taking your job away from you? Or spreading un-American values?*

Again, emotions per se are not the problem; they become problematic when they are irrelevant to the claim being advanced. If you get emotional enough, angry enough, or scared enough, you may forget about logical reasons and evidence and jump right to an unwarranted conclusion. Remember: Just because you feel strongly about a claim, that doesn't necessarily mean the claim is true. In critical thinking, the best decisions happen when emotions are guided by reason.

Red Herring

Perhaps the most blatant fallacy of irrelevance is the **red herring**, the deliberate raising of an irrelevant issue during an argument. This fallacy gets its name from the practice of dragging a smelly fish across a trail to throw a fox hunting dog off the scent. The basic pattern is to put forth a claim and then couple it with additional claims that may seem to support it but in fact are mere distractions. For instance:

> *Every woman should have the right to an abortion on demand. There's no question about it. These antiabortion activists block the entrances to abortion clinics, threaten abortion doctors, and intimidate anyone who wants to terminate a pregnancy.*

> *The legislators should vote for the three-strikes-and-you're-out crime control measure. I'm telling you, crime is a terrible thing when it happens to you. It causes death, pain, and fear. And I wouldn't want to wish these things on anyone.*

Notice what's happening here. In the first example, the issue is whether women should have the right to abortion on demand. But the arguer shifts the subject to the behavior of antiabortion activists, as though their behavior has some bearing on the original issue. Their behavior, of course, has nothing to do with the main issue. The argument is bogus. In the second example, the issue is whether the legislators should vote for a three-strikes crime bill. But the subject gets changed to the terrible costs of crime, which is only remotely related to the main issue. (There's also an appeal to fear.) We can all agree that crime can have awful consequences, but this fact has little to do with the merits and demerits of enacting a three-strikes law.

Another example—a famous one—comes from candidate Donald Trump during his second presidential debate with Hillary Clinton in 2016.

Responding to a question about his coarse remarks captured on tape earlier in his career, he abruptly shifts the focus to another subject entirely:

> Yes, I'm very embarrassed by it [the tape]. I hate it. But it's locker room talk, and it's one of those things. I will knock the hell out of ISIS. We're going to defeat ISIS. ISIS happened a number of years ago in a vacuum that was left because of bad judgment. And I will tell you, I will take care of ISIS.

Straw Man

If appeal to the person is the most widely used fallacy in American politics, this fallacy must be a close second. **Straw man** is the distorting, weakening, or oversimplifying of someone's position so it can be more easily attacked or refuted. A straw-man argument works like this: Reinterpret claim X so that it becomes the weak or absurd claim Y. Attack claim Y. Conclude that X is unfounded. For example,

> David says that he's opposed to the new sodomy laws that make it illegal for consenting adult homosexuals to engage in sex acts in their own homes. Obviously he thinks that gay sex is something special and should be protected so it's allowed to take place just about anywhere. Do you want gays having sex all over town in full view of your children? David does, and he's dead wrong.
>
> Senator Jones is opposed to the military spending bill, saying that it's too costly. Why does he always want to slash everything to the bone? He wants a pint-sized military that couldn't fight off a crazed band of terrorists, let alone a rogue nation.
>
> Lawyers for the ACLU have sued to remove the massive Ten Commandments monument from the lobby of the courthouse. As usual, they are as anti-religious as ever. They want to remove every vestige of religion and faith from American life. Don't let them do it. Don't let them win yet another battle in their war to secularize the whole country.

In the first passage, David is opposed to laws prohibiting sexual activity between consenting, homosexual adults in their own homes. His opponent, however, distorts his view, claiming that David is actually in favor of allowing gay sex virtually anywhere, including in public. David, of course, is not asserting this (few people would). This distorted version of David's position is easy to ridicule and reject, allowing his actual view to be summarily dismissed.

In the second passage, Senator Jones is against the military spending bill on the grounds that it costs too much. His position, though, is twisted into the claim that the military should be pared down so drastically that it would be ineffective even against small groups of terrorists. The senator's views on military spending are thus made to appear extreme or ludicrous. But it is unlikely that Senator Jones (or any other senator) wants to see the U.S. military reduced to such a level. He simply wants a less expensive military—not necessarily an ineffective one.

The third passage is typical of the kind of fallacious arguments that crop up in debates over church-state separation. Here, the ACLU wants a monument displaying the Ten Commandments removed from the lobby of a government building, a view that is characterized as anti-religious. But a request that a religious symbol be removed from a government context is not, in itself, necessarily anti-religious. Many have argued, for example, that such requests should be made to protect freedom of religion by preventing the government from giving preferential treatment to one religion over another. Also, wanting to get rid of a religious display on public property is a far cry from wanting to remove "every vestige of religion and faith from American life." Characterizing the ACLU suit as anti-religious, though, is a way to generate strong opposition to it. Note that in church-state debates, the straw-man tack is also used to bolster the other side of the dispute. Those who favor religious displays on government property are sometimes characterized as fanatics who want to turn the government into a theocracy. But, of course, from the fact that people want to allow such a religious display it does not follow that they want anything like a theocracy.

Fallacies with Irrelevant Premises

- **Genetic fallacy:** Arguing that a claim is true or false solely because of its origin
- **Composition:** Arguing that what is true of the parts must be true of the whole
- **Division:** Arguing that what is true of the whole must be true of the parts or that what is true of a group is true of individuals in the group
- **Appeal to the person:** Rejecting a claim by criticizing the person who makes it rather than the claim itself
- **Equivocation:** The use of a word in two different senses in an argument
- **Appeal to popularity:** Arguing that a claim must be true merely because a substantial number of people believe it
- **Appeal to tradition:** Arguing that a claim must be true or good just because it's part of a tradition
- **Appeal to ignorance:** Arguing that a lack of evidence proves something
- **Appeal to emotion:** The use of emotions as premises in an argument
- **Red herring:** The deliberate raising of an irrelevant issue during an argument
- **Straw man:** The distorting, weakening, or oversimplifying of someone's position so it can be more easily attacked or refuted
- **Two wrongs make a right:** Arguing that your doing something morally wrong is justified because someone else has done the same (or similar) thing.

Two Wrongs Make a Right

Two wrongs make a right is a piece of fallacious reasoning that we are all probably guilty of. It is arguing that doing something morally wrong is justified because someone else has done the same (or similar) thing:

> *I have a clear conscience. I stole his laptop because he took mine a month ago.*
>
> *My wife had an affair, so I'm within my rights to have one, too.*
>
> *Okay, I snatched a few of those little Brach candies at the supermarket. So what? Three other people did, too.*

The idea is that someone else's wrong acts can somehow make yours right. But if your action is morally impermissible, someone else's deed cannot make it otherwise. If your action lacks justification, it cannot acquire justification by what someone else does.

That is not to say that justification for your behavior is impossible to obtain. Most ethicists would say that self-defense against other people's injurious actions can be a legitimate reason for your doing something that normally would be wrong. It surely must be permissible, they would argue, to knock down a mugger who is busy trying to knock you down. Likewise, a nation surely must be justified in going to war against a foreign power that first made war against it. And to many, in the name of justice, punishment by the state for criminal acts can also be justified.

But what about "an eye for an eye" justice? Can't we avenge a wrong done to us by someone else—can't we do unto him as he has done to us? In many cultures, the answer is an emphatic *yes*. If a man kills your goat, you are justified in killing his. If a woman steals your coat, you can legitimately steal hers. But most ethicists would probably say *no*: This "eye for an eye" principle (and similar "two wrongs make a right" views) is not justice but personal vengeance, which is immoral.

Section Query

What would constitute a reasonable and effective response to someone using an ad hominem fallacy against you?

6.2 Fallacies: Unacceptable Premises

Begging the Question

The fallacy of **begging the question** (or arguing in a circle) is the attempt to establish the conclusion of an argument by using that conclusion as a premise. To beg the question is to argue that a proposition is true because the very same proposition supports it:

> *p*
> Therefore, *p*.

The classic question-begging argument goes like this:

> God exists. We know that God exists because the Bible says so, and we should believe what the Bible says because God wrote it.

Or, more formally:

> *The Bible says that God exists.*
> *The Bible is true because God wrote it.*
> *Therefore, God exists.*

This argument assumes at the outset the very proposition ("God exists") that it is trying to prove. Any argument that does this is fallacious.

Unfortunately, most question-begging arguments are not as obviously fallacious as "*p* is true because *p* is true." They may be hard to recognize because they are intricate or confusing. Consider this argument:

> *It is in every case immoral to lie to someone, even if the lie could save a life. Even in extreme circumstances a lie is still a lie. All lies are immoral because the very act of prevarication in all circumstances is contrary to ethical principles.*

At first glance, this argument may seem reasonable, but it's not. It reduces to this circular reasoning: "Lying is always immoral because lying is always immoral."

Among the more subtle examples of question-begging is this famous one, a favorite of critical thinking texts:

> *To allow every man unbounded freedom of speech must always be, on the whole, advantageous to the state; for it is highly conducive to the interests of the community that each individual should enjoy a liberty, perfectly unlimited, of expressing his sentiments.*[5]

This argument, as well as the one preceding it, demonstrates the easiest way to subtly beg the question: Just repeat the conclusion as a premise, but use different words.

False Dilemma

The fallacy of **false dilemma** is asserting that there are only two alternatives to consider when there are actually more than two. For example,

> Look, either you support the war or you are a traitor to your country. You don't support the war. So you're a traitor.

This argument contends that there are only two alternatives to choose from: Either you back the war, or you are a traitor. And since you don't back the war, you must be a traitor. But this argument works only if there really are just two alternatives. Actually there are other plausible possibilities here. Maybe you are loyal to your country but don't want to see it get involved in a costly war. Maybe you are a patriot who simply disagrees with your government's rationale for going to war. Because these possibilities are excluded, the argument is fallacious.

This argument is like some famous false dilemmas in politics and diplomacy that have been used to try to force the undecided or reluctant to make a choice:

> "You are either with us or against us in the fight against terror." (President George W. Bush, after the September 11 attacks, demanding support from the rest of the world against terrorism)

> America: Love It or Leave It! (A popular bumper sticker during the Vietnam War asserting that people should fully support government war policy or get out of the country)

Now consider this argument:

> Either those lights you saw in the night sky were alien spacecraft (UFOs), or you were hallucinating. You obviously weren't hallucinating. So they had to be UFOs.

This argument says that there are only two possibilities: The lights were UFOs, or you hallucinated the whole thing. And they must have been UFOs because you weren't hallucinating. But as is the case with the majority of alleged paranormal events, there are many more possible explanations than most people realize. The lights could have been commercial aircraft, military aircraft, meteors, atmospheric conditions, or the planet Venus (which, believe it or not, is often mistaken for a UFO). Since the argument ignores these reasonable possibilities, it's fallacious.

Finally:

> We must legalize drugs. We either legalize them or pay a heavy toll in lives and the taxpayer's money to continue the war on drugs. And we cannot afford to pay such a high price.

At first glance, these two alternatives may seem to exhaust the possibilities. But there is at least one other option—to launch a massive effort to prevent drug use and thereby reduce the demand for illegal drugs. The argument does not work because it fails to consider this possibility.

Note that these arguments are expressed in disjunctive (either-or) form. But they can just as easily be expressed in a conditional (if-then) form, which says the same thing:

> Look, if you don't support the war, then you are a traitor to your country. You don't support the war. So you're a traitor.
>
> If those lights you saw in the night sky were not alien spacecraft (UFOs), then you were hallucinating. You obviously weren't hallucinating. So they had to be UFOs.
>
> We must legalize drugs. If we don't legalize them, then we will pay a heavy toll in lives and the taxpayer's money to continue the war on drugs. And we cannot afford to pay such a high price.

Sometimes we encounter stand-alone disjunctive phrases, rather than full-blown false dilemma arguments. These are false choices often presented as one-liners or headlines on websites, blogs, tabloid newspapers, TV news programs, and magazines. For example,

> *Syria: Quagmire or Failure?*
> *Microsoft: Bad Cop or Evil Giant?*
> *Barack Obama: Socialist or Nouveau Fascist?*

By limiting the possibilities, these headlines can imply that almost any outlandish state of affairs is actual—without even directly asserting anything. People are often taken in by false dilemmas because they don't think beyond the alternatives laid before them. Out of fear, the need for simple answers, or a failure of imagination, they don't ask, "Is there another possibility?" To ask this is to think outside the box and reduce the likelihood of falling for simplistic answers.

Decision-Point Fallacy

Here's a variation on the false-dilemma ploy that you will encounter sooner or later, if you haven't already: the **decision-point fallacy** (also called the line-drawing fallacy). For the sake of clarity, let's start with a silly example:

> *Joe lost the hair on his head. When he had a full head of hair and he lost just a hair or two, he clearly was not bald. If we are to say truthfully that he is bald, there must have been a point in the hair-loss process (a decision point) in which he became bald. (Maybe the loss of one more hair was*

enough to render him bald.) But obviously there is no such point at which we can legitimately decide that Joe went from not being bald to being bald. Therefore, we must infer that Joe did not become bald at all.

And here are two opposing arguments that are far more serious:

The abortion-rights version: *At conception, an embryo is not a person (not an entity with full moral rights, including a right to life). And in the long process of gestation, there is no precise point at which we can definitively say that the fetus has gone from being a nonperson to being a person. Therefore, the fetus does not become a person at any point in gestation—the fetus is simply not a person.*

The right-to-life version: *In the long process of gestation, there is no point at which we can definitively say that the fetus has become a person. People have suggested different points at which personhood arises (at viability, for example), but none of these is plausible. Conception, however, is plausible as the beginning of personhood, for at that instant the embryo receives what will make it fully human—DNA. Therefore, personhood arises at the moment of conception.*

What's wrong with these decision-point arguments? In many processes, there is no decision point, no dynamic moment that suddenly transforms something into something else—and our concepts are fuzzy to reflect this fact. *Bald* and *hairy* are such terms. But none of this means that those concepts don't sometimes apply. Even though we can't say at what point a man becomes bald, we can normally use the word *bald* just fine to accurately describe a man who has hair loss.

The decision-point fallacy would have us assume that there must be a specific transforming point even though no such point exists or needs to exist. It is often an easy assumption to make—and to avoid.

Slippery Slope

The fallacy of **slippery slope** is arguing, without good reasons, that taking a particular step will inevitably lead to a further, undesirable step (or steps). The idea behind the metaphor, of course, is that if you take the first step on a slippery slope, you will have to take others because, well, the slope is slippery. A familiar slippery-slope pattern is "Doing action A will lead to action B, which will lead to action C, which will result in calamitous effect D. Therefore, you should not do action A." It's fallacious when there is no good reason to think that doing action A will actually result in undesirable effect D. Take a look at this classic example:

We absolutely must not lose the war in Vietnam. If South Vietnam falls to the communists, then Thailand will fall to them. If Thailand falls to

them, then South Korea will fall to them. And before you know it, all of
Southeast Asia will be under communist control.

This argument was commonplace during the Cold War. It was known as the domino theory because it asserted that if one country in Southeast Asia succumbed to communism, they all would succumb, just as a whole row of dominoes will fall if the first one is pushed over. It was fallacious because there was no good evidence that the dominoes would inevitably fall as predicted. In fact, after South Vietnam was defeated, they did not fall as predicted.

Here are some more examples:

If assault rifles are banned in this country, then handguns will be next. Then sporting rifles will be banned. And ultimately all guns will be banned, and our fundamental freedom to own guns will be canceled out altogether. So if assault rifles are banned, we might as well strike the Second Amendment from the Constitution because it will be worthless.

We must ban pornography in all forms. Otherwise, rape and other sex crimes will be as common as jaywalking.

All Americans should be against laws permitting consensual homosexual sex in one's own home. If that kind of thing is allowed, before you know it anything goes—bestiality, prostitution, illegal drug use, and violence.

These arguments follow the basic slippery-slope pattern. They are fallacies not because they assert that one event or state of affairs can inevitably lead to others, but because there is no good reason to believe the assertions. Some arguments may look like slippery-slope fallacies but are not because there is good reason to think that the steps are connected as described. Observe:

If you have Lyme disease, you definitely should get medical treatment. Without treatment, you could develop life-threatening complications. Man, you could die. You should see your doctor now.

This is not a fallacious slippery-slope argument. There are good reasons to believe that the series of events mentioned would actually happen.

Now you can have a laugh at *The Onion*'s satirical and very funny slippery slope argument about gay marriage.

Condemning the decision as "dangerously reasonable" and "beyond level-headed," vocal opponents of same-sex marriage strongly cautioned that this morning's Supreme Court rulings supporting gay rights could put the United States on a one-way, slippery slope to rationality. "I don't think people fully understand that letting homosexuals legally marry one another

Fallacies with Unacceptable Premises

- **Begging the question:** The attempt to establish the conclusion of an argument by using that conclusion as a premise
- **False dilemma:** Asserting that there are only two alternatives to consider when there are actually more than two
- **Decision-point fallacy:** Arguing that because a line or distinction cannot be drawn at any point in a process, there are no differences or gradations in that process.
- **Slippery slope:** Arguing, without good reasons, that taking a particular step will inevitably lead to a further, undesirable step (or steps)
- **Hasty generalization:** The drawing of a conclusion about a target group based on an inadequate sample size
- **Faulty analogy:** An argument in which the things being compared are not sufficiently similar in relevant ways

is just the very beginning of a dangerous road to clear logic and sound, sensible decision making," said anti-gay protester Kevin Moore, 43, who warned that the landmark ruling will likely lead to "an unspeakable amount of enlightened discourse and thoughtful compromises across the country."[6]

Hasty Generalization

In Chapter 2 we pointed out the connection between the availability error and the fallacy known as **hasty generalization**. Here we need only recall that we are guilty of hasty generalization when we draw a conclusion about a whole group based on an inadequate sample of the group. This mistake is a genuine fallacy of unacceptable premises because the premises stating the sample size are relevant to the conclusion, but they provide inadequate evidence. For example,

> You should buy an iPhone. They're great. I bought one last year, and it has given me nothing but flawless performance.
>
> The only male professor I've had this year was a chauvinist pig. All the male professors at this school must be chauvinist pigs.
>
> Psychology majors are incredibly ignorant about human psychology. Believe me, I know what I'm talking about: My best friend is a psych major. What an ignoramus!
>
> The French are snobby and rude. Remember those two high-and-mighty guys with really bad manners? They're French. I rest my case.
>
> The food at Pappy's Restaurant is awful. I had a sandwich there once, and the bread was stale.

Faulty Analogy

Like hasty generalizations, defective arguments by analogy, or **faulty analogies**, are also fallacies involving unacceptable premises. An analogy is a comparison of two or more things alike in specific respects. An argument by analogy reasons this way: Because two or more things are similar in several respects, they must be similar in some further respect. For example,

> *In the Vietnam War, the United States had not articulated a clear rationale for fighting there, and the United States lost. Likewise, in the present war the United States has not articulated a clear rationale for fighting. Therefore, the United States will lose this war too.*
>
> *A watch is a mechanism of exquisite complexity with numerous parts precisely arranged and accurately adjusted to achieve a purpose—a purpose imposed by the watch's designer. Likewise the universe has exquisite complexity with countless parts—from atoms to asteroids—that fit together precisely and accurately to produce certain effects as though arranged by plan. Therefore, the universe must also have a designer.*

In a faulty analogy, the things being compared are not sufficiently similar in relevant ways. Such analogical arguments are said to be weak. For instance, you could argue the following:

> *Dogs are warm-blooded, nurse their young, and give birth to puppies.*
>
> *Humans are warm-blooded and nurse their young. Therefore, humans give birth to puppies too.*

This argument by analogy is about as weak as they come—and a little silly. Dogs and humans are not sufficiently similar in relevant ways (in physiology, for one thing) to justify such a strange conclusion.

Section Query

Are there slippery slope arguments that are not fallacious? Give an example.

6.3 Persuaders: Rhetorical Moves

Rhetoric presents us with a large repertoire of techniques for influencing hearts and minds through emotion—while proving nothing through reason. Very often rhetorical devices do nothing more than promote a negative (or positive) attitude toward someone or something, but this ploy can be extraordinarily persuasive. Here are a few of the better known examples.

Whose Pants Are on Fire?

In case you wanted more convincing that critical thinking is badly needed in political discourse, here is some unsettling evidence. Every day PolitiFact.com, a project of the *Tampa Bay Times*, fact-checks the statements of politicians, lobbyists, and others making assertions about political issues. The project participants then rate the statements using the Truth-O-Meter scale: an assertion is either True, Mostly True, Half True, Mostly False, False, and—for the really outrageously wrong—Pants on Fire. Here are a few statements that earned the latter rating. (For a more detailed analysis of them, go to PolitiFact.com.)

> **Facebook post:** Says Alexandria Ocasio-Cortez said, "We'll never have to worry about China attacking us! They are 12 hours ahead, so we'll have plenty of time to shoot down their missiles!"
> **Facebook post:** Says Bernie Sanders marched with Fidel Castro and Che Guevara in Cuba.
> **Facebook post:** Says Donald Trump was photographed wearing blackface.
> **Bloggers:** Courts have "quietly confirmed" that the MMR vaccine causes autism.
> **Facebook post:** A Virginia principal "expelled two kids for wearing a crucifix around their necks saying, 'there is no place for religion at school.'"
> **Facebook post:** Says U.S. Rep. Rashida Tlaib was photographed in front of a picture of Osama bin Laden and an ISIS flag.
> **Facebook post:** Quotes Mike Pence as saying that people with pre-existing conditions need "more Jesus care," not health care.
> **thelastlineofdefense.org:** "Nancy Pelosi Removed From Benefit for 'Being So Drunk She Couldn't Stand Up'"
> **asamericanasapplepie.org:** "Hillary (Clinton) caught on tape laughing about (hurricane) Irma 'wiping out all of those Florida hillbillies.'"
> **Tucker Carlson:** "The United States ended slavery around the world, and maybe we should get some credit for that, too."
> **Donald Trump:** Says troops recently received "one of the biggest pay raises" ever, and that it was the first pay increase in "more than 10 years."
> **Bloggers:** Quotes Sen. Elizabeth Warren as saying "If women need to be raped by Muslims to prove our tolerance, so be it. Then thank goodness for Planned Parenthood."
> **Infowars:** "Election fraud: Democrats are voting twice in Maryland"
> **WorldNewsDailyReport.com:** "Canadians face major donut shortage after first day of cannabis legalization."
> **Bloggers:** Says a photo shows Brett Kavanaugh passed out.
> **Bloggers:** Says "Sasha Obama's racist anti-white rant just got her expelled."
> **Donald Trump Jr.:** "You see the Nazi platform from the early 1930s . . . look at it compared to the (Democratic Party) platform of today, you're saying, 'Man, those things are awfully similar.'"
> **Vladimir Putin:** "The Russian state has never interfered . . . into internal American affairs including election process."
> **Common Sense News:** Says the "Pope calls for world-wide gun confiscation except for the UN."
> **TheNewYorkEvening.com:** "Pope Francis: Gun owners 'can't call themselves Christian'"
> **Rick Perry:** "More than 3,000 homicides were committed by 'illegal aliens' over the past six years."
> **Rudy Giuliani:** "We had no domestic attacks under Bush."

Innuendo

Innuendo is suggesting something denigrating about a person without explicitly stating it. Through innuendo you can indirectly convey the false claim that someone is bad, though you make only true statements. For example,

> *I'm fairly sure that Senator Johnson's youthful indiscretions involving alcohol, marijuana, and crack cocaine probably have no influence on her current public service.*
>
> *It's time we restored honesty and integrity to the office of mayor.*
>
> *I think we can assume that Mr. Abernathy absolutely does not embezzle—anymore.*
>
> *I'm not saying my opponent will rig this election. I'm just saying we should have people watching the polling places and vote-counters very, very carefully.*
>
> *Judge Sharon Jones should not be reelected. In her court, she has sided with child predators.*

Innuendo was employed in a notorious smear of Senator John McCain in the South Carolina Republican primary in 2000. In a sham telephone survey, voters were asked, "Would you be more or less likely to vote for John McCain if you knew he had fathered an illegitimate black child?"

Euphemisms and Dysphemisms

Euphemisms are words used to convey positive or neutral attitudes or emotions in place of more negative ones; **dysphemisms** are words used to convey negative attitudes or emotions in place of neutral or positive ones. These rhetorical devices work by using the persuasive force of a word's connotations, the feelings and attitudes linked to the word's literal meaning. The devices can mislead, obscure, and confuse. To hide the truth, political, economic, or military leaders might use the euphemism *meaningful downturn in aggregate output* for *recession*; *revenue enhancement* for *tax increase*; *downsizing* for *firing*; *armed reconnaissance* for *bombing*; *neutralize* for *kill*; *enhanced interrogation methods* for *torture*; *collateral damage* for *civilian casualties*; or *soft targets* for *people to kill*.

In debates about gun ownership, those who want to restrict gun ownership may characterize their position as "anti-assault weapon." Those opposed to this position may label it as "anti-self-defense." Both these labels are meant to provoke certain attitudes toward the subject matter—attitudes that may not be supported by any evidence or argument.

Consider the disparate impact on the reader of these pairs of terms, both of which refer to the same thing:

full-figured	fat
guerrillas	freedom fighters
resolute	pigheaded
emphatic	pushy
sweat	perspire

But keep in mind that euphemisms often perform a useful social purpose by allowing us to discuss sensitive subjects in an inoffensive way. We may spare people's feelings by saying that their loved ones have "passed" rather than that they have "died," or that their dog was "put to sleep" rather than "killed." Nevertheless, as critical thinkers, we should be on guard against the deceptive use of connotations. As critical writers, we should rely primarily on argument and evidence to make our case.

Stereotyping

A stereotype is an unwarranted conclusion or generalization about all the members of a group. **Stereotyping** someone is judging her not as an individual, but as part of a group whose members are thought to be all alike. We think because she is a member of the group, and we assume without good reason that all the members of that group are rude and arrogant, that she must also be rude and arrogant. We wrongly assume that because all members of _____ (insert of any political, ethnic, or class group) are _____ (insert name of any negative attribute), the member of that group standing before us also must have that attribute.

By asserting that someone is part of a hated stereotyped group, a speaker or writer can induce others to form a baseless, negative opinion of that person. This slanted opinion in turn can cause people to react dismissively, disdainfully, or angrily to any member of the disparaged group. This is the well-worn path of bigots of all stripes—and a painful indication that critical thinking is needed.

Stereotyping comes in many forms—cultural, gender, racial, sexual, class, political, and more. Much of it is negative, characterizing groups as bad in one way or another. Stereotyping is especially prevalent in politics, where it is often mixed in with dysphemisms, the straw-man fallacy, innuendo, appeal to the person, and other fallacious thinking:

> Common stereotypes about Democrats: *They're pro-taxes and anti-rich; they're obsessed with being politically correct; they don't support the troops; they live in their own liberal, elite bubbles; they're all looking for handouts from the government; they're all socialists; they listen only to the lamestream media and don't think for themselves; they're anti-family.*[7]

Who Is More Intolerant—Liberals or Conservatives?

The answer might surprise you. Here's a snapshot of some of the relevant research.

Are conservatives more prejudiced than liberals, or vice versa? Research over the years has shown that in industrialized nations, social conservatives and religious fundamentalists possess psychological traits, such as the valuing of conformity and the desire for certainty, that tend to predispose people toward prejudice. Meanwhile, liberals and the nonreligious tend to be more open to new experiences, a trait associated with lower prejudice. So one might expect that, whatever each group's own ideology, conservatives and Christians should be inherently more discriminatory on the whole.

But more recent psychological research ... shows that it's not so simple. These findings confirm that conservatives, liberals, the religious and the nonreligious are each prejudiced against those with opposing views. But surprisingly, each group is about *equally* prejudiced. While liberals might like to think of themselves as more open-minded, they are no more tolerant of people unlike them than their conservative counterparts are.

Political understanding might finally stand a chance if we could first put aside the argument over who has that bigger problem. The truth is that we all do.

When Mark Brandt, an American-trained psychologist now at Tilburg University in the Netherlands, first entered graduate school, he wondered why members of groups that espouse tolerance are so often intolerant. "I realized that there was a potential contradiction in the literature," he told me. "On the one hand, liberals have a variety of personality traits and moral values that should protect them from expressing prejudice. On the other hand, people tend to express prejudice against people who do not share their values." So, if you value open-mindedness, as liberals claim to do, and you see another group as prejudiced, might their perceived prejudice actually increase your prejudice against them?

Brandt approached this question with Geoffrey Wetherell and Christine Reyna in a 2013 paper published in *Social Psychological and Personality Science*. They asked a variety of Americans about their political ideologies; how much they valued traditionalism, egalitarianism and self-reliance; and their feelings toward eight groups of people, four of them liberal (feminists, atheists, leftist protesters and pro-choice people) and four of them conservative (supporters of the traditional family, religious fundamentalists, Tea Party protesters and pro-life people). Participants reported how much each group violated their "core values and beliefs," and they assessed how much they supported discrimination toward that group, by rating their agreement with statements such as "Feminists should not be allowed to make a speech in this city" and "Prolife people deserve any harassment they receive."

As predicted, conservatives were more discriminatory than liberals toward liberal groups, and liberals were more discriminatory than conservatives toward conservative groups. Conservatives' discrimination was driven by their higher traditionalism and by liberal groups' apparent violation of their values. Liberals' discrimination was driven by their lower traditionalism and by conservative groups' apparent violation of *their* values. Complicating matters, conservatives highly valued self-reliance, which weakened their discrimination toward liberal groups, perhaps because self-reliance is associated with the freedom to believe or do what one wants. And liberals highly valued universalism, which weakened their discrimination toward conservative groups, likely because universalism espouses acceptance of all.

But these differences didn't affect the larger picture: Liberals were as discriminatory toward conservative groups as conservatives were toward liberal groups. And Brandt's findings have been echoed elsewhere: Independently and concurrently, the labs of John Chambers at St. Louis University and Jarret Crawford at The College of New Jersey have also found approximately equal prejudice among conservatives and liberals.[9]

Common stereotypes about Republicans: *All they want is a free ride for rich people and no entitlements for the less well off; they're all bigots and racists; they're gun fanatics; they're pro-life; they hate immigrants; they didn't like Obama because he was black; they don't care about the poor; they're not compassionate; they're evangelical crazies; they hate science; they don't believe in global warming.*[8]

Ridicule

Ridicule is the use of derision, sarcasm, laughter, or mockery to disparage a person or idea. Ridicule succeeds when it gets an emotional reaction from you that leads you to dismiss people or their claims for no good reason. Its aim is to put people or beliefs in a ridiculous or absurd light, to make them a laughingstock. Look:

Trust the New York Times *to report the news fairly? Right, just like I trust the airlines to be always on time.*

You think Fox News is fair and balanced? Ha!

Now, is it on your mother's side or your father's that your ancestors were apes?

Throughout history, ridicule has been a powerful weapon against political figures, ideas, and regimes:

"So now they're telling us that—get this, folks—global warming is caused by cows farting! Priceless!"

"[Donald Trump is] Jabba the Hut's out-of-shape stunt double." (Stephen Colbert)

"Suppose you were an idiot and suppose you were a member of Congress. But I repeat myself." (Mark Twain)

"And in a gutless act of political correctness, 'Pizza Day' will now be known as 'Italian-American Sauced Bread Day.'" (Principal Seymour Skinner, *The Simpsons*)

Anti-liberal poster: "If you think it's a good idea to bring in refugees who hate your country, your religion, and your country, you must be a moron."

Anti-liberal poster: "You say that everything I don't like must be banned, and everything I do like is a human right and must be paid for by others."

Anti-conservative poster: "How many Republicans does it take to change a lightbulb? None—they'd rather sit in the dark and blame Obama."

Anti-conservative poster: "Dad, what's science? I don't know, son, we're Republicans."

Remember, when ridicule does its work, it makes no appeal to evidence or argument. It may be interesting or amusing, but it gives you no good reason to believe anything. When the credibility of claims is at stake, ridicule is best seen as an emotional trick.

Rhetorical Definitions

One of the more subtle means of persuasion uses **rhetorical definition**. The point of this tactic is not to accurately define but to influence through an emotion-charged skewed definition. Usually we are most interested in what is called a *lexical definition*, which reports the meaning that a term has among those who use the language. For example, among English-speaking people, the word *rain* is used to refer to (or mean) condensed atmospheric moisture falling in drops, which is the lexical definition. A *stipulative definition* reports a meaning that a term is deliberately assigned, often for the sake of convenience or economy of expression. If you assign a meaning to a familiar term or to a term that you invent, you give a stipulative definition. A *precising* definition reports a meaning designed to decrease ambiguity or vagueness. It qualifies an existing term by giving it a more precise definition. Someone, for example, might offer a precising definition for the word *old* (as it applies to the age of humans) by specifying that "old" refers to anyone over eighty. A rhetorical definition, on the other hand, wants to sway you toward particular attitudes or beliefs.

Someone who opposes abortions for any reason, for example, might rhetorically define *abortion* as "the murder of innocent human beings and the rejection of God." Someone who believes that some abortions are morally permissible might define *abortion* as "the termination of a human embryo or fetus."

Now take a look at these politically motivated rhetorical definitions:

Government entitlements should be discontinued. They're just handouts to people who don't want to work.

For conservatives, tax reform means making the rich richer and the middle class poorer.

Gun control is code for "Let's get rid of every gun in America."

Capital punishment is legalized murder.

Section Query

In the past six months, what stereotypes have you heard or read about racial, social, or religious groups?

REVIEW NOTES

6.1 FALLACIES: IRRELEVANT PREMISES

- Propaganda and **demagoguery** are powerful, dishonest forces allied against all who want to know what's really going on in the world. They are powerful and dishonest in large part because of the fallacies and rhetorical tricks they employ.
- We must distinguish between fallacies that have irrelevant premises and those that have unacceptable premises.
- Just because an argument is fallacious, that doesn't necessarily mean its conclusion is false.
- It's generally not a good idea to dismiss an opponent outright by declaring that he or she has just used a **fallacy**. (Assuming the argumentative exchange is worth your time, the better strategy is to respectfully explain why the fallacious argument cannot prove what it purports to prove.)
- Fallacies with irrelevant premises include the **genetic fallacy, composition** and **division, appeal to the person, ad hominem, appeal to pity, apple polishing, argument from outrage, whataboutism, equivocation, appeal to popularity, appeal to tradition, appeal to ignorance, appeal to emotion, red herring, straw man**, and **two wrongs make a right**.

6.2 FALLACIES: UNACCEPTABLE PREMISES

- Fallacies with unacceptable premises include **begging the question, false dilemma, decision-point fallacy, slippery slope, hasty generalization**, and **faulty analogy**.

6.3 PERSUADERS: RHETORICAL MOVES

- **Rhetoric** presents us with a large repertoire of techniques for influencing hearts and minds through emotion—while proving nothing through reason.
- Rhetorical devices include **innuendo, euphemisms** and **dysphemisms, stereotyping, ridicule**, and **rhetorical definitions**.

KEY TERMS

ad hominem	decision-point fallacy	red herring
appeal to emotion	demagoguery	rhetoric
appeal to ignorance	division	rhetorical definition
appeal to pity	dysphemism	ridicule
appeal to popularity (or appeal to the masses)	equivocation	scare tactics
	euphemism	slippery slope
appeal to the person	fallacy	stereotyping
appeal to tradition	false dilemma	straw man
apple polishing	faulty analogy	*tu quoque*
argument from outrage	genetic fallacy	two wrongs make a right
begging the question	hasty generalization	whataboutism
burden of proof	innuendo	
composition	prejudice	

EXERCISES

Exercises marked with an asterisk (*) have answers in "Answers to Exercises" (Appendix B).

Exercise 6.1

1. What are fallacies of irrelevant premises? What makes them irrelevant?
2. What is the genetic fallacy?
3. Can the origin of a claim ever be relevant to deciding its truth or falsity?
*4. What is the fallacy of composition?
5. What are the two forms of the fallacy of division?
6. Why are appeals to the person fallacious?
7. What type of ad hominem argument is put forth as a charge of hypocrisy?
8. What is whataboutism? Why is it fallacious?
9. What is the fallacy of equivocation?
*10. Why are appeals to popularity fallacious?
11. Why are appeals to tradition fallacious?
12. What are the two forms of the appeal to ignorance?
13. What are appeals to emotion? What is the argument from outrage?
14. What is rhetoric?
*15. According to the text, is it ever legitimate to use rhetoric and argument together?
16. What is the fallacy of red herring?
17. Why is an argument that relies on the straw-man fallacy a bad argument?
18. What is the fallacy of begging the question?
*19. Why are people often taken in by false dilemmas?
20. What is the burden of proof?
21. What is the fallacy of slippery slope? Can the argument used in the slippery-slope fallacy ever be used legitimately? Why or why not?
22. What is the rhetorical device of innuendo?
23. What is the rhetorical device of stereotyping?
24. What are euphemisms and dysphemisms?
25. What is the rhetorical device of ridicule?

Exercise 6.2

In the following passages, identify any fallacies of irrelevance (genetic fallacy, composition, division, appeal to the person, equivocation, appeal to popularity, appeal to tradition, appeal to ignorance, appeal to emotion, red herring, and straw man). Some passages may contain more than one fallacy, and a few may contain no fallacies at all. Also identify any rhetorical devices highlighted in this chapter.

*1. "Seeing that the eye and hand and foot and every one of our members has some obvious function, must we not believe that in like manner a human being has a function over and above these particular functions?" (Aristotle)
2. The federal budget deficits are destroying this country. Just ask any working stiff; he'll tell you.
3. The hippies of the sixties railed against the materialistic, capitalistic system and everyone who prospered in it. But all their bellyaching was crap because they were a bunch of hypocrites, living off their rich mothers and fathers.
4. Anthony argues that capital punishment should be abolished. But why should we listen to him? He's a prisoner on death row right now.
*5. The *New York Times* reported that one-third of Republican senators have been guilty of Senate ethics violations. But you know that's false—the *Times* is a notorious liberal rag.
6. Geraldo says that students who cheat on exams should not automatically be expelled from school. But it's ridiculous to insist that students should never be punished for cheating.
7. Of course the death penalty is a just punishment. It has been used for centuries.
8. My sweater is blue. Therefore, the atoms that make up the sweater are blue.

9. The prime minister is lying about his intelligence briefings since almost everyone surveyed in national polls thinks he's lying.

*10. Kelly says that many women who live in predominantly Muslim countries are discriminated against. But how the heck would she know? She's not a Muslim.

11. A lot of people think that football jocks are stupid and boorish. That's a crock. Anyone who had seen the fantastic game that our team played on Saturday, with three touchdowns before halftime, would not believe such rubbish.

12. Does acupuncture work? Can it cure disease? Of course. It has been used in China by folk practitioners for at least three thousand years.

13. The arguments of right-to-lifers cannot be believed. They're hypocrites who scream about dead babies but then murder abortion doctors.

*14. "The only proof capable of being given that an object is visible, is that people actually see it. The only proof that a sound is audible, is that people hear it: and so of the other sources of our experience. In like manner, I apprehend, the sole evidence it is possible to produce that anything is desirable, is that people actually desire it." (John Stuart Mill)

15. The new StratoCar is the best automobile on the road. Picture the admiring glances you'll get when you take a cruise in your StratoCar through town. Imagine the power and speed!

16. Gremlins exist, that's for sure. No scientist has ever proved that they don't exist.

17. "The most blatant occurrence of recent years is all these knuckleheads running around protesting nuclear power—all these stupid people who do not research at all and who go out and march, pretending they care about the human race, and then go off in their automobiles and kill one another." (Ray Bradbury)

18. Is the theory of evolution true? Yes. Polls show that most people believe in it.

*19. The former mayor was convicted of drug possession, and he spent time in jail. So you can safely ignore anything he has to say about legalizing drugs.

20. I don't believe in heaven and hell because no one—not even scientists—has ever produced proof that they exist.

21. Professor, I deserve a better grade than a D on my paper. Look, my parents just got a divorce. If they see that I got a D, they will just blame each other, and the fighting will start all over again. Give me a break.

22. Only man has morals. No woman is a man. Therefore, no woman has morals.

23. Every player on the team is the best in the league. So the team itself is the best in the league.

*24. Why are Asians so good at math?

25. I'm sure Senator Braxton would never take a large bribe.

*26. Our administration may need to consider trying some form of revenue enhancement.

Exercise 6.3

In the following passages, identify any fallacies of unacceptable premises (begging the question, false dilemma, slippery slope, and hasty generalization). Some passages may contain more than one fallacy, and a few may contain no fallacies at all.

1. Random drug testing in schools is very effective in reducing drug use because the regular use of the testing makes drug use less likely.

2. If today you can make teaching evolution in public schools a crime, then tomorrow you can make it a crime to teach it in private schools. Then you can ban books and other educational materials that mention evolution. And then you can ban the very word from all discourse. And then the anti-science bigots will have won.

3. Three thieves are dividing up the $7000 they just stole from the First National Bank. Robber number one gives $2000 to robber number two, $2000 to robber number three, and $3000 to

himself. Robber number two says, "How come you get $3000?" Robber number one says, "Because I am the leader." "How come you're the leader?" "Because I have more money."

*4. Either God exists or he does not exist. If he exists, and you believe, you will gain heaven; if he exists and you don't believe, you will lose nothing. If he does not exist, and you believe, you won't lose much. If he does not exist, and you don't believe, you still won't lose much. The best gamble then is to believe.

5. John is now on trial for murder, but the proceedings are a waste of time and money. Everyone knows he's guilty.

*6. I used to work with this engineering major. And, man, they are really socially inept.

7. I met these two guys on a plane, and they said they were from Albuquerque. They were total druggies. Almost everyone in that city must be on drugs.

8. Some people are fools, and some people are married to fools.

9. Bill is an investment banker, drives a Cadillac, is overweight, and votes Republican. John is also an investment banker, drives a Cadillac, and is overweight. So John probably votes Republican, too.

*10. Either we fire this guy or we send a message to other employees that it's okay to be late for work. Clearly, we need to fire him.

Exercise 6.4

For each of the following claims, devise an argument using the fallacy shown in parentheses. Make the argument as persuasive as possible.

1. The federal budget deficit will destroy the economy. (red herring)
2. *The Hunger Games* is the best movie ever made. (appeal to popularity)
*3. Mrs. Anan does not deserve the Nobel Prize. (appeal to the person)
4. Vampires—the blood-sucking phantoms of folklore—are real. (appeal to ignorance)
5. Internet pornography can destroy this country. (slippery slope)
*6. The Boy Scouts of America should allow gay kids to be members. (begging the question)
7. The United States should attack Iran. (false dilemma)
8. That economics seminar is absolutely the worst course offered at the university. (hasty generalization)
9. Pope John Paul II was a moral giant. (appeal to emotion)
10. The Nigerian court was right to sentence that woman to be stoned to death for adultery. (appeal to popularity)
*11. There are too many guns on the streets because our politicians are controlled by the National Rifle Association and other gun nuts. (red herring)
12. All efforts should be made to ban trade in exotic pets such as tigers. (genetic fallacy)

CAPSTONE

Find one example each of three different fallacies. Choose the three from the following list, and look for your examples in social media posts, blog posts, comment streams, and letters to the editor. Identify each fallacy and rewrite the passage to eliminate the fallacy and strengthen the argument. (To effectively rework the argument, you may have to make up some facts.)

Appeal to the person
Straw man
Red herring
Appeal to popularity
False dilemma
Hasty generalization
Appeal to ignorance
Slippery slope

Experts and Evidence

Chapter Objectives

7.1 Experts and Nonexperts
- Understand that an expert is someone who is more knowledgeable in a particular subject area or field than most others are.
- Know that if a claim conflicts with other claims we have good reason to accept, we have good grounds for doubting it.
- Understand that if a claim conflicts with our background information, we have good reason to doubt it.
- Remember that we are justified in doubting a claim when it comes from someone deemed to be an expert who in fact is *not* an expert. Relying on bogus expert opinion is known as the fallacious appeal to authority.

7.2 Judging Experts
- Recognize the two indicators for being considered an expert: (1) education and training from reputable institutions or programs in the relevant field and (2) experience in the field.
- Recognize two additional indicators of true expertise: (1) reputation among peers and (2) professional accomplishments.
- Understand that if we have reason to believe that an expert is biased, we are not justified in accepting the expert's opinion.
- Know that even though qualified, unbiased, honest experts can be wrong, in general, genuine experts are more likely to be right about things in their fields than we are.

7.3 Experts and Personal Experience
- Know that it's reasonable to accept the evidence provided by personal experience only if there's no good reason to doubt it.
- Be aware that our personal experience is susceptible to error: Under certain circumstances, our senses, memory, and judgment can't be trusted.

(Continued)

(Continued)

7.4 Innumeracy and Probability
- *Understand that we are not good at off-the-cuff judgments about the chances of something happening.*
- *Know that thinking that previous events can affect the probabilities in the random event at hand is a common error known as the gambler's fallacy.*

Attitudes toward experts and expertise are changing. Many people, for example, seem to confidently believe the following:

- If you read a book, do a Google search, and see what people are saying on social media, you will be an expert.
- Experts have been wrong so often that they have no credibility.
- Experts can't be trusted, because they contradict my beliefs.
- On the internet, there are no experts: Everyone's opinion on any issue is equal to everyone else's.

This chapter (combined with the preceding ones) shows that these beliefs are in fact false. The probability of becoming an instant expert is pretty low, and experts are not—and never have been—infallible, but neither are they clueless. Nonexperts can come to know a lot about some complex issues if they respect evidence, expertise, and critical thinking. And the insight and know-how of experts—when approached critically and used wisely—can help us live more intelligently and avoid mistakes.

An **expert** is someone who is more knowledgeable in a particular subject area or field than most others are. Experts in professions and fields of knowledge provide us with reasons for believing a claim because, in their specialty areas, they are more likely to be right than we are. They are more likely to be right because (1) they have mastered particular skills or bodies of knowledge, and (2) they practice those skills or use that knowledge as their main occupation in life.[1] Experts make mistakes, but in general they are much less likely to err than nonexperts are. True experts are familiar with the established facts and existing data in their field, understand how to properly evaluate that information, and know how to apply it. Essentially, this means that they know how to assess the evidence and arguments for particular claims involving that information. They are true authorities on a specified subject. Someone who knows the lore of a field but can't evaluate the reliability of a claim is no expert.

7.1 Experts and Nonexperts

In a complex world where we can never be knowledgeable in every field, we must rely on experts—a perfectly legitimate state of affairs. But good critical thinkers are careful about expert opinion, guiding their use of experts by some commonsense principles. Some of these principles apply to critical thinking generally and some to assessments of opinion and evidence offered by putative experts. The most basic principle is this:

> If a claim conflicts with other claims we have good reason to accept, we have good grounds for doubting it.

When two claims conflict (as when one says A, and another says not-A), they simply cannot *both* be true; at least one of them has to be false. You are not justified in believing either one of them until you resolve the conflict. Sometimes this job is easy. If, for example, the competing claims are reports of personal observations, you can often decide between them by making further observations. If your friend says that your dog is sleeping atop your car, and you say that your dog is not sleeping atop your car (because you checked a short time ago), you can see who's right by simply looking at the roof of your car.

Many times, however, sorting out conflicting claims requires a deeper inquiry. You may need to do some research to see what evidence exists for each of the claims. In the best-case scenario, you may quickly discover that one of the claims is not credible because it comes from an unreliable source.

Now suppose that you're confronted with another type of conflict—this time between a claim and your **background information**. Background information is that huge collection of very well supported beliefs that we all rely on to inform our actions and choices. A great deal of this lore consists of basic facts about everyday things, beliefs based on overwhelming evidence (including our own reliable personal observations and the statements of excellent authorities), and strongly justified claims that we would regard as "common sense" or "common knowledge." Background beliefs include obvious claims such as "The sun is hot," "The Easter bunny is not real," "Humans are mortal," "Fire burns," and "George Washington lived in the 18th century."

Suppose, then, that you're asked to accept this unsupported claim:

> Some babies can bench-press a 500-pound weight.

You are not likely to give much credence to this claim for the simple reason that it conflicts with an enormous number of your background beliefs concerning human physiology, gravity, weightlifting, and who knows what else.

Or how about this claim:

> The U.S. president is entirely under the control of the chief justice of the United States.

This claim is not as outlandish as the previous one, but it, too, conflicts with our background beliefs, specifically those having to do with the structure and workings of the U.S. government. So we would have good reason to doubt this one also.

The principle exemplified here is this:

> *If a claim conflicts with our background information, we have good reason to doubt it.*

Other things being equal, the more background information the claim conflicts with, the more reason we have to doubt it. We would normally—and rightfully—assign a low probability to any claim that conflicts with a great deal of our background information.

You would be entitled, for example, to have some doubt about the claim that Joan is late for work if it conflicts with your background information that Joan has never been late for work in the 10 years you've known her. But you are entitled to have very strong doubts about, and to assign very low credibility to, the claim that Luis can turn a stone into gold just by touching it. You could even reasonably dismiss the claim out of hand. Such a claim conflicts with too much of what we know about the physical world.

It's always possible, of course, that a conflicting claim is true and some of our background information is unfounded. So many times it's reasonable for us to examine a conflicting claim more closely. If we find that it has no good reasons in its favor, that it is not credible, we may reject it. If, on the other hand, we discover that there are strong reasons for accepting the new claim, we may need to revise our background information. For example, we may be forced to accept the claim about Luis's golden touch (and to rethink some of our background information) if it is backed by strong supporting evidence. Our background information would be in need of some serious revision if Luis could produce this stone-to-gold transformation repeatedly under scientifically controlled conditions that rule out error, fraud, and trickery.

We need to keep in mind that although our background information is generally trustworthy, it is not infallible. What we assume is a strongly justified belief may be nothing more than prejudice or dogma. We should therefore be willing to re-examine background beliefs that we have doubts about—and to be open to reasonable doubts when they arise.

So it is not reasonable to accept a claim if there is good reason to doubt it. And sometimes, if the claim is dubious enough, we may be justified in dismissing a claim out of hand. But what should we believe about a claim that is not quite dubious enough to summarily discard yet not worthy of complete acceptance? We should measure out our belief according to the strength of reasons. That is,

We should proportion our belief to the evidence.

The more evidence a claim has in its favor, the stronger our belief in it should be. Weak evidence for a claim warrants weak belief; strong evidence warrants strong belief. And the strength of our beliefs should vary across this spectrum as the evidence dictates.

Implicit in all of the foregoing is a principle already mentioned, but it deserves to be repeated because it's so often ignored:

It's not reasonable to believe a claim when there is no good reason for doing so.

The famous 20th-century philosopher Bertrand Russell tried hard to drive this idea home. As he put it, "It is undesirable to believe a proposition when there is no ground whatever for supposing it true."[2] Russell claimed that if the use of this principle became widespread, social life and political systems would be transformed.

Now, when a claim runs counter to a consensus among experts, this principle holds:

If a claim conflicts with expert opinion, we have good reason to doubt it.

This tenet follows from our definition of experts. If they really are more likely to be right than nonexperts about claims in their field, then any claim that conflicts with expert opinion is at least initially dubious.

Here's the companion principle:

When the experts disagree about a claim, we have good reason to doubt it.

If a claim is in dispute among experts, then nonexperts can have no good reason for accepting (or rejecting) it. Throwing up your hands and arbitrarily deciding to believe or disbelieve the claim is not a reasonable response. The claim must remain in doubt until the experts resolve the conflict or you resolve the conflict yourself by becoming informed enough to competently decide on the issues and evidence involved—a course that's possible but usually not feasible for nonexperts.

But when is a claim considered in dispute among experts? It's in dispute when *substantial* numbers of experts disagree with one another—but not when a mere handful of dissidents disagree with almost all of the others. We cannot reasonably consider a claim in dispute when, say, three experts disagree with five thousand of their fellows. It is disingenuous and misleading to declare that an issue is undecided when a few experts disagree with the opinions of the overwhelming majority—which was the case in 2019 when 97 percent of climate scientists agreed that climate-warming trends are extremely likely to be caused by human activities.[3]

Sometimes we may have good reason to be suspicious of unsupported claims even when they are purportedly derived from expert opinion. Our doubt is justified when a claim comes from someone deemed to be an expert who in fact is *not* an expert. When we rely on such bogus expert opinion, we make the mistake known as the **fallacious appeal to authority**.

The fallacious appeal to authority usually happens in one of two ways. First, we may find ourselves disregarding this important rule of thumb: *Just because someone is an expert in one field, he or she is not necessarily an expert in another.* The opinion of experts generally carries more weight than our own—but only in their areas of expertise. Any opinions that they proffer outside their fields are no more authoritative than those of nonexperts. Outside their fields, they are not experts.

We needn't look far for real-life examples of such skewed appeals to authority. Any day of the week we may be urged to accept claims in one field based on the opinion of an expert from an unrelated field. An electrical engineer or Nobel Prize–winning chemist may assert that herbs can cure cancer. A radio talk show host with a degree in physiology may give advice in psychology. A former astronaut may declare that archeological evidence shows that Noah's ark now rests on a mountain in Turkey. A botanist may say that the evidence for the existence of ESP is conclusive. The point is not that these experts can't be right, but that their expertise in a particular field doesn't give us reason to believe their pronouncements in another. There is no such thing as a general expert, only experts in specific subject areas.

Second, we may fall into a fallacious appeal to authority by regarding a nonexpert as an expert. We forget that a nonexpert—even one with prestige, status, or sex appeal—is still a nonexpert. Movie stars, famous actors, YouTube celebs, renowned athletes, and well-known politicians endorse products of all kinds in online, TV, and print advertising.

> ### Are Doctors Experts?
>
> Yes and no. Physicians are certainly experts in the healing arts, in diagnosing and treating disease and injury. They know and understand the relevant facts, and they have the wherewithal to make good judgments regarding those facts. But are physicians experts in determining whether a particular treatment is safe and effective? Contrary to what many believe, the answer is, in general, *no*. Determining the safety and efficacy of treatments is a job for scientists (who may also be physicians). Medical scientists conduct controlled studies to try to ascertain whether treatment X can safely alleviate disease A—something that usually cannot be determined by a doctor interacting with her patients in a clinical setting. Medical studies are designed to control all kinds of extraneous variables that can skew the study results, the same extraneous variables that are often present in the doctor's office.
>
> Critical thinkers should keep this distinction in mind because they will often hear people assert that treatment Y works just because Dr. Wonderful says so.

But when they speak outside their areas of expertise—when they back their claims by nothing more than their own opinion—they give us no good reason for believing that the products are as advertised. Advertisers, of course, know this, but they hope that we will buy the products anyway because of the appeal or attractiveness of the celebrity endorsers.

Historically, the regarding of a nonexpert as an expert has probably been the most prevalent form of the appeal to authority—with disastrous results. Political, religious, tribal, and cultural leaders often have been designated as authorities not because they knew the facts and could correctly judge the evidence, but because culture, tradition, or whim dictated that they be regarded as authorities. When these "authorities" spoke, people listened and believed—then went to war, persecuted unbelievers, or undertook countless other ill-conceived projects. If we are to avoid this trap, we must look beyond mere labels and titles and ask, *"Does this person provide us with any good reasons or evidence?"*

Section Query

Have you ever fallen for a fallacious appeal to authority online—that is, have you ever accepted the claims of a bogus expert? If so, why?

7.2 Judging Experts

This question about good reasons, of course, is just another way of asking if someone is a true expert. How can we tell? To be considered an expert, someone must have shown that he or she has the knowledge, judgment, and competence required in a particular field. What are the indicators that someone has this essential kind of expertise? There are several that provide clues to someone's ability but *do not guarantee* the possession of true expertise.

In most professional fields, the following two indicators are considered minimal prerequisites for being considered an expert:

1. **Education and training from reputable institutions or programs** in the relevant field (usually evidenced by degrees or certificates). Teachers, airline pilots, plumbers, electricians, and many others are required to have credentials to show that they have met standards of knowledge and competence.
2. **Experience in the field.** Long experience (generally the more years the better) suggests that the expert is good enough to have outlasted others who are unsuited to, or unskilled in, the work. He or she has had chances to learn from mistakes and to handle challenges that less experienced practitioners may yet to encounter.

But, unfortunately, people can have the requisite education and experience and still not know what they're talking about in the field in question. Woe be to us, for in the real world there are well-trained, experienced auto mechanics who do terrible work—and tenured PhD's whose professional judgment is shaky. Two additional indicators, though, are more revealing:

1. **Reputation among peers** (as reflected in the opinions of others in the same field, relevant prestigious awards, and positions of authority)
2. **Professional accomplishments**

These two indicators are more helpful because they are very likely to be correlated with the intellectual qualities expected in true experts. People with excellent reputations among their professional peers and with significant accomplishments to their credit usually are true experts.

As we've seen, we are often justified in believing an unsupported claim because it's based on expert opinion. But if we have reason to doubt the opinion of the experts, then we are not justified in believing the claim based on that opinion. And chief among possible reasons for doubt (aside from conflicting expert opinion) is bias. When experts are biased, they are motivated by something other than the search for the truth—perhaps financial gain, loyalty to a cause, professional ambition, emotional needs, political outlook, sectarian dogma, personal ideology, or some other judgment-distorting factor. Therefore, if we have reason to believe that an expert is biased, we are not justified in accepting the expert's opinion.

But how can we tell when experts are biased? There are no hard-and-fast rules here. In the more obvious cases, we often suspect bias when an expert is being paid by special-interest groups or companies to render an opinion, or when the expert expresses very strong belief in a claim even though there is no evidence to support it, or when the expert stands to gain financially from the actions or policies that he or she supports.

It's true that many experts can render unbiased opinions and do high-quality research even when they have a conflict of interest. Nevertheless, in such situations we have reasonable grounds to suspect bias—unless we have good reason to believe that the suspicion is unwarranted. These good reasons might include the fact that the expert's previous opinions in similar circumstances have been reliable or that he or she has a solid reputation for always offering unbiased assessments.

There are, of course, many other possible reasons to doubt the opinion of experts. Any blatant violation of the critical thinking principles discussed in this text, for example, would give us good reason to question an authority's reliability. Among the more common tip-offs of dubious authority are these:

- The expert is guilty of simple factual or formal errors.
- The expert's claims conflict with what you have good reason to believe.
- The expert does not adequately support his or her assertions.
- The expert's writing contains logical contradictions or inconsistent statements.
- The expert does not treat opposing views fairly.
- The expert is strongly biased, dogmatic, dismissive, or intolerant.
- The expert relies on information you know is out of date.
- The expert cherry-picks data to support his or her claims.
- Most other experts in the same field disagree.

The amount of weight you give to any one of these factors—and the subsequent degree of doubt you attach to an expert's opinion—will vary in each case. In general, a single minor error of fact or style does not justify dismissing an expert's entire article that is otherwise excellent.

But doubt is cumulative, and as reasons for doubt are added, you may rightfully decide that you are not justified in believing any part of an expert's testimony, regardless of his or her credentials. Depending on your aims, you may decide to check the expert's assertions against other sources or to consult an authority with much less evidential or rhetorical baggage.

Keep in mind that there are certain kinds of issues that we probably don't want experts to settle for us. Indeed, in most cases the experts *cannot* settle them for us. These issues usually involve moral, social, or political questions. If we're intellectually conscientious, we want to provide our own final answers to such questions, though we may draw heavily on the analyses and arguments provided by experts. We may study what the experts have to say and the conclusions they draw. But we want ultimately to come to our own conclusions. We prefer this approach in large part because the questions are so important and because the answers we give help define who we are. What's more, the experts typically disagree on these issues. So even if we wanted the experts to settle one of these questions for us, they probably couldn't.

Do Nonexperts Know Best?

Some people have a bias against experts—*all* experts. Their thoughts on the subject might run something like this: "It's the uneducated ones, the simple seekers of knowledge who are the truly wise, for their thinking has not yet been corrupted by ivory-tower learning and highbrow theorizing that's out of touch with the real world. Thus the wisdom of the nonexpert is to be preferred over the expert whenever possible." This attitude is, oddly enough, sometimes embraced by very educated people.

This nonexpertism is related to the appeal to ignorance discussed in Chapter 6. (A variation of the appeal to ignorance says that since there's no evidence refuting a position, it must be true.) The problem is that both tacks, though psychologically compelling, are fallacious. A lack of good reasons—evidence or expert testimony—does not constitute proof of a claim. In addition, when we as nonexperts try to judge scientific and medical claims using only our personal experience, we are likely to reach conclusions that are wrong (as explained in the next section).

The history of science shows that virtually all notable scientific discoveries have been made by true experts—men and women who were fully knowledgeable about their subject matter. There have been many more instances, however, of cocksure nonexperts who proposed theories, cures, and solutions to problems that turned out to be worthless.

Here's an obvious truth that's easy to forget: Even qualified, unbiased, honest experts can be wrong. In fact, they are often wrong. Error is in the nature of expertise, especially in attempts at prediction. Experts were wrong when they made these predictions:

- Fast-moving trains would kill passengers by asphyxiation.
- Rockets will never be able to leave Earth's atmosphere.
- Flying cars will soon become common.
- The Soviet Union is in no danger of collapsing.
- We will find weapons of mass destruction (WMDs) in Iraq.
- People will never want a computer in their homes.
- The Internet will be a spectacular flop.
- The iPhone will be a market failure.
- The American economy is basically healthy (it collapsed in 2008).
- Donald Trump will not win the presidential election of 2016.
- An AI computer program will not be able to beat a human player at the board game Go until around 2025 (it happened in 2016).

But the mistakes of experts do not invalidate our earlier premise that, in general, genuine experts are more likely to be right about things in their fields than we are. When errors do occur, they usually happen because experts depart from investigating and explaining the facts and jump to trying to predict the facts. Prediction in any field is hard, and most experts aren't very good at it, although some are better at it than others. Prediction is notoriously iffy in the social sciences (notably economics, history, and political science) and in public policy. The natural sciences have a much better track record.

Tom Nichols reminds us,

> Predictive failure, however, does not retroactively strip experts of their claim to know more than laypeople. Laypeople should not jump to the assumption that a missed call by the experts therefore means all opinions are equally valid (or equally worthless). The polling expert Nate Silver, who made his reputation with remarkably accurate forecasts in the 2008 and 2012 presidential elections, has since admitted that his predictions about Republican presidential nominee Donald Trump in 2016 were based on flawed assumptions. But Silver's insights into the other races remain solid, even if the Trump phenomenon surprised him and others.[4]

Fallacious Appeal to (Questionable) Authority

Why do so many people listen to the advice and endorsements of famous people who may be no more knowledgeable than the least informed among us? If you have ever fallen for the celebrity version of the fallacious appeal to authority, maybe the following quotes will do you good. They prove that some really famous people can say some really stupid things—and knowing that might help you think twice before getting stung by this fallacy.

"I make Jessica Simpson look like a rock scientist." (Tara Reid)

"Whenever I watch TV and see those poor starving kids all over the world, I can't help but cry. I mean I'd love to be skinny like that, but not with all those flies and death and stuff." (Mariah Carey)

"I get to go overseas places, like Canada." (Britney Spears)

"I'm not anorexic, I'm from Texas. Are there people from Texas that are anorexic? I've never heard of one, and that includes me." (Jessica Simpson)

"Circumcision is barbaric and stupid. Who are you to correct nature? Is it real that GOD requires a donation of foreskin? Babies are perfect." (Russell Crowe)

"I don't think there is anything particularly wrong about hitting a woman. An open-handed slap is justified if all other alternatives fail and there has been plenty of warning. If a woman is a bitch, or hysterical, or bloody-minded continually, then I'd do it." (Sean Connery)

"The media is—really, the word, I think one of the greatest of all terms I've come up with—is fake." (Donald Trump)

"Uh, uh, Chuck Graham, state senator [who is wheelchair-bound], is here. Stand up, Chuck, let 'em see you. Oh, God love you. What am I talking about?" (Joe Biden)

"I think that gay marriage is something that should be between a man and a woman." (Arnold Schwarzenegger)

"So where's the Cannes Film Festival being held this year?" (Christina Aguilera)

Section Query

What should be your attitude toward the claims of an authority who seems knowledgeable but is strongly biased and dogmatic?

7.3 Experts and Personal Experience

We accept a great many claims because they are based on personal experience—our own or someone else's. Personal experience, broadly defined, arises from our senses, our memory, and our judgment involved in those faculties. In countless cases, our personal experience (or the personal experience of someone else, online or off) is our evidence (or part of the evidence) that something is or is not the case. You think the herbal tea cured your headache because the pain went away after you drank it. Or you're sure your headache *will* go away because people calling themselves experts online say their experience proves that it will. You believe that Jack caused the traffic accident because you, or someone else, witnessed it. You believe that your friend can bend spoons with her mind because you saw her do it at a party. You're sure that the other guy threw the first punch, not you, because that's how you remember the incident. Or you share a grainy photo on Instagram and Facebook because the original poster says the picture shows the assailant running from the scene of a mass shooting. Or you vote to convict the alleged assailant because eyewitness testimony puts him at the scene of the crime with a gun in his hand.

But can we trust personal experience to reveal the truth?

The answer is a *qualified* yes. And here's the qualification in the form of an important principle:

> *It's reasonable to accept the evidence provided by personal experience only if there's no good reason to doubt it.*

In the simplest cases, if we have no good reason to doubt what our personal experience reveals to us, then we're justified in believing it. This means that if our faculties are working properly and our use of them is unimpeded by anything in our environment, we're entitled to accept what our personal experience tells us. If we seem to see a cat on the mat under good viewing conditions—that is, we have no reason to believe that our observations are impaired by, say, poor lighting, cracked glasses, or too many beers—then we're justified in believing that there's a cat on the mat.

But many cases—maybe most of them—are not simple, and there's plenty of room for doubt. Identifying what causes something inside the human body is difficult at best. Tracking cause and effect or multiple factors in complex situations is never easy, even for careful observers. When deliberate deception is likely to be at play (as in the spoon-bending demonstration and in the online mountains of fake photos and phony testimony), discerning what's real and what isn't takes critical inquiry.

The main problem is that our personal experience is susceptible to error in all sorts of ways. Under certain circumstances, our senses, memory, and judgment can't be trusted. It's easy enough to identify these circumstances in an abstract way. The harder job is (1) determining when they actually occur in real-life situations and (2) avoiding them or taking them into account. Here's a rundown of the major difficulties.

Impairment

This should be obvious: If our perceptual powers are somehow impaired or impeded, we have reason to doubt them. The unambiguous cases are those in which our senses are debilitated because we are ill, injured, tired, stressed out, excited, drugged, drunk, distracted, or disoriented. And just as clear are the situations that interfere with sensory input—when our environment is, say, too dark, too bright, too noisy, or too hazy. If any of these factors are in play, the risk of misperception is high, which gives us reason to doubt the trustworthiness of what we experience.

Memories can be affected by many of the same factors that interfere with accurate perception. They are especially susceptible to distortion if they are formed during times of stress—which helps explain why the memories of people who witness crimes or alleged ghosts are so often unreliable. These situations are understandably stressful.

The impairment of our faculties is complicated by the peculiar way they operate. Contrary to what many believe, they are not like recording devices that make exact mental copies of objects and events in the world. Research suggests that they are more like artists who use bits of sensory data or memory fragments to concoct creative representations of things, not exact replicas. Our perception and memory are *constructive*, which means that what we perceive and remember is to some degree fabricated by our minds. Here are some of the more blatant examples: You see a man standing in the shadows by the road—then discover when you get closer that the man is a tree stump. You anxiously await a phone call from Aunt Mary, and when the call comes and you hear the person's voice, you're sure it's her—then realize that it's some guy asking for a charitable donation. While in the shower you hear the phone ring—but no one is calling, and the ringing is something your mind is making up.

The constructive workings of our minds help us solve problems and deal effectively with our environment. But they can also hinder us by manufacturing too much of our experiences using too little data. Unfortunately, the constructive tendency is most likely to lead us astray precisely when our powers of perception and memory are impaired or impeded. Competent investigators of alleged paranormal phenomena understand this and are rightfully skeptical of paranormal claims based on observations made under dubious conditions like those mentioned here. Under the right conditions, the mind is very good at showing us UFOs and midnight ghosts that aren't there. Likewise, juries are expected to be suspicious of the testimony of eyewitnesses who swear they plainly saw the dirty deed committed but were frightened, enraged, or a little tipsy at the time.

Expectation

A tricky thing about perception is that we often perceive exactly what we expect to perceive—regardless of whether there's anything there to detect. Ever watch the second hand on an electric clock move—then suddenly realize that the clock is not running at all? Ever been walking through a crowd looking for a friend and hear her call your name—then find out later that she was 10 blocks away at the time? Such experiences—the result again of the constructive tendencies of mind—are common examples of how expectation can distort your perceptions.

Scientific research shows that expectation can have a more powerful effect on our experiences than most people think. In numerous studies, subjects who expected to see a flash of light, smell a certain odor, or feel an electric shock did indeed experience these things—even though the appropriate stimuli were never present. The mere suggestion that the stimuli would occur was enough to cause the subjects to perceive, or apparently perceive, things that did not exist.

Our tendency to sometimes perceive things that are not really there is especially pronounced when the stimuli are vague or ambiguous. For example, we may perceive completely formless stimuli—clouds, smoke, "white noise," garbled voices, random-patterned wallpaper, blurry photos, lights in the night sky, stains on the ceiling—yet think we observe very distinct images or sounds. In the formlessness we may see ghosts, faces, and words and hear songs, screams, or verbal warnings. We may see or hear exactly what we expect to see or hear. Or the mere suggestion of what we should perceive helps us perceive it. This phenomenon is a kind of illusion known as *pareidolia*. It's the reason some people claim to hear Satanic messages when rock music is played backward, or to observe a giant stone face in fuzzy pictures of the surface of Mars, or to see the perfect likeness of Jesus in the skillet burns on a tortilla.

Scientists are keenly aware of the possible distorting influence of expectancy, so they try to design experiments that minimize it. We, too, need to minimize it as much as possible. Our strong expectations are a signal that we should double-check our sensory information and be careful about the conclusions we draw from it. We should also be alert to when other people (such as alleged experts) are not as careful.

Causal Confusions

In our lives, we are constantly challenged to sort out causes and effects. We know that mistaking the one for the other, or simply being confused by the causal commotion, can be disadvantageous at best and fatal at worst. Here are some of the more common mistakes.

MISIDENTIFYING RELEVANT FACTORS
A key issue in any type of causal reasoning is whether the factors preceding an effect are truly relevant to that effect. It's easy to find a preceding factor common to all occurrences of a phenomenon, but that factor may

Eyewitness Testimony and Wrongful Convictions

Eyewitness testimony is unreliable. So says a raft of scientific evidence. Consider this report published in *Scientific American*:

> In 1984 Kirk Bloodworth was convicted of the rape and murder of a nine-year-old girl and sentenced to the gas chamber—an outcome that rested largely on the testimony of five eyewitnesses. After Bloodworth served nine years in prison, DNA testing proved him to be innocent. Such devastating mistakes by eyewitnesses are not rare, according to a report by the Innocence Project, an organization affiliated with the Benjamin N. Cardozo School of Law at Yeshiva University that uses DNA testing to exonerate those wrongfully convicted of crimes. Since the 1990s, when DNA testing was first introduced, Innocence Project researchers have reported that 73 percent of the 239 convictions overturned through DNA testing were based on eyewitness testimony. One third of these overturned cases rested on the testimony of two or more mistaken eyewitnesses. How could so many eyewitnesses be wrong? . . .
>
> The uncritical acceptance of eyewitness accounts may stem from a popular misconception of how memory works. Many people believe that human memory works like a video recorder: the mind records events and then, on cue, plays back an exact replica of them. On the contrary, psychologists have found that memories are reconstructed rather than played back each time we recall them. The act of remembering, says eminent memory researcher and psychologist Elizabeth F. Loftus of the University of California, Irvine, is "more akin to putting puzzle pieces together than retrieving a video recording." Even questioning by a lawyer can alter the witness's testimony because fragments of the memory may unknowingly be combined with information provided by the questioner, leading to inaccurate recall.
>
> Many researchers have created false memories in normal individuals; what is more, many of these subjects are certain that the memories are real.[5]

be irrelevant. *Relevant* factors include only those things that could possibly be *causally connected* to the occurrence of the phenomenon being studied.

Your ability to identify relevant factors depends mostly on your background knowledge—what you know about the kinds of conditions that could produce the occurrences in which you're interested. Lack of background knowledge might lead you to dismiss or ignore relevant factors or to assume that irrelevant factors must play a role. The only cure for this inadequacy is deeper study of the causal possibilities in question.

MISHANDLING MULTIPLE FACTORS

Most of the time, the biggest difficulty in evaluating causal connections is not that there are so few relevant factors to consider—but that there are so many. We are in trouble if we cannot narrow the possibilities to just one or a few, but at the same time, ordinary causal reasoning is frequently flawed because of the failure to consider *all* the relevant antecedent factors.

Sometimes this kind of oversight happens because we simply don't look hard enough for possible causes. At other times, we miss relevant factors because we don't know enough about the causal processes involved. This again is a function of skimpy background knowledge. Either way, there is no countermeasure better than your own determination to dig out the whole truth.

BEING MISLED BY COINCIDENCE

Sometimes ordinary events are paired in unusual or interesting ways: You think of Hawaii, then suddenly a Twitter ad announces low-cost fares to Maui; you receive some email just as your doorbell sounds and your phone rings; or you stand in the lobby of a hotel thinking of an old friend—then see her walk by. Plenty of interesting pairings can also show up in scientific research. Scientists might find, for example, that men with the highest rates of heart disease may also have a higher daily intake of water. Or women with the lowest risk of breast cancer may own Toyotas. Such pairings are very probably just coincidence, merely interesting correlations of events. A problem arises, though, when we think that there nevertheless must be a causal connection involved.

For several reasons, we may very much want a coincidence or correlation to be a cause-and-effect relationship, so we come to believe that the pairing is causal. Just as often we may mistake causes for coincidences because we're impressed or excited about the conjunction of events. The pairing of events may seem "too much of a coincidence" to be coincidence, so we conclude that one event must have caused the other. You may be thinking about how nice it would be for your sister to call you from her home in Alaska—then the phone rings, and it's her! You're tempted to conclude that your wishing caused her to call. But such an event, though intriguing and seemingly improbable, is not really so extraordinary. Given the ordinary laws of statistics, incredible coincidences are common and *must occur*. Any event, even one that seems shockingly improbable, is actually very probable over the long haul. Given enough opportunities to occur, events like this surprising phone call are virtually certain to happen to *someone*.

People are especially prone to "it can't be just coincidence" thinking because, for several psychological reasons, they misjudge the probabilities involved. They may think, for example, that a phone call from someone at the moment they're thinking of that person is incredible—but only because they've forgotten about all the times they've thought of that person and the phone *didn't* ring. Such probability misjudgments are a major source of beliefs about the paranormal or supernatural.

If you observe that the longer you boil eggs, the harder they get (and no other relevant factors complicate this relationship), you can safely conclude that this correlation between boiling and hardening is a causal connection. You have good evidence that the boiling causes the hardening. But most causal connections are not so easily established.

In medical science, consistent correlations are highly prized because direct evidence of cause and effect is so hard to come by. Correlations are often indirect evidence of one thing causing another. In exploring the link between cigarette smoking and lung cancer, for example, researchers discovered first that people who smoke cigarettes are more likely to get lung cancer than those who don't smoke. But later research also showed that the more cigarettes people smoke, the higher their risk of lung cancer. Medical scientists call such a correlation a *dose-response relationship*. The higher the dose of the element in question (smoking), the higher the response (the more cases of lung cancer). This dose-response relationship between cigarette smoking and lung cancer is, when combined with other data, strong evidence that smoking causes lung cancer.

So the important lesson here is this: Correlation does not always mean that a causal relationship is present. A correlation could just be a coincidence. An increase in home PC sales is correlated with a rise in the incidence of AIDS in Africa, but this doesn't mean that one is in any way causally linked with the other.

Unfortunately, there is no foolproof way to distinguish coincidence from cause and effect. But this rule of thumb can help:

> *Don't assume that a causal connection exists unless you have good reason for doing so.*

Usually, when a cause-effect connection is uncertain, only further evaluation or research can clear things up.

CONFUSING CAUSE WITH TEMPORAL ORDER

A particularly prevalent type of misjudgment about coincidences is the logical fallacy known as **post hoc, ergo propter hoc** ("after that, therefore because of that"). We believe that a cause must precede its effect. But just because one event precedes another that doesn't mean that the earlier one *caused* the later. To think so is to be taken in by this fallacy. Outrageous examples of post hoc arguments include: "The rooster crowed, then the sun came up, so the rooster's crowing caused sunrise!" and "Jasmine left her umbrella at home Monday, and this caused it to rain." You can clearly see the error in such cases, but consider these arguments:

ARGUMENT 1

After the training for police officers was enhanced, violent crime in the city decreased by 10 percent. So enhanced training caused the decline in violent crime.

ARGUMENT 2

An hour after Julio drank the cola, his headache went away. The cola cured his headache.

ARGUMENT 3

As soon as Smith took office and implemented policies that reflected his conservative theory of economics, the economy went into a downward slide characterized by slow growth and high unemployment. Therefore, the Smith policies caused the current economic doldrums.

ARGUMENT 4

I wore my black shirt on Tuesday and got an F on a math quiz. I wore the same shirt the next day and flunked my psych exam. That shirt's bad luck.

The conclusion of argument 1 is based on nothing more than the fact that the enhanced training preceded the reduction in violent crime. But crime rates can decrease for many reasons, and the enhanced training may have had nothing to do with the decline in crime. For the argument to be strong, other considerations besides temporal order would have to apply—for example, that other possible causes or antecedent factors had been ruled out; that there was a close correlation between amount of training and decline in crime rates; or that in previous years (or in comparable cities) enhanced training was always followed by decreased violent crime (or no change in training was always followed by steady crime rates).

Argument 2 is also purely post hoc. Such reasoning is extremely common and underlies almost all folk remedies and a great deal of quackery and bogus self-cures. You take a vitamin E capsule, and eight hours later your headache is gone. But was it really the vitamin E that did the trick? Or was it some other overlooked factor such as something you ate, the medication you took (or didn't take), the nap you had, the change in environment (from, say, indoors to outdoors), the natural variation in bodily sensations experienced in any illness, or the stress reduction you felt when you had pleasant thoughts? Would your headache have gone away on its own anyway? Was it the *placebo effect*—the tendency for people to feel better when treated even when the treatment is fake or inactive? A chief function of controlled medical testing is to evaluate cause-and-effect relationships by systematically ruling out post hoc thinking and irrelevant factors.

Argument 3 is typical post hoc reasoning from the political sphere. Unless there are other good reasons for thinking that the economic policy is causally connected to specific economic events, the argument is weak and the conclusion unreliable.

Argument 4 is 100 percent post hoc and undiluted superstition. There is no difference in kind between this argument and much of the notorious post hoc reasoning of centuries ago: "That girl gave me the evil eye. The next day I broke my leg. That proves she's a witch, and the Elders of Salem should put her to death!"

CONFUSING CAUSE AND EFFECT

Sometimes we may realize that there's a causal relationship between two factors—but we may not know which factor is the cause and which is the effect. We may be confused, in other words, about the answers to questions like these:

> *Does your coffee drinking cause you to feel stressed out—or do your feelings of being stressed out cause you to drink coffee?*

The Deadly *Post Hoc* Fallacy

Despite a growing body of scientific research showing no connection between a measles vaccine and autism in young children, many people have insisted that the vaccine causes the disorder. Some parents of autistic children reasoned that since autism symptoms arose after the children were vaccinated, the vaccine was to blame. As evidence builds against a causal link, the reasoning looks more and more *post hoc*—and dangerous. Here's a recent statement from the National Institutes of Health:

> Study after study has found no link between autism spectrum disorders (ASD) and the measles-mumps-rubella (MMR) vaccine—or any vaccine for that matter. Yet many parents still refuse or delay vaccinations for their young children based on misplaced fear of ASD, which can be traced back to a small 1998 study that's since been debunked and retracted. Such decisions can have a major negative impact on public health. With vaccination rates in decline, we've recently seen the resurgence of measles and other potentially fatal childhood infectious diseases.

Among the parents most likely to avoid getting their kids vaccinated are those who already have a child with ASD. So, it's especially important and timely news that researchers have once again found no link between MMR vaccines and ASD—even among children known to be at greater risk for autism because an older sibling has the developmental brain disorder.[6]

> *Does participation in high school sports produce desirable virtues such as courage and self-reliance—or do the virtues of courage and self-reliance lead students to participate in high school sports?*
>
> *Does regular exercise make people healthy—or are healthy people naturally prone to regular exercise?*
>
> *Did the misbehaving kid cause the parents to yell at each other—or did the parents' yelling cause the kid to misbehave?*

As you can see, it's not always a simple matter to discern what the nature of a causal link is. Again, we must rely on our rule of thumb: *Don't assume that a causal connection exists unless you have good reason for doing so.* This tenet applies not only to our ordinary experience but to all states of affairs involving cause and effect, including scientific investigations.

In everyday life, sorting cause from effect is often easy because the situations we confront are frequently simple and familiar—as when we're trying to discover what caused the kettle to boil over. But as we've seen, in many other common circumstances, things aren't so simple. We often cannot be sure that we've identified all the relevant factors, or ruled out the influence of coincidence, or correctly distinguished cause and effect. Our rule of thumb, then, should be our guide in all the doubtful cases.

Science faces all the same kinds of challenges in its pursuit of causal explanations. And despite its sophisticated methodology and investigative tools, it must expend a great deal of effort to pin down causal connections. Identifying the cause of a disease, for example, usually requires not one study or experiment, but many. The main reason is that uncovering relevant factors and excluding irrelevant or misleading factors is always tough. This is why we should apply our rule of thumb even to scientific research that purports to identify a causal link.

Section Query

What is the most amazing coincidence you have (or someone you know has) ever experienced? How do you explain this event?

7.4 Innumeracy and Probability

When we make an off-the-cuff judgment about the chances of something happening (whether an event in the past or one in the future), we should be extra careful. Why? Because, generally, we humans are terrible at figuring probabilities.

Here's a classic example. Imagine that your classroom has 23 students present including yourself. What are the chances that at least two of the students have exactly the same birthday? (Not the same *date of birth*, but the same birthday out of the 365 possible ones.) The answer is neither 1 chance in 365 (1/365), nor 1 in 52 (1/52). It's *1 chance in 2 (1/2, or 50-50)*—a completely counterintuitive result.

As we've seen, a common error is misjudging the probability of coincidences. Many of us often believe that an event is simply too improbable to be a mere coincidence, that something else surely must be going on—such as secret intervention by someone else. But amazing coincidences occur all the time. The probability that a particular strange event will occur—say, that an ice cube tossed out of an airplane will hit the roof of a barn—may be extremely low, maybe one in a billion. But that same event given enough opportunities to occur may be highly probable over the long haul. It may be unlikely in any given instance for you to flip a coin and get tails seven times in a row. But this "streak" is virtually certain to happen if you flip the coin enough times.

What are the odds that someone will be thinking of a person she knew, or knew of, from the past 25 years then suddenly learn that the person is seriously ill or dead? Believe it or not, such a strange event is likely to occur several times a day. If we make the reasonable assumption that someone would recognize the names of a few thousand people (both famous and not so famous) from the past 25 years and that a person would learn of the illness or death of each of those few thousand people in the 25 years, then the chances of our eerie coincidence happening to someone somewhere are pretty good. We could reasonably expect that each day several people would have this experience.

Another error is to think that previous events can affect the probabilities in the random event at hand. This mistake is known as the **gambler's fallacy**. Let's say you toss an unbiased coin six times in a row. On the first toss, the odds are, of course, 1 in 2, or 50-50, that it will land tails. It lands tails. Astoundingly, on the other five tosses the coin also lands tails. That's six tails in a row. So what are the odds that the coin will land tails on the seventh toss? Answer: 50-50. Each toss has exactly the same probability of landing tails (or heads): 50-50. The coin does not remember previous tosses. To think otherwise is to commit the gambler's fallacy. You see it a lot in casinos, sporting events, and—alas—everyday decision making.

The lesson here is not that we should mistrust all judgment about probabilities, but that we shouldn't rely solely on our intuitive sense in evaluating them. Relying entirely on intuition, or "gut feeling," in assessing probabilities is usually not a reason to trust the assessment, but to doubt it.

If we require greater precision in judging probabilities, we're in luck because mathematicians have worked out how to quantify and evaluate them. In the simplest case, calculating the probability of the occurrence

Hierarchy of Reliability

Every source of information must be judged on its own merits and in the context of other available evidence. But it's possible to provide a very general ranking of trustworthiness for the sources we rely on for most of our knowledge—a kind of hierarchy of reliability. Here is one such ranking, ranging from most reliable sources to the least. The hierarchy is a general guide, not a precision tool, for even highly ranked sources can sometimes be wrong, low-ranking sources can be right, and some sources may generally be better or worse than their category might suggest.

Tier 1

- Articles and reports in peer-reviewed journals and conference proceedings
- Books published by academic and highly credible publishers (e.g., Harvard University Press, Cambridge University Press, Oxford University Press, Columbia University Press, Basic Books, Blackwell, John Wiley, Routledge, Rowman and Littlefield)
- Official government and university reports and web pages (.gov, .edu, NASA, FDA, NIH, GAO, etc.)

Tier 2

- News agencies. (e.g., AP, UPI, Reuters, AFP)
- Highly rated newspapers, magazines, and websites* (e.g., the *Economist*, World News, *Chicago Tribune*, Politico, *Commentary* magazine, the *New York Times*, *National Affairs* magazine, *National Journal*, Washington Blade, the *Washington Post*, *U.S. News and World Report*, *Barron's*, *Fortune* magazine)
- Highly rated broadcast news organizations* (PBS NewsHour, NPR, ABC News, CBS News, NBC News, C-SPAN, Spectrum News NY1)
- Major trade book publishers (e.g., Hachette Book Group, HarperCollins, Macmillan, Simon & Schuster, W. W. Norton, Penguin Random House)

Tier 3

- Nongovernmental organizations, advocacy groups, and political action committees (PACs)
- TV, radio, and podcast shows
- Advertising, marketing, publicity (paid sponsored content online—social media, search engines, promotional blogs, websites, etc.; print ads; TV and radio ads)

* Rated high for factual reporting by MediaBiasFactCheck.com.

of an event or outcome is a matter of division. For example, the probability of getting heads in the toss of an unbiased coin is one chance out of two—1/2 or 0.50. There is one toss and only two possible outcomes, heads or tails. Likewise, the probability of randomly drawing the jack of spades out of a standard deck of 52 cards is 1 chance in 52—1/52, or 0.192. And the probability of drawing one of the hearts out of the deck is 13 in 52, or 0.25 (because there are 13 cards in each suit).

But suppose we want to know the probability of getting a 10 by throwing two dice (two unbiased six-sided dice). Here we are talking about two events that are *independent* of each other—the event of the first die showing a 5, and the event of the second die showing a 5. The one event has no effect on the other. The probability of the first event occurring is 1 chance out of 6—1/6, and the other event has the same probability, 1/6. To determine the probability of *both* events happening in one throw of the dice, we find the mathematical product of the two: 1/6 × 1/6 = 1/36. Just as you would expect, the chances of these dual events happening (1/36) are much lower than that of just one of them happening (1/6). So to calculate the probability of two independent events happening together, we *multiply* the probability of the first event occurring by the probability of the second event occurring.

Now let's say the events in question are *not independent* of one another—each event can affect the other. Suppose we want to know the probability of drawing two hearts one after another from one standard (shuffled) deck of cards. Note that the deck will be light by one card after the first draw, thereby giving the second draw slightly different odds. The probability of drawing the first heart is 13/52 (13 hearts in the deck of 52), and the probability of drawing the next one is 12/51. To determine the probability of drawing two hearts in a row, we multiply: 13/52 × 12/51 = 1/17. So even when two events *are* affected by each other, to figure the odds of joint occurrence, we still *multiply* the probability of the first event occurring by the probability of the second event occurring.

Sometimes we may want to know the chances of *either* one of two events happening. Here we are not looking merely for two events to occur jointly as in the previous examples. We are interested in the odds of either one happening when they are mutually exclusive (if one occurs, the other cannot). Say we want to know the probability of pulling either a diamond or a club from a 52-card deck in one draw. The odds of drawing a diamond is 1 chance out of 4 (1/4), and the odds of drawing a club is also 1 in 4 (1/4). To figure the odds of drawing either one, we *add* the two probabilities: 1/4 + 1/4 = 1/2.

 ## Section Query

Suppose you toss an unbiased coin, and it lands tails three times in a row. What are the odds that your next toss will also be tails?

REVIEW NOTES

7.1 EXPERTS AND NONEXPERTS

- An **expert** is someone who is more knowledgeable in a particular subject area or field than most others are. Experts in professions and fields of knowledge provide us with reasons for believing a claim because, in their specialty areas, they are more likely to be right than we are.

- If a claim conflicts with other claims we have good reason to accept, we have good grounds for doubting it. If a claim conflicts with our **background**

- **information**, we have good reason to doubt it. Although our background information is generally trustworthy, it is not infallible. We should therefore be willing to re-examine background beliefs that we have doubts about—and to be open to reasonable doubts when they arise.
- If a claim is not quite dubious enough to summarily discard yet not worthy of complete acceptance, we should measure out our belief according to the strength of reasons—that is, we should proportion our belief to the evidence.
- We are justified in doubting a claim when it comes from someone deemed to be an expert who in fact is *not* an expert. When we rely on such bogus expert opinion, we make the mistake known as the **fallacious appeal to authority**.

7.2 JUDGING EXPERTS

- In most professional fields, the following two indicators are considered minimal prerequisites for being considered an expert: (1) education and training from reputable institutions or programs in the relevant field and (2) experience in the field.
- Two additional indicators of true expertise may be even more revealing: (1) reputation among peers (as reflected in the opinions of others in the same field, relevant prestigious awards, and positions of authority) and (2) professional accomplishments.
- If we have reason to believe that an expert is biased, we are not justified in accepting the expert's opinion.
- We may suspect bias when an expert is being paid by special-interest groups or companies to render an opinion, or when the expert expresses very strong belief in a claim even though there is no evidence to support it, or when the expert stands to gain financially from the actions or policies that he or she supports.
- Even qualified, unbiased, honest experts can be wrong, but the mistakes of experts do not disprove that, in general, genuine experts are more likely to be right about things in their fields than we are.

7.3 EXPERTS AND PERSONAL EXPERIENCE

- It's reasonable to accept the evidence provided by personal experience only if there's no good reason to doubt it. If our faculties are working properly and our use of them is unimpeded by anything in our environment, we're entitled to accept what our personal experience tells us.
- Our personal experience is susceptible to error in all sorts of ways; under certain circumstances, our senses, memory, and judgment can't be trusted.
- The major factors that can distort our personal experience include impairment, expectation, and causal confusions.

7.4 INNUMERACY AND PROBABILITY

- Humans are not good at off-the-cuff judgments about the chances of something happening. A common error is the misjudging of coincidences, in which we wrongly assume that an event is too unlikely to be mere coincidence.
- Assuming that previous events can affect the probabilities in the random event at hand is a common error known as the **gambler's fallacy**.
- *Post hoc, ergo propter hoc* ("after that, therefore because of that") is the fallacy of reasoning that just because B followed A, A must have caused B.

KEY TERMS

background information
expert

fallacious appeal to authority
gambler's fallacy

post hoc, ergo propter hoc

EXERCISES

Exercises marked with an asterisk (*) have answers in "Answers to Exercises" (Appendix B).

Exercise 7.1

1. What kinds of beliefs are part of a person's background information?
2. What is the most reasonable attitude toward a claim that conflicts with other claims you have good reason to believe?
3. What degree of probability should we assign to a claim that conflicts with our background information?
*4. What is the most reasonable attitude toward a claim that is neither worthy of acceptance nor deserving of outright rejection?
5. What is an expert?
6. What should be our attitude toward a claim that conflicts with expert opinion?
7. What should be our attitude toward a claim when experts disagree about it?
8. What is the fallacy of the appeal to authority?
9. According to the text, in most fields, what are the two minimal prerequisites for being considered an expert?
*10. According to the text, beyond the minimal prerequisites, what are two more telling indicators that someone is an expert?
11. Under what three circumstances should we suspect that an expert may be biased?
12. When is it reasonable to accept the evidence provided by personal experience?
13. What are two factors that can give us good reason to doubt the reliability of personal experience?
14. In what ways are our perception and memory constructive?

Exercise 7.2

Based on claims you already have good reason to believe, your background information, and your assessment of the credibility of any cited experts, indicate for each of the following claims whether you would accept it, reject it, or proportion your belief to the evidence. Give reasons for your answers. If you decide to proportion your belief to the evidence, indicate generally what degree of plausibility you would assign to the claim.

1. Israeli psychic Uri Geller can bend spoons with his mind.
2. In Russia, some people live to be 150 years old.
3. Every year in the United States over three hundred people die of leprosy.
*4. According to Dr. Feelgood, the spokesperson for Acme Mattresses, the EasyRest 2000 from Acme is the best mattress in the world for back-pain sufferers.
5. Some bars in the suburbs of Chicago have been entertaining their nightly patrons with pygmy hippo tossing.
*6. Every person has innate psychic ability that, when properly cultivated, can enable him or her to read another person's mind.
7. The prime minister of Canada works with the government of the United States to suppress the economic power of French Canadians.
8. Molly, a 34-year-old bank manager, says that stock prices will plummet dramatically in two months and will trigger another deep, year-long recession.
9. Humans use only about 10 percent of the brain's capacity for thinking and creating.

*10. Fifteen women have died after smelling a free perfume sample that they received in the mail.

11. A Facebook post describing the struggles of a nine-year-old girl with incurable cancer is circulating on the internet. The more people who receive the post, the better the little girl's chances of survival.

12. A report from the National Institutes of Health says that there is no evidence that high doses of the herb ephedra can cure cancer.

13. Giant albino alligators crawl through the underground sewers of New York City.

*14. Crop circles—large-scale geometric patterns pressed into crop fields—are the work of space aliens.

15. Crop circles are the work of human hoaxers.

16. North Korea is a communist paradise where everyone prospers and human rights are respected.

*17. Dr. Xavier, a world-famous astrologer, says that the position of the sun, planets, and stars at your birth influences your choice of careers and your marital status.

18. Eleanor Morgan, a Nobel Prize–winning economist, says that modern democratic systems (including developed nations) are not viable.

19. Eating meat rots your colon.

20. The highway speed limit in New York is 65 mph.

Exercise 7.3

For each of the following situations and the claim associated with it, indicate whether there may be good reasons to doubt the claim and, if so, specify the reasons.

*1. Standing on a street corner in heavy fog, Eve thinks she sees an old friend walking away from her on the other side of the street. She says to herself, "That's Julio Sanchez."

*2. While playing an old rock tune backward, Elton thinks that he hears a sentence on the tape. It's almost inaudible, but he thinks it says, "Hello, Elton, long time no see."

3. Detective Jones views the videotape of the robbery at the 7-Eleven, which occurred last night. He sees the robber look into the camera. "I know that guy," he says. "I put him away last year on a similar charge."

Exercise 7.4

For each of the following claims, indicate whether it is: (a) probably true, (b) probably false, (c) almost certainly true, (d) almost certainly false, or (e) none of the above.

*1. "Most people are not aware that the cartoonish 'Bigfoot' figure is a distorted product of ancient and modern stories describing a real but unacknowledged species that is still occasionally observed today in North American forests." (The Bigfoot Field Researchers Organization)

2. "The actual risk of falling ill from a bioterrorist attack is extremely small." (American Council on Science and Health)

3. Nobody in the world is truly altruistic. Everyone is out for himself alone.

4. School violence is caused mainly by hypocrisy on the part of teachers and school administrators.

*5. "The world shadow government behind the U.S. government is at it again, destroying U.S. buildings and killing people with staged acts of terrorism [on 9/11/01], the intent of which being—among other things—to start WW III." (Website devoted to 9/11 theories)

*6. "What is Pre-Birth Communication? It's something that many people experience, yet very few talk about—the sense that somehow we are in contact with a being who is not yet born! It may be a vivid dream, the touch of an invisible presence, a telepathic message announcing pregnancy, or many other types of encounter. It is a mystery, one that challenges our ideas about ourselves and our children." (Website on "pre-birth communication")

*7. Physicians, drug companies, the food industry, the National Cancer Institute, and the American Cancer Society are all fighting to prevent "natural" cancer cures such as vitamin supplements and herbs from being used by cancer patients.

8. Medieval history is a lie—or, rather, it doesn't exist. Monks made it up based on a corrupt copy of ancient history.

Exercise 7.5

Analyze each of the following causal arguments. Identify the conclusion and whether the argument is weak or strong. If it's weak, explain why with reference to the material in this chapter.

*1. School violence is caused mainly by teens playing violent video games. Incidents of violence in schools have increased as more and more teens are playing violent video games, as the video games themselves have become more graphically and realistically violent, and as the number and variety of video games have expanded dramatically.

2. Smoking and exposure to secondhand smoke among pregnant women pose a significant risk to both infants and the unborn. According to numerous studies, each year the use of tobacco causes thousands of spontaneous births, infant deaths, and deaths from SIDS. Death rates for fetuses are 35 percent higher among pregnant women who smoke than among pregnant women who don't smoke.

*3. Why are crime rates so high, the economy so bad, and our children so prone to violence, promiscuity, and vulgarity? These social ills have arisen—as they always have—from the "moral vacuum" created when Americans turn away from religion. Our current slide into chaos started when prayer was banned from public schools and secular humanism swooped in to replace it. And as God has slowly faded from public life, we have got deeper in the hole.

*4. Ever since I started drinking herbal tea in the morning, my energy level has improved and I'm a lot calmer during the day. That stuff works.

5. Yesterday my astrological chart—prepared by a top astrologer—said that I would meet an attractive person today, and I did. Last week, it said I'd come into some money, and I did. (Jack paid me that hundred dollars he owed me.) Now I'm a believer. The stars really do rule.

CAPSTONE

List five sources that you consider highly reliable in a field or profession that you're interested in. Then list five of the least reliable sources. For each source, give reasons for your rating. Your lists can be composed of websites, blogs, books, articles, TED talks, or podcasts.

8

Science, Nonscience, and the Media

Chapter Objectives

8.1 What Science Is and Is Not
- *Define* science *and understand why it is neither ideology, motivated reasoning, nor technology.*
- *Identify at least four signs of bogus science.*

8.2 How Science Is Done
- *Know the five steps in the scientific method and understand how and why scientists derive test implications of a hypothesis.*
- *Understand how a hypothesis is confirmed or disconfirmed and why this process cannot yield conclusive results.*

8.3 Judging Scientific Theories
- *Explain the reasoning process known as inference to the best explanation and how science uses it to judge the worth of theories.*
- *Understand the minimum requirement of consistency used in judging scientific theories. Define internal and external consistency.*
- *Explain how the criteria of adequacy are used by scientists to judge the merits of theories. Define* testability, fruitfulness, scope, simplicity, conservatism, *and* ad hoc hypothesis.
- *Know why conspiracy theories fail as explanations of phenomena.*

8.4 Telling Good Theories from Bad
- *Understand how to use the TEST formula to judge the relative worth of theories.*
- *Explain why Copernicus's theory of planetary motion is better than Ptolemy's.*
- *Explain why scientists think evolution is a better theory than creationism.*
- *Understand how scientists know that climate change is happening.*

(Continued)

(Continued)

8.5 How the Media Get Science Wrong
- *Understand* that health news is often hyped, exaggerated, and false.
- *Learn* to recognize when a study does not establish that a treatment is effective or that a cause-and-effect relationship exists.
- *Understand* why cause and effect generally cannot be established by single studies, small studies, anecdotes, case studies, nonintervention studies, and animal studies.

8.6 Scientific Opinion Polls
- *Define* random sampling, self-selecting sample, margin of error, *and* confidence level.
- *Understand* why a poll cannot be trusted if the sample is not random or not representative, the questions are phrased improperly, or the sample is self-selected.

Science and technology are making and unmaking the planet, shaping machines and minds, increasing our power and our peril, while we struggle to adapt. Science gives us knowledge—knowledge that some people embrace, some resent, some fear, and some deny. But do we understand this knowledge? More to the point, do we even understand science? This question is not, Do we know that Earth rotates around the sun once a year, or do we know how to use a quantum computer, or can we pass a course in biology or physics? The question has several parts: Do we understand how science is done, how to evaluate the knowledge it yields, and how to use that knowledge to make sense of our world, guide our lives, and plot our futures?

The challenge of answering these questions is not merely theoretical. It's pressing on us right now. Science writer Shawn Otto explains our predicament:

> Science and technology have come to affect every aspect of life on the planet. There is a phase change going on in the scientific revolution: a shifting from one state to another, as from a solid to a liquid. There is a sudden, *quantitative* expansion of the number of scientists and engineers around the globe, coupled with a sudden *qualitative* expansion of their ability to collaborate with each other over the Internet.

These two changes are dramatically speeding up the process of discovery and the convergence of knowledge across once-separate fields, a process Harvard entomologist Edward O. Wilson named consilience. We now have fields where economics merges with environmental science, electrical engineering with neuroscience and physics, computer science with biology and genetics, astronomy with biology, and many more. This consilience is shedding new light on long-held assumptions about the world we live in and the nature of life.

Over the course of the next forty years, science is poised to create more knowledge than humans have created in all of recorded history, completely redefining our concepts about—and power over—life and the physical and mental worlds as we assume editing control over the genetic code and mastery in our understanding of the brain. One only has to recall the political battles fought over past scientific advances to see that we are in for a rocky ride. How that rush of new knowledge will impact life, how it will be applied through technology and law, and whether our societies and governments will be able to withstand the immense social and economic upheavals it will bring depends upon whether we can update our political process to accommodate it. Can we manage the next phase of the scientific revolution to our advantage, or will we become its unwilling victims?[1]

Into this maelstrom of change, whole armies of interested parties are marching, twisting science to their own uses, misinterpreting data, quashing evidence, cherry-picking results, contradicting established facts, pretending that scientific consensus doesn't exist, and ignoring reality altogether. The soldiers in these anti-science brigades include politicians, legislators, U.S. presidents, PR firms, journalists, political parties, special interest groups, industry hacks, partisan bloggers, talk radio hosts, conspiracy theorists, policymakers, and countless others.

How can we safely make our way through this storm? Let's see what we can do in the following pages.

8.1 What Science Is and Is Not

Science is the careful, systematic search for knowledge and understanding of reality through the formulation, testing, and evaluation of theories. It has proven itself through the centuries to be the most powerful tool we have for uncovering truths about the world and distinguishing between what is real and what is not. It has been successful in helping us acquire knowledge because it methodically guards against the common biases and prejudices of the human mind, resists partisan pressure and popular opinion, accepts nothing on faith, and demands hard evidence and solid reasons. Science embodies to a high degree what is essential to reliable knowing of empirical facts: systematic consideration of alternative solutions or theories, rigorous testing of them, and careful checking and rechecking of the conclusions.

Some would say that science is reliable because it is self-correcting. Science does not grab hold of an explanation and never let go. Science is not dogma. Instead, it looks at alternative ways to explain a phenomenon, tests these alternatives, and opens up the conclusions to criticism from scientists everywhere. Eventually, after much testing and thinking, scientists may hit upon a theory that does hold up under scrutiny. They are then justified in accepting that theory, even though no conclusion in science can be proved beyond doubt, and there is no guarantee that future research will not reveal a better theory.

We will look more closely at the scientific method and the nature of scientific theories shortly, but we first need to say what science is not.

Science Is Not Ideology

Some people say that science is not a way of finding out how the world works, but a worldview affirming how the world is, just as Catholicism or socialism affirms a view of things. To some, science is not only an ideology, but a most objectionable one—one that posits a universe that is entirely material, mechanistic, and deterministic. On this "scientific view," the world—including us—is nothing more than bits of matter forming a big machine that turns and whirs in predetermined ways. This mechanistic notion is thought to demean humans and human endeavors by reducing us to the role of cogs and sprockets.

But we can't identify science with a specific worldview. At any given time, a particular worldview may predominate in the scientific community, but this fact doesn't mean that the worldview is what science is all about. Predominant worldviews among scientists have changed over the centuries, but the general nature of science as a way of searching for truth has not. For example, the mechanistic view of the universe, so common among scientists in the 17th century, has now given way to other views. Discoveries in quantum mechanics (the study of subatomic particles) have shown that the old mechanistic perspective is incorrect.

Science is, above all, a *process*. Over the centuries the process has yielded findings that have contradicted prevailing ideologies, but that doesn't make science an ism.

Scientific facts can become political. Because science, by its very nature, questions traditional beliefs and unchallenged assumptions about the world, it often provokes opposition to its findings, opposition that is political, even if the scientific facts themselves are just objective descriptions of reality. Thus we can honestly say that science is not partisan, but it may be political whether it likes it or not.

Science Is Not Motivated Reasoning

Recall that motivated reasoning is reasoning for the purpose of supporting a predetermined conclusion, not to uncover the truth (Chapter 3). Many people are guilty of this backward "research," amassing evidence that agrees with their preferred opinions and ignoring or dismissing evidence that supports contrary views. Science does *not* work this way. Scientific inquiry begins with a question to answer, formulates hypotheses to answer the question, and then tests those hypotheses to see if any of them are true. This approach commits scientists to following the evidence wherever it leads, even to conclusions that might conflict with their expectations or wishes. Scientific research is initiated precisely because the conclusions are unknown.

Among scientists, in universities and research facilities throughout the world, motivated reasoning is considered an egregious violation of scientific practice and professional ethics. Researchers found guilty of flagrant motivated reasoning are censured by the community of scientists and disciplined by scientific organizations.

Science Is Not Technology

Science is a way of searching for truth. Technology is not a search for truth; it's the production of products—cell phones, GPS, social media, robots, self-driving cars, better mousetraps. Technology applies knowledge acquired through science to practical problems that science generally doesn't care about, such as the creation of electronic gadgets. Technology seeks facts to use in producing stuff. Science tries to understand how the world works not by merely cataloging specific facts but by identifying general principles that both explain and predict phenomena.

This nice distinction gets blurry sometimes when technologists do scientific research in order to build a better product or scientists create gadgets in order to do better scientific research. But in general, science pursues knowledge; technology makes things.

Seven Warning Signs of Bogus Science

What would a distinguished scientist tell trial judges who must try to discern whether scientific testimony by an expert is credible? Robert L. Park is that scientist (as well as an author and professor of physics), and he has identified the following clues "that a scientific claim lies well outside the bounds of rational scientific discourse." He cautions, though, that "they are only warning signs—even a claim with several of the signs could be legitimate."

1. The discoverer pitches the claim directly to the media. The integrity of science rests on the willingness of scientists to expose new ideas and findings to the scrutiny of other scientists. Thus, scientists expect their colleagues to reveal new findings to them initially. An attempt to bypass peer review by taking a new result directly to the media, and then to the public, suggests that the work is unlikely to stand up to close examination by other scientists.

2. The discoverer says that a powerful establishment is trying to suppress his or her work. The idea is that the establishment will presumably stop at nothing to suppress discoveries that might shift the balance of wealth and power in society. Often, the discoverer describes mainstream science as part of a larger conspiracy that includes industry and government. Claims that the oil companies are frustrating the invention of an automobile that runs on water, for instance, are a sure sign that the idea of such a car is baloney.

3. The scientific effect involved is always at the very limit of detection. Alas, there is never a clear photograph of a flying saucer, or the Loch Ness monster. All scientific measurements must contend with some level of background noise or statistical fluctuation. But if the signal-to-noise ratio cannot be improved, even in principle, the effect is probably not real and the work is not science.

Thousands of published papers in parapsychology, for example, claim to report verified instances of telepathy, psychokinesis, or precognition. But those effects show up only in tortured analyses of statistics. The researchers can find no way to boost the signal, which suggests that it isn't really there.

4. Evidence for a discovery is anecdotal. If modern science has learned anything in the past century, it is to distrust anecdotal evidence. Because anecdotes have a very strong emotional impact, they serve to keep superstitious beliefs alive in an age of science. The most important discovery of modern medicine is not vaccines or antibiotics; it is the randomized double-blind test, by means of which we know what works and what doesn't. Contrary to the saying, the word "data" is not the plural of "anecdote."

5. The discoverer says a belief is credible because it has endured for centuries. There is a persistent myth that hundreds or even thousands of years ago, long before anyone knew that blood circulates throughout the body or that germs cause disease, our ancestors possessed miraculous remedies that modern science cannot understand. Much of what is termed "alternative medicine" is part of that myth.

6. The discoverer has worked in isolation. The image of a lone genius who struggles in secrecy in an attic laboratory and ends up making a revolutionary breakthrough is a staple of Hollywood's science-fiction films, but it is hard to find examples in real life. Scientific breakthroughs nowadays are almost always syntheses of the work of many scientists.

7. The discoverer must propose new laws of nature to explain an observation. A new law of nature, invoked to explain some extraordinary result, must not conflict with what is already known. If we must change existing laws of nature or propose new laws to account for an observation, it is almost certainly wrong.[2]

Section Query

Do you think science is an ideology—or a process for discovering facts about the world? Explain your answer.

8.2 How Science Is Done

The **scientific method** cannot be identified with any particular set of experimental or observational procedures because there are many different methods to evaluate the worth of a hypothesis. In some sciences such as physics and biology, hypotheses can be assessed through controlled experimental tests. In other sciences such as astronomy and geology, hypotheses usually must be tested through observations. For example, an astronomical hypothesis may predict the existence of certain gases in a part of the Milky Way, and astronomers can use their telescopes to check whether those gases exist as predicted.

The scientific method, however, does involve several steps, regardless of the specific procedures involved:

1. Identify the problem or pose a question.
2. Devise a hypothesis to explain the event or phenomenon.
3. Derive a test implication or prediction.
4. Perform the test.
5. Accept or reject the hypothesis.

Scientific inquiry begins with a problem to solve or a question to answer. So in step 1 scientists may ask: What causes X? Why did Y happen? Does hormone therapy cause breast cancer? Does aspirin lower the risk of stroke? How is it possible for whales to navigate over long distances? How did early hominids communicate with one another? Was the Big Bang an uncaused event?

In step 2 scientists formulate a hypothesis that will constitute an answer to their question. In every case there are facts to explain, and the hypothesis is an explanation for them. The hypothesis guides the research, suggesting what kinds of observations or data would be relevant to the problem at hand. Without a hypothesis, scientists couldn't tell which data are important and which are worthless.

Where do hypotheses come from? One notion is that hypotheses are generated through induction—by collecting the data and drawing a generalization from them to get a hypothesis. But this can't be the way that most hypotheses are formulated because they often contain concepts that aren't in the data. Hypotheses or theories generally reach beyond the known data to posit the existence of things unknown. The construction of hypotheses is not usually based on any such mechanical procedure. In many ways, they are created just as works of art are created. Scientists dream them up. They, however, are guided in hypothesis creation by certain criteria—namely, the criteria of adequacy mentioned earlier.

Remember, though, that scientists must consider not just their favorite hypothesis, but alternative hypotheses as well. The scientific method calls for consideration of competing explanations and for their examination or testing at some point in the process. Sometimes applying the criteria of adequacy can immediately eliminate some theories from the running, and sometimes theories must be tested along with the original hypothesis.

In step 3 scientists derive implications, or consequences, of the hypothesis to test. As we've seen, sometimes we can test a theory directly, as when we simply check the lawnmower's gas tank to confirm the theory that it won't run because it's out of gas. But often theories cannot be tested directly. How would we directly test, for example, the hypothesis that chemical X is causing leukemia in menopausal women? We can't.

So scientists test indirectly by first deriving a test implication from a hypothesis and then putting that implication to the test. Deriving such an observational consequence involves figuring out what a hypothesis implies or predicts. Scientists ask, "If this hypothesis were true, what consequences would follow? What phenomena or events would have to obtain?"

The logic of hypothesis testing, then, works like this. When we derive a test implication, we know that if the hypothesis to be tested (H) is true, then there is a specific predicted consequence (C). If the consequence turns out to be false (it does not obtain as predicted), then the hypothesis is probably false, and we can reject it. The hypothesis, in other words, is disconfirmed. We can represent this outcome in a conditional, or hypothetical, argument:

If H, then C.

not-C.

Therefore, not-H.

This is, remember, an instance of *modus tollens*, a valid argument form. In this case, H would be false even if only one of several of its consequences (test implications) turned out to be false.

On the other hand, we would get a very different situation if C turned out to be true:

If H, then C.
C.
Therefore, H.

Notice that this is an instance of affirming the consequent, an invalid argument form. So just because C is true, that doesn't necessarily mean that H is true. If a consequence turns out to be true, that doesn't *prove* that the hypothesis is correct. In such a result, the hypothesis is confirmed and the test provides at least some evidence that the hypothesis is true. But the hypothesis isn't then established. If other consequences for the hypothesis are tested, and all the results are again positive, then there is more evidence that the hypothesis is correct. As more and more consequences are tested, and they are shown to be true, we can have increasing confidence that the hypothesis is in fact true. As this evidence accumulates, the likelihood that the hypothesis is actually false decreases—and the probability that it's true increases.

In step 4 scientists carry out the testing. Usually this experimentation is not as simple as testing one implication and calling it quits. Scientists may test many consequences of several competing hypotheses. As the testing proceeds, some hypotheses are found wanting, and they're dropped. If all goes well, eventually one hypothesis remains, with considerable evidence in its favor. Then step 5 can happen, as the hypothesis or hypotheses are accepted or rejected.

Because scientists want to quickly eliminate unworthy hypotheses and zero in on the best one, they try to devise the most telling tests. This means that they are on the lookout for situations in which competing hypotheses have different test consequences. If hypothesis 1 says that C is true, and hypothesis 2 says that C is false, a test of C can then help eliminate one of the hypotheses from further consideration.

Implicit in all this is the fact that no hypothesis can ever be *conclusively* confirmed. It's always possible that we will someday find evidence that undermines or conflicts with the evidence we have now. Likewise, no hypothesis can ever be *conclusively* confuted. But our inability to conclusively confirm or confute a hypothesis does not mean that all hypotheses are equally acceptable. Maintaining a hypothesis in the face of mounting negative evidence is unreasonable, and so is refusing to accept a hypothesis despite accumulating confirming evidence. Through the use of carefully controlled experiments, scientists can often affirm or deny a hypothesis with a high degree of confidence.

Let's see how we might use the five-step procedure to test a fairly simple hypothesis. Suppose you hear reports that some terminal cancer patients have lived longer than expected because they received high doses of vitamin C. And say that the favored hypothesis among many observers is that the best explanation for the patients' surviving longer is that vitamin C is an effective treatment against cancer. So you decide to test this hypothesis: High doses of vitamin C can increase the survival time of people with terminal cancer. (Years ago, this hypothesis was actually proposed and tested in three well-controlled clinical trials.[3]) An obvious alternative hypothesis is that vitamin C actually has no effect on the survival of terminal cancer patients and that any apparent benefits are due mainly to the placebo effect (the tendency for people to temporarily feel better after they're treated, even if the treatment is a fake). The placebo effect could be leading observers to believe that people taking vitamin C are being cured of cancer and are thus living longer. Or the placebo effect could be making patients feel better, enabling them to take better care of themselves (by eating right or complying with standard medical treatment, for example), increasing survival time.

Now, if your hypothesis is true, what would you expect to happen? That is, what test implication could you derive? If your hypothesis is true, you would expect that terminal cancer patients given high doses of vitamin C would live longer than terminal cancer patients who didn't receive the vitamin (or anything else).

How would you conduct such a test? To begin with, you could prescribe vitamin C to a group of terminal cancer patients (called the experimental group) but not to another group of similar cancer patients (called the control group) and keep track of their survival times. Then you could compare the survival rates of the two groups. But many people who knowingly receive a treatment will report feeling better—even if the treatment is an inactive placebo. So any positive results you see in the treated group might be due not to vitamin C but to the placebo effect.

To get around this problem, you would need to treat both groups, one with vitamin C and the other with a placebo. That way, if most of the people getting the vitamin C live longer than expected and fewer of those in the placebo group do, you can have slightly better reason for believing that vitamin C works as advertised.

But even this study design is not good enough. It's possible for the people conducting the experiment, the experimenters, to unknowingly bias the results. Through subtle behavioral cues, they can unconsciously inform the test subjects which treatments are real and which ones are placebos—and this, of course, would allow the placebo effect to have full rein. Also, if the experimenters know which treatment is the real one, they can unintentionally misinterpret or skew the study results in line with their own expectations.

This problem can be solved by making the study *double-blind*. In double-blind experiments, neither the subjects nor the experimenters know who receives the real treatment and who the inactive one. A double-blind protocol for your vitamin study would ensure that none of the subjects would know who's getting vitamin C, and neither would the experimenters.

What if you have a double-blind setup but most of the subjects in the vitamin C group were sicker to begin with than those in the placebo control group? Obviously, this would bias the results, making the vitamin C treatment look less effective—even if it *is* effective. To avoid this skewing, you would need to randomly assign subjects to each group. This *randomization* helps ensure that each group is as much alike as possible to start.

Finally, you would need to run some statistical tests to ensure that your results are not a fluke. Even in the most tightly controlled studies, it's possible that the outcome is the result of random factors that cannot be controlled. Statisticians have standard methods for determining when experiment results are likely, or not likely, to be due to chance.

Suppose you design your study well, conduct it, and the results are that the patients receiving the high doses of vitamin C did not live longer than the placebo group. In fact, all the subjects lived about the same length of time. Therefore, your hypothesis is disconfirmed. On the other hand, the alternative hypothesis—that vitamin C has no measurable effect on the survival of terminal cancer patients—is confirmed.

Should you now reject the vitamin C theory? Not yet. Even apparently well-conducted studies can have hidden mistakes in them, or there can be factors that the experimenters fail to take into account. This is why scientists insist on study *replication*—the repeating of an experiment by different groups of scientists. If the study is replicated by other scientists, and the study results hold up, then you can be more confident that the results are solid. In such a case, you could safely reject the vitamin C hypothesis. (This is, in fact, what scientists did in the real-life studies of vitamin C and cancer survival.)

At this point, when evidence has been gathered that can bear on the truth of the hypothesis in question, good scientific judgment is crucial. It's here that consideration of other competing hypotheses and the criteria of adequacy again come into play. At this stage, scientists need to decide whether to reject or accept a hypothesis—or modify it to improve it.

Nonintervention (Population) Studies

Not all medical hypotheses are tested by treating (or not treating) groups of patients and analyzing the results (as in the vitamin C example). Many are tested without such direct intervention in people's lives. The former type of study is known as an intervention, or controlled, trial, while the latter is called, not surprisingly, a *nonintervention* study (also an *observational* or *population* study). The basic idea in a nonintervention study is to track the interplay of disease and related factors in a specified population, uncovering associations among these that might lead to better understanding or control of the disease process.

A typical nonintervention study might go like this: For seven years scientists monitor the vitamin E intake (from food and supplements) and the incidence of heart disease of 90,000 women. Evaluation of this data shows that the women with the highest amounts of vitamin E in their diets have a 40 percent lower incidence of heart disease. That is, for reasons unknown, a lower risk of heart disease is associated with a higher intake of vitamin E in women. This study does not show that higher intakes of vitamin E *cause* less heart disease, only that there is a link between them. Perhaps some other factor merely associated with vitamin E is the true protector of hearts, or maybe women who take vitamin E are more likely to do other things (such as exercise) that lower their risk of heart disease.

Generally, nonintervention studies cannot establish cause-and-effect relationships, though they may hint that a causal relationship is present. And sometimes multiple nonintervention studies yielding the same results can make a strong case for a causal connection. Intervention trials, however, *can* establish cause and effect.

Nonintervention studies have led scientists to some of the most important findings in preventive health. It was a series of such studies done over decades, coupled with other kinds of scientific data, that revealed that cigarette smoking caused cancer. And it was such investigations that showed that high blood pressure, high cholesterol, overweight, and smoking are risk factors for heart disease.

Note to critical thinkers: Very often the media misreport the results of nonintervention studies, reading cause and effect into a mere association. For example, if a single nonintervention study finds a link between chewing gum and better eyesight, a headline in a blog, or the morning paper, or a TV newscaster may proclaim, "Gum-chewing improves your eyesight!" Maybe, maybe not—but the study would not justify that conclusion.

Section Query

Have you ever accepted health or medical claims in a news story that was based on a nonintervention study? If so, why? If not, why not?

8.3 Judging Scientific Theories

Theory testing is part of the broader effort to assess the merits of one theory against a field of alternatives. This broader effort—the central task of science—comes down to asking (and answering) one question: What is the best explanation (theory) for this phenomenon or state of affairs? The best explanation is the one most likely to be true. Science does its most important work, then, through the inductive form of reasoning known as inference to the best explanation (Chapter 2).

Inference to the best explanation probably seems very familiar to you. That's because you use it all the time—and need it all the time. Often when we try to understand something in the world, we construct explanations for why this something is the way it is, and we try to determine which of these is the best. Devising explanations helps increase our understanding by fitting our experiences and background knowledge into a coherent pattern. At every turn we are confronted with phenomena that we can fully understand only by explaining them.

Sometimes we're barely aware that we're using inference to the best explanation. If we awaken and see that the streets outside are wet, we may immediately posit this explanation: It's been raining. Without thinking much about it, we may also quickly consider whether a better explanation is that a street-sweeper machine has wet the street. Just as quickly we may dismiss this explanation because we see that the houses and cars are also wet. After reasoning in this fashion, we may decide to carry an umbrella that day.

In science, where inference to the best explanation is an essential tool, usually the theories of interest are causal theories, in which events are the things to be explained and the proposed causes of the events are the explanations. Just as we do in everyday life, scientists often consider several competing theories for the same event or phenomenon. Then—through scientific testing and careful thinking—they systematically eliminate inadequate theories and eventually arrive at the one that's rightly regarded as the best of the bunch. Using this form of inference, scientists discover planets, viruses, cures, subatomic particles, black holes—and many things that can't even be directly observed.

As you can see, the term *theory* as it's used in science is not synonymous with *conjecture* or *guess*. A theory is an explanation, and if it is the best explanation to explain something, it is a fact. Thus we refer to the germ *theory* of disease, the heliocentric (sun-centered) *theory* of planetary motion, Einstein's *theory* of relativity, the oxygen *theory* of combustion, the *theory* of gravitation—these are facts about the way the world is because they have been established scientifically. So to dismiss a scientific finding by calling it just a theory—as in "evolution is just a theory"—is to misunderstand the scientific meaning of the word.

Theories and Consistency

Of course, it's easy to make up theories to explain things we don't understand. People do it all the time. The harder job is sorting out good theories from bad. The work can be demanding, but there are special criteria we can use to get the job done. Before we apply these criteria, though, we have to make sure that the theory in question meets the minimum requirement of *consistency*. A theory that does not meet this minimum requirement is worthless, so there is no need to use the special criteria to evaluate the theory. A theory that meets the requirement is eligible for further consideration. Here we are concerned with both *internal* and *external* consistency. A theory that is internally consistent is consistent with itself—it's free of contradictions. A theory that is externally consistent is consistent with the data it's supposed to explain—it fully accounts for the phenomenon to be explained.

If we show that a theory contains a contradiction, we have refuted it. A theory that implies that something both is and is not the case cannot possibly be true. By exposing an internal contradiction, Galileo once refuted Aristotle's famous theory of motion, a venerable hypothesis that had stood tall for centuries. He showed that the theory implied that one falling object falls both faster and slower than another one.

If a theory is externally inconsistent, we have reason to believe that it's false. Suppose you leave your car parked on the street overnight and the next morning discover that (1) the windshield is broken, (2) there's blood on the steering wheel, and (3) there's a brick on the front seat. And let's say that your friend Charlie offers this theory to explain these facts: Someone threw a brick through your windshield. What would you think about this theory?

You would probably think that Charlie had not been paying attention. His theory accounts for the broken windshield and the brick—but not the blood on the steering wheel. You would likely toss his theory out and look for one that was complete. Like this one: A thief broke your windshield with a brick and then crawled through the broken window, cutting himself in the process. An adequate theory must fully account for the facts to be explained.

Theories and Criteria

A simplified answer to the problem of theory choice is this: Just weigh the evidence for each theory, and the theory with the most evidence wins. As we will soon see, the amount or degree of evidence that a theory has is indeed a crucial factor—but it cannot be the sole criterion by which we assess explanations. Throughout the history of science, major theories—from the heliocentric theory of the solar system to

Einstein's general theory of relativity—have never been established by empirical evidence alone.

The task of determining the best explanation has another complication. There could be no end to the number of theories that we could devise to explain the data at hand. In fact, we could come up with an infinite number of possible theories for any phenomenon simply by repeatedly adding one more element. For example, to explain why your cell phone died, you could propose the one-poltergeist theory (a single entity causing the trouble), a two-poltergeist theory, a three-poltergeist theory, and so on.

Fortunately, despite these complications, we can use the **criteria of adequacy** to help us judge the merits of eligible theories and to arrive at a defensible judgment of which theory is best. The criteria of adequacy are the essential tools of science and have been used by scientists throughout history to uncover the best explanations for all sorts of events and states of affairs. Science, though, doesn't own these criteria. They are as useful—and as used—among nonscientists as they are among men and women of science.

Applying the criteria of adequacy to a set of theories constitutes the ultimate test of a theory's value, for *the best theory is the eligible theory that meets the criteria of adequacy better than any of its competitors*. Here, *eligible* means that the theory has already met the minimum requirement for consistency.

All of this implies that the evaluation of a particular theory is not complete until alternative, or competing, theories are considered. As we've seen, there is an indefinite number of theories that could be offered to explain a given set of data. The main challenge is to give a fair assessment of the relevant theories in relation to each other. To fail to somehow address the alternatives is to overlook or deny relevant evidence, to risk biased conclusions, and to court error. Such failure is probably the most common error in the appraisal of theories.

A theory judged by these criteria to be the best explanation for certain facts is worthy of our belief, and we may legitimately claim to know that such a theory is true. But the theory is not then necessarily or certainly true in the way that a sound deductive argument's conclusion is necessarily or certainly true. Inference to the best explanation, like other forms of induction, cannot guarantee the truth of the best explanation. That is, it is not truth-preserving. The best theory we have may actually be false. Nevertheless, we would have excellent reasons for supposing our best theory to be a true theory.

The criteria of adequacy are *testability*, *fruitfulness*, *scope*, *simplicity*, and *conservatism*. Let's examine each one in detail.

TESTABILITY

Most of the theories that we encounter every day and all the theories that scientists take seriously are **testable**—*there is some way to determine whether the theories are true or false.* If a theory is untestable—if there is no possible procedure for checking its truth—then it is of little or no help in increasing our understanding. Suppose someone says that an invisible, undetectable spirit is causing your headaches. What possible test could we perform to tell if the spirit actually exists? None. So the spirit theory is entirely empty. We can assign no weight to such a claim.

Here's another way to look at it. Theories are explanations, and explanations are designed to increase our understanding of the world. But an untestable theory does not—and cannot—explain anything. It is equivalent to saying that an unknown thing with unknown properties acts in an unknown way to cause a phenomenon—which is the same thing as offering no explanation at all.

We often run into untestable theories in daily life, just as scientists sometimes encounter them in their work. Many practitioners of alternative medicine claim that health problems are caused by an imbalance in people's *chi*, an unmeasurable form of mystical energy that is said to flow through everyone. Some people say that their misfortunes are caused by God or the Devil. Others believe that certain events in their lives happen (and are inevitable) because of fate. And parents may hear their young daughter say that she did not break the lamp, but her invisible friend did.

Many theories throughout history have been untestable. Some of the more influential untestable theories include the theory of witches (some people called witches are controlled by the Devil), the moral fault theory of disease (immoral behavior causes illness), and the divine placement theory of fossils (God created geological fossils to give the false impression of an ancient Earth).

But what does it mean for a theory to be testable or untestable? A theory is testable *if it predicts something other than what it was introduced to explain.* Suppose your electric clock stops each time you touch it. One theory to explain this event is that there is an electrical short in the clock's wiring. Another theory is that an invisible, undetectable demon causes the clock to stop. The wiring theory predicts that if the wiring is repaired, the clock will no longer shut off when touched. So it is testable—there is something that the theory predicts other than the obvious fact that the clock will stop when you touch it. But the demon theory makes no predictions about anything, *except* the obvious, the very fact that the theory was introduced to explain. It predicts that the clock will stop if you touch it, but we already know this. So our understanding is not increased, and the demon theory is untestable.

Now, if the demon theory says that the demon can be detected with x-rays, then there is something the theory predicts other than the clock's stopping when touched. You can x-ray the clock and examine the film for demon silhouettes. If the theory says that the demon can't be seen but can be heard with sensitive sound equipment, then you have a prediction, something to look for other than clock stoppage.

So other things being equal, testable theories are superior to untestable ones; they may be able to increase our understanding of a phenomenon. But an untestable theory is just an oddity.

FRUITFULNESS

Imagine that we have two testable theories, theory 1 and theory 2, that attempt to explain the same phenomenon. Theory 1 and theory 2 seem comparable in most respects when measured against the criteria of adequacy. Theory 1, however, successfully predicts the existence of a previously unknown entity, say, a star in an uncharted part of the sky. What would you conclude about the relative worth of these two theories?

If you thought carefully about the issue, you would probably conclude that theory 1 is the better theory—and you would be right. Other things being equal, theories that perform this way—that successfully predict previously unknown phenomena—are more credible than those that don't. They are said to be **fruitful**, to yield new insights that can open up whole new areas of research and discovery. This fruitfulness suggests that the theories are more likely to be true.

If a friend of yours is walking through a forest where she has never been before, yet she seems to be able to predict exactly what's up ahead, you would probably conclude that she possessed some kind of accurate information about the forest, such as a map. Likewise, if a theory successfully predicts some surprising state of affairs, you are likely to think that the predictions are not just lucky guesses.

All empirical theories are testable (they predict something beyond the thing to be explained). But fruitful theories are testable and then some. They not only predict something, they predict something that no one expected. The element of surprise is hard to ignore.

Decades ago Einstein's theory of relativity gained a great deal of credibility by successfully predicting a phenomenon that was extraordinary and entirely novel. The theory predicts that light traveling close to massive objects (such as stars) will appear to be bent because the space around such objects is curved. The curve in space causes a curve in nearby light rays. At the time, however, the prevailing opinion was that light always travels in straight lines—no bends, no curves, no breaks. In 1919 the physicist Sir Arthur Eddington devised a way to test this prediction.

He managed to take two sets of photographs of exactly the same portion of the sky—when the sun was overhead (in daylight) and when it was not (at night). He was able to get a good photo of the sky during daylight because there was a total eclipse of the sun at the time. If light rays really were bent when they passed near massive objects, then stars whose light passes near the sun should appear to be shifted slightly from their true position (as seen at night). Eddington discovered that stars near the sun did appear to have moved and that the amount of their apparent movement was just what the theory predicted. This novel prediction then demonstrated the fruitfulness of Einstein's theory, provided a degree of confirmation for the theory, and opened up new areas of research.

So the moral is that other things being equal, fruitful theories are superior to those that aren't fruitful. Certainly many good theories make no novel predictions but are accepted nonetheless. The reason is usually that they excel in other criteria of adequacy.

SCOPE

Suppose theory 1 and theory 2 are two equally plausible theories to explain phenomenon X. Theory 1 can explain X well, and so can theory 2. But theory 1 can explain or predict *only* X, whereas theory 2 can explain or predict X—as well as phenomena Y and Z. Which is the better theory?

We must conclude that theory 2 is better because it explains more diverse phenomena. That is, it has more **scope** than the other theory. The more a theory explains or predicts, the more it extends our understanding. And the more a theory explains or predicts, the less likely it is to be false because it has more evidence in its favor.

A major strength of Newton's theory of gravity and motion, for example, was that it explained more than any previous theory. Then came Einstein's theory of relativity. It could explain everything that Newton's theory could explain plus many phenomena that Newton's theory could not explain. This increased scope of Einstein's theory helped convince scientists that it was the better theory.

Here's a more down-to-earth example. For decades psychologists have known about a phenomenon called *constructive perception* (discussed in Chapter 7). In constructive perception what we perceive (see, hear, feel, etc.) is determined in part by what we expect, know, or believe. Studies have shown that when people expect to perceive a certain stimulus (say, a flashing light, a certain color or shape, a shadow), they often *do* perceive it, even if there is no stimulus present. The phenomenon of constructive perception then can be used to explain many instances in which people seem to perceive something when it is not really there or when it is actually very different from the way people think it is.

One kind of case that investigators sometimes explain as an instance of constructive perception is the UFO sighting. Many times people report seeing lights in the night sky that look to them like alien spacecraft, and they explain their perception by saying that the lights were caused by alien spacecraft. So we have two theories to explain the experience: constructive perception and UFOs from space. If these two theories differ only in the degree of scope provided by each one, however, we must conclude that the constructive-perception theory is better. (In reality, theories about incredible events usually differ on several criteria.) The constructive-perception theory can explain not only UFO sightings but all kinds of ordinary and extraordinary experiences—hallucinations, feelings of an unknown "presence," misidentification of crime suspects, contradictory reports in car accidents, and more. The UFO theory, however, is (usually) designed to explain just one thing: an experience of seeing strange lights in the sky.

Scope is often a crucial factor in a jury's evaluation of theories put forth by both the prosecution and the defense. The prosecution will have a very powerful case against the defendant if the prosecutor's theory (that the defendant did it) explains all the evidence and many other things while the defense theory (innocence) does not. The defendant would be in big trouble if the prosecutor's theory explains the blood on the defendant's shirt, the eyewitness accounts, the defendant's fingerprints on the wall, and the sudden change in his usual routine—*and* the innocence theory renders these facts downright mysterious.

Other things being equal, then, the best theory is the one with the greatest scope. And if other things aren't equal, a theory with superior scope doesn't necessarily win the day because it may do poorly on the other criteria—or another theory might do better.

SIMPLICITY

Suppose you want to explain why your car didn't start this morning, and you consider the theory that the car's battery is dead (theory 1), along with four other theories:

> Theory 2: Each night, you are sabotaging your own car while you sleepwalk.
>
> Theory 3: Your 90-year-old uncle, who lives a thousand miles away from you, has secretly been going for joyrides in your car, damaging the engine.
>
> Theory 4: A poltergeist (a noisy, mischievous ghost) has damaged the car's carburetor.
>
> Theory 5: Yesterday, you accidentally drove the car through an alternative space-time dimension, scrambling the electrical system.

By now you probably suspect that these explanations are somehow unacceptable, and so they are. One important characteristic that they each lack is **simplicity**. Other things being equal, the best theory is the one that is the simplest—that is, the one that makes the fewest assumptions. The theory making the fewest assumptions is less likely to be false because there are fewer ways for it to go wrong. Another way to look at it is that since a simpler theory is based on fewer assumptions, less evidence is required to support it.

Theories 4 and 5 lack simplicity because they each must assume the existence of an unknown entity (poltergeists and another dimension that scrambles electrical circuits). Such assumptions about the existence of unknown objects, forces, and dimensions are common in occult or paranormal theories. Theories 2 and 3 assume no new entities, but they do assume complex chains of events. This alone makes them less plausible than theory 1, the dead battery explanation.

The criterion of simplicity has often been a major factor in the acceptance or rejection of important theories. For example, scientists eventually accepted Copernicus's theory of planetary motion (heliocentric orbits) over Ptolemy's (Earth-centered orbits) because the former was simpler (see the next section). In order to account for apparent irregularities in the movement of certain planets, Ptolemy's theory had to assume that planets have extremely complex orbits (orbits within orbits). Copernicus's theory, however, had no need for so much extra baggage. His theory could account for the observational data without so many orbits-within-orbits.

Sometimes a theory's lack of simplicity is the result of constructing ad hoc hypotheses. An **ad hoc hypothesis** is one that cannot be verified independently of the phenomenon it's supposed to explain. If a theory is in trouble because it is not matching up with the observational data of the phenomenon, you might be able to rescue it by altering it—by positing additional entities or properties that can account for the data. Such tinkering is legitimate (scientists do it all the time) if there is an independent way of confirming the existence of these proposed entities and properties. But if there is no way to verify their existence, the modifications are ad hoc hypotheses. Ad hoc hypotheses always make a theory less simple—and therefore less credible.

CONSERVATISM

What if a trusted friend told you that—believe it or not—some dogs lay eggs just as chickens do? Let's assume that your friend is being perfectly serious and believes what she is saying. Would you accept this claim about egg-laying dogs? Not likely. But why not?

Probably your main reason for rejecting such an extraordinary claim would be that it fails the criterion of **conservatism**, though you probably wouldn't state it that way. (Note: This sense of "conservatism" *has nothing to do with political parties*.) This criterion says that other things being equal, *the best theory is the one that fits best with our well-established beliefs*—that is, with beliefs backed by excellent evidence or very good arguments. We would reject the canine-egg theory because, among other things, it conflicts with our well-founded beliefs about mammals, evolution, canine anatomy, and much more. Humans have an enormous amount of experience with dogs (scientific and otherwise), and none of it suggests that dogs can lay eggs. In fact, a great deal of what we know about dogs suggests that they *cannot* lay eggs. To accept the canine-egg theory despite its conflicting with a mountain of solid evidence would be irrational—and destructive of whatever understanding we had of the subject.

Perhaps one day we may be shocked to learn that—contrary to all expectations and overwhelming evidence—dogs do lay eggs. But given that this belief is contrary to a massive amount of credible experience, we must assign a very low probability to it.

What kind of beliefs fall into the category of "well-established" knowledge? For starters, we can count beliefs based on our own everyday observations that we have no good reasons to doubt (such as "it's raining outside," "the parking lot is empty," and "the train is running late today"). We can include basic facts about the world drawn from excellent authority ("Earth is round," "men have walked on the moon," and "Cairo is the capital of Egypt"). And we can include a vast array of beliefs solidly supported by scientific evidence, facts recognized as such by most scientists ("cigarettes cause lung cancer," "vaccines prevent disease," "dinosaurs existed," and "germs cause infection").

Many of our beliefs, however, cannot be regarded as well established. Among these, of course, are all those we have good reasons to doubt. But there is also a large assortment of beliefs that occupy the middle ground between those we doubt and those we have excellent reasons to believe. We may have some reasons in favor of these beliefs, but those reasons are not so strong that we can regard the beliefs as solid facts. We can only proportion our belief to the evidence and be open to the possibility that we may be wrong. Very often such claims reside in areas that are marked by controversy—politics, religion, ethics, economics, and more. Among these notions, we must walk cautiously, avoid dogmatism, and follow the evidence as best we can. We should not assume that the claims we have absorbed from our upbringing and culture are beyond question.

That being said, there are good reasons for respecting the criterion of conservatism, properly understood. We are naturally reluctant to accept explanations that conflict with what we already know, and we should be. Accepting beliefs that fly in the face of our well-supported knowledge has several risks:

1. The chances of the new belief being true are not good (because it has no evidence in its favor, while our well-established beliefs have plenty of evidence on their side).
2. The conflict of beliefs undermines our knowledge (because we cannot know something that is in doubt, and the conflict would be cause for doubt).
3. The conflict of beliefs lessens our understanding (because the new beliefs cannot be plausibly integrated into our other beliefs).

So everything considered, the more conservative a theory is, the more plausible it is.[4]

Here's another example. Let's say that someone claims to have built a perpetual motion machine. This type of machine is supposed to function without ever stopping and without requiring any energy input from outside the machine; it is designed to continuously supply its own energy.

Now, this is an intriguing idea—that we shouldn't take too seriously. The problem is that the notion of a perpetual motion machine is not conservative at all. It conflicts with a very well-established belief—namely, one of the scientific laws of thermodynamics. The law of conservation of mass-energy says that mass-energy cannot be created or destroyed. A perpetual motion machine, though, would have to create energy out of nothing. Like any law of nature, however, the law of conservation of mass-energy is supported by a vast amount of empirical evidence. We must conclude, then, that it is extremely unlikely that anyone could escape the law of conservation of mass-energy through the use of any machine. (This fact, however, has not stopped countless optimistic inventors from claiming that they've invented such devices. When the devices are put to the test, they invariably fail to perform as advertised.)

It's possible, of course, that a new theory that conflicts with what we know could turn out to be right and a more conservative theory wrong. But we would need good reasons to show that the new theory was correct before we would be justified in tossing out the old theory and bringing in the new.

Science looks for conservative theories, but it still sometimes embraces theories that are departures (sometimes *radical* departures) from the well-worn, accepted explanations. When this dramatic change happens, it's frequently because other criteria of adequacy outweigh conservatism.

We will look at other examples shortly, but before going further, we need to understand two crucial points about the nature of theory appraisal.

First, there is no strict formula or protocol for applying the criteria of adequacy. In deductive arguments there are rules of inference that are precise and invariable. But inference to the best explanation is a different animal. There are no precise rules for applying the criteria, no way to quantify how a theory measures up according to each criterion, and no way to rank each criterion according to its importance. Sometimes we may assign more weight to the criterion of scope if the theory in question seems comparable to other theories in terms of all the remaining criteria. Other times we may weight simplicity more when considering theories that seem equally conservative or fruitful. The process of theory evaluation is not like solving a math problem—but more like diagnosing an illness or making a judicial decision. It is rational but not formulaic, and it depends on the dynamics of human judgment. The best we can do is follow some guidelines for evaluating theories generally and for applying the criteria of adequacy. Fortunately, this kind of help is usually all we need.

Second, despite the lack of formula in theory assessment, the process is far from subjective or arbitrary. There are many distinctions that we successfully make every day that are not quantifiable or formulaic—but they are still objective. We cannot say exactly when day turns into night or when a person with a full head of hair becomes bald or when a puddle in the rain becomes a pond, but our distinctions between night and day or baldness and hirsuteness or puddles and ponds are clearly objective. Of course, there are cases that are not so clear-cut that give rise to reasonable disagreement among reasonable people. But there are also many instances that are manifestly unambiguous. Pretending that these states of affairs are unclear would be irrational. It would simply be incorrect to believe that broad daylight is nighttime or that a puddle is a pond.

What's Wrong with Conspiracy Theories?

Conspiracy theories try to explain events by positing the secret participation of numerous conspirators. The assassination of JFK, the terrorist attacks of 9/11, the death of Elvis Presley, the UFO crash at Roswell, the Great Recession of 2008, the NASA moon landings, the bloodline of Jesus Christ—all these and more have been the subject of countless conspiracy theories, both elaborate and provocative. Online they are everywhere. Some conspiracy theories, of course, have been found to be true after all. But most of them are implausible or absurd. The main problem with them is that they fail the criteria of adequacy, especially the criterion of *simplicity*. They would have us make numerous assumptions that raise more questions than they answer: How do the conspirators manage to keep their activities secret? How do they control all the players? Where is the evidence that all the parts of the conspiracy have come together just so?

As we have seen, for any set of facts, it is shockingly easy to devise a theory that fits them, but this fit alone cannot establish the truth of the theory. That's why we must apply the criteria of adequacy to sort out the plausible theories from the implausible. Very often the set of alleged facts that are supposed to back up the theory are not facts at all. They are unsupported assertions coughed up by a fevered social media and red-hot political conflicts.

For those who eagerly believe them, conspiracy theories are what scientists call *nonfalsifiable hypotheses*: There is no possible evidence that believers would accept as counting against their beloved theory. Every piece of counterevidence is dismissed, ignored, chalked up to a government cover-up, or interpreted as actually confirming the theory.

There is no escape from this prison of the mind except through critical thinking—through a fair weighing of the evidence, a careful consideration of alternative theories, and an unwillingness to believe without good reason.

 **Section Query**

Have you ever accepted a conspiracy theory? If so, how well did it pass the criterion of simplicity? To you, was the theory nonfalsifiable?

8.4 Telling Good Theories from Bad

Many (perhaps most) theories that you run into every day are easy to assess. They are clearly the best (or not the best) explanations for the facts at hand. The dog barked because someone approached the house. Your friend blushed because he was embarrassed. The senator resigned because of a scandal. In such cases, you may make inferences to the best explanation (using some or all of the criteria of adequacy) without any deep reflection. But at other times, you may need and want to be more deliberate, to think more carefully about which explanation is really best. In either case, it helps to have a set of guidelines that tells you how your inquiry *should* proceed if you're to make cogent inferences. Here, then, is the **TEST formula**, four steps to finding the best explanation:

Step 1. State the **T**heory and check for consistency.
Step 2. Assess the **E**vidence for the theory.
Step 3. **S**crutinize alternative theories.
Step 4. **T**est the theories with the criteria of adequacy.

Step 1. State the theory and check for consistency. Before you can evaluate a theory, you must express it in a statement that's as clear and specific as possible. Once you do this, you can check to see if the theory meets the minimum requirement for consistency. If it fails the consistency test, you can have no good grounds for believing that it's correct. And, obviously, if the theory fails step 1, there's no reason to go to step 2.

Step 2. Assess the evidence for the theory. To critically evaluate any theory, you must understand any reasons in its favor—the empirical evidence or logical arguments that may support or undermine it. Essentially, this step involves an honest assessment of the empirical evidence relevant to the truth (or falsity) of the theory. To make this assessment, you must put to use what you already know about the credibility of sources, logical argument, and evidence from personal and scientific observations (topics covered in Chapters 2 and 7).

In this step, you may discover that the evidence in favor of a theory is strong, weak, or nonexistent. You may find that there is good evidence that seems to count against the theory. Or you may learn that the phenomenon under investigation did not occur at all. Whatever the case, you must have the courage to face up to reality. You must be ready to admit that your favorite theory has little to recommend it.

Step 3. Scrutinize alternative theories. Inference to the best explanation will not help us very much if we aren't willing to consider alternative explanations. Simply examining the evidence relevant to an eligible theory is not enough. To get to the truth, we must abandon motivated reasoning.

Theories can often appear stronger than they really are if we don't bother to compare them with others. To take an outrageous example, consider this theory designed to explain the popularity and seeming omnipresence of an American icon: Mickey Mouse is not an animated character but a living, breathing creature that lives in Hollywood.

The evidence for this explanation is the following: (1) Millions of people (mostly children) worldwide believe that Mickey is real; (2) Walt Disney (Mickey's alleged creator) always talked about Mickey as if the mouse was real; (3) millions of ads, books, movies, and TV shows portray Mickey as real; (4) it's possible that through millions of years of Earth's history a biological creature with Mickey's physical characteristics could have evolved; and (5) some say that if enough people believe that Mickey is real, then—through psychic wish fulfillment or some other paranormal process—he will become real.

Now, you don't believe that Mickey is real (do you?), even in the face of reasons 1–5. But you might admit that the Mickey theory is starting to sound more plausible. And if you never hear any alternative explanations—and in motivated reasoning, you *never* hear any alternative explanations—you might eventually become a true believer. (Anthropologists can plausibly argue that various cultures have come to believe in many very unlikely phenomena and exotic deities in large part because of *a lack of alternative explanations*.)

When you do consider an alternative explanation—for example, that Mickey is an imaginary character of brilliant animation marketed relentlessly to the world—the Mickey-is-real theory looks ridiculous. And once you consider the evidence for this alternative theory (for example, documentation that Walt Disney created Mickey with pen and ink and that countless marketing campaigns have been launched to promote his creation), the other explanation looks even sillier.

Step 3 requires us to have an open mind, to think outside the box, to ask if there are other ways to explain the phenomenon in question and to consider the evidence for those theories. Specifically, in this step we must conscientiously look for competing theories *and then apply both step 1 and step 2 to each one of them*. This process may leave us with many or few eligible theories to examine. In any case, it's sure to tell us something important about the strength or weakness of competing theories.

Many times the criteria of adequacy can help us do a preliminary assessment of a theory's plausibility without our surveying alternative theories. For example, a theory may do so poorly regarding a particular criterion that we can conclude that, whatever the merits of alternative explanations, the theory at hand is not very credible. Such a clear lack of credibility is often apparent when a theory is obviously neither simple nor conservative.

Skipping step 3 is an extremely common error in the evaluation of explanations of all kinds. It is a supreme example of many types of errors discussed in earlier chapters—overlooking evidence, preferring available evidence, looking only for confirming evidence, and denying the evidence.

Step 3 goes against our grain. The human tendency is to grab hold of a favorite theory—and to halt any further critical thinking right there. Our built-in bias is to seize on a theory immediately—because we find it comforting or because we just "know" it's the right one—and then ignore or resist all other possibilities. The result is a greatly increased likelihood of error and delusion and a significantly decreased opportunity to achieve true understanding.

Step 4. Test the theories with the criteria of adequacy. As we've seen, simply toting up the evidence for each of the competing theories and checking to see which one gets the highest score will not do. We need to measure the plausibility of the theories using the criteria of adequacy. The criteria can help us put any applicable evidence in perspective and allow us to make a judgment about theory plausibility even when there's little or no evidence to consider.

By applying the criteria to all the competing theories, we can often accomplish several important feats. We may be able to eliminate some theories immediately, assign more weight to some than others, and distinguish between theories that at first glance seem equally strong.

The best way to learn how to do step 4, as well as steps 1–3, is by example. Watch what happens when we assess the plausibility of the following theories—Copernican planetary motion, evolution, and climate change—using the TEST formula.

Copernicus versus Ptolemy

Consider the historic clash between the geocentric (Earth-centered) and the heliocentric (sun-centered) theories of planetary motion. It's difficult to imagine two rival theories that have more profoundly influenced how humanity views itself and its place in the universe.

In the beginning was the geocentric view. Aristotle got things going by putting forth the theory that a spherical Earth was at the center of a spherical universe consisting of a series of concentric, transparent spheres. On one celestial sphere we see the sun, the moon, and the known planets. On the outermost sphere we behold the stars. All the heavenly bodies rotate in perfect circles around the stationary Earth. The heavenly bodies are pure, incorruptible, and unchanging; Earth is impure, corruptible, and transient.

Then came the great astronomer and mathematician Ptolemy, who flourished in Alexandria between 127 and 148 CE. He discovered inconsistencies in the traditional geocentric system between the predicted and observed motions of the planets. He found, in other words, that Aristotle's theory was not conservative, a crucial failing. So he fine-tuned the old view, adding little circular motions (called epicycles) along the planet orbits and many other minor adjustments. He also allowed for an odd asymmetry in which the center of planet orbits was not exactly the center of Earth—all this so the theory would match up to astronomical observations. By the time Ptolemy finished tinkering, he had posited 80 circles and epicycles—80 different planetary motions—to explain the movements of the sun, moon, and five known planets.

The result was a system far more complex than Aristotle's was. But the revised theory worked well enough for the times, and it agreed better than the earlier theory did with observational data. Despite the complications, learned people could use Ptolemy's system to calculate the positions of the planets with enough accuracy to effectively manage calendars and astrological charts. So for 15 centuries, astronomers used Ptolemy's unwieldy, complex theory to predict celestial events and locations. In the West, at least, Earth stood still in the center of everything as the rest of the universe circled around it.

The chief virtue of the Ptolemaic system, then, was conservatism. It fit, mostly, with what astronomers knew about celestial goings-on. It was also testable, as any scientific theory should be. Its biggest failing was simplicity—or the lack thereof. The theory was propped up by numerous assumptions for the purpose of making the theory fit the data.

Enter Nicolaus Copernicus (1473–1543). He was disturbed by the complexity of Ptolemy's system. It was a far cry from the simple theory that Aristotle bequeathed to the West. Copernicus proposed a heliocentric theory in which Earth and the other planets orbit the sun, the true center of the universe. In doing so, he greatly simplified both the picture of the heavens and the calculations required to predict the positions of planets.

Copernicus's theory was simpler than Ptolemy's on many counts, but one of the most impressive was retrograde motion, a phenomenon that had stumped astronomers for centuries. From time to time, certain planets seem to reverse their customary direction of travel across the skies—to move backward! Ptolemy explained this retrograde motion by positing yet more epicycles, asserting that planets orbiting Earth will often orbit around a point on the larger orbital path. Seeing these orbits within orbits from Earth, an observer would naturally see the planets sometimes backing up.

But the Copernican theory could easily explain retrograde motion without all those complicated epicycles. As the outer planets (Mars, Jupiter, Saturn) orbit the sun, so does Earth, one of the inner planets. The outer planets, though, move much slower than Earth does. On its own orbital track, Earth sometimes passes the outer planets as they lumber along on their orbital track, just as a train passes a slower train on a parallel track. When this happens, the planets appear to backward, just as the slower train seems to reverse course when the faster train overtakes it.

Copernicus's theory, however, was not superior on every count. It explained a great many astronomical observations, but Ptolemy's theory did too, so they were about even in scope. It had no big advantage in fruitfulness over the Ptolemaic system. It made no impressive predictions of unknown phenomena. Much more troubling, it seemed to conflict with some observational data.

One test implication of the Copernican theory is the phenomenon known as *parallax*. Critics of the heliocentric view claimed that if the theory were true, then as Earth moved through its orbit, stars closest to it should seem to shift their position relative to stars farther away. There should, in other words, be parallax. But no one had observed parallax.

Copernicus and his followers responded to this criticism by saying that stars were too far away for parallax to occur. As it turned out, they were right about this, but confirmation didn't come until 1832 when parallax was observed with more powerful telescopes.

Another test implication seemed to conflict with the heliocentric model. Copernicus reasoned that if the planets rotate around the sun, then they should show phases just as the moon shows phases due to the light of the sun falling on it at different times. But in Copernicus's day, no one could see any such planetary phases. Fifty years later, though, Galileo used his new telescope to confirm that Venus had phases.

Ultimately, scientists accepted the Copernican model over Ptolemy's because of its simplicity—despite what seemed at the time like evidence against the theory. As Copernicus said, "I think it is easier to believe this [sun-centered view] than to confuse the issue by assuming a vast number of Spheres, which those who keep the Earth at the center must do."[5]

Evolution versus Creationism

Few scientific theories have been more hotly debated among nonscientists than evolution and its rival, creationism (or creation science). Both theories purport to explain the origin and existence of biological life on Earth, and each claims to be a better explanation than the other. Can science decide this contest? Yes. Despite the complexity of the issues involved and the mixing of religious themes with the nonreligious, good science can figure out which theory is best. Remember that the best theory is the one that explains the phenomenon and measures up to the criteria of adequacy better than any of its competitors. There is no reason that the scientific approach cannot provide an answer here—even in this thorniest of thorny issues.

Neither the term "evolution" nor the concept began with Charles Darwin (1809–1882), the father of evolutionary theory. The word showed up in English as early as 1647. The ancient Greek philosopher Anaximander (c. 611–547 BCE) was actually the first evolutionary theorist, inferring from some simple observations that humans must have evolved from an animal and that this evolution must have begun in the sea. But in his famous book *On the Origin of Species* (1859), Darwin distilled the theory of evolution into its most influential statement.

Scientists have been fine-tuning the theory ever since, as new evidence and new insights pour in from many different fields, such as biochemistry and genetics. But the basic idea has not changed: Living organisms adapt to their environments through inherited characteristics; this adaptation results in changes in succeeding generations. Specifically, the offspring of organisms differ physically from their parents in various ways, and these differences can be passed on genetically to their offspring. If an offspring has an inherited trait (such as sharper vision or a larger brain) that increases its chances of surviving long enough to reproduce, the individual is more likely to survive and pass the trait on to the next generation. After several generations, this useful trait, or adaptation, spreads throughout a whole population of individuals, differentiating the population from its ancestors. *Natural selection* is the name that Darwin gave to this process.

Creation science, on the other hand, maintains that (1) the universe and all life was created suddenly, out of nothing, only a few thousand years ago (6000 to 10,000 is the usual range); (2) natural selection could not have produced living things from a single organism; (3) species change very little over time; (4) man and apes have a separate ancestry; and (5) Earth's geology can be explained by catastrophism, including a worldwide flood.[6]

The first thing we should ask about these two theories is whether they're testable. The answer is *yes*. Recall that a theory is testable if it predicts or explains something other than what it was introduced to explain. On this criterion, evolution is surely testable. It explains, among other things, why bacteria develop resistance to antibiotics, why there are so many similarities between humans and other primates, why new infectious diseases emerge, why the chromosomes of closely related species are so similar, why the fossil record shows the peculiar progression of fossils that it does, and why the embryos of related species have such similar structure and appearance.

Creationism is also testable. It, too, explains something other than what it was introduced to explain. It claims that Earth's geology was changed in a worldwide flood, that the universe is only a few thousand years old, that all species were created at the same time, and that species change very little over time.

Innumerable test implications have been derived from evolutionary theory, and innumerable experiments have been conducted, confirming the theory. For example, if evolution is true, then we would expect to see systematic change in the fossil record from simple creatures at the earlier levels to more complex individuals at the more recent levels. We would expect not to see a reversal of this configuration. And this sequence is exactly what scientists see time and time again.

Creationism, however, has not fared as well. Its claims have not been borne out by evidence. In fact, they have consistently conflicted with well-established scientific findings.

This latter point means that creationism fails the criterion of conservatism—it conflicts with what we already know. For example, the scientific evidence shows that Earth is not 6000 to 10,000 years old—but billions of years old. According to the National Academy of Sciences,

> There are no valid scientific data or calculations to substantiate the belief that Earth was created just a few thousand years ago. [There is a] vast amount of evidence for the great age of the universe, our galaxy, the Solar system, and Earth from astronomy, astrophysics, nuclear physics, geology, geochemistry, and geophysics. Independent scientific methods consistently give an age for Earth and the Solar system of about 5 billion years, and an age for our galaxy and the universe that is two to three times greater.[7]

Creationism also fails the criterion of conservatism on the issue of a geology-transforming universal flood:

> Nor is there any evidence that the entire geological record, with its orderly succession of fossils, is the product of a single universal flood that occurred a few thousand years ago, lasted a little longer than a year, and covered the highest mountains to a depth of several meters. On the contrary, intertidal and terrestrial deposits demonstrate that at no recorded time in the past has the entire planet been under water.... The belief that Earth's sediments, with their fossils, were deposited in an orderly sequence in a year's time defies all geological observations and physical principles concerning sedimentation rates and possible quantities of suspended solid matter.[8]

Has either theory yielded any novel predictions? Evolution has. It has predicted, for example, that new species should still be evolving today; that the fossil record should show a movement from older, simpler organisms to younger, more complex ones; that proteins and chromosomes of related species should be similar; and that organisms should adapt to changing environments. These and many other novel predictions have been confirmed. Creationism has made some novel claims, as we saw earlier, but none of these have been supported by good evidence. Creationism is not a fruitful theory.

The criterion of simplicity also draws a sharp contrast between the two theories. Simplicity is a measure of the number of assumptions that a theory makes. Both theories make assumptions, but creationism assumes much more. Creationism assumes the existence of a creator and unknown forces. Proponents of creationism readily admit that we do not know how the creator created nor what creative processes were used.

In this contest of theories, the criterion of scope—the amount of diverse phenomena explained—is probably more telling than any of the others. Biological evolution explains a vast array of phenomena in many

Can We See Evolution?

Critics of the theory of evolution often ask, "If evolution occurs, why can't we see it?" Here's how the National Academy of Sciences responds to this objection:

> Scientific conclusions are not limited to direct observation but often depend on inferences that are made by applying reason to observations. Even with the launch of Earth-orbiting spacecraft, scientists could not directly see the Earth going around the Sun. But they inferred from a wealth of independent measurements that the Sun is at the center of the solar system. Until the recent development of extremely powerful microscopes, scientists could not observe atoms, but the behavior of physical objects left no doubt about the atomic nature of matter. Scientists hypothesized the existence of viruses for many years before microscopes became powerful enough to see them.
>
> Thus, for many areas of science, scientists have not directly observed the objects (such as genes and atoms) or the phenomena (such as the Earth going around the Sun) that are now well-established facts. Instead, they have confirmed them indirectly by observational and experimental evidence. Evolution is no different. . . .
>
> This contention that nobody has seen evolution occurring further ignores the overwhelming evidence that evolution has taken place and is continuing to occur. The annual changes in influenza viruses and the emergence of bacteria resistant to antibiotics are both products of evolutionary forces. Another example of ongoing evolution is the appearance of mosquitoes resistant to various insecticides, which has contributed to a resurgence of malaria in Africa and elsewhere. The transitional fossils that have been found in abundance since Darwin's time reveal how species continually give rise to successor species that, over time, produce radically changed body forms and functions. It also is possible to directly observe many of the specific processes by which evolution occurs. Scientists regularly do experiments using microbes and other model systems that directly test evolutionary hypotheses.[9]

fields of science. In fact, a great deal of the content of numerous scientific fields—genetics, physiology, biochemistry, neurobiology, and more—would be deeply perplexing without the theory of evolution. As the eminent geneticist Theodosius Dobzhansky put it, "Nothing in biology makes sense except in the light of evolution."[10]

Virtually all scientists would agree—and go much further:

> It helps to explain the emergence of new infectious diseases, the development of antibiotic resistance in bacteria, the agricultural relationships among wild and domestic plants and animals, the composition of Earth's atmosphere, the molecular machinery of the cell, the similarities between human beings and other primates, and countless other features of the biological and physical world.[11]

And

> Evolution provides a scientific explanation for why there are so many different kinds of organisms on Earth and how all organisms on this planet are part of an evolutionary lineage. It demonstrates why some organisms that look quite different are in fact related, while other organisms that may look similar are only distantly related. It accounts for the appearance of humans on Earth and reveals our species' biological connections with other living things. It details how different groups of humans are related to each other and how we acquired many of our traits. It enables the development of effective new ways to protect ourselves against constantly evolving bacteria and viruses.[12]

Creationism, however, can explain none of this. And it provokes, not solves, innumerable mysteries: What caused the worldwide flood? Where did all that water come from? Where did it all go? Why does Earth seem so ancient (when it's said to be so young)? How did the creator create the entire universe suddenly—out of nothing? Why does the fossil record seem to suggest evolution and not creation? So many questions are an indication of diminished scope and decreased understanding.

Good scientists must be prepared to admit this much: If creationism meets the criteria of adequacy as well as evolution does, then creationism must be as good a theory as evolution. But creationism fails to measure up to the criteria of adequacy. On every count it shows itself to be inferior. Scientists, then, are justified in rejecting creationism in favor of evolution. And this is exactly what they do.

For some people, all this talk about science, criteria, and evidence is irrelevant. They reject evolution because they think it's incompatible

Evolution and Intelligent Design

A controversial view known as intelligent design (ID) is a common conceptual challenge to evolution, maintaining that biological life is much too complex to be fully explained by evolutionary processes. Some claim that life on Earth is best explained by the intervention of a supreme intelligence. Michael Behe, professor of biochemistry at Lehigh University, famously argues that some biological systems are so profoundly intricate—so "irreducibly complex"—that they could not have been produced by gradual evolutionary changes. Only an intelligent designer can account for such complexity. He says that an irreducibly complex system (for example, the eye) is composed of several interconnected, perfectly matched parts such that if even one part is missing, the system will not function. An eye can improve the survival prospects of organisms only if it functions, and proper functioning requires that each of its parts is there to do its job. According to evolution, the eye came about through slow, incremental changes. But, Behe asks, how can an unfinished, nonfunctioning eye improve survival? This shows, he argues, that the eye and all other irreducibly complex systems were created whole—not through evolution, but by some great intelligence.

But most biologists deny that the development of irreducibly complex systems through natural selection is physically impossible. Behe thinks natural selection requires that a complex system be formed by gradual addition of components until a functioning model is achieved. But critics point out that the components can be present all along or arise at different times, performing tasks that improve various processes. Then, because of a change in the genome, the parts may be put to new uses, forming an irreducibly complex structure. For example,

> Evolutionary biologists also have demonstrated how complex biochemical mechanisms, such as the clotting of blood or the mammalian immune system, could have evolved from simpler precursor systems. With the clotting of blood, some of the components of the mammalian system were present in earlier organisms, as demonstrated by the organisms living today (such as fish, reptiles, and birds) that are descended from these mammalian precursors. Mammalian clotting systems have built on these earlier components.
>
> Existing systems also can acquire new functions. For example, a particular system might have one task in a cell and then become adapted through evolutionary processes for different use.[13]

From the fact that biologists generally do not know precisely how each step of such a process happens, it does not follow that the process is impossible or unknowable. Philip Kitcher, professor of philosophy at Columbia, thinks that the remedy for our ignorance of these matters is more and better research, not the presumption of an intelligent designer:

> Even if intelligent designers were right in supposing that the phenomena they indicate couldn't have evolved by natural selection, only a more explicit identification of the causal mechanism that was at work could justify the conclusion that that mechanism is intelligent.[14]

with religion. Many religious believers, religious scientists, and religious denominations, however, would strongly disagree. Science does prove that some religious beliefs are unfounded—like the notions that Earth is only a few thousand years old, that Earth underwent a worldwide flood, and that new species of living things cannot evolve over time. But millions of religious people—many Christians, Hindus, Muslims, Jews, and Buddhists—see no contradiction between evolution and their religious beliefs. Denominations that have accepted evolution include the Roman Catholic Church, the Presbyterian Church, the United Methodist Church, the United Church of Christ, the Episcopal Church, the Evangelical Lutheran Church of America, and others.

A letter signed by more than 15,000 Christian clergy members, compiled by the Clergy Letter Project, declares,

> We the undersigned, Christian clergy from many different traditions, believe that the timeless truths of the Bible and the discoveries of modern science may comfortably coexist. We believe that the theory of evolution is a foundational scientific truth, one that has stood up to rigorous scrutiny and upon which much of human knowledge and achievement rests. To reject this truth or to treat it as "one theory among others" is to deliberately embrace scientific ignorance and transmit such ignorance to our children. We believe that among God's good gifts are human minds capable of critical thought and that the failure to fully employ this gift is a rejection of the will of our Creator.[15]

Some religious scientists hold similar views. For example, Francis Collins, director of the Human Genome Project and of the National Human Genome Research Institute at the National Institutes of Health, says,

> In my view, there is no conflict in being a rigorous scientist and a person who believes in a God who takes a personal interest in each one of us. Science's domain is to explore nature. God's domain is in the spiritual world, a realm not possible to explore with the tools and language of science. It must be examined with the heart, the mind, and the soul.[16]

Climate Change

The first thing to understand about the empirical question of climate change—whether it's happening and, if so, why—is that it's a *scientific* question. What people should *do* about it is a moral, political, or policy question. An elementary mistake in critical thinking comes from letting your views on the latter dictate your assessment of the former.

A larger difficulty in sorting out the facts is that much of the media coverage does not do the science justice. Matthew C. Nisbet, professor of communication, public policy, and urban affairs at Northeastern

University and editor-in-chief of the journal *Environmental Communication*, explains the problem like this:

> At the opinion-leading legacy print publications such as *The Guardian* or *Washington Post*, and at newer digital-native outlets such as *HuffPost* (formerly *The Huffington Post*) or *Buzzfeed*, the challenge in most instances is not the amount of coverage but how the risks and solutions to climate change are characterized. Studies conducted by social scientists in the United States and Europe using statistical techniques to rigorously evaluate hundreds of news stories show that journalists frequently gloss over the uncertainties and caveats inherent in a single study or line of climate change research, neglect to report on the varying predictions offered by different climate models, and fail to include in their reporting the careful language that the Intergovernmental Panel on Climate Change (IPCC) has developed to qualify the likelihood of various consequences of climate change. In coverage of major climate change-related events such as a new IPCC report or United Nations summit, journalists also tend to dramatize their significance by emphasizing the most calamitous future climate change scenarios, framing a new scientific report's findings in terms of disastrous and fear-inducing risks, rather than emphasizing in the face of those risks opportunities to protect health or sustainably grow economies. Reviewing available studies, the German journalism researcher Michael Bruggeman concludes that reporting too often "simplifies science and turns context-dependent and preliminary findings into established facts."[17]

So to make headway in understanding climate change, we must proceed as we would when delving into any other politically inflamed, complex issue that science addresses. We must be especially alert to fake news and media bias, fallacious appeals to authority and unsupported claims, confirmation bias and evidence denial. And we must, of course, apply the criteria of adequacy to competing theories.

For years, scientists throughout the world have been issuing unsettling reports and dire warnings about changes in Earth's climate. The Climate Science Special Report (CSSR), one of many statements issued by scientific organizations worldwide, says, "Global annually averaged surface air temperature has increased by about 1.8 degrees Fahrenheit (1.0 degrees C) over the last 115 years (1901–2016). This period is now the warmest in the history of modern civilization."[18]

Such a rise may seem small, but it can lead to huge, potentially cataclysmic effects worldwide. According to the Intergovernmental Panel on Climate Change (IPCC), a group of 1300 independent scientific experts worldwide,

Each of the last three decades has been successively warmer at the Earth's surface than any preceding decade since 1850. The period from 1983 to 2012 was likely the warmest 30-year period of the last 1400 years in the Northern Hemisphere, where such assessment is possible (medium confidence).[19]

Earth has always undergone natural eras of warming and cooling, but scientists say this current period of planet-heating is different. They assert that there is a greater than 95 percent probability that it is caused by human activity, and the changes are happening at an unprecedented rate.

Climate scientists say the planet is heating up because of the greenhouse effect: The heat of solar radiation is being trapped in the lower atmosphere by so-called greenhouse gases. These include carbon dioxide (CO_2), methane, and nitrous oxide, all of which have increased dramatically in the atmosphere since before the Industrial Revolution. Some of the increase comes from natural sources like volcanic eruptions, but most of it has been traced to human activity such as the burning of fossil fuels (coal, oil, and gas), as well as to deforestation and land use changes. The IPCC asserts,

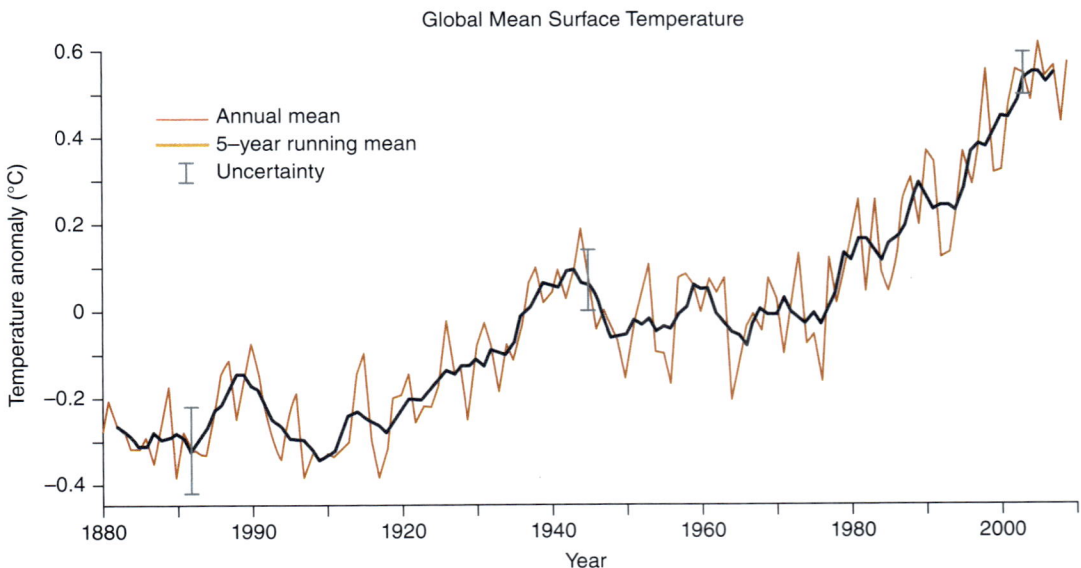

Fig. 8.1 Despite ups and downs from year to year, global average surface temperature is rising. By the beginning of the 21st century, Earth's temperature was roughly 0.5 degrees Celsius above the long-term (1951–1980) average. (NASA figure adapted from Goddard Institute for Space Studies Surface Temperature Analysis.)

Anthropogenic [human-caused] greenhouse gas emissions have increased since the pre-industrial era, driven largely by economic and population growth, and are now higher than ever. This has led to atmospheric concentrations of carbon dioxide, methane and nitrous oxide that are unprecedented in at least the last 800,000 years. Their effects, together with those of other anthropogenic drivers, have been detected throughout the climate system and are extremely likely to have been the dominant cause of the observed warming since the mid-20th century.[20]

This global warming has already had powerful effects on the planet. These have been both positive and negative but, on balance, mostly negative. NASA declares in its report "Global Climate Change: Vital Signs of the Planet,"

Glaciers have shrunk, ice on rivers and lakes is breaking up earlier, plant and animal ranges have shifted and trees are flowering sooner.

Effects that scientists had predicted in the past would result from global climate change are now occurring: loss of sea ice, accelerated sea level rise and longer, more intense heat waves.[21]

According to the U.S. Global Change Research Program, there are many effects of climate change that are happening now in the United States and are likely to continue:

Northeast. Heat waves, heavy downpours and sea level rise pose growing challenges to many aspects of life in the Northeast. Infrastructure,

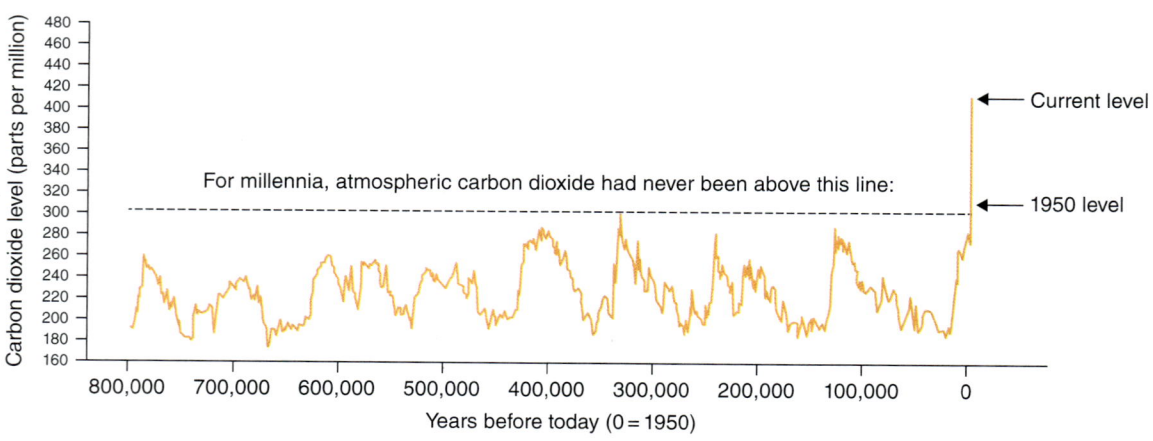

Fig. 8.2 This graph, based on the comparison of atmospheric samples contained in ice cores and more recent direct measurements, provides evidence that atmospheric CO_2 has increased since the Industrial Revolution. (Published by NASA. Credit: Luthi, D., et al., 2008; Etheridge, D.M., et al., 2010; Vostok ice core data/J.R. Petit et al.; NOAA Mauna Loa CO_2 record.)

agriculture, fisheries and ecosystems will be increasingly compromised. Many states and cities are beginning to incorporate climate change into their planning.

Northwest. Changes in the timing of streamflow reduce water supplies for competing demands. Sea level rise, erosion, inundation, risks to infrastructure and increasing ocean acidity pose major threats. Increasing wildfire, insect outbreaks and tree diseases are causing widespread tree die-off.

Southeast. Sea level rise poses widespread and continuing threats to the region's economy and environment. Extreme heat will affect health, energy, agriculture and more. Decreased water availability will have economic and environmental impacts.

Midwest. Extreme heat, heavy downpours and flooding will affect infrastructure, health, agriculture, forestry, transportation, air and water quality, and more. Climate change will also exacerbate a range of risks to the Great Lakes.

Southwest. Increased heat, drought and insect outbreaks, all linked to climate change, have increased wildfires. Declining water supplies, reduced agricultural yields, health impacts in cities due to heat, and flooding and erosion in coastal areas are additional concerns.[22]

Climate change and global warming are controversial mostly because of their political and policy implications. If the planet really is becoming overheated, and if the main cause of the warming is increased levels of greenhouse gases produced by the burning of fossil fuels, then it seems that the obvious solution is to implement major reductions in the burning of these fuels. But such reductions would disrupt or drastically alter the economic, commercial, and industrial systems that now run on the fuels—changes that many people strongly oppose.

There is little doubt that climate change is happening, but there is considerable disagreement among many nonscientists about *why* it's happening. So the question is, What is the best explanation of the climate-change data? Let's consider a few of the more popular theories.

Theory 1: *Global warming is due to Earth's natural cycles of warming and cooling over time and doesn't have much to do with human activities.* Evidence for this view comes from Earth's climate history, which scientists have documented:

> Earth has experienced climate change in the past without help from humanity. We know about past climates because of evidence left in tree rings, layers of ice in glaciers, ocean sediments, coral reefs, and layers of sedimentary rocks. For example, bubbles of air in glacial ice trap tiny samples of Earth's atmosphere, giving scientists a history of greenhouse gases that stretches

Is It Too Late to Prevent Climate Change?

Here is NASA's answer:

Humans have caused major climate changes to happen already, and we have set in motion more changes still. Even if we stopped emitting greenhouse gases today, global warming would continue to happen for at least several more decades, if not centuries. . . .

In the absence of major action to reduce emissions, global temperature is on track to rise by an average of 6 °C (10.8 °F), according to the latest estimates. Some scientists argue a "global disaster" is already unfolding at the poles of the planet; the Arctic, for example, may be ice-free at the end of the summer melt season within just a few years. Yet other experts are concerned about Earth passing one or more "tipping points"—abrupt, perhaps irreversible changes that tip our climate into a new state.

But it may not be too late to avoid or limit some of the worst effects of climate change.

Responding to climate change will involve a two-tier approach: 1) "mitigation"—reducing the flow of greenhouse gases into the atmosphere; and 2) "adaptation"—learning to live with, and adapt to, the climate change that has already been set in motion. The key question is: what will our emissions of carbon dioxide and other pollutants be in the years to come? Recycling and driving more fuel-efficient cars are examples of important behavioral change that will help, but they will not be enough. Because climate change is a truly global, complex problem with economic, social, political and moral ramifications, the solution will require both a globally-coordinated response (such as international policies and agreements between countries, a push to cleaner forms of energy) and local efforts on the city- and regional-level (for example, public transport upgrades, energy efficiency improvements, sustainable city planning, etc.). It's up to us what happens next.[23]

back more than 800,000 years. The chemical make-up of the ice provides clues to the average global temperature.

Using this ancient evidence, scientists have built a record of Earth's past climates, or "paleoclimates." The paleoclimate record combined with global models shows past ice ages as well as periods even warmer than today.[24]

But this support for theory 1 is weak because these warming/cooling cycles cannot explain Earth's relatively recent surge in global temperatures:

The paleoclimate record also reveals that the current climatic warming is occurring *much more rapidly* than past warming events.

As the Earth moved out of ice ages over the past million years, the global temperature rose a total of 4 to 7 degrees Celsius over about 5,000 years. In the past century alone, the temperature has climbed 0.7 degrees Celsius, roughly ten times faster than the average rate of ice-age-recovery warming.

Models predict that Earth will warm between 2 and 6 degrees Celsius in the next century. When global warming has happened at various times in the past two million years, it has taken the planet about 5,000 years to warm 5 degrees. The predicted rate of warming for the next century is at least 20 times faster. This rate of change is extremely unusual.[25]

Theory 2: *Global warming is caused not by human activity but by surges in the sun's energy*. We know that the sun affects Earth's climate system. Subtle changes in Earth's orbit around the sun have caused the advances and retreats of the ice ages, and scientists have documented the sun's natural 11-year cycle of decreases and increases in solar radiation. But these facts do not show that global warming is propelled by the sun and not human activity. NASA scientists explain why:

> The warming we've seen over the last few decades is too rapid to be linked to changes in Earth's orbit, and too large to be caused by solar activity.
>
> One of the "smoking guns" that tells us the Sun is not causing global warming comes from looking at the amount of the Sun's energy that hits the top of the atmosphere. Since 1978, scientists have been tracking this using sensors on satellites and what they tell us is that there has been no upward trend in the amount of the Sun's energy reaching Earth.
>
> A second smoking gun is that if the Sun were responsible for global warming, we would expect to see warming throughout all layers of the atmosphere, from the surface all the way up to the upper atmosphere (stratosphere). But what we actually see is warming at the surface and cooling in the stratosphere. This is consistent with the warming being caused by a build-up of heat-trapping gases near the surface of the Earth, and not by the Sun getting "hotter."[26]

Theory 3: *The idea that human-caused global warming exists is a fraud perpetuated by a conspiracy of scientists*. The evidence for this charge is nonexistent. In 2009, a controversy, now labeled Climategate, arose when servers at the University of East Anglia in the United Kingdom were hacked and emails between climate scientists were stolen and published on the internet. Many people alleged that the stolen emails showed that the scientists had suppressed or falsified climate data and that this revelation was proof that global warming was a conspiracy. Pennsylvania State University, the U.K. House of Commons Science and Technology Committee, the U.S. Department of Commerce Inspector General, and the National Science Foundation launched inquiries and concluded that no scientific misconduct was involved. But even if the allegations against the scientists were true, that alone would not prove that there is no human-made global warming nor that there is a conspiracy of scientists bent on promoting a lie. Conspiracy or no conspiracy, the case for human-caused warming is backed by a vast array of evidence gathered for decades by independent scientists throughout the world.

In addition, theory 3 suffers from the same weaknesses that plague conspiracy theories generally: It fails criteria of adequacy. It fails the criterion of scope because it provides no evidence about who the conspirators are and how they were able to conspire together to fake or suppress evidence and to fool thousands of other scientists. So it doesn't really explain anything. It fails the criterion of simplicity because it makes a host of assumptions—that there are conspiring scientists, that they can follow a global-warming agenda in their research without raising suspicions, that they can coordinate their activities, that they can keep their conspiracy secret, that the scientific community would not discover the deception, that they would risk their careers and reputation to falsify their findings, that their employers and institutions would not figure out what they were really up to, and so on. The theory is not conservative because it conflicts with human nature, with what we know about the way scientists and scientific organizations work, and with the behavior and values of scientists themselves. It also conflicts with what science has already firmly established—that human activity caused and is causing global warming.

Theory 4: *Global warming is happening, and human activity is the cause.* An enormous number of scientific studies and observations demonstrate that Earth is getting warmer. According to the National Academy of Sciences,

> Earth's average surface air temperature has increased by about 0.8 °C (1.4 °F) since 1900, with much of this increase taking place since the mid-1970s. A wide range of other observations (such as reduced Arctic sea ice extent and increased ocean heat content) and indications from the natural world (such as poleward shifts of temperature-sensitive species of fish, mammals, insects, etc.) together provide incontrovertible evidence of planetary-scale warming.
>
> The clearest evidence for surface warming comes from widespread thermometer records. In some places, these records extend back to the late 19th century. Today, temperatures are monitored at many thousands of locations, over both the land and ocean surface. Indirect estimates of temperature change from such sources as tree rings and ice cores help to place recent temperature changes in the context of the past. In terms of the average surface temperature of Earth, these indirect estimates show

that 1983 to 2012 was probably the warmest 30-year period in more than 800 years.

A wide range of other observations provides a more comprehensive picture of warming throughout the climate system. For example, the lower atmosphere and the upper layers of the ocean have also warmed, snow and ice cover are decreasing in the Northern Hemisphere, the Greenland ice sheet is shrinking, and sea level is rising. These measurements are made with a variety of monitoring systems, which gives added confidence in the reality that Earth's climate is warming.[27]

The evidence that this warming is human-caused is extensive, consistent, and multidimensional. From 1800 to 2012, the a major greenhouse gas carbon dioxide has increased in the atmosphere by about 40 percent—from about 280 parts per million by volume to about 380 parts per million. As carbon dioxide has increased, so has global surface temperature, and scientists have been able to link the carbon dioxide directly to human activities:

> Measurements of different forms of carbon (isotopes) reveal that this increase is due to human activities. Other greenhouse gases (notably methane and nitrous oxide) are also increasing as a consequence of human activities. The observed global surface temperature rise since 1900 is consistent with detailed calculations of the impacts of the observed increase in atmospheric CO_2 (and other human-induced changes) on Earth's energy balance.
>
> Different influences on climate have different signatures in climate records. These unique fingerprints are easier to see by probing beyond a single number (such as the average temperature of Earth's surface), and looking instead at the geographical and seasonal patterns of climate change. The observed patterns of surface warming, temperature changes through the atmosphere, increases in ocean heat content, increases in atmospheric moisture, sea level rise, and increased melting of land and sea ice also match the patterns scientists expect to see due to rising levels of CO_2 and other human-induced changes.[28]

Some people have claimed that this global warming must be due to natural (nonhuman) causes. But scientists have demonstrated that this is not the case:

> The expected changes in climate are based on our understanding of how greenhouse gases trap heat. Both this fundamental understanding of the physics of greenhouse gases and fingerprint studies show that natural

causes alone are inadequate to explain the recent observed changes in climate. Natural causes include variations in the Sun's output and in Earth's orbit around the Sun, volcanic eruptions, and internal fluctuations in the climate system (such as El Niño and La Niña). Calculations using climate models have been used to simulate what would have happened to global temperatures if only natural factors were influencing the climate system. These simulations yield little warming, or even a slight cooling, over the 20th century. Only when models include human influences on the composition of the atmosphere are the resulting temperature changes consistent with observed changes.[29]

Most actively publishing climate scientists—97 percent—affirm that global warming is happening now and that humans are causing it. Eighteen American scientific societies and 11 international science academies concur. A joint statement from the American scientific organizations says,

> Observations throughout the world make it clear that climate change is occurring, and rigorous scientific research demonstrates that the greenhouse gases emitted by human activities are the primary driver.[30]

Now let's apply the criteria of adequacy to our four theories.

Theory 1 (natural cycles of warming and cooling) is testable and simple, and it has some scope, since natural variations in Earth's climate can explain ice ages and some warming periods. But it is not fruitful, because it has predicted no previously unknown entities or processes. Its worst fault, however, is that it fails the criterion of conservatism: It conflicts with established facts about the magnitude and pattern of global warming. Scientists understand the nature of Earth's normal cycles of warming and cooling, but these climate variations do not match the scientific data regarding the planet's abnormal rise in temperature.

Theory 2 (solar energy changes) is testable and simple and has some scope, since it explains phenomena involved in Earth's 11-year cycle of decreases and increases in solar radiation. But it isn't fruitful since it has predicted no new phenomena. Worst of all, like theory 1, it falls short on the criterion of conservatism because solar radiation cycles don't correspond to the documented patterns of global warming.

Theory 3 (conspiracy of scientists) is the worst of the competing theories. As noted earlier, it is neither simple nor conservative, and it is without scope—it explains nothing.

If the World Is Warming, Why Are Some Winters and Summers Still Very Cold?

Snow, ice, and frigid weather may occur even while global warming is happening. The U.S. National Academy of Sciences and the United Kingdom's Royal Society explain why:

> Global warming is a long-term trend, but that does not mean that every year will be warmer than the previous one. Day to day and year to year changes in weather patterns will continue to produce some unusually cold days and nights, and winters and summers, even as the climate warms.
>
> Climate change means not only changes in globally averaged surface temperature, but also changes in atmospheric circulation, in the size and patterns of natural climate variations, and in local weather. La Niña events shift weather patterns so that some regions are made wetter, and wet summers are generally cooler. Stronger winds from polar regions can contribute to an occasional colder winter. In a similar way, the persistence of one phase of an atmospheric circulation pattern known as the North Atlantic Oscillation has contributed to several recent cold winters in Europe, eastern North America, and northern Asia.
>
> Atmospheric and ocean circulation patterns will evolve as Earth warms and will influence storm tracks and many other aspects of the weather. Global warming tilts the odds in favour of more warm days and seasons and fewer cold days and seasons. For example, across the continental United States in the 1960s there were more daily record low temperatures than record highs, but in the 2000s there were more than twice as many record highs as record lows. Another important example of tilting the odds is that over recent decades heatwaves have increased in frequency in large parts of Europe, Asia and Australia.[31]

Theory 4 is by far the best of the four theories. It is testable, simple, fruitful, and conservative. It has successfully predicted some previously unknown phenomena, including global sea level rise, melting of land and sea ice, retreating glaciers, and warming of the atmosphere. These successful predictions make the theory fruitful. And of course it is conservative because it is consistent with scientific laws, well-supported theories, and established facts.

Section Query

1. Do you think evolution can be compatible with religious beliefs? Why or why not?
2. Do you believe climate change is being caused by human activity? Why or why not?

8.5 How the Media Get Science Wrong

Science sheds its light on the world and helps us distinguish between what is real and what is not. But the media are prisms that can sometimes distort that light. Too often the science news that floods our feeds is not just slightly inaccurate; it's not even close to what the science actually says. The resulting headlines can range from silly to ludicrous to morbid:

- Scientists Say Smelling Farts Might Prevent Cancer (*Time Magazine*)
- Why Oreos May Be as Addictive as Cocaine (*Forbes*)
- "Horns" are growing on young people's skulls. Phone use is to blame, research suggests. (*Washington Post*)
- More people have died from selfies than shark attacks this year. (*Mashable*)

But false or misleading science news, whether amusing or not, can also alarm us unnecessarily and lead us to change our lives for no good reason. For example,

- Bacon Gives Kids Cancer (U.K. *Daily Mirror*)
- Asparagus link to breast cancer is discovered by scientists. (*Evening Standard*)
- Junk Food in Pregnancy Leaves Children Fat for Life (U.K. *Daily Mirror*)
- Sugar as Addictive as Cocaine, Heroin (*New York Daily News*)
- Eat Less Meat, Live Longer? (*New York Times*)

And some science news can lead to harm by encouraging unproven or risky treatments and unsafe habits:

- Vitamin D: Supplement Linked to Weight Loss in Overweight and Obese Children (*Newsweek*)
- Ketamine Shows Promise as Treatment for Adolescents with Depression (*Newsweek*)
- Does Echinacea Really Work Against Colds? (*Time Magazine*)

We can add to this list a few stories highlighted by comedian John Oliver in his funny and right-on-target takedown of bad science reporting:

- Drinking a glass of red wine is equivalent to an hour at the gym.
- Sugar might make cancer grow.

- Pregnant women who eat chocolate every day can improve blood flow to the placenta and benefit the growth and development of their baby.
- Drinking champagne every week may delay dementia and Alzheimer's disease.
- Driving while dehydrated is just as dangerous as driving drunk.

What's going on here? Two things: *hyping the science* and *misunderstanding the science*.

Hyping the Science

Health and medical studies are produced by universities, government and commercial labs, and independent health organizations. When a study is completed, the sponsoring organization announces it to the world by distributing press releases. The point of the releases is to enhance the organization's prestige, gain publicity, or attract future funding. So those who write the releases are under pressure to highlight the most interesting, media-attracting aspects of the research, even when it is highly technical, complicated, and (to most nonscientists) yawn-inducing. The result is often just what you might expect: news releases that are as much hyperbole and distortion as fact.

When news outlets get the releases, they pounce on them, looking for science news they can turn into eye-opening headlines or clickbait and stories that have immediate relevance to the readers. The better reporters from the more responsible news organizations will look beyond the press release for the facts. They will read the original study, talk to the scientists involved,

Fig. 8.3 Screen grab from Fox News report on red wine and exercise.

Fig. 8.4 Screen grab from *Today Show* report on sugar and cancer.

Fig. 8.5 Screen grab from Channel 4 WBZ News report on chocolate and health of mothers and babies.

Fig. 8.6 Screen grab from KTVU report on champagne and dementia.

Fig. 8.7 Screen grab from Fox News report on the dangers of driving while dehydrated.

see what other studies have been done, and ask other scientists in the field what they think of the new research. But other news outfits won't go to all that trouble. They will report what's in the press release, exaggerations and all, and might even add a sexy (and misleading) twist or two of their own. So in too many cases, the original research—which may be solid but preliminary or exploratory—gets distorted twice.

A now infamous example of this double whammy of misrepresentation is the chocolate story mentioned earlier. The story was based on a preliminary study of the effect of high- and low-flavonoid chocolate on the risk of the pregnancy complication known as preeclampsia. The result: The researchers found no significant difference in the rate of preeclampsia between women who ate the two kinds of chocolate. In other words, chocolate didn't help prevent preeclampsia. But the press release issued by a medical society put a more positive spin on the study with the headline "The benefits of chocolate during pregnancy." Several news outlets then covered the story, reporting that chocolate decreases the risk of preeclampsia.[32]

Often the hype in a science story needs no nudge at all from a press release. Consider the *Washington Post* report about horns growing on young people's skulls due to phone use. The study in question was not about phone use, and the "horns" came from a bit of speculation at the end of the study.[33] Steven Novella, science news critic and clinical neurologist at Yale University School of Medicine, puts the study in perspective:

> When I see headlines like that my first questions is always—what did the research actually show? What was the data? In this case the researchers were looking at X-rays of the skull, and particularly at the occipital protuberances. This is a pair of bumps at the back of the head where the posterior neck muscles insert. They found that the risk of having bony spurs or calcifications in the ligaments attaching to the skull (not horns) increased in men, with

forward tilt of the head, and in younger subjects. That's the data. Everything else is the authors' speculation about what these results mean.[34]

Misunderstanding the Science

Scientific studies drive science news reporting, and scientific studies are frequently misunderstood and misconstrued by nonscientists, whether they're journalists or not. But nonscientists don't need to be experts to make some reasonable judgments about the evidence that studies purportedly offer. Many times you can see, as well as any expert can, when a study *does not* establish that a treatment is effective or that factor A causes factor B. You can see this if you understand some basic facts about the nature and limitations of this kind of research.

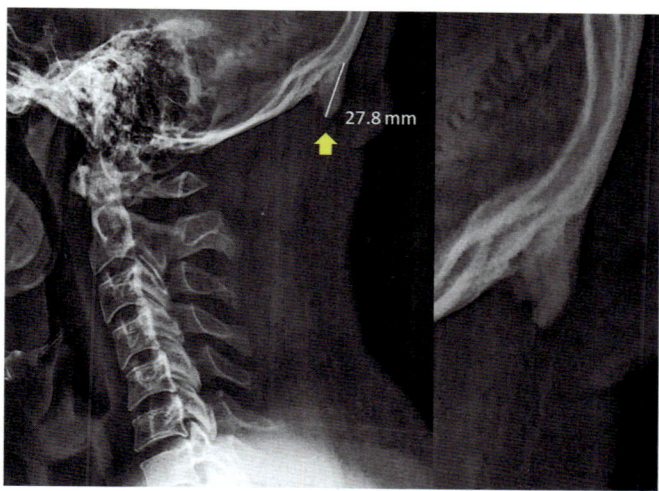

Fig. 8.8 X-rays of bone spurs at the back of the skull.

Recall that the gold standard in medical and health research is the double-blind, randomized, controlled clinical trial, a study configured to minimize bias and error at every step. When this kind of study is conscientiously designed and conducted, it can offer strong and clear support for claims about treatments and cause-and-effect relationships. For all the reasons enumerated earlier, it has both an experimental (treatment) group and a control group; the subjects in the control group get a placebo or a different treatment; neither the subjects nor the experimenters know who receives the real treatment and who receives the placebo; and each group is as much alike as possible to start. If one of these elements is missing, *we have good reason to doubt the results of the study.* (Of course, even if all these elements are present, the study's results can still be comprised by errors in collecting, analyzing, and interpreting the data.)

Other kinds of research can help scientists understand human physiology and disease, but these studies alone also typically *cannot* establish cause and effect. These include the following:

- *Single studies*. In most instances, a single study cannot prove very much. Research is exacting work, and many things can—and do—go wrong. The probability that researchers in any given study have reached false conclusions is high. That's why scientists seek replication—the redoing of a study by different researchers to see if they get the same results. Usually it takes many studies to confirm conclusions. The media like to give the impression that a medical breakthrough has just popped out of a single study, but real breakthroughs almost never happen that way. All of the dubious headlines noted earlier were based on single studies.

- *Small studies.* Studies with only a handful of subjects are very preliminary, usually designed just to probe a question and to see if larger clinical trials should be done. They are *unlikely* to yield strong evidence of cause-and-effect connections. The smaller the study, the greater the chance that some confounding factor will skew the results. The study about dehydration and drunk driving was done on just 12 men; the study on ketamine and depression included just 13 adolescents. The reaction of a conscientious scientist to the findings of a small study is likely to be something like "Gee, I wonder if that's true" or "Let's look into that," not "Wow! A new cure!"

- *Anecdotes and case studies.* Anecdotes are individual stories of personal experience ("Whiskey cured my warts" or "Ginseng boosted my IQ"). But for all the reasons discussed in Chapter 7, anecdotes are very weak evidence. Case studies (or case reports) are doctor's observations of individual patients. These reports can give us important clues about the nature of an illness, but they cannot establish the cause of a disease or confirm the value of a treatment. A doctor's attempt to draw firm conclusions about the effectiveness of a treatment is undermined by all the same confounding factors that controlled studies try to avoid—the placebo effect, overlooked causes, the variable nature of illness, and more.

- *Nonintervention studies.* As we saw earlier, nonintervention studies don't involve intervening in subjects' lives. Their purpose is to search for associations between disease and health habits, body weight, diet, medical conditions, and countless other factors. Nonintervention studies (also known as case-control, cohort, and prospective studies) can involve thousands of subjects, examine scores of factors, and run for years. But despite their size, they *cannot* prove cause-and-effect relationships. They can only reveal correlations that merely suggest possible cause and effect. They can show that vitamin X supplements are consistently linked to liver disease, but they can't demonstrate that vitamin X supplements cause liver disease. Only controlled clinical trials can do that.

  Scientists know it is extremely easy to find correlations among all sorts of things in such studies. It is easy to examine dozens of factors and sift them until associations are found that are "statistically significant" but probably merely coincidental (a practice known as "*p*-hacking"). Through *p*-hacking, we might find links between cell phone use and pregnancy, shirt size and IQ, pet ownership and diabetes, law degrees and cancer, eating bananas and impotence. But probably none of these associations would be causal. The headline about eating meat is based on an observational study that has been accused of *p*-hacking.[35]

- *Animal studies.* Animal studies are invaluable preliminary research, providing clues to the possible effectiveness of drugs, the hazards of chemicals, and the nature of disease. But by themselves, they cannot show that a treatment works in humans or that a food or drug is safe for human consumption. Treatments proven effective in animals usually do not work as hoped in humans. These facts, however, have not stopped the media from insisting that a substance that worked wonders for a rat can do the same for a human being. Studies in mice and rats were the starting points for the headlines about red wine and gym workouts, asparagus and breast cancer, sugar and cancer, champagne and dementia, and Oreos and addiction.

Is All Health News Wrong?

Considering the mountains of hyped and distorted science reporting that we encounter every day, we might be tempted to answer *yes*. But we don't know that for sure. We do know, however, that a disconcertingly large proportion of health news on social media is misleading or untrue.

In 2019, a coalition of scientists, clinicians, and science editors published a study of the scientific accuracy of health news articles. They focused on the top 100 most popular health articles—that is, those that had the highest number of social media "engagements" (shares, comments, and likes). These experts assessed the credibility of each article as Very High, High, Neutral, Low, or Very Low. They found that of the top 10 most popular articles (representing 6.6 million shares), only 3 of them got a high credibility rating. Three of them received a very low credibility rating, meaning that they contained major inaccuracies. Four of them got a medium credibility score: They contained no major inaccuracies but did give misleading information. Perhaps not surprisingly, the most inaccurate articles got the most attention on social media. As the researchers pointed out,

> This result is expected: sensational headlines (as exemplified by these 3 [very low rating] articles) are much more likely to attract social media engagements, as opposed to headlines in which a balanced tone is struck. Coupled with the

fact that clickbait headlines have a tendency to be factually inaccurate (often involving exaggerations and logical fallacies), it is therefore not surprising that scientifically inaccurate stories tend to be more popular on social media than accurate stories. This also highlights a major concern in online credibility, as this means that the general public is more likely to come into contact with misleading information than accurate ones on social media.[36]

These were the top 10 articles ranked by popularity:[37]

1. Federal Study Finds Marijuana 100X Less Toxic Than Alcohol, Safer Than Tobacco
2. Video shows difference between healthy lungs and those of a smoker
3. Benefits of Walking: 8 Ways Walking Regularly Improves Your Health
4. Everything You Know About Obesity Is Wrong
5. World Health Organization Officially Declares Bacon is as Harmful as Cigarettes
6. Have Cold or Flu Symptoms? Here's How to Tell the Difference
7. Stem Cell Treatment Could Be A Game-Changer for MS Patients
8. How Cycling In Old Age Can Keep Your Immune System Young
9. Is everything you think you know about depression wrong?
10. Cause of polycystic ovary syndrome discovered at last

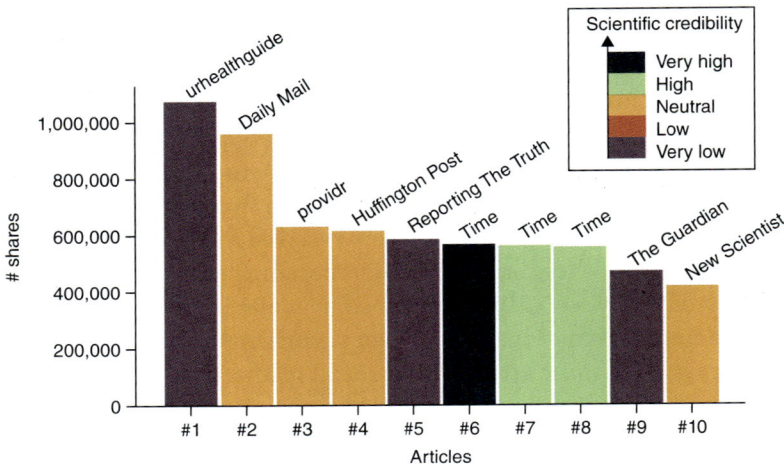

Fig. 8.9   Credibility ratings for the 10 most popular health articles on social media in 2018.

8.5 HOW THE MEDIA GET SCIENCE WRONG

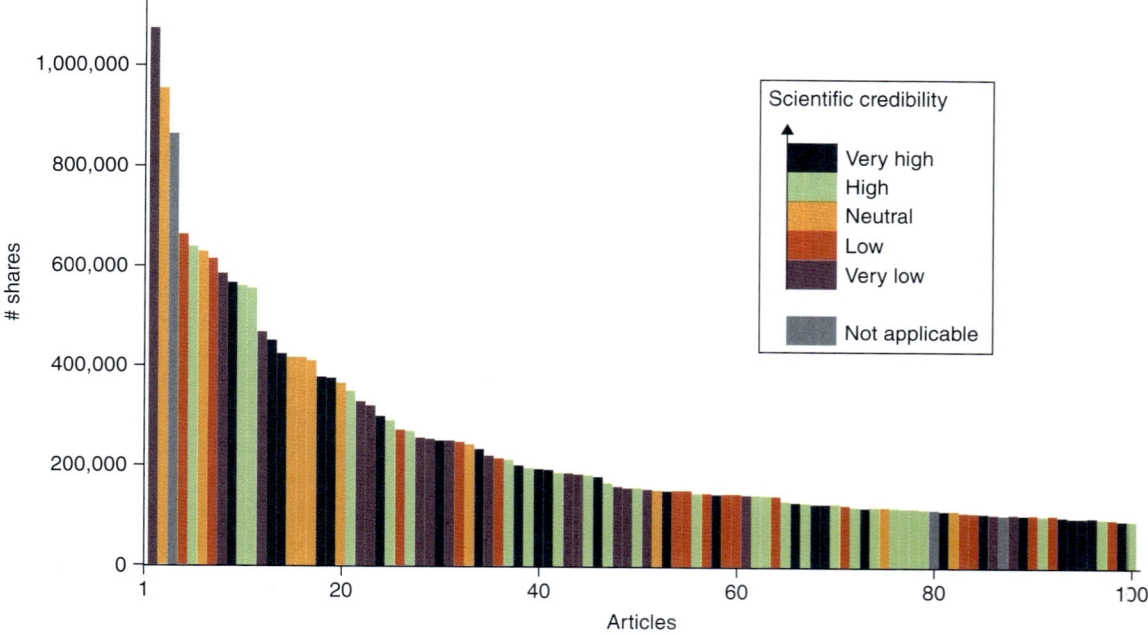

Fig. 8.10 Credibility rating for each of the 100 most popular health articles on social media in 2018.

Less than half of the 100 most popular articles achieved a high credibility rating. The rest had problematic content ranging from exaggerated to confused to false. The number of shares for these dubious articles accounted for almost half of the total shares.

Expert Review of Article 9: "Is Everything You Think You Know about Depression Wrong?"

This article, published in the *Guardian* and shared 469,000 times, was judged by experts as "not credible and potentially harmful." According to their online report,

> This article discusses current scientific thinking behind clinical depression and raises the possibility that clinicians may be treating the condition using the wrong approach, suggesting that most cases of depression are the result of feeling a lack of fulfilment in one's life, instead of a chemical imbalance in the brain. While there are some grains of truth in this, the article is highly misleading in many ways.[38]

One reviewer, whose comments are included on the site, concurs:

> This article is an excerpt from a provocative book written by a lay person who is clearly anti-psychiatry, so there is no pretense of providing evidence (except cherry-picking evidence which supports his views) or a balanced viewpoint. It is full of wild exaggerations, oversimplifications and inaccuracies. Just a few include: . . .
>
> - That all psychiatrists believe that depression is caused only by biochemical changes in the brain—NOT TRUE. All psychiatrists are taught a biopsychosocial model of illness, comprised of biological factors, psychological factors and social factors all working in a complex intertwined relationship (with each factor amenable to evidence-based treatments). . . .
> - That all psychiatrists believe depression is caused by low serotonin and that antidepressant medications work by increasing serotonin—NOT TRUE. That theory was dispelled over 30 years ago and no one believes that there is a single cause for depression. The prevailing theory now is that antidepressant medications work by altering complex biochemical pathways that lead to formation of new brain cells and brain pathways, in effect to allow the brain to better compensate for stress.
> - That all psychiatrists only treat depression with medications—NOT TRUE. All psychiatrists are trained in psychotherapy and use supportive psychotherapy in management of depression. Many psychiatrists also deliver evidence-based psychotherapies (for example, cognitive behavioural therapy or interpersonal psychotherapy).[39]

 **Section Query**

Find one news story that you think does *not* hype or exaggerate the scientific research it's based on.

8.6 Scientific Opinion Polls

Recall from Chapter 2 that in the kind of argument called enumerative induction, we reason from premises about individual members of a group to conclusions about the group as a whole. Enumerative inductions reach a high level of sophistication in the form of scientific opinion polls conducted by professional polling organizations. Opinion polls are used to arrive at generalizations about everything from the outcome of presidential elections to public sentiments about cloning babies to the consumer's appetite for tacos. But as complex as they are, opinion polls are still essentially inductive arguments (or the basis of inductive arguments) and must be judged accordingly.

So, as inductive arguments, opinion polls should (1) be strong and (2) have true premises. More precisely, any opinion poll worth believing must (1) use a large enough sample that accurately represents the target population in all the relevant population features and (2) generate accurate data (the results must correctly reflect what they purport to be about). A poll can fail to meet this latter requirement through data-processing errors, botched polling interviews, poorly phrased questions, and the like.

In national polling, samples need not be enormous to be accurate reflections of the larger target population. Modern sampling procedures used in national polls can produce representative samples that are surprisingly small. Polling organizations such as Gallup and Pew regularly conduct polls in which the target group is American adults (a population of more than 327 million in 2018), and the representative sample consists of only 1000 to 1500 individuals.

How can a sample of 1000 be representative of almost 200 million people? This can be achieved by using **random sampling**. To ensure that a sample is truly representative of the target group, the sample must be selected *randomly* from the target group. In a simple random selection, every member of the target group has an equal chance of being selected for the sample. Imagine that you want to select a representative sample from, say, 1000 people at a football game, and you know very little about the characteristics of this target population. Your best bet for getting a representative sample of this group is to choose the sample members at random. Any nonrandom selection based on preconceived notions about what characteristics are representative will likely result in a biased sample.

Selecting a sample in truly random fashion is easier said than done (humans have a difficult time selecting anything in a genuinely random way). Even a simple process such as your trying to arbitrarily pick names from a list of registered voters is not likely to be truly random. Your choices may be skewed, for example, by unconscious preferences for certain names or by boredom and fatigue. Researchers and pollsters use various techniques to help them get close to true randomization. They may, for instance, assign a number to each member of a population and then use a random-number generator to make the selections.

One approach that definitely does *not* yield a random sample is allowing survey subjects to choose themselves. The result of this process is called a **self-selecting sample**—a type of sample that usually tells you very little about the target population. We would get a self-selecting sample if we publish a questionnaire on a website and ask readers to fill it out and send it in, or if during a TV or radio news broadcast we ask people to cast their vote on a particular issue by clicking options on a website or emailing their responses. In such cases, the sample is likely to be biased in favor of subjects who, for example, just happen to be especially opinionated or passionate; who may have strong views about the topic of the survey and are eager to spout off; or who may simply like to fill out questionnaires. Magazines, newspapers, talk shows, and news programs

How Survey Questions Go Wrong

Many opinion polls are untrustworthy because of flaws in the way the questions are asked. The sample may be large enough and representative in all the right ways, but the poll is still dubious. Here are a few of the more common problems.

Question Phrasing

Poll results can be dramatically skewed simply by the way the questions are worded. A poll might ask, for example, "Are you in favor of a woman's right to kill her unborn child?" The question is ostensibly about a woman's right to terminate a pregnancy through abortion and is supposed to be a fair measure of attitudes on the question. But the wording of the question practically guarantees that a very large percentage of respondents will answer *no*. The controversial and emotionally charged characterization of abortion as the killing of an unborn child would likely persuade many respondents to avoid answering *yes*. More neutral wording of the question would probably elicit a very different set of responses.

Another example: A 1995 poll of African Americans discovered that 95 percent of the sample group approved of a local school voucher program. To get this huge approval rating, the survey question was worded like this: "Do you think that parents in your area should or should not have the right to choose which local schools their children will attend?" Who would want to give up such a right? No wonder the question elicited an overwhelming number of "shoulds."

Such biased wording is often the result of pollster sloppiness. Many other times it's a deliberate attempt to manipulate the poll results. The crucial test of polling questions is whether they're likely to bias responses in one direction or another. Fair questions aren't skewed this way—or are skewed as little as possible.

Question Ordering

The order in which questions are asked in a poll can also affect the poll results. Pollsters know that if the economy is in bad shape and they ask people about the economic mess first and then ask them how they like the president, respondents are likely to give the president lower marks than if the order of the questions were reversed. Likewise, if you're asked specific questions about crimes that have been committed in your hometown and then you're asked if you feel safe from crime, you're more likely to say *no* than if you're asked the questions in reverse order.

Restricted Choices

Opinion polls frequently condense broad spectrums of opinions on issues into a few convenient choices. Some of this condensation is necessary to make the polling process manageable. But some of it is both unnecessary and manipulative, seriously distorting the opinions of those polled. Daniel Goleman of the *New York Times* offers this example: "In one survey... people were asked if they felt 'the courts deal too harshly or not harshly enough with criminals.' When offered just the two options, 6 percent said 'too harshly' and 78 percent answered 'not harshly enough.' But when a third alternative was added—'don't have enough information about the courts to say'—29 percent took that option, and 60 percent answered 'not harshly enough.'"

sometimes acknowledge the use of self-selecting samples by labeling the survey in question as "unscientific." But whether or not that term is used, the media frequently tout the results of such distorted surveys as though the numbers actually proved something.

So a well-conducted poll using a random sample of 1000 to 1500 people can reliably reflect the opinions of the whole adult population. Even so, if a second well-conducted poll is done in exactly the same way, the results will not be identical to those of the first poll. The reason is that every instance of sampling is only an approximation of the results that you would get if you polled every single individual in a target group. And, by chance, each attempt at sampling will yield slightly different results. If you dipped a bucket into a pond to get a one-gallon sample of water, each bucketful would be slightly different in its biological and chemical content—even if the pond's content was very uniform.

Such differences are referred to as the **margin of error** for a particular sampling or poll. Competently executed opinion polls will state their results along with a margin of error. A presidential poll, for example, might say that candidate X will receive 62 percent of the popular vote, plus or minus 3 points (a common margin of error for presidential polls). The usual way of expressing this number is 62 percent ±3. This means that the percentage of people in the target population who will likely vote for candidate X is between 59 and 65 percent.

Connected to the concept of margin of error is the notion of **confidence level**. In statistical theory, the confidence level is the probability that the sample will accurately represent the target group within the margin of error. A confidence level of 95 percent (the usual value) means that there is a 95 percent chance that the results from polling the sample (taking into account the margin of error) will accurately reflect the results that we would get if we polled the entire target population. So if our aforementioned presidential poll has a 95 percent confidence level, we know that there's a 95 percent chance that the sampling results of 62 percent ±3 points will accurately reflect the situation in the whole target group. Of course, this confidence level also means that there's a 5 percent chance that the poll's results will *not* be accurate.

Note that *confidence level* refers only to sampling error, the probability of the sample not accurately reflecting the true values in the target population. It doesn't tell you anything about any other kinds of polling errors such as bias that can occur because of poorly worded questions or researchers who may consciously or unconsciously influence the kinds of answers received.

Sample size, margin of error, and confidence level are all related in interesting ways.

- Up to a point, the larger the sample, the smaller the margin of error because the larger the sample, the more representative it is likely to be. Generally, for national polls, a sample size of 600 yields a margin of error of ±5 points; a sample of 1000, ±4 points; and a sample of 1500, ±3 points. But increasing the sample size substantially to well beyond 1000 does not substantially decrease the margin of error. Boosting the

Mean, Median, and Mode

If you read enough opinion polls, you will surely encounter one of these terms: *mean*, *median*, or *mode*. These concepts are invaluable in expressing statistical facts, but they can be confusing. Mean is simply an average. The mean of these four numbers—6, 7, 4, and 3—is 5 (6 + 7 + 4 + 3 = 20 divided by 4). The median is the middle point of a series of values, meaning that half the values are above the point and half the values are below the point. The median of these eleven values—3, 5, 7, 13, 14, 17, 21, 23, 24, 27, 30—is 17 (the number in the middle). The mode is the most common value. The mode in this series of values—7, 13, 13, 13, 14, 17, 21, 21, 27, 30, 30—is 13 (the most frequently appearing value).

The notions of mean, median, and mode are often manipulated to mislead people. For example, let's say that the dictator of Little Island Nation (population 1000) proposes a big tax cut for everyone, declaring that the mean tax savings will be $5000 (the total tax cut divided by 1000 taxpayers). The Islanders begin to gleefully envision how they will spend their $5000. But then they learn that the mean figure has been skewed higher because of a few millionaires whose tax savings will be $100,000 or more. The tax savings for the vast majority of taxpayers is actually less than $500. The $5000 figure that the dictator tossed out is the true mean—but painfully misleading. To the Islanders, the median tax savings is much more revealing: The median is $400. The mode, the most common figure, is $300. When they get all the facts, the Islanders stage a revolt—the first one in history caused by a better understanding of statistics.

sample from 1500 to 10,000, for example, pushes the margin of error down to only 1 percent.

- The lower the confidence level, the smaller the sample size can be. If you're willing to have less confidence in your polling results, then a smaller sample will do. If you can accept a confidence level of only 90 percent (a 10 percent chance of getting inaccurate results), then you don't need a sample size of 1500 to poll the adult population.
- The larger the margin of error, the higher the confidence level can be. With a large margin of error (±8, for example), you will naturally have more confidence that your survey results will fall within this wide range. This idea is the statistical equivalent of a point made earlier: You can have more confidence in your enumerative inductive argument if you qualify, or decrease the precision of, the conclusion.

An enumerative induction, like any other inductive argument, must be strong and have true premises for us to be justified in accepting the conclusion. A strong enumerative induction must be based on a sample that is both large enough and representative. An opinion poll, as a sophisticated enumerative induction, must use a sufficiently large and representative sample and ensure that the gathered data accurately reflect what's being measured.

Trustworthy Sources in Science and Medicine

American Association for the Advancement of Science (AAAS)
American Physical Society (APS)
Centers for Disease Control and Prevention (CDC)
Committee for Skeptical Inquiry
HealthNewsReview.org
Howtogeek
James Randi Educational Foundation (JREF)
Johns Hopkins Medicine
Live Science
Mayo Clinic
MIT Technology Review
NASA
National Academy of Sciences (NAS)
National Center for Science Education (NCSE)
National Geographic
National Institutes of Health
National Oceanic and Atmospheric Administration (NOAA)
Nature
New Scientist
Public Library of Science (PLOS)
PubMed
Quackwatch
SciCheck
Science
Science Based Medicine
Science Daily
Science.gov
Scientific American
Skeptic
Skeptical Inquirer
Skeptical Raptor
Understanding Science
Union of Concerned Scientists

Section Query

Do you see any disadvantages in trusting the results of an opinion poll based on a self-selecting sample?

REVIEW NOTES

8.1 WHAT SCIENCE IS AND IS NOT

- Science is the careful, systematic search for knowledge and understanding of reality through the formulation, testing, and evaluation of theories.

- Science is not ideology. We can't identify science with a specific worldview. Science is, above all, a *process*.

- Science is not motivated reasoning. Scientific inquiry begins with a question to answer, formulates hypotheses to answer the question, and then tests those hypotheses to see if any of them are true.

- Science is not technology. Science is a way of searching for truth. Technology is not a search for truth; it's the production of products.

8.2 HOW SCIENCE IS DONE

- The **scientific method** cannot be identified with any particular set of experimental or observational procedures because there are many different methods to evaluate the worth of a hypothesis.
- The scientific method involves these steps: identifying a problem or posing a question, devising a hypothesis, deriving a test implication, performing the test, and accepting or rejecting the hypothesis.
- A proper test of a health or medical hypothesis would involve an experimental group and a control group (with either a placebo or alternative treatment), a double-blind design, randomization, and replication.

8.3 JUDGING SCIENTIFIC THEORIES

- The central task of science comes down to asking (and answering) one question: What is the best explanation (theory) for this phenomenon or state of affairs? The best explanation is the one most likely to be true. Science does its most important work, then, through the inductive form of reasoning known as inference to the best explanation.
- Theories must meet the minimum requirement of consistency. They must be both internally consistent and externally consistent.
- An **ad hoc hypothesis** is one that that cannot be verified independently of the phenomenon it's supposed to explain. Ad hoc hypotheses always make a theory less simple—and therefore less credible.
- To judge the worth of theories, scientists use the **criteria of adequacy**, which are **testability**, **fruitfulness**, **scope**, **simplicity**, and **conservatism**.
- The main problem with conspiracy theories is that they fail the criteria of adequacy, especially the criterion of *simplicity*. They would have us make numerous assumptions that raise more questions than they answer.

8.4 TELLING GOOD THEORIES FROM BAD

- The **TEST formula** requires four steps: (1) State the **T**heory and check for consistency, (2) assess the **E**vidence for the theory, (3) **S**crutinize alternative theories, and (4) **T**est the theories with the criteria of adequacy.
- Copernicus's theory was simpler than Ptolemy's on many counts, but one of the most impressive was retrograde motion, a phenomenon that had stumped astronomers for centuries.
- As a theory, creationism fails the criteria of simplicity, conservatism, fruitfulness, and scope. Evolution, however, excels in all the criteria.
- Millions of religious people—many Christians, Hindus, Muslims, Jews, and Buddhists—see no contradiction between evolution and their religious beliefs.
- The empirical question of climate change—whether it's happening and, if so, why—is a *scientific* question. What people should *do* about it is a *moral, political, or policy* question. An elementary mistake in critical thinking comes from letting your views on the latter dictate your assessment of the former.
- There is general agreement that climate change is happening. The central dispute is over why.
- Theories to explain why climate change is happening include (1) Earth's natural cycles of warming and cooling, (2) surges in the sun's activity, (3) a conspiracy of scientists, and (4) human activity. The first three theories fail several of the criteria of adequacy. Theory 4 (human activity) comes out a winner on all the criteria.

- Most actively publishing climate scientists—97 percent—affirm that global warming is happening now and that humans are causing it. Eighteen American scientific societies and 11 international science academies concur.

8.5 HOW THE MEDIA GET SCIENCE WRONG

- Science news is often hyped twice—once by press releases from universities and science organizations and once by news media that then add their own hype.
- Nonscientists don't need to be experts to make some reasonable judgments about the evidence that studies purportedly offer. Many times you can see, as well as any expert can, when a study *does not* establish that a treatment is effective or that factor A causes factor B.
- Cause and effect generally cannot be established by single studies, small studies, anecdotes, case studies, nonintervention studies, and animal studies.
- It is not the case that all health news is wrong, but research shows that a large proportion of it is misleading or untrue.

8.6 SCIENTIFIC OPINION POLLS

- Important concepts in scientific opinion polling include **random sampling**, **self-selecting sample**, **margin of error**, and **confidence level**.
- A poll cannot be trusted if the sample is not random or not representative, the questions are phrased improperly, or the sample is self-selected.

KEY TERMS

ad hoc hypothesis
confidence level
conservatism
criteria of adequacy
fruitfulness

margin of error
random sampling
scientific method
scope
self-selecting sample

simplicity
TEST formula
testability

EXERCISES

Exercises marked with an asterisk (*) have answers in "Answers to Exercises" (Appendix B).

Exercise 8.1

1. How does science differ from technology?
2. What is the scientific method?
3. Can science be identified with a particular worldview?
4. According to the text, what is motivated reasoning?
5. According to the text, why is science such a reliable way of knowing?
*6. What are the five steps of the scientific method?
7. Can hypotheses be generated through induction? Why or why not?

8. What does it mean to derive a test implication from a theory?

*9. What is the conditional argument reflecting the fact that a theory is disconfirmed?

10. What is the conditional argument reflecting the fact that a theory is confirmed?

11. Can theories be conclusively confirmed? Why or why not?

*12. Can theories be conclusively disconfirmed? Why or why not?

13. What are the essential elements of a clinical trial testing whether high doses of vitamin C can increase the survival time of people with terminal cancer?

14. What's the point of including a placebo group in a clinical trial?

15. What is a nonintervention study?

*16. Asking what is the best explanation, or theory, for this state of affairs is to engage in what form of inductive reasoning?

17. What are the scientific criteria of adequacy?

18. What is the TEST formula?

19. What are three kinds of scientific studies that cannot establish cause and effect?

*20. In terms of critical thinking, what is the main problem with conspiracy theories?

Exercise 8.2

For each of the following phenomena, devise a hypothesis to explain it and derive a test implication to test the hypothesis.

1. In a recent study of scientific literacy, women performed better than men in understanding the scientific process and in answering questions about basic scientific facts and concepts.

*2. Jamal found giant footprints in his backyard and mysterious tufts of brown fur clinging to bushes in the area. Rumors persist that Bigfoot, the giant primate unknown to science, is frequenting the area. Two guys living nearby also claim to be perpetrating a hoax about the existence of the creature.

3. A man with a gun entered a mall in Chicago and began shooting randomly at shoppers, shouting something about demons using his body to commit horrible acts.

4. For years after the tragedy of September 11, 2001, there were no major terrorist attacks in the United States.

5. The CIA reviewed the president's State of the Union speech before he gave it and verified that the intelligence information in the speech was correct. Later it was found that some of the information was erroneous and based on dubious sources.

*6. Weight trainers swear that the supplement creatine dramatically increases their performance.

7. Many people who take B vitamins for their headaches report a lower incidence of headaches.

8. There is currently no evidence supporting the idea that garlic can lower the risk of coronary artery disease.

9. When John got home, he found that the lock on his door had been broken and his TV was missing.

10. The economic gap between the very rich and the very poor widened considerably in 2018.

11. Automobile accidents on Blind Man's Curve have increased lately, especially since the streetlight was broken and not replaced.

*12. Juan was found two hours after the fatal stabbing, sitting in Central Park with blood on his shirt.

Exercise 8.3

Using your background knowledge and reliable information gleaned from internet searches, devise a competing theory for each of the following and then apply the criteria of adequacy to both of them—that is, ascertain how well each theory does in relation to its competitor on the criteria of testability, fruitfulness, scope, simplicity, and conservatism.

1. Phenomenon: People report feeling less pain after trying acupuncture.
   Theory: Treatment with acupuncture needles can alleviate pain.

2. Phenomenon: In the United States in 2014, a few people contracted the Ebola virus even though none of them had traveled recently to places in Africa known to be the source of the virus.
   Theory: The virus was carried from Africa to the United States by trade winds in the Atlantic Ocean.

*3. Phenomenon: The unexpected melting of massive chunks of the world's glaciers.
   Theory: Global climate change.

4. Phenomenon: A rare species of fungus grows in only one place in the world—the wing tips of a beetle that inhabits caves in France.
   Theory: Evolution.

5. Phenomenon: As the job market worsens, blacks lose jobs faster than whites.
   Theory: Racial prejudice.

6. Phenomenon: The psychic was able to recount a number of personal details about a recently deceased person he never met.
   Theory: Psychic ability.

*7. Phenomenon: A large proportion of the terrorist attacks in the world in the past five years have been perpetrated by religious fanatics.
   Theory: Religion fosters terrorism.

8. Phenomenon: Twenty patients with severe arthritis pain were prayed for by 50 people, and 14 out of those 20 reported a significant lessening of pain.
   Theory: Prayer heals.

9. Phenomenon: Over the past year, two terminally ill cancer patients in Broderick Hospital were found to be cancer-free.
   Theory: Treatment with a new type of chemotherapy works.

10. Phenomenon: Air pollution levels in San Francisco are at their highest levels in years.
    Theory: Increased numbers of SUVs being driven in the San Francisco area.

Exercise 8.4

For each of the following theories, derive a test implication and indicate whether you believe that such a test would likely confirm or disconfirm the theory.

1. Elise has the power to move physical objects with her mind alone.

*2. Ever since the city installed brighter street lights, the crime rate has been declining steadily.

3. The Ultra-Sonic 2000 pest-control device can rid a house of roaches by emitting a particular sound frequency that humans can't hear.

4. The Dodge Intrepid is a more fuel-efficient car than any other on the road.

5. Practitioners of transcendental meditation (TM) can levitate—actually ascend unaided off the ground without physical means of propulsion.

*6. Eating foods high in fat contributes more to overweight than eating foods high in carbohydrates.

7. Lemmings often commit mass suicide.

8. The English sparrow will build nests only in trees.

Exercise 8.5
Read the following passages and answer the following questions for each one:

1. What is the phenomenon being explained?
2. What theories are advanced to explain the phenomenon? (Some theories may be unstated.)
3. Which theory seems the most plausible and why? (Use the TEST formula.)
4. Regarding the most credible theory, is there a test implication mentioned? If so, what is it? If not, what would be a good test implication for the theory?
5. What test results would convince you to change your mind about your preferred theory?

Passage 1

In the past several years, a researcher named David Oates has been advocating his discovery of a most interesting phenomenon. Oates claims that backward messages are hidden unintentionally in all human speech. The messages can be understood by recording normal speech and playing it in reverse. . . .

[According to Oates,] "Any thought, any emotion, any motive that any person has can appear backwards in human speech. The implications are mind boggling because reverse speech opens up the Truth."

> . . . To our knowledge there is not one empirical investigation of reverse speech in any peer-reviewed journal. If reverse speech did exist it would be, at the very least, a noteworthy scientific discovery. However, there are no data to support the existence of reverse speech or Oates's theories about its implications.[40]

Passage 2

A Ouija board is used in divination and spiritualism. The board usually has the letters of the alphabet inscribed on it, along with words such as "yes," "no," "goodbye" and "maybe." A planchette (a slidable 3-legged device) or pointer of some sort is manipulated by those using the board. The users ask the board a question and together or one of them singly moves the pointer or the board until a letter is "selected" by the pointer. The selections "spell" out an answer to the question asked.

Some users believe that paranormal or supernatural forces are at work in spelling out Ouija board answers. Skeptics believe that those using the board either consciously or unconsciously select what is read. To prove this, simply try it blindfolded for some time, having an innocent bystander take notes on what letters are selected. Usually, the result will be unintelligible nonsense.

The movement of the planchette is not due to paranormal forces but to unnoticeable movements by those controlling the pointer, known as the *ideomotor* effect. The same kind of unnoticeable movement is at work in dowsing.

The Ouija board was first introduced to the American public in 1890 as a parlor game sold in novelty shops.[41]

Passage 3

Trickery aside, what about reports of apparent animal ESP? Anecdotal evidence suggests some animals may have precognitive awareness of various types of natural catastrophes, becoming agitated before earthquakes, volcanic eruptions, cyclones, and other events. However, the creatures may actually be responding to subtle sensory factors—like variations in air pressure and tremors in the ground—that are beyond the range of human perception.

Something of the sort may explain some instances of apparent animal prescience. For example, a Kentucky friend of mine insists that his dogs seem to know when he has decided to go hunting, exhibiting a marked excitement even though they are lodged some distance away from the house. However, it seems possible that they are either responding to some unintended signal (such as recognizing certain noises associated with his getting ready for a hunting trip) or that he is selectively remembering those occasions when the dogs' excitement happens to coincide with his intentions. Another friend says he once had dogs who seemed to know when he was going to take them for a walk, but he decided he must have unconsciously signaled them (such as by glancing in the direction of their hanging leashes).[42]

Exercise 8.6

Read each of the following passages containing science news and determine (1) what claim is being made, (2) what scientific evidence (if any) is being offered to support that claim, and (3) whether or not you would accept the claim. Explain your reasoning.

Passage 1

Magnesium Treats Depression Better than Antidepressant Drugs

A new option has recently debuted in the medical world. A natural medication that can help treat depression as well, if not better than previous depression medications. This new miracle is magnesium. Magnesium is a mineral that the body naturally craves and recent studies have shown that 248 mg of magnesium per day can lead to an astounding reversal of depression symptoms.

Thanks to a rise in pharmaceutical prices, medication is often pricey and it can be tough to afford necessary medications. Depression medication can cost anywhere from $30.00–$200.00 per month. Over the course of a year this amount can build up to quite an expense. Unfortunately many people can not afford these rises and therefore can no longer afford their medications. One of the greatest things about the recent discovery of magnesium and its medicinal properties is that people can take magnesium for just pennies a day. Magnesium is an effective approach to treating depression and eliminating side effects. It is safer and cheaper than other prescription therapies and drugs.[43]

Passage 2

Cannabis Oil (THC, CBD) Kills Cancer Cells, Leaving Healthy Cells in Perfect Harmony

Cannabis is without any doubt a miracle treatment for illnesses of all kinds. This is still an important thing to spread awareness of, because the shock waves produced by American enforced prohibition, decades of the drug war, are still being felt around the planet despite states legalizing it.

It is capable of causing cancer cells to die, while leaving normal cells working in perfect harmony....

This evidence goes way back, and you know it was suppressed. In 1974, a research team from the Medical College of Virginia discovered that malignant tumor cell growth in mice was inhibited by cannabis, also in cell cultures.

At the time the Washington Post reported on it, stating that THC *"slowed the growth of lung cancers, breast cancers and a virus-induced leukemia in laboratory mice, and prolonged their lives by as much as 36%."*[44]

Passage 3

Moringa Leaves Benefits: 10 Surprising Benefits of Drinking Moringa

For hundreds of years, moringa and ginger were among the top choices for treating various ailments.

Native to India, Afghanistan, and Pakistan, the Moringa tree was commonly used in the traditional Ayurveda. Today, however, it is famous all around the world for its medicinal properties.

According to the Ayurveda, the leaves of the tree can effectively treat over 300 health issues as the leaves are a rich source of nutrition and natural energy boosters.

The moringa soothes the body, lowers blood pressure, and treats sleeping difficulties. Plus, this potent natural remedy will cleanse the body from the accumulated toxins.

The moringa contains over 90 nutrients, and provides seven times the vitamin C of oranges, four times the calcium of milk and the vitamin A of carrots, three times the potassium of bananas, and two times the protein of yogurt.[45]

CAPSTONE

Read the following science article and answer the questions at the end.

Disabling One Gene Allows You to Eat as Much as You Want without Gaining Weight

Scientists have discovered that tweaking a single gene in mice allows them to eat as much food as they desire without gaining weight. With the holiday season upon us, it sounds too good to be true, but the researchers claim their discovery could be used as a basis for a human treatment in the near future.

Reporting in the journal EMBO Reports, scientists at the University of Texas Southwestern Medical Center and Flinders University in Australia found that the single gene, known as RCAN1, acts as a feedback inhibitor for all kinds of metabolic processes and the production of body heat. After disabling this gene from the mice, they curiously discovered that they become were resistant to diet-induced weight gain. Effectively, their metabolism was given a supercharge, allowing them to "burn up" more calories.

The experiment has so far only been tested with mice. Nevertheless, the researchers claim that their findings hold potential as a new drug therapy for humans with obesity or metabolic conditions.

"We know a lot of people struggle to lose weight or even control their weight for a number of different reasons. The findings in this study could mean developing a pill which would target the function of RCAN1 and may result in weight loss," lead author, Professor Damien Keating of Flinders University, said in a statement. "These results show we can potentially make a real difference in the fight against obesity."

"We have already developed a series of drugs that target the protein that this gene makes, and we are now in the process of testing them to see if they inhibit RCAN1 and whether they might represent potential new anti-obesity drugs," he added.

The human body contains two types of fat: white fat and brown fat. White fat, used to store energy, is the stuff you imagine when you hear the word fat. Brown fat cells, packed full of mitochondria, burn up energy and produce heat. We tend to lose our small supplies of brown fat as we age, and obese individuals and people with diabetes have even less. According to the researchers, disabling the RCAN1 can help turn the white fat into brown fat.

"In light of our results, the drugs we are developing to target RCAN1 would burn more calories while people are resting," Professor Keating explained. "It means the body would store less fat without the need for a person to reduce food consumption or exercise more."

Of course, even if the researchers did squeeze these findings into a human treatment, you would still need a balanced diet for your wider health's sake. However, for people with chronic obesity or metabolic conditions, this could serve as a very helpful tool.

1. Does the claim in the headline accurately reflect what the evidence shows? Is the headline misleading? Explain.
2. Is the description of the research findings accurate? Does the article help you understand the limitations of the study?
3. What information would you add to the article to make it less misleading and more helpful?

9

Advertising
Commercial and Political

Chapter Objectives

9.1 How Advertising Works
- Understand that the advertising industry is motivated by profit.
- Know that online advertising has become the most precise, calibrated, targeted, and stealthy form of advertising in history.
- Learn how to approach all advertising with an attitude of reasonable skepticism.
- Realize that although advertising can be both truthful and helpful, its primary function is neither to provide objective and accurate information nor to help consumers make fully informed, rational choices.

9.2 Internet Advertising
- Be aware that data science is used to optimize the impact of online advertising through micro-targeting.
- Understand how advertising messages are communicated through paid search ads, social media ads, and display ads.
- Distinguish between editorial content and native advertising.

9.3 Political Advertising
- Understand the factors that can make political videos so powerful.
- Understand some of the ways that political videos can present false or misleading messages through fallacies and rhetoric.
- Appreciate the power of Facebook political ads to target users based on their psychological and behavioral characteristics.

Advertising is the practice of calling the public's attention to something to induce them to buy products or services or otherwise change their opinions or behavior. Advertising exists because interested parties—companies, governments, organizations, political groups, and individuals—pay for it to exist. They pay to advance their own ends, agendas, and ideas. Unlike many other communicators—journalists, scholars, and serious authors, for example—advertisers are not necessarily obliged to adhere to standards of objectivity, fairness, or reliability. Advertising is motivated reasoning on stimulants and thus should be viewed through the lens of critical thinking.

Advertising is like air: It is everywhere, so pervasive and so natural that we forget it's there, yet penetrating and changing us every day. Advertising messages hit us rapid-fire and nonstop from social media, email, websites, podcasts, movie theaters, magazines, newsletters, newspapers, television, radio, book covers, junk mail, product labels, billboards, vehicle signs, T-shirts, wall posters, flyers, and who knows what else. Ads permeate all media—print, broadcasting, publishing, and the internet. Caught in this whirl of words and sounds and images, we can easily overlook the obvious and disconcerting facts behind them: (1) All advertising is designed to influence, persuade, or manipulate us; (2) to an impressive degree and in many ways, it *does* successfully influence, persuade, or manipulate us; and (3) we are often oblivious to—or in outright denial about—how effectively advertising influences, persuades, or manipulates us.

9.1 How Advertising Works

How well advertising does its job can be measured in money. Advertising in traditional media can cost a great deal. A single full-page magazine ad can cost tens of thousands of dollars; a thirty-second TV ad can run into the millions (especially on Super Bowl Sunday). But companies are willing to pay the price because advertising works. The revenues garnered from advertising can outweigh its costs by wide margins; in the case of a magazine ad or a TV spot, the gain could easily be hundreds of thousands or millions of dollars. In addition, advertisers and advertising agencies invest heavily each year in scientific consumer research to determine how to configure ads precisely to elicit the desired response from people. Again, they make these investments because there is a sure payoff: Consumers usually respond just as the research says they will. How do your eyes track across a newspaper ad when you are looking at it? Would you respond better to a TV commercial if the voice-over came from Rihanna,

Michelle Obama, Taylor Swift, or Dwayne Johnson? Would the magazine ad be more likely to sell you the cottage cheese if the headline used the word *creamy* instead of *smooth*? You may not care about any of this, but advertisers do because such seemingly trivial bits of information can help them influence you in ways you barely suspect.

Advertising online is even more powerful and pervasive. It has become the most precise, calibrated, targeted, and sneaky form of advertising in history. Pop-up ads, banner ads, display ads, click-through ads (ads that you click through to the advertiser's chosen destination), and more—all these digital enticements never sleep. Digital advertising revenue rose to more than $100 billion in 2018. In a typical week of working and playing online, you are likely to encounter thousands of online ads. A single video ad can rack up millions of shares in record time. And every choice, click, or view gets logged and analyzed so advertisers can come at you again and again.

However averse we are (or think we are) to advertising or to its aims, we cannot deny its appeal. We like advertising, at least some of it. We easily can point to ads that annoy us or insult our intelligence, but most of us can also recall ones that are entertaining, funny, inspiring, even informative.

How, then, should critical thinkers think about advertising? What should our attitude be as we are exposed to countless come-ons per minute? The principle that should guide us is the same one we noted in Chapter 4 on fake news: **reasonable skepticism**. Recall that this principle asks us to give up the habit of automatically accepting claims in the media, to reject the assumption that most of what's said online is true, to stop taking the word of online sources on faith. It says that we should not believe a claim unless there are legitimate reasons for doing so.

And we generally do have good reasons to doubt advertising claims and to be wary of advertising's persuasive powers. This means that usually the most reasonable response to advertising is a degree of suspicion. If we prefer truth over falsehood, if we would rather not be mistaken or bamboozled, if we want to make informed choices involving our time and money, then a general wariness toward advertising ploys is justified. This principle does not assume that all ad claims are false or that advertising cannot be genuinely informative or useful. It simply says that we should not accept uncritically an ad's message or impact on us.

The good reasons for suspicion include the obvious fact that the purpose of advertising is to sell or promote something. To put the point bluntly, though advertising can be both truthful and helpful, its primary function is *not* to provide objective and accurate information to consumers. Advertisers will tell you many good things about their products but are unlikely to mention all the bad. Their main job is *not* to help consumers make fully informed, rational choices about available options. Advertising is advertising—it is not intended to be an impartial search for facts or a program of consumer protection. We are therefore justified in maintaining the same attitude toward advertising that we would toward a complete stranger who wants to sell us a widget: His motives are obviously pecuniary while his commitment to honesty is unknown.

Another obvious reason for suspicion is that advertising has a reputation for—and a history of—misleading messages. The world is filled with ads that make dubious or false claims, use fallacious arguments (stated or implied), and employ psychological tricks to manipulate consumer responses.

Some of these methods fit neatly in our rundown of fallacies and rhetorical ploys in Chapter 6. Ads frequently employ fallacious appeals to authority ("As an Olympic gold medal winner, I can tell you that PowerVitamin 2000 really works!"), appeals to emotion ("Enjoy the goodness and warmth of Big-Brand Soup, just like mother used to make"), appeals to popularity ("CNN, America's number-one source for news"), hasty generalizations ("Mothers everywhere will love Softie Diapers—our test mothers sure did!"), and faulty analogies ("As a businessman, I saved General Motors. As president, I can save this country").

Section Query

Lately, have you doubted the truthfulness or reliability of an online ad? If so, why? If not, why do you trust so many ads?

9.2 Internet Advertising

Internet advertising is like the ocean. There may be a lot of things to see on the surface, but most of the action, power, and danger is down below. Below the surface, data scientists and computer programmers use statistics and linear algebra to optimize the impact of advertising and micro-target you as a potential prospect. A simple click-through Facebook ad sits there on your screen, enticing you to buy a new pair of running shoes. But this little enticement is not random. Beneath the digital appearance of the ad, algorithms and cookies have already identified you as someone who has an interest in running and fitness, who earns more than $45,000 per year, who votes for Democrats, who frequents dating sites, who has bought shoes online before—and who is more likely than not to buy these particular shoes right now.

Here's an explanation of how all this works by Dina Srinivasan, a former advertising executive and antitrust scholar:

> Digital advertising is automated, data-driven, and opaque in its mechanics. That 22-year-old [media buyer] has had to make way for data scientists, mathematicians, and computer programmers who, behind the scenes, use statistics, calculus, and linear algebra to optimize advertising campaigns, by micro-targeting users and constantly tweaking algorithms.
>
> Does that car manufacturer still want to reach men looking to buy a car? A data scientist may tell them the optimal target is a 39-year-old man, carrying on an extramarital affair, who's on the brink of divorce. They can model this hypothesis (and prove it works), and advertising companies like Google and Facebook can put that into execution, finding ways to home in and target those types of people online.
>
> When you go to a website and load a page, in the milliseconds that it takes for that page to load, there are real-time auctions running in the background that determine which ads to load on *your* page. Almost all online ads are delivered in this way, where highly complex auction markets make their money by competing on who can better track users and invade their privacy more thoroughly.
>
> The targeting begins the moment you as a reader visit any website. Typically, your IP address, your location, and the URL of the page you are on are swiped from your browser without your explicit knowledge, and shared with advertising companies that run these ad auctions. The goal, of course, is to build as specific a portrait about you as possible—by linking your device with your identity—and cookies are a common tool for doing so.[1]

Internet advertising began in 1994 with simple banner ads, which were followed over the years by a stunning proliferation of other kinds of ads, each seemingly more sophisticated and effective than the last. We can divide them into three types: paid search ads, social media ads, and display ads.

Paid search ads show up in search engine results

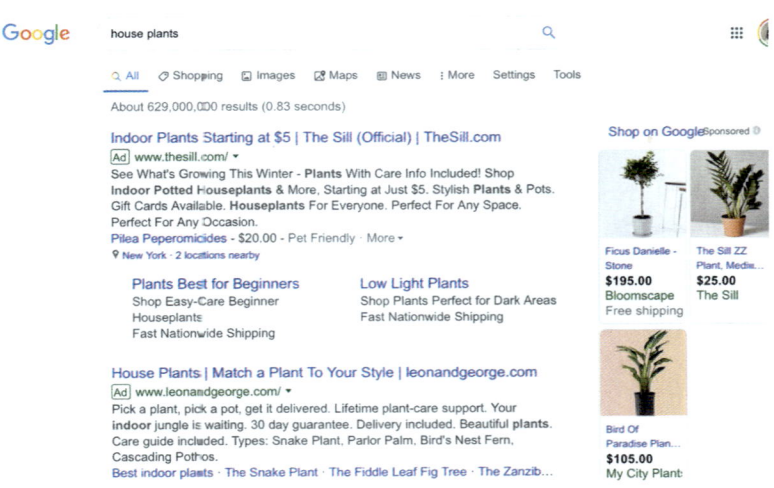

Fig. 9.1 Google search results for "house plants."

Fig. 9.2　Paid Facebook ad.

Fig. 9.3　Paid Twitter ad.

on Google, Bing, Dogpile, Webopedia, Yahoo, and other search sites. If you search for "house plants" on any of these platforms, the first results will likely consist of ads for house plants or gardening products, usually labelled "AD" or "Sponsored." The non-advertising results—articles by plant experts, for example—will follow. That the ads appear near the top of the list is, of course, not an indication of their accuracy or reliability. Someone pays to have those ads ranked first.

Social media ads appear on—you guessed it—social media platforms, including Facebook, Instagram, YouTube, Twitter, Snapchat, TikTok, Pinterest, and LinkedIn. Advertisers pay to have their ads not just posted on social media, but posted to a specific targeted audience defined by people's personal, demographic, and behavioral characteristics. These ads, often labeled "Sponsored" or "Promoted," appear as banners, display ads, click-through ads, and auto-play videos (essentially digital TV ads).

Display ads are the billboards of the online world, appearing in many guises, including static images, floating banners, sidebar ads, pop-ups, background wallpaper, and autoplay or user-play videos. These ads are presented on websites (or topic-specific sections of websites) that are related to the product or service being touted and may or not be targeted at specific demographic or behavioral visitors.

Native advertising is paid advertising designed to imitate the tone, style, and look of a publication's editorial or journalistic content. Indeed, the effectiveness of native advertising depends on *not* looking like ads—or rather, looking like just another editorial feature. These ads attempt to persuade not by overt sales pitches but indirectly, through informative and engaging stories, vignettes, and personal profiles, showing up on social media feeds and web pages as videos, slide shows, or text. The Federal Trade Commission (FTC) has guidelines for ensuring that the nature of the ads is transparent, and so the ads are usually tagged as "Sponsored content," "Promoted," "Recommended for You," or "Promoted Stories." But critics complain that they still mislead, for many people don't seem to be able to tell the difference between them and genuine editorial content. (Recall the Stanford media literacy study discussed in Chapter 1.)

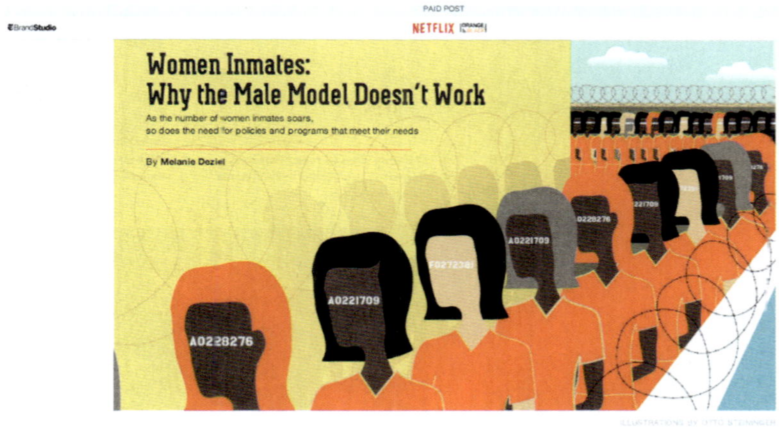

Fig. 9.4 A native ad promoting the second season of Netflix's *Orange Is the New Black* that appeared on the *New York Times* website.

Suppose you click on an article titled "The 7 Worst Financial Mistakes I Made before I Turned 30," which takes you to the Jones Investment Company blog. You obviously will get a different kind of coverage of the subject than you might get from, say, the *Wall Street Journal*, the *Economist*, or a bestselling book by experts on the topic. Or say you click on a video about "The 10 Best Scuba Diving Sites in the World," which takes you to the Acme Beach Travel Agency website. You were maybe hoping for a more independent and less biased source? The point is that it does matter whether you are aware that the story you are enjoying is native advertising.

Native advertising takes many forms, ranging from simple and straightforward to sophisticated and nearly indistinguishable from editorial content (see Figs. 9.4-9.6).

Fig. 9.5 Buzzfeed's native ad "A Cat's Guide to Taking Care of Your Human," produced in partnership with Purina, the pet food company. The video begins, "Despite being huge and having the ability to open canned goods, humans are frail in both body and mind and we must care for them."

Fig. 9.6 A bank of native ads hosted on CNN.com.

Old School Advertising Tricks

Advertisers have been deploying the same fallacies and rhetorical tricks for ages, many of which do not involve making explicit claims or providing good reasons for acting or choosing. Here are a few of the old standbys.

Identification

Many ads persuade by simply inviting the consumer to identify with attractive people (real or imagined) or groups. Most ads featuring celebrity endorsements use this ploy. The idea is to get you to identify so strongly with a celebrity that you feel his or her product choices are *your* preferred choices. Without providing a single good reason or argument, endorsement ads say, in effect, that if Brad Pitt likes Chanel No. 5, if Selena Gomez likes designer brand Coach, if Justin Timberlake likes McDonald's, then maybe you should, too.

Slogans

Catchy, memorable phrases are the stock-in-trade of advertising. How can we forget "Nike. Just do it" (Nike); "Think Different" (Apple); "Because you're worth it" (L'Oréal); "Like a rock" (Chevrolet); "Don't leave home without it" (American Express); "Built Ford tough!" (Ford); "Quality never goes out of style" (Levi's); or "The happiest place on earth" (Disney)? Such catchphrases may not say much, but they do get our attention, engender appealing emotions or concepts, and associate them with products or companies—again and again and again. Through repetition that seems to embed themselves in our brains, slogans surreptitiously get us to feel that one product or brand is better than another.

Misleading Comparisons

In advertising, comparisons can mislead in many ways. Consider these examples:

1. Cutting Edge Razors shave 30 percent better.
2. Big sale! Apple iPad for less than the suggested retail price!
3. Simply better-tasting tacos. No question.

The problem with example 1 is its vagueness, which is of course deliberate. What does "30 percent better" mean? Thirty percent better than they used to be? Thirty percent better than other razors do? If the latter, what other products are we talking about? Are Cutting Edge Razors being compared to the *least* effective razors on the market? The *30 percent* may seem impressive—until we know to what it actually refers. (Another relevant question is how shaving effectiveness was determined. As you might imagine, there are many ways to perform such tests, some of them likely to yield more impressive numbers than others.)

The claim in example 2 may or may not be touting a true bargain. We would probably view the "big sale" in a different light if we knew whether the store's *regular* prices are below the suggested retail prices or if *all* stores sell the Apple iPad below the suggested retail.

Example 3 contains the same sort of vagueness we find in example 1 plus an additional sort of emptiness. The phrase "better-tasting tacos" is a claim about a subjective state of affairs—a claim that *anyone* could make about his or her own gustatory experience. You and a thousand other people might try the tacos and think they taste terrible. So the claim tells you nothing about whether you will like the tacos. The claim would be empty even if it were stretched to "The best-tasting tacos on Earth!" In the ad world, such exaggerations are known as *puffery*, which is regarded in advertising law as hype that few people take seriously.

Weasel Words

When advertisers want to *appear* to make a strong claim but avoid blatant lying or deception, they use what are known as *weasel words*. Weasel words water down a claim in subtle ways—just enough to ensure that it is technically true but superficially misleading. Consider these examples:

1. You may have already won a new 2020 Ford pickup truck!
2. Some doctors recommend ginseng for sexual dysfunction.
3. Relieves up to 60 percent of headaches in chronic headache sufferers.

Example 1 is typical junk-mail hype that seems to promise a valuable prize. But the weasel word *may* weakens the claim. Technically, you *may* have actually won since your winning is at least (remotely) possible. But in the typical sweepstakes, the odds of your winning anything are millions to one. Yes, you may have already won—and you are just as likely to get hit by an asteroid tomorrow. Example 2 plays on the weasel word *some*. It is probably true that *some* (meaning at least one) doctors recommend ginseng for sexual dysfunction, but a huge majority of them do not. Using *some*, we could craft an infinite number of technically true but misleading (and ridiculous) claims about what doctors do and don't do. In example 3 the weasel words are *up to*. Notice that many states of affairs would be consistent with this (vague) statement. It would be true even if just 1 percent of headaches were relieved in almost all headache sufferers.

Other weasels include *as many as*, *reportedly*, *possibly*, *virtually*, *many*, *seems*, and *perhaps*. Such words, of course, can have perfectly respectable uses as necessary qualifiers in many contexts. The problems arise when they are used not to qualify but to misguide.

Section Query

Go to Buzzfeed.com or Upworthy.com. Can you pick out the native ads from the editorial features?

9.3 Political Advertising

Political advertising is a far bigger challenge (or a far bigger affront) to critical thinking than most other forms of advertising. It is often difficult to tell the difference between political advertising and propaganda (as defined in Chapter 4), for the former can be just as deliberately biased and misleading as the latter. And now that political ads have gone digital and started micro-targeting us on social media feeds, they can be more insidious and potent than ever.

Back in the media stone age (the 1950s), political TV ads consisted of cartoons and videos of speeches or testimonials, all designed to portray a candidate in a positive light. Very tame stuff. But in the run-up to the 1964 presidential election, political advertising took a radical turn when a TV ad for Democratic presidential candidate Lyndon B. Johnson aired. Johnson's opponent was Barry Goldwater, a conservative Republican and militant anti-communist. The ad featured a little girl picking the petals from a daisy and counting to 10 as she plucks them. When she reaches 10, the camera zooms into the girl's eye and freezes as a man's booming voice starts counting down from 10. Suddenly a nuclear bomb explodes, and a roaring, white-hot mushroom cloud fills the screen. A voiceover declares, "These are the stakes. To make a world in which all of God's children can live or to go into the dark. We must either love each other or we must die. Vote for President Johnson on November 3. The stakes are too high for you to stay home."

Barry Goldwater isn't mentioned, but the implication is that if he is elected, a nuclear holocaust will result, killing millions of children like the one in the ad.

Thus the negative political ad was born. After this, political opponents were portrayed in TV attack ads as unsavory, dangerous, untrustworthy, wishy-washy, or worse. Smearing a politician or distorting a political idea was easy. As editing technology has evolved, lying and misleading through video has become easier still. It is now possible not merely to put logical fallacies and rhetorical gimmicks to work in political videos, but to magnify their impact a hundredfold. It is now commonplace for political videos to make someone look as if he or she is saying or doing something that is completely made up.

Fig. 9.7 The 60-second "Peace, Little Girl" ad that aired during the 1964 presidential campaign.

Reputable fact-checking organizations have been sounding the alarm about the problem for some time. According to Glenn Kessler of the *Washington Post*'s Fact Checker,

> If a picture says a thousand words, video can be even more powerful. But the Internet is increasingly populated with false and misleading videos—spread by politicians, advocacy groups and others—viewed by millions. That poses a challenge not only to fact checkers but to anyone relying on social media or web searches to get information or find the latest news.
>
> Advancements in technology make it easier for just about anyone to create convincingly falsified video. Moreover, people in today's polarized political climate seem increasingly willing to believe what they want to believe—especially when it aligns with their political values and is shown in video. This potent combination of advancements in technology, the spread of social media and an impressionable population allows video misinformation to spread rapidly.[2]

Political videos can present false or misleading messages through the words they use (lies, half-truths, exaggerations, etc.), or through technical manipulation of the videos themselves. Here are some examples of the former: political ads from the 2018 election, with comments and analysis by FactCheck.org:

Falsely Portraying a Democratic Candidate as Anti-ICE

TV ads in Arkansas' 2nd Congressional District falsely portray Democratic candidate Clarke Tucker as wanting to abolish the U.S. Immigration and Customs Enforcement.

Rep. French Hill, a two-term congressman, is airing a TV ad called "We Must Enforce the Law" that shows images of tattooed members of a transnational gang known as the Mara Salvatrucha, or MS-13, and warns that they are "infiltrating America." (As we have written, the MS-13 gang has had a presence in the U.S. since the early 1980s, beginning in Southern California, and currently numbers about 10,000—a figure the Department of Justice has been using since 2006.)

The announcer says, "MS-13, the most dangerous gang infiltrating America, but Washington liberals want to get rid of ICE, the police enforcing our immigration laws and protecting our border from MS-13." Photos of House

Fig. 9.8 TV attack ad directed at Democratic candidate Clarke Tucker.

Minority Leader Nancy Pelosi and Senate Minority Leader Chuck Schumer appear on the screen as the announcer says "Washington liberals," even though neither Pelosi nor Schumer support abolishing ICE.

The ad then says that Tucker "attended an anti-ICE rally" and "refused to take a position" on the "abolish ICE" movement. It quotes Tucker as saying, "I don't know what it is." This is misleading. Tucker did not attend an "anti-ICE rally," and he has taken a position on ICE.[3]

Misleading the Public about a Politician's Voting Record

A Republican TV ad claims Sen. Joe Manchin of West Virginia is "fighting the Trump agenda," even though he has voted with the president nearly 61 percent of the time.

In fact, Manchin has voted with Trump more often than any Democratic senator.

The ad was released by the National Republican Senatorial Committee on Aug. 14, and is the second in its series of commercials attacking Manchin, who is running for reelection in a state that Trump won by more than 40 percentage points in 2016.

The narrator starts by pointing out that Manchin backed Hillary Clinton for president despite her once saying that her plan for renewable energy production was "going to put a lot of coal miners and coal companies out of business." (Her full comments, however, included a promise to bring renewable energy jobs to coal country to replace those lost jobs, as we wrote during the presidential campaign.)

Manchin told Politico he threatened to pull his support for Clinton after those remarks, but her pledge to invest $20 billion in West Virginia won him over. Looking back, Manchin said, "it was a mistake politically" to endorse Clinton.

The ad's narrator, however, isn't being fully transparent when he says, "now Manchin's fighting the Trump agenda."

That is followed by a video clip of Trump saying of the senator, "But he votes against everything. And he voted against our tax cuts."

Manchin did vote against the Tax Cuts and Jobs Act, as did all Democrats in the House and Senate. He also voted against other Trump-supported legislation, including bills to repeal or replace parts of the Affordable Care Act, which even some Republicans opposed.

Fig. 9.9 TV ad accusing Sen. Joe Manchin of "fighting the Trump agenda."

But Manchin has voted *with* Trump more often than against him.[4]

Telling an Old Lie about Medicare

This ad from the Democratic Senatorial Campaign Committee dredges up an old claim we haven't heard much in recent years—saying Republican Rep. Martha McSally of Arizona "voted to essentially end Medicare." That's a reference to a budget plan, first proposed by Rep. Paul Ryan, that calls for changing Medicare—not *ending* it—to a system in which seniors would use premium-support payments to select their own plan from a Medicare exchange. . . .

Fig. 9.10   Democratic attack ad falsely accusing Republican Rep. Martha McSally of voting "to essentially end Medicare."

Democratic Rep. Kyrsten Sinema also tweeted the claim in mid-October. Both the tweet and the ad include the words "essentially end Medicare" in quotes and refer to a *Wall Street Journal* article. But that's a truncated quote from the 2011 *Journal* article, which said Ryan's plan "would essentially end Medicare, which now pays most of the health-care bills for 48 million elderly and disabled Americans, **as a program that directly pays those bills**." (The emphasis is ours.)

So it wouldn't terminate the Medicare program, as the ad says. Instead, it would change how the program operates.[5]

Manipulated videos have become the go-to tactic for political smearing, propaganda, and hatchet jobs. Here are four examples, examined and categorized by type of manipulation by the *Washington Post*'s Fact Checker:[6]

Paying Women and Children to Cross the U.S. Border?

Misrepresentation: Presenting unaltered video in an inaccurate manner misrepresents the footage and misleads the viewer. President Trump and Rep. Matt Gaetz (R-Fla.) claimed a video showed men giving money to women and children in Honduras to cross the U.S. border ahead of the 2018 midterm elections; Gaetz suggested that the money came from U.S. organizations and George Soros. However, the video was

Fig. 9.11   A video claimed by President Trump and Rep. Matt Gaetz to show men giving money to women and children in Honduras to cross the U.S. border.

Fig. 9.12 A spliced video showing alleged interview with Rep. Alexandria Ocasio-Cortez.

shot in Guatemala, not Honduras, and it was unclear why the men were handing out money to women and children.

The Mashup of Two Separate Interviews?

Splicing: Editing together disparate videos fundamentally alters the story that is being told. CRTV took soundbites from an interview Rep. Alexandria Ocasio-Cortez conducted with another news outlet and edited together footage of its own anchor asking questions. In less than 24 hours, the video had nearly 1 million views. CRTV later said the video was satire. [The question to Rep. Ocasio-Cortez was "Do you have any knowledge whatsoever about how our political system works?" Rep. Ocasio-Cortez is shown shaking her head.]

President Trump Loves Nuclear War?

Splicing: During the 2016 presidential campaign, a pro-Clinton political ad combined President Trump's quotes over footage and excluded key context. The video plays Trump saying: "This is the Trump theory on war. I'm really good at war. I love war, in a certain way." And then after a quick dip to black, immediately plays, "Including with nukes, yes, including with nukes." But his comment about nuclear weapons was actually in reference to Japan using nuclear weapons to defend itself from North Korea.

Phillip Picardi
@pfpicardi

At left is @tyler_mitchell's photo of @Emma4Change for the cover of @TeenVogue. At right is what so-called "Gun Rights Activists" have photoshopped it into. #MarchForOurLives

Fig. 9.13 A photoshopped GIF showing Emma Gonzalez doing something she never did.

Emma Gonzalez Tears Up the U.S. Constitution?

Doctoring: Altering the frames of a video—cropping, changing speed, using Photoshop, dubbing audio, or adding or deleting visual information—can deceive the viewer. A photoshopped gif was circulated on social media showing Parkland student and gun-control advocate Emma Gonzalez tearing the U.S. Constitution in half. The original image was posted in a Teen Vogue story about teenage activists and shows Gonzalez ripping up a gun-range target.

The most influential, beguiling, and relentless political ads on the planet may be the ones you see on Facebook. That's because they can micro-target millions of users based on their psychological and behavioral characteristics, hit those users again and again with tailored messages, and run the whole operation indefinitely and below the radar.

Consider the case of the 2016 election of Donald Trump. Brad Parscale, President Trump's digital marketing expert, claims that his Facebook advertising campaign won the election. Whether or not this is true, his methods of precisely targeting millions of people on Facebook with political ads helped to usher in a new era of stealth political influence through social media. The *Guardian* reports on how Parscale did it and why it matters:

> Parscale claims he typically ran 50,000 to 60,000 variations of Facebook ads each day during the Trump campaign, all targeting different segments of the electorate. Understanding the meaning of a single one of those ads would require knowing what the ad actually said, who the campaign targeted to see that ad, and how that audience responded. Multiply that by 100 and you have a headache; by 50,000 and you'll start to doubt your grasp on reality. Then remember that this is 50,000 a day over the course of a campaign that lasted more than a year. . . .
>
> Any candidate using Facebook can put a campaign message promising one thing in front of one group of voters while simultaneously running an ad with a completely opposite message in front of a different group of voters. The ads themselves are not posted anywhere for the general public to see (this is what's known as "dark advertising"), and chances are, no one will ever be the wiser.
>
> That undermines the very idea of a "marketplace of ideas," says Ann Ravel, a former member of the Federal Election Commission who has long advocated stricter regulations on digital campaigning. "The way to have a robust democracy is for people to hear all these ideas and make decisions and discuss," Ravel said. "With microtargeting, that is not happening."[7]

Fortunately, there are ways to take at least some of the mystery out of how we are being targeted on Facebook. On any Facebook ad, we can see (some) of the information used to target us by clicking on the dots in the upper right corner of the ad and selecting "Why am I seeing this?" Also, ProPublica, the independent investigative newsroom, has been compiling a searchable database of political ads—ads that are hardly ever seen outside the targeted audience of Facebook users (https://projects.propublica.org/facebook-ads/). It allows us to see what ads are being displayed to users sorted by age, gender, city or state, and political orientation (liberal, conservative, or neither liberal nor conservative). It shows us, for example, the ads targeting a 45-year-old woman living in California who is a liberal, and the ads aimed at a 65-year-old man living in Washington DC who is a conservative.

 **Section Query**

If you had seen the video of Emma Gonzalez tearing the U.S. Constitution in half, would you have believed it—that is, would you have believed that the video was authentic? Why or why not? Be honest: Would your belief or disbelief have been based on your political preconceptions?

REVIEW NOTES

9.1 HOW ADVERTISING WORKS

- **Advertising** runs on money, with billions of dollars spent on it every year and billions of dollars earned as a result.
- Online advertising has become the most precise, calibrated, targeted, and insidious form of advertising in history, hitting us with thousands of targeted ads per week.
- It's important to approach all advertising with an attitude of **reasonable skepticism**.
- Although advertising can be both truthful and helpful, its primary function is *not* to provide objective and accurate information to consumers; its purpose is *not* to help consumers make fully informed, rational choices about available options.

9.2 INTERNET ADVERTISING

- Behind every ad you see online, data scientists and computer programmers are using statistics and linear algebra to optimize the impact of the ad by micro-targeting you as a potential prospect.
- Advertising messages can appear in paid search ads, social media ads, and display ads.
- It's essential to distinguish between editorial content and **native advertising**.
- Common advertising ploys include identification, slogans, misleading comparisons, and weasel words.

9.3 POLITICAL ADVERTISING

- Political videos can present false or misleading messages through fallacies and rhetoric and through the manipulation of the videos themselves.
- Facebook political ads are used to target millions of users based on their psychological and behavioral characteristics.

KEY TERMS

advertising
native advertising
reasonable skepticism

EXERCISES

Exercises marked with an asterisk (*) have answers in "Answers to Exercises" (Appendix B).

Exercise 9.1

1. What is advertising? What is its purpose?
2. How is the success of advertising measured?
3. What is reasonable skepticism?
*4. What is usually the best response to advertising?
5. How do data scientists and computer programmers optimize the impact of online advertising?
*6. What are paid search ads? What are display ads?
7. What is native advertising?
8. How do advertisers use identification, slogans, and weasel words to promote their products?
*9. With what famous TV ad did negative political advertising begin?
10. In video manipulation, what is the technique of misrepresentation?
11. How can splicing be used to create a false or misleading video?
12. How can doctoring be used to create a false or misleading video?

Exercise 9.2

Answer the following questions. (The techniques and resources you'll need for this exercise are discussed in Chapter 4: Fake News.)

1. Consider the "paying women and children to cross the U.S. border" video mentioned in this chapter. If you were seeing this video for the first time, how would you go about checking its accuracy? Describe each step in the process.

2. Consider the "President Trump loves nuclear war" video mentioned in this chapter. If you were seeing this video for the first time, how would you go about checking its accuracy? Describe each step in the process.

Exercise 9.3

I. Answer the questions at the end after reading the report by FactCheck.org assessing the accuracy of the following 2018 political ad targeting Rep. Beto O'Rourke (https://www.factcheck.org/2018/11/republican-closing-ads-immigration/).

Fig. 9.14 A 2018 political ad targeting Rep. Beto O'Rourke.

Texans Are, a super PAC that supports Sen. Ted Cruz, is running an ad that makes the false claim that Rep. Beto O'Rourke is "against background checks for refugees from terrorist hotbeds."

The ad starts with scenes of Central Americans walking in the street, leaving their countries to seek asylum from Mexico and the United States. "The caravan is coming," the announcer says. "Some say criminals among them."

To support its claim about O'Rourke opposing background checks for refugees, the TV ad cites O'Rourke's vote in 2015 against H.R. 4038, the American Security Against Foreign Enemies Act, or the American SAFE Act. That bill, which passed the House but failed in the Senate, would have added additional screening for refugees coming from Iraq and Syria, and required the FBI to investigate applicants in addition to the Department of Homeland Security.

O'Rourke argued that the process at the time was already thorough.

In a post on the blogging platform Medium, O'Rourke explained his "no" vote, in part, by saying: "The process proposed in today's bill would create unnecessary, duplicative work and processes for U.S. security agencies. This would significantly delay the current rigorous process by up to 2 years, according to the Administration. In effect, it would close the door on refugees during the single greatest humanitarian crisis of our time."

In 2015, the U.S. Citizenship and Immigration Services said refugees already receive "the highest degree of security screening and background checks for any category of traveler to the United States."

The process includes fingerprinting and checking records against databases maintained by the National Counterterrorism Center, the Department of Defense, the FBI and Interpol. Each refugee applicant is also interviewed personally by specially trained USCIS officers. And those from Syria are subjected to special measures including iris scans and an "enhanced review" by Homeland Security.[8]

1. According to FactCheck.org, how is the ad inaccurate or misleading?
2. What sources does FactCheck.org cite in its report?
3. How confident are you that FactCheck.org has arrived at the correct answer? Give reasons for your answer.
4. Before reading FactCheck.org's assessment, would you have deemed the ad persuasive? Why or why not?

II. Answer the questions at the end after reading the report by FactCheck.org assessing the accuracy of the following 2018 political ad targeting U.S. Senate candidate Kelli Ward, an Arizona Republican (https://www.factcheck.org/2018/08/pac-attack-on-kelli-ward-badly-misfires/).

Fig. 9.15 Attack ad targeting Republican Senate candidate Kelli Ward.

The ad [from a group calling itself DefendArizona] starts with powerful images of armed masked terrorists, while the narrator talks about ISIS—the terrorist group also known as the Islamic State. The vilifying visuals continue throughout the 30-second ad.

"ISIS killed thousands. Plotted attacks on U.S. soil. They're a real threat," the narrator says. "But Kelli Ward called for restraint in fighting terrorism."

On the screen, viewers see: "Kelli Ward on fighting ISIS '... restraint and realism,'" with a notation citing an interview that Ward gave to Seth Leibsohn on June 28, 2016.

We listened to the interview and Ward did not call for "restraint in fighting terrorism." Quite the opposite. She said the U.S. has "to be willing to decimate ISIS," not merely contain them.

The partial quote used in the ad—"restraint and realism"—wasn't about fighting terrorists. It was directed at past presidents who, she claimed, overreached by trying to "spread democracy" and "do nation building." . . .

Ward did not explain how she would "decimate ISIS," but she also did not say that she would pursue a policy of "restraint in fighting terrorism," as the ad claims.

The ad's narrator goes on to say, "Kelli Ward would cut military funding, putting the war on terror at risk." Again, DefendArizona misstates the facts.

On the screen, the ad cites "Vote Smart, 2016" as its source. But that source, in fact, contradicts the ad.

A 2016 Vote Smart survey asked candidates if they would be willing to cut defense spending to balance the budget. Ward answered "no." She did say that "everything has to be on the table" when it comes to cutting spending, "including waste and bureaucracy in the Defense Department," but she went on to say the U.S. "must fund our troops and maintain the strongest military in the world."[9]

1. According to FactCheck.org, how is this ad misleading and inaccurate?
2. What sources does FactCheck.org cite in its report?
3. How confident are you that FactCheck.org has arrived at the correct answer? Give reasons for your answer.

Exercise 9.4

Identify the native ads on the following websites.

1.

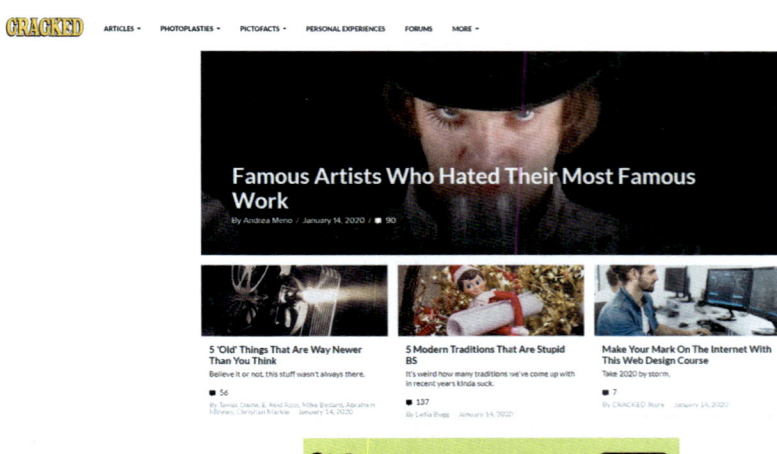

Fig. 9.16 Homepage of Cracked.com.

2.

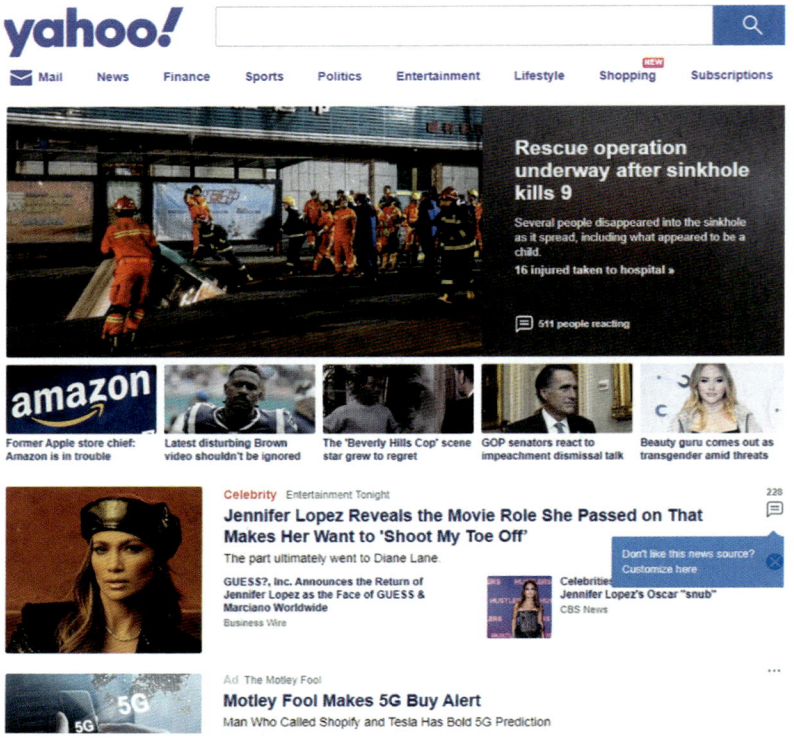

Fig. 9.17 Homepage of Yahoo.com.

CAPSTONE

Research each of the following political ads to determine who the advertiser is, what the purpose of the ad is, whom the ad may be targeting (age, political orientation, part of country), and whether any claims made are inaccurate or misleading.

1.
> **Ten Commandments Amendment**
> Sponsored · Paid for by Ten Commandments Amendment PAC, PO Box 1762, Orange Beach AL 36561 · 🌐
>
> Gubernatorial candidate Walt Maddox comes out against Amendment One, the Ten Commandments Amendment, on your Nov. 6 ballot.
>
> Orange Beach resident Dean Young, who is heading up a political action committee to campaign for it, slammed Maddox for his statements.
>
> Said Young: "It's because of people like him that our nation is spiraling out of control, morally. I'd like to congratulate him on at least telling the truth and letting the people of Alabama know where he stands and tha...
>
> See More

Fig. 9.18 Political ad archived at https://projects.propublica.org/facebook-ads/ad/6094108019834.

2.
> **Linda Meigs for District 20**
> Sponsored · Paid for by Linda Meigs for Alabama House LLC P.O. Box 4181 Huntsville, AL 35815 · 🌐
>
> Not even 1/3 of 4-year-olds in Alabama can attend the pre-k program. I will fight for an Education Lottery to fund pre-K expansion. Shouldn't all children in Alabama be given the building blocks they need to build a bright future? Vote for Linda Meigs on Nov. 6th!

LINDAMEIGS.COM
Vote Linda Meigs Nov 6
She will fight for our kids' future!
Learn More

Fig. 9.19 Political ad archived at https://projects.propublica.org/facebook-ads/ad/6106304085542.

Appendix A: For Further Reading

Chapter 1: Critical Thinking and the Challenges of Modern Media

Bartlett, Bruce. *The Truth Matters*. New York: Ten Speed Press, 2017.

Davis, Evan. *Post-Truth*. London: Little, Brown, 2017.

Harrison, Guy P. *Think Before You Like: Social Media's Effect on the Brain and the Tools You Need to Navigate Your Newsfeed*. Amherst, NY: Prometheus Books, 2017.

Potter, W. James. *Media Literacy*, 8th ed. New York: Sage, 2016.

Vaughn, Lewis. *The Power of Critical Thinking*, 6th ed. New York: Oxford University Press, 2019.

Chapter 2: Claims, Reasons, and Arguments

Davis, Evan. *Post-Truth*. London: Little, Brown, 2017.

Nichols, Tom. *The Death of Expertise*. New York: Oxford University Press, 2017.

Vaughn, Lewis. *Concise Guide to Critical Thinking*. New York: Oxford University Press, 2018.

Chapter 3: Obstacles to Critical Thinking

Eagleman, David. *The Brain: The Story of You*. New York: Vintage Books, 2015.

Gilovich, Thomas. *How We Know What Isn't So*. Amherst, NY: Prometheus Books, 1991.

Kahneman, Daniel. *Thinking, Fast and Slow*. New York: Farrar, Straus, and Giroux, 2011.

Nichols, Tom. *The Death of Expertise*. New York: Oxford University Press, 2017.

Singer, P. W., and Emerson T. Brooking. *LikeWar: The Weaponization of Social Media*. Boston: Houghton, Mifflin, Harcourt, 2018.

Chapter 4: Fake News

Bartlett, Bruce. *The Truth Matters: A Citizen's Guide to Separating Facts from Lies and Stopping Fake News in Its Tracks*. New York: Ten Speed Press, 2017.

Bender, John R., Lucinda D. Davenport, et al. *Writing and Reporting for the Media*. New York: Oxford University Press, 2016.

Dvorkin, Jeffrey. *Critical New Literacy*. New York: Routledge, 2019.

Green, John (MediaWise and the Stanford History Education Group). "CrashCourse: Navigating Digital Information." YouTube.com.

Harrison, Guy P. *Think Before You Like: Social Media's Effect on the Brain and the Tools You Need to Navigate Your Newsfeed*. Amherst, NY: Prometheus Books, 2017.

Holdstein, Deborah H., and Danielle Aquiline. *Who Says? The Writer's Research*. New York: Oxford University Press, 2017.

Klaidman, Stephen, and Tom L. Beauchamp. *The Virtuous Journalist*. New York: Oxford University Press, 1987.

Lanier, Jaron. *Ten Arguments for Deleting Your Social Media Accounts*. New York: Henry Holt, 2018.

Levitin, Daniel J. *Weaponized Lies: How to Think Critically in the Post-Truth Era*. New York: Dutton, 2016.

McManus, John. *Don't Be Fooled: A Citizen's Guide to News and Information in the Digital Age*. Sunnyvale, CA: Unvarnished Press, 2012.

Novella, Steven, et al. *The Skeptics' Guide to the Universe.* New York: Grand Central, 2018.

Schick, Theodore, and Lewis Vaughn. *How to Think about Weird Things,* 8th ed. New York: McGraw-Hill, 2019.

Chapter 5: Media Bias

Atkins, Larry. *Skewed: A Critical Thinker's Guide to Media Bias.* Amherst, NY: Prometheus Books, 2016, chap. 2.

Bender, John R., Lucinda D. Davenport, et al. *Writing and Reporting for the Media.* New York: Oxford University Press, 2016.

Dvorkin, Jeffrey. *Critical New Literacy.* New York: Routledge, 2019.

Green, John (MediaWise and the Stanford History Education Group). "CrashCourse: Navigating Digital Information." YouTube.com.

Klaidman, Stephen, and Tom L. Beauchamp. *The Virtuous Journalist.* New York: Oxford University Press, 1987.

Lazere, Donald. *Thinking Critically about Media and Politics.* Boulder, CO: Paradigm, 2013.

Schiffer, Adam J. *Evaluating Media Bias.* Lanham, MD: Rowman & Littlefield, 2018.

Chapter 6: Manipulation through Fallacies and Rhetoric

Lazere, Donald. *Thinking Critically about Media and Politics.* Boulder, CO: Paradigm, 2013.

Roberts-Miller, Patricia. *Patricia Roberts-Miller* (blog). http://www.patriciarobertsmiller.com/.

Roberts-Miller, Patricia. *Demagoguery and Democracy.* New York: The Experiment, 2017.

Chapter 7: Experts and Evidence

Holdstein, Deborah H., and Danielle Aquiline. *Who Says? The Writer's Research.* New York: Oxford University Press, 2017.

Levitin, Daniel J. *Weaponized Lies: How to Think Critically in the Post-Truth Era.* New York: Dutton, 2016.

Nichols, Tom. *The Death of Expertise.* New York: Oxford University Press, 2017.

Novella, Steven, et al. *The Skeptics' Guide to the Universe.* New York: Grand Central, 2018.

Otto, Shawn. *The War on Science.* Minneapolis: Milkweed, 2016.

Chapter 8: Science, Nonscience, and the Media

Dawkins, Richard. *Climbing Mount Improbable.* New York: Norton, 1996.

Dennett, Daniel C. *Darwin's Dangerous Idea: Evolution and the Meanings of Life.* New York: Simon & Schuster, 1995.

Dvorkin, Jeffrey. *Critical News Literacy.* New York: Routledge, 2019.

Holdstein, Deborah H., and Danielle Aquiline. *Who Says? The Writer's Research.* New York: Oxford University Press, 2017.

IPCC. "2014: Summary for Policymakers." In *Climate Change 2014: Mitigation of Climate Change. Contribution of Working Group III to the Fifth Assessment Report of the Intergovernmental Panel on Climate Change,* edited by O. Edenhofer et al. Cambridge: Cambridge University Press, 2015.

Kitcher, Philip. *Living with Darwin: Evolution, Design, and the Future of Faith.* New York: Oxford University Press, 2006.

Levitin, Daniel. *A Field Guide to Lies and Statistics.* New York: Viking, 2016.

Levitan, Dave. *Not a Scientist.* New York: W. W. Norton, 2017.

Mooney, Chris, and Sheril Kirshenbaum. *Unscientific America: How Scientific Literacy Threatens Our Future.* New York: Basic Books, 2009.

National Academies of Sciences, Engineering, and Medicine. *Science Literacy: Concepts, Contexts, and Consequences.* Washington, DC: National Academies Press, 2016.

National Academies of Sciences, Institute of Medicine, *Science, Evolution, and Creationism.* Washington, DC: National Academies Press, 2008.

NASA. "Global Climate Change." NASA's Jet Propulsion Laboratory and California Institute of Technology. https://climate.nasa.gov/. Accessed July 14, 2019.

Otto, Shawn. *The War on Science*. Minneapolis: Milkweed, 2016.

Schick, Theodore, and Lewis Vaughn. *How to Think about Weird Things*, 8th ed. New York: McGraw-Hill, 2019.

Tyson, Neil D., and Donald Goldsmith. *Origins: Fourteen Billion Years of Cosmic Evolution*. New York: W. W. Norton, 2004.

Vaughn, Lewis. *The Power of Critical Thinking*, 6th ed. New York: Oxford University Press, 2019.

Chapter 9: Advertising: Commercial and Political

Bassham, Gregory, William Irwin, Henry Nardone, and James M. Wallace. *Critical Thinking: A Student's Introduction*, 5th ed. New York: McGraw-Hill, 2012.

McManus, John. *Don't Be Fooled: A Citizen's Guide to News and Information in the Digital Age*. Sunnyvale, CA: Unvarnished Press, 2012.

Appendix B: Answers to Exercises

Chapter 1
EXERCISE 1.1
2. Critical thinking is the systematic evaluation or formulation of beliefs or statements by rational standards. Information becomes knowledge when we process it through critical thinking.
6. Confirmation bias is the tendency to look for and recognize only information that confirms our existing views.
8. Homophily is the tendency to give more credence to a statement if it comes from our friends.
13. Filter bubbles shore up existing beliefs (whether true or false) and prevent contrary evidence or opposing views from piercing the bubble, often leading to positions that are misinformed, one-sided, bigoted, and hardened to stone.

CAPSTONE
1. Probably False
2. Probably False
3. Probably False
4. Probably True
5. Probably False
6. Probably True
7. Probably True
8. Probably False
9. Probably True
10. Probably False

Chapter 2
EXERCISE 2.1
4. Deductive.
8. Sound.
12. No.

EXERCISE 2.3
3. Valid.
6. Valid.
11. Invalid.
15. Valid.
20. Invalid.

Chapter 3
EXERCISE 3.1
3. Reasoning for the purpose of supporting a predetermined conclusion, not to uncover the truth.
6. The dead giveaway that you are skewing your thinking is a surge of strong emotions.
11. Group pressure can affect your attempts to think critically by allowing your need to be part of a group or your identification with a group undermine critical thinking.
14. The phenomenon of being ignorant of how ignorant you are.

EXERCISE 3.2
1. Self-interest.
4. Group pressure (in this case, the we-are-better-than-them type).
7. Group pressure.
10. Self-interest.

EXERCISE 3.3
1. a. The charges are false.
   c. Important evidence that would exonerate Father Miller was not mentioned in the newspaper account.

3. a. A study from Harvard shows that women are less violent and less emotional than men.
6. No good reasons listed.

EXERCISE 3.4
1. Better-than-others group pressure. Possible negative consequence: failure to consider other points of view; discrimination against people who disagree with Ortega.
3. It's not entirely clear what the group's motivations are. This passage could easily be an example of better-than-others group pressure.
7. Appeal to popularity. Possible negative consequence: overlooking other factors that might be a lot more important than popularity.

EXERCISE 3.5
3. Do not agree. Persuasive evidence would include the body of an alien or the alien craft itself, both scientifically documented as being of extraterrestrial origin.
8. Do not agree. Persuasive evidence would include several double-blind, controlled trials demonstrating that meditation and controlled breathing shrink tumors.

Chapter 6
EXERCISE 6.1
4. The fallacy of composition is arguing that what is true of the parts must be true of the whole.
10. They are fallacious because they assume that a proposition is true merely because a great number of people believe it; however, as far as the truth of a claim is concerned, what many people believe is irrelevant.
15. Yes.
19. People are often taken in by false dilemmas because they don't think beyond the alternatives laid before them.

EXERCISE 6.2
1. Composition.
5. Genetic fallacy.
10. Appeal to the person.
14. Equivocation.
19. Appeal to the person.
24. Stereotyping.
26. Euphemism.

EXERCISE 6.3
4. False dilemma.
6. Hasty generalization.
10. False dilemma.

EXERCISE 6.4
3. Jones says that Mrs. Anan deserves the Nobel Prize. But he's a friend of hers.

   Clearly then Mrs. Anan does not deserve the Nobel Prize.
6. In light of ethical considerations, the Boy Scouts of America should allow gay kids to be members. The reason is that banning gay kids from the organization would be in conflict with basic moral principles.
11. There are too many guns on the streets because our politicians are controlled by the National Rifle Association and other gun nuts. We don't want the NRA telling us what to do.

Chapter 7
EXERCISE 7.1
4. We should proportion our belief to the evidence.
10. Two additional indicators are reputation among peers and professional accomplishments.

EXERCISE 7.2
4. Proportion belief to the evidence; the claim is not dubious enough to dismiss out of hand, and not worthy of complete acceptance. Low plausibility.

6. Reject it; it conflicts with a great deal of background information.
10. Proportion belief to the evidence; the claim is not dubious enough to dismiss out of hand, and not worthy of complete acceptance. Moderate plausibility.
14. Reject it; it conflicts with a great deal of background information.
17. Reject it; it conflicts with a great deal of background information.

EXERCISE 7.3
1. Reasons for doubt due to low visibility.
2. Reasons for doubt due to vague stimuli.

EXERCISE 7.4
1. Almost certainly false.
5. Almost certainly false.
6. Almost certainly false.
7. Almost certainly false.

EXERCISE 7.5
1. School violence is caused mainly by teens playing violent video games. Incidents of violence in schools have increased as more and more teens are playing violent video games, as the video games themselves have become more graphically and realistically violent, and as the number and variety of video games have expanded dramatically.

   Conclusion: School violence is caused mainly by teens playing violent video games. Weak. Overlooking relevant factors, failing to rule out coincidence.

3. Why are crime rates so high, the economy so bad, and our children so prone to violence, promiscuity, and vulgarity? These social ills have arisen—as they always have—from the "moral vacuum" created when Americans turn away from religion. Our current slide into chaos started when prayer was banned from public schools and secular humanism swooped in to replace it. And as God has slowly faded from public life, we have got deeper in the hole.

   Conclusion: Serious social ills occur because Americans turn away from religion. Weak. Overlooking relevant factors, failing to rule out coincidence.

4. Ever since I started drinking herbal tea in the morning, my energy level has improved and I'm a lot calmer during the day. That stuff works.

   Conclusion: Herbal tea boosts energy and calms the nerves. Weak. Overlooking relevant factors, failing to rule out coincidence, possibly confusing cause and effect.

Chapter 8
EXERCISE 8.1
6. (1) Identify the problem or pose a question, (2) devise a hypothesis to explain the event or phenomenon, (3) derive a test implication or prediction, (4) perform the test, (5) accept or reject the hypothesis.
9. If H, then C. Not-C. Therefore, not-H.
12. No. Hypotheses are tested together with other hypotheses. A hypothesis can always be saved from refutation by making changes in one of the accompanying hypotheses.
16. Inference to the best explanation.
20. The main problem with conspiracy theories is that they fail the criteria of adequacy, especially the criterion of simplicity.

EXERCISE 8.2
2. Hypothesis: Two guys are perpetrating a Bigfoot hoax. Test implication: If the two guys are perpetrating a hoax, then monitoring their behavior day and night should yield evidence of hoaxing activity.
6. Hypothesis: Creatine dramatically increases the performance of weight trainers. Test implication: If creatine increases

performance, then giving creatine to weight trainers in a controlled way (in a double-blind controlled trial) would result in dramatically enhanced performance.

12. Hypothesis: Juan did the fatal stabbing. Test implication: If the hypothesis is true, at least some of the blood on his shirt is likely to belong to the victim, which a DNA test can confirm.

EXERCISE 8.3

3. Theory: Global climate change. Competing theory: Heat from volcanic activity around the planet is melting the glaciers. Both theories are about equal in terms of testability, fruitfulness, and scope. The volcanic theory, however, is neither simple nor conservative. It's not simple because it assumes an unknown process. It's not conservative because it is not consistent with what is known about the effects of heat from volcanoes.

7. Theory: Religion fosters terrorism. Competing theory: Terrorists commit terrorist acts because they are insane. Both theories are about equal in terms of testability, fruitfulness, scope, and simplicity. The insanity theory, though, is not conservative. It conflicts with what we know about those who commit terrorist acts. In general, terrorists may be fanatical, but they do not seem to be clinically insane.

EXERCISE 8.4

2. Test implication: If brighter street lights decrease the crime rate, then reducing the brightness of the lights (while keeping constant all other factors, such as police patrols) should increase the crime rate. The test would likely confirm the theory.

6. Test implication: If eating foods high in fat contributes more to overweight than eating foods high in carbohydrates, then over time people should gain more body weight when they are eating X number of grams of fat per day than when they are eating the same number of grams of carbohydrates per day.

Chapter 9

EXERCISE 9.1

4. The best response is reasonable skepticism.

6. Paid search ads are ads that show up in search engine results. Display ads are ads that are presented on websites (or topic-specific sections of websites) that are related to the product or service being touted.

9. The 1964 "Peace, Little Girl" ad.

Glossary

ad hoc hypothesis: A hypothesis, or theory, that cannot be verified independently of the phenomenon it's supposed to explain. Ad hoc hypotheses always make a theory less simple—and therefore less credible.

ad hominem (appeal to the person): The fallacy of rejecting a claim by criticizing the person who makes it rather than the claim itself. *Ad hominem* means "to the man."

advertising: The practice of calling the public's attention to something to induce them to buy products or services or otherwise change their opinions or behavior.

affirming the antecedent: See *modus ponens*.

affirming the consequent: An invalid argument form:

If *p*, then *q*.
q.
Therefore, *p*.

analogical induction: See **argument by analogy**.

antecedent: In the first part of a conditional statement (If *p*, then *q*), the component that begins with the word *if*. See also **conditional statement**.

appeal to authority, fallacious: See **fallacious appeal to authority**.

appeal to common practice: The fallacy of accepting or rejecting a claim based solely on what groups of people generally do or how they behave (when the action or behavior is irrelevant to the truth of the claim).

appeal to emotion: The fallacy of using emotions in place of relevant reasons as premises in an argument.

appeal to ignorance: The fallacy of arguing that a lack of evidence proves something. In one type of this fallacy, the problem arises by thinking that a claim must be true because it hasn't been shown to be false. In another type, the breakdown in logic comes when you argue that a claim must be false because it hasn't been proved to be true.

appeal to pity: The attempt to persuade people to accept a conclusion by evoking their pity, compassion, or empathy.

appeal to popularity (or bandwagon fallacy): The fallacy of arguing that a claim must be true merely because a substantial number of people believe it.

appeal to the person: See **ad hominem**.

appeal to tradition: The fallacy of arguing that a claim must be true just because it's part of a tradition.

apple polishing: The attempt to persuade people to accept a conclusion by flattering them.

argument: A group of statements in which some of them (the premises) are intended to support another of them (the conclusion).

argument by analogy (analogical induction): An argument making use of analogy, reasoning that because two or more things are similar in several respects, they must be similar in some further respect.

argument from outrage: The attempt to influence people to accept a claim by getting them intensely angry at a particular situation.

authority, fallacious appeal to: See **fallacious appeal to authority**.

availability error: Relying on evidence not because it's trustworthy but because it's memorable or striking—that is, psychologically available.

background information: Background information is that huge collection of very well supported beliefs that we all rely on to inform our actions and choices. A great deal of this lore consists of basic facts about everyday things, beliefs based on very good evidence (including our own personal observations and the statements of excellent authorities), and strongly justified claims that we would regard as "common sense" or "common knowledge." Background beliefs include obvious claims such as "The sun is hot," "The Easter bunny is not real," "Humans are mortal," "Fire burns," and "George Washington lived in the 18th century."

begging the question: The fallacy of attempting to establish the conclusion of an argument by using that conclusion as a premise. Also called *arguing in a circle*.

bias: A distorted and unfair perspective caused by the values of the writer or editor.

burden of proof: The weight of evidence or argument required by one side in a debate or disagreement.

causal argument: An inductive argument whose conclusion contains a causal claim.

causal claim: A statement about the causes of things.

claim: A statement; an assertion that something is or is not the case.

cogent argument: A strong inductive argument with all true premises.

commercial bias: Bias in news organizations that arises from their financial and institutional interests.

composition: The fallacy of arguing that what is true of the parts must be true of the whole. The error is thinking that the characteristics of the parts are somehow transferred to the whole, something that is not always the case.

compound statement: A statement composed of at least two constituent, or simple, statements.

conclusion: In an argument, the statement that the premises are intended to support.

conditional statement: An "if-then" statement; it consists of the antecedent (the part introduced by the word *if*) and the consequent (the part introduced by the word *then*).

confidence level: In statistical theory, the probability that the sample will accurately represent the target group within the margin of error.

confirmation bias: The tendency to look for and recognize only information that confirms our existing views.

consequent: The part of a conditional statement (If *p*, then *q*) introduced by the word *then*.

conservatism: A criterion of adequacy for judging the worth of theories. A conservative theory is one that fits with our established beliefs.

criteria of adequacy: The standards used to judge the worth of theories. They include *testability*, *fruitfulness*, *scope*, *simplicity*, and *conservatism*.

critical thinking: The systematic evaluation or formulation of beliefs, or statements, by rational standards.

decision-point fallacy: Arguing that because a line or distinction cannot be drawn at any point in a process, there are no differences or gradations in that process.

deductive argument: An argument intended to provide logically conclusive support for its conclusion.

deepfake: A counterfeit video that has been manipulated with artificial intelligence (AI) to show people doing or saying things they never actually did or said.

demagoguery: Demagoguery refers to the actions of political leaders who seek support by appealing to the desires and prejudices of ordinary people rather than by using rational argument.

denying the antecedent: An invalid argument form:

If p, then q.
Not p.
Therefore, not q.

denying the consequent: *See* **modus tollens**.

denying contrary evidence: The cognitive error of refusing to accept or acknowledge evidence that undermines our existing beliefs.

disjunctive syllogism: A valid argument form:

> Either *p* or *q*.
> Not *p*.
> Therefore, *q*.

In the syllogism's second premise, either disjunct can be denied.

division: The fallacy of arguing that what is true of the whole must be true of the parts. The error is thinking that characteristics of the whole must transfer to the parts or that traits of the group must be the same as traits of individuals in the group.

Dunning-Kruger effect: The phenomenon of being ignorant of how ignorant you are.

dysphemism: Words used to convey negative attitudes or emotions in place of neutral or positive ones.

enumerative induction: An inductive argument pattern in which we reason from premises about individual members of a group to conclusions about the group as a whole.

equivocation: The fallacy of using a word in two different senses in an argument.

euphemism: Words used to convey positive or neutral attitudes or emotions in place of more negative ones.

evidence: Something that makes a statement more likely to be true. (It does not mean "something that I feel or perceive is true.")

expert: Someone who is more knowledgeable in a particular subject area or field than most others are.

explanation: A statement or statements intended to tell why or how something is the case.

fake news: Deliberately false or misleading news stories that masquerade as truthful reporting.

fallacious appeal to authority: The mistake in which we rely on bogus expert opinion.

fallacy: An argument form that is both common and defective; a recurring mistake in reasoning.

false consensus effect: The tendency to overestimate the degree to which other people share our opinions, attitudes, and preferences.

false dilemma: The fallacy of asserting that there are only two alternatives to consider when there are actually more than two.

faulty analogy: A defective argument by analogy.

fruitfulness: A criterion of adequacy for judging the worth of theories. A fruitful theory is one that makes novel predictions.

gambler's fallacy: The error of thinking that previous events can affect the probabilities in the random event at hand.

genetic fallacy: The fallacy of arguing that a claim is true or false solely because of its abstract or nonhuman origins.

hasty generalization: The fallacy of drawing a conclusion about a target group based on an inadequate sample size.

homophily: The tendency to give more credence to a statement if it comes from our friends.

hypothetical syllogism: A valid argument made up of three hypothetical, or conditional, statements:

> If *p* then *q*.
> If *q*, then *r*.
> Therefore, if *p*, then *r*.

illusion-of-truth effect: The phenomenon in which you come to believe that a false claim is actually true simply because it is familiar.

indicator words: Words that frequently accompany arguments and signal that a premise or conclusion is present.

inductive argument: An argument in which the premises are intended to provide probable, not conclusive, support for its conclusion.

inference: The process of reasoning from a premise or premises to a conclusion based on those premises.

inference to the best explanation: A form of inductive reasoning in which we reason from premises about a state of affairs to an explanation for that state of affairs:

> Phenomenon *Q*.
> *E* provides the best explanation for *Q*.
> Therefore, it is probable that *E* is true.

innuendo: Suggesting something denigrating about a person without explicitly stating it.

invalid argument: A deductive argument that fails to provide conclusive support for its conclusion.

knowledge: True belief that is supported by sufficient evidence or reasoning.

logic: The study of good reasoning, or inference, and the rules that govern it.

margin of error: The variation between the values derived from a sample and the true values of the whole target group.

media literacy: The ability to access and understand media messages, apply critical thinking to them, and use them responsibly.

mere exposure effect: The idea that just being exposed repeatedly to words or images (even without registering them consciously) can induce a favorable or comfortable feeling toward them, whether or not there is any good reason for doing so.

***modus ponens* (affirming the antecedent):** A valid argument form:

If p, then q.
p.
Therefore, q.

***modus tollens* (denying the consequent):** A valid argument form:

If p, then q.
Not q.
Therefore, not p.

moral statement: A statement asserting that an action is right or wrong (moral or immoral) or that something (such as a person or motive) is good or bad.

motivated reasoning: Reasoning for the purpose of supporting a predetermined conclusion, not to uncover the truth.

native advertising: Paid advertising designed to imitate the tone, style, and look of a publication's editorial or journalistic content.

objectivity: In journalism, ensuring that the story exhibits no explicit or implicit preference for one set of values over another.

opinion: In news, expressions of views that often cannot be verified entirely through objective evidence—they are explanations, interpretations, judgments, speculations, and the like.

pandering: In journalism, a bias that involves slanting the news merely to increase the size of the audience rather than to enhance the readers' understanding or appreciation of an issue.

peer pressure: Group pressure to accept or reject a claim based solely on what one's peers think or do.

philosophical skepticism: The view that we know much less than we think we do or nothing at all.

philosophical skeptics: Those who embrace philosophical skepticism.

***post hoc, ergo propter hoc* ("after that, therefore because of that"):** The fallacy of reasoning that just because B followed A, A must have caused B.

prejudice: A negative or adverse belief about someone without sufficient reasons.

premise: In an argument, a statement, or reason, given in support of the conclusion.

random sampling: A method of selecting randomly from a target group in such a way as to ensure that the sample is representative. In a simple random selection, every member of the target group has an equal chance of being selected for the sample.

reasonable skepticism: An attitude that involves giving up the habit of automatically accepting claims in the media, rejecting the questionable assumption that most of what's said online is true, and refusing to believe a claim unless there are legitimate reasons for doing so.

red herring: The fallacy of deliberately raising an irrelevant issue during an argument. The basic pattern is to put forth a claim and then couple it with additional claims that may seem to support it but in fact are mere distractions.

representative sample: In enumerative induction, a sample that resembles the target group in all relevant ways.

rhetoric: The use of nonargumentative, emotive words and phrases to persuade or influence an audience.

rhetorical definitions: Influencing someone through an emotion-charged skewed definition.

ridicule: The use of derision, sarcasm, laughter, or mockery to disparage a person or idea.

sample (sample member): In enumerative induction, the observed members of the target group.

scare tactics: The attempt to persuade people to accept a conclusion by scaring them.

scientific method: Systematic observation and experimentation in the testing of theories.

scope: A criterion of adequacy for judging the worth of theories. A theory with scope is one that explains or predicts phenomena other than that which it was introduced to explain.

self-selecting sample: A type of sample that usually tells you very little about the target population.

sensationalism: In journalism, the covering or hyping of events (often trivial) to rouse emotions that distract from more important subjects or issues.

simplicity: A criterion of adequacy for judging the worth of theories. A simple theory is one that makes minimal assumptions.

slippery slope: The fallacy of arguing, without good reasons, that taking a particular step will inevitably lead to further, undesirable steps.

social relativism: The view that truth is relative to societies.

sound argument: A deductively valid argument that has true premises.

statement (claim): An assertion that something is or is not the case.

stereotyping: Judging someone not as an individual, but as part of a group whose members are thought to be all alike.

straw man: The fallacy of distorting, weakening, or oversimplifying someone's position so it can be more easily attacked or refuted.

strong argument: An inductive argument that succeeds in providing very probable—but not conclusive—support for its conclusion.

subjective relativism: The idea that truth depends on what someone believes.

subjectivist fallacy: Accepting the notion of subjective relativism or using it to try to support a claim.

syllogism: A deductive argument made up of three statements—two premises and a conclusion. *See also **modus ponens** and **modus tollens**.*

testability: A criterion of adequacy for judging the worth of theories. A testable theory is one in which there is some way to determine whether the theory is true or false—that is, it predicts something other than what it was introduced to explain.

TEST formula: A four-step procedure for evaluating the worth of a theory: (1) state the **T**heory and check for consistency, (2) assess the **E**vidence for the theory, (3) **S**crutinize alternative theories, and (4) **T**est the theories with the criteria of adequacy.

truth-preserving: A characteristic of a valid deductive argument in which the logical structure guarantees the truth of the conclusion if the premises are true.

***tu quoque* ("you're another"):** A type of ad hominem fallacy that argues that a claim must be true (or false) just because the claimant is hypocritical.

two wrongs make a right: Arguing that your doing something morally wrong is justified because someone else has done the same (or similar) thing.

valid argument: A deductive argument that succeeds in providing conclusive support for its conclusion.

weak argument: An inductive argument that fails to provide strong support for its conclusion.

whataboutism: The reversing of an accusation by arguing that an opponent is guilty of an equally bad or worse offense.

worldview: A philosophy of life; a set of beliefs and theories that helps us make sense of a wide range of issues in life.

Notes

Chapter 1: Critical Thinking and the Challenges of Modern Media

1. P. W. Singer and Emerson T. Brooking, *LikeWar: The Weaponization of Social Media* (Boston: Houghton, Mifflin, Harcourt, 2018), 123–124.
2. Guy P. Harrison, *Think Before You Like* (Amherst, NY: Prometheus Books, 2017), 74.
3. Singer and Brooking, *LikeWar*, 138–139.
4. Singer and Booking, *LikeWar*, 140.
5. Singer and Booking, *LikeWar*, 147.
6. Jacques Steinberg, "2005: In a Word; Truthiness," *New York Times*, December 25, 2005.
7. Amanda Taub, "The Real Story about Fact News Is Partisanship," *New York Times*, January 11, 2017.
8. Nathan P. Kalmoe and Lilliana Mason, "Lethal Mass Partisanship: Prevalence, Correlates, and Electoral Contingencies" (paper prepared for the January 2019 NCAPSA American Politics Meeting), https://www.dannyhayes.org/uploads/6/9/8/5/69858539/kalmoe___mason_ncapsa_2019_-_lethal_partisanship_-_final_lmedit.pdf.
9. Sam Wineburg, Sarah McGrew, Joel Breakstone, and Teresa Ortega, "Evaluating Information: The Cornerstone of Civic Online Reasoning," November 22, 2016, Stanford Digital Repository, http://purl.stanford.edu/fv751yt5934.
10. Wineburg et al., "Evaluating Information."
11. Wineburg et al., "Evaluating Information."
12. Stephen Law, *Believing Bullshit: How Not to Get Sucked into an Intellectual Black Hole* (Amherst, NY: Prometheus Books, 2011).

Chapter 2: Claims, Reasons, and Arguments

1. Walter Sinnott-Armstrong, "How to Win Every Argument," *Time*, July 2, 2018, Ideas and Society section.
2. Guy P. Harrison, *Think Before You Like* (Amherst, NY: Prometheus Books, 2017), 240–243.

Chapter 3: Obstacles to Critical Thinking

1. W. K. Clifford, "The Ethics of Belief," in *The Rationality of Belief in God*, ed. George I. Mavrodes (Englewood Cliff, NJ: Prentice-Hall, 1970), 159–160.
2. Bertrand Russell, *Let the People Think* (London: William Clowes, 1941), 2.
3. Guy P. Harrison, *Think Before You Like* (Amherst, NY: Prometheus Books, 2017), 186–187.
4. Lawrence Blum, *"I'm Not a Racist But . . .": The Moral Quandary of Race* (Ithaca, NY: Cornell University Press), 8–9.
5. Blum, *"Not a Racist,"* 1–2.
6. Thomas Gilovich, *How We Know What Isn't So* (New York: Free Press, 1991), 54.
7. Tom Nichols, *The Death of Expertise* (New York: Oxford University Press, 2017), 53.
8. Daniel Kahneman, *Thinking, Fast and Slow* (New York: Farrar, Straus, and Giroux, 2011), 66.
9. Kahneman, *Thinking*, 67.
10. Nichols, *Death of Expertise*, 44.
11. David Dunning, "Confident Idiots," *Pacific Standard*, October 27, 2014.

12. Nichols, *Death of Expertise*, 37.
13. Harrison, *Think Before You Like*, 185.
14. Steven Novella, "More on the Backfire Effect," NeuroLogica Blog, August 15, 2017, https://theness.com/neurologicablog/index.php/backfire-effect-not-significant/#more-10502.
15. Elizabeth Kolbert, "Why Facts Don't Change Our Minds," *New Yorker*, February 19, 2017.

Chapter 4: Fake News

1. Sabrina Tavernise, "As Fake News Spreads, More Readers Shrug at the Truth," in *Fake News: Read All About It* (New York: New York Times Company, 2017).
2. Center for Information Technology and Society, "The Danger of Fake News in Inflaming or Suppressing Social Conflict," CITS, https://www.cits.ucsb.edu/fake-news/danger-social (accessed April 28, 2019).
3. Scott Shane, "From Headline to Photograph, a Fake News Masterpiece," *New York Times*, January 18, 2017.
4. Shane, "Headline to Photograph."
5. Shane, "Headline to Photograph."
6. Sam Wineburg and Sarah McGrew, "Lateral Reading: Reading Less and Learning More When Evaluating Digital Information," Working Paper No. 2017 A1, Stanford History Education Group, September 2017, https://purl.stanford.edu/yk133ht8603.
7. Wineburg and McGrew, "Lateral Reading," 9.
8. Wineburg and McGrew, "Lateral Reading," 12.
9. Wineburg and McGrew, "Lateral Reading," 13–14.
10. Wineburg and McGrew, "Lateral Reading," 18.
11. Alex Kasprak, "Disguising Hate: How Radical Evangelicals Spread Anti-Islamic Vitriol on Facebook," Snopes.com, May 15, 2019, https://www.snopes.com/news/2019/05/15/radical-evangelical-facebook/ (May 19, 2019).
12. Dan Evon, "Is the 'Haiku Bird' a Real Creature?" Snopes.com, April 8, 2019, https://www.snopes.com/fact-check/haiku-bird/.
13. David Mikkelson, "Does This Photograph Show a Girl Forced into Child Marriage by Muslims?," Snopes.com, March 18, 2019, https://www.snopes.com/fact-check/girl-forced-child-marriage-meme/.
14. Dan Evon, "Does This Photograph Show a Migrant Caravan Member Urinating on the U.S. Flag?," Snopes.com, November 6, 2018, https://www.snopes.com/fact-check/caravan-urinate-flag-photo/.
15. Dan Evon, "Does This Photograph Show John McCain with Osama bin Laden?," Snopes.com, August 27, 2018, https://www.snopes.com/fact-check/mccain-bin-laden-photo/.
16. Dan Evon, "Does This Image Show a Peaceful Meeting of a Lion and a Zebra at a Watering Hole?," Snopes.com, July 31, 2018, https://www.snopes.com/fact-check/zebra-lion-watering-hole/.
17. Dan Evon, "Does This Photograph Show Border Agents Forcibly Separating Children from Families?," Snopes.com, June 21, 2018, https://www.snopes.com/fact-check/is-photograph-border-agents-separating-children/.
18. Cristiano Lima, "'Nightmarish': Lawmakers Brace for Swarm of 2020 Deepfakes," *Politico*, June 13, 2019, https://www.politico.com/story/2019/06/13/facebook-deepfakes-2020-1527268.
19. Kevin Roose, "Here Come the Fake Videos, Too," *New York Times*, March 4, 2018, https://www.nytimes.com/2018/03/04/technology/fake-videos-deepfakes.html?module=inline.
20. Miles O'Brien, "Why 'Deepfake' Videos Are Becoming More Difficult to Detect," June 12, 2019, PBS NewsHour, PBS.org, https://www.pbs.org/newshour/show/why-deepfake-videos-are-becoming-more-difficult-to-detect.

Chapter 5: Media Bias

1. Stephen Klaidman and Tom L. Beauchamp, *The Virtuous Journalist* (New York: Oxford University Press, 1987), 50.
2. Klaidman and Beauchamp, *Virtuous Journalist*, 35.
3. John McManus, *Don't Be Fooled!* (Sunnyvale, CA: Unvarnished Press, 2012).
4. Klaidman and Beauchamp, *Virtuous Journalist*, 46.
5. Klaidman and Beauchamp, *Virtuous Journalist*, 46–47.
6. Much of this material is based on comments by Klaidman and Beauchamp.
7. W. James Potter, *Media Literacy* (Thousand Oaks, CA: Sage, 2016), 197.
8. Amy Mitchell, Jeffrey Gottfried, Michael Barthel, and Nami Sumida, "Distinguishing between Factual and Opinion Statements in the News," Pew Research Center, June 18, 2018, https://www.journalism.org/2018/06/18/distinguishing-between-factual-and-opinion-statements-in-the-news/.
9. Paul Krugman, "Trump's Taking Us from Temper Tantrum to Trade War," *New York Times*, July 2, 2018.
10. Larry Atkins, *Skewed: A Critical Thinker's Guide to Media Bias* (Amherst, NY: Prometheus Books, 2016), chap. 2.
11. Atkins, *Skewed*, chap. 1.
12. Adam J. Schiffer, *Evaluating Media Bias* (Lanham, MD: Rowman & Littlefield, 2018), 33.
13. Schiffer, *Evaluating Media Bias*, 54.
14. Schiffer, *Evaluating Media Bias*, 24.
15. Schiffer, *Evaluating Media Bias*, 2.
16. McManus, *Don't Be Fooled!*, 44.
17. McManus, *Don't Be Fooled!*, 58.
18. Schiffer, *Evaluating Media Bias*, 61–62.
19. McManus, *Don't Be Fooled!*, 72.

Chapter 6: Manipulation through Fallacies and Rhetoric

1. Patricia Roberts-Miller, "Characteristics of Demagoguery," http://www.patriciarobertsmiller.com/characteristics-of-demagoguery/ (accessed March 31, 2019).
2. The inspiration for this unconventional categorization comes primarily from Ludwig F. Schlecht, "Classifying Fallacies Logically," *Teaching Philosophy* 14, no. 1 (1991): 53–64; and Greg Bassham et al., *Critical Thinking: A Student's Introduction* (San Francisco: McGraw-Hill, 2002).
3. Itamar Shatz, "How to Counter Ad Hominem Arguments," *Effectiviology*, https://effectiviology.com/ad-hominem-fallacy/ (accessed April 3, 2019).
4. W. Ross Winterowd and Geoffrey R. Winterowd, *The Critical Reader, Thinker, and Writer* (Mountain View, CA: Mayfield, 1992), 447–448.
5. Reported in Richard Whately, *Elements of Logic* (London: Longman, Greens, 1826).
6. "Gay Marriage Opponents Warn Supreme Court Ruling Could Put Nation on Slippery Slope to Rationality," *The Onion*, June 26, 2013.
7. Ideas from Elise Hennigan, "Stereotypes That Democrats Are Tired of Hearing," *Ranker*, 2019, https://www.ranker.com/list/stereotypes-democrats-are-sick-of/elise (accessed April 8, 2019).
8. Ideas from Elise Hennigan, *Ranker*, "Stereotypes That Republicans Are Tired of Hearing," 2019, https://www.ranker.com/list/stereotypes-republicans-are-sick-of/elise (accessed April 8, 2019).
9. Matthew Hutson, "Why Liberals Aren't as Tolerant as They Think," *Politico.com*, May 9, 2017, https://www.politico.com/magazine/story/2017/05/09/why-liberals-arent-as-tolerant-as-they-think-215114.

Chapter 7: Experts and Evidence

1. From Tom Nichols, *The Death of Expertise* (New York: Oxford University Press, 2017), 29.
2. Bertrand Russell, *Let the People Think* (London: William Clowes, 1941), 1.
3. NASA and the California Institute of Technology, "Climate Change: How Do We Know?," https://climate.nasa.gov/evidence/ (accessed July 3, 2019).
4. Nichols, *Death of Expertise*, 202–203.
5. Hal Arkowitz and Scott O. Lilienfield, "Why Science Tells Us Not to Rely on Eyewitness Accounts," *Scientific American*, January 1, 2010.
6. Francis Collins, "No Link between MMR Vaccine and Autism, Even in Higher Risk Kids," National Institutes of Health, NIH Director's Blog, April 28, 2015, https://directorsblog.nih.gov/2015/04/28/no-link-between-mmr-vaccine-and-autism-even-in-high-risk-kids/.

Chapter 8: Science, Nonscience, and the Media

1. Shawn Lawrence Otto, *The War on Science: Who's Waging It, Why It Matters, What We Can Do About It* (Minneapolis: Milkweed Editions, 2016), chap. 1.
2. Excerpted from Robert L. Park, "The Seven Warning Signs of Bogus Science," *Chronicle of Higher Education*, January 31, 2003, http://chronicle.com/free/v49/i21/21b02001.htm.
3. See Stephen Barrett et al., *Consumer Health*, 6th ed. (New York: WCB/McGraw-Hill, 1993), 239–240.
4. W. V. Quine and J. S. Ullman, *The Web of Belief* (New York: Random House, 1970), 43–44.
5. Thomas S. Kuhn, *The Copernican Revolution: Planetary Astronomy in the Development of Western Thought* (Cambridge, MA: Harvard University Press, 1957), 179.
6. Paraphrased from section 4a of Act 590 of the Acts of Arkansas of 1981, "Balanced Treatment for Creation-Science and Evolution-Science Act."
7. National Academy of Sciences, *Science and Creationism* (Washington, DC: National Academy Press, 1998).
8. National Academy of Sciences, *Science and Creationism*.
9. National Academy of Sciences, Institute of Medicine, *Science, Evolution, and Creationism* (Washington, DC: National Academies Press, 2008), 39.
10. Theodosius Dobzhansky, quoted in National Academy of Sciences, *Science and Creationism*, www.nap.edu/openbook.php?record_id=6024.
11. National Academy of Sciences, "Preface," in *Science and Creationism*.
12. National Academy of Sciences, Institute of Medicine, *Science, Evolution, and Creationism* (Washington, DC: National Academies Press, 2008), 4.
13. National Academy of Sciences, *Science, Evolution*, 41.
14. Philip Kitcher, *Living with Darwin: Evolution, Design, and the Future of Faith* (New York: Oxford University Press, 2006), p. 103.
15. Clergy Letter Project, "The Clergy Letter from American Christian Clergy: An Open Letter Concerning Religion and Science," https://www.theclergyletterproject.org/Christian_Clergy/ChrClergyLtr.htm (accessed July 13, 2019).
16. Francis Collins, *The Language of God: A Scientist Presents Evidence for Belief* (New York: Free Press, 2007), 6.
17. Matthew C. Nisbet, "Sciences, Publics, Politics: The Trouble with Climate Emergency Journalism," *Issues in Science and Technology* 35, no. 4 (Summer 2019): 23–26.

18. D. J. Wuebbles et al., "2017: Executive Summary," in *Climate Science Special Report: Fourth National Climate Assessment, Volume I*, ed. D. J. Wuebbles et al. (Washington, DC: U.S. Global Change Research Program), 12–34, doi: 10.7930/J0DJ5CTG.
19. Intergovernmental Panel on Climate Change (IPCC), *Climate Change 2014: Synthesis Report, Summary for Policymakers*, https://www.ipcc.ch/site/assets/uploads/2018/02/AR5_SYR_FINAL_SPM.pdf, 2 (accessed July 15, 2019).
20. IPCC, *Climate Change 2014*, 4.
21. NASA, *Global Climate Change*, "Global Climate Change: Vital Signs of the Planet," https://climate.nasa.gov/ (accessed July 15, 2019).
22. Wuebbles, "Executive Summary."
23. NASA, "Global Climate Change."
24. Earth Observatory NASA, "How Is Today's Warming Different from the Past?" https://earthobservatory.nasa.gov/features/GlobalWarming/page3.php (accessed July 15, 2019).
25. Earth Observatory NASA, "Today's Warming."
26. NASA, "Is the Sun Causing Global Warming?," https://climate.nasa.gov/faq/14/is-the-sun-causing-global-warming/ (accessed February 20, 2020).
27. National Academy of Sciences/The Royal Society, *Climate Change: Evidence and Causes*, http://dels.nas.edu/resources/static-assets/exec-office-other/climate-change-full.pdf, 3 (accessed July 17, 2019).
28. National Academy, *Climate Change*, 5.
29. National Academy, *Climate Change*, 5.
30. American Association for the Advancement of Science, "AAAS Reaffirms Statements on Climate Change and Integrity," December 4, 2009, https://www.aaas.org/news/aaas-reaffirms-statements-climate-change-and-integrity.
31. National Academy, *Climate Change*, 13.
32. HealthNewsReview.org, "Chocolate Prevents Preeclampsia? How a Medical Society's Poor PR Helped Drive This Misleading Message," February 8, 2016, https://www.healthnewsreview.org/2016/02/chocolate-prevents-preeclampsia-how-a-medical-societys-poor-pr-helped-drive-this-misleading-message/.
33. David and Mark G. L. Sayers, "Prominent Exostosis Projecting from the Occipital Squama More Substantial and Prevalent in Young Adult than Older Age Groups," *Nature*, February 20, 2018, https://www.nature.com/articles/s41598-018-21625-1#Sec4.
34. Steven Novella, "People Growing Horns? More Bad Science Reporting," NeuroLogica Blog, June 21, 2019, https://theness.com/neurologicablog/index.php/people-growing-horns-more-bad-science-reporting/#more-11484.
35. Stan Young, "'Meat Kills' Study Is Rotten to the Bone, but NYT Swallows It Anyway," American Council on Science and Health, April 24, 2019, https://www.acsh.org/news/2019/04/24/meat-kills-study-rotten-bone-nyt-swallows-it-anyhow-13948.
36. Health Feedback and Credibility Coalition, "The Most Popular Health Articles of 2018, a Scientific Credibility Review," January 28, 2019, https://healthfeedback.org/the-most-popular-health-articles-of-2018-a-scientific-credibility-review/.
37. Health Feedback and Credibility Coalition, "Most Popular Health Articles."
38. Johann Hari, "Is Everything You Think You Know about Depression Wrong?," *Guardian*, January 7, 2018, https://www.theguardian.com/society/2018/jan/07/is-everything-you-think-you-know-about-depression-wrong-johann-hari-lost-connections.
39. Hari, "Everything You Think."
40. Tom Byrne and Matthew Normand, "The Demon-Haunted Sentence," *Skeptical Inquirer* 24, no. 2 (March/April 2000): 46–47.

41. Robert T. Carroll, "Ouija Board," Skeptic's Dictionary, http://skepdic.com (accessed October 27, 2003).
42. Joe Nickell, "Psychic Pets and Pet Psychics," *Skeptical Inquirer* 26, no. 6 (November/December 2002): 13.
43. Jenna Barrington, "Study Finds Magnesium Treats Mild-to-Moderate Depression without the Side Effects of Drugs," Healthy Holistic Living, May 11, 2018, https://www.healthy-holistic-living.com/magnesium-treats-depression-better-antidepressant-drugs/.
44. Adam Goldberg, "Cannabis Oil (THC, CBD) Kills Cancer Cells, Leaving Healthy Cells in Perfect Harmony," anonews.com, October 18, 2018, https://web.archive.org/web/20190124094328/http://www.anonews.co/cannabis-oil-thc-cbd-kills-cancer-cells-leaving-healthy-cells-in-perfect-harmony/.
45. BonBon, "Moringa Leaves Benefits: 10 Surprising Benefits of Drinking Moringa," Tinhtamvn [blog], September 14, 2018, https://tinhtamvn.net/moringa-leaves-benefits-10-surprising-benefits-of-drinking-moringa/.

Chapter 9: Advertising: Commercial and Political

1. Dina Srinivasan, "How Digital Advertising Markets Really Work," *American Prospect*, June 24, 2019, https://prospect.org/article/how-digital-advertising-markets-really-work.
2. Glenn Kessler, "Introducing the Fact Checker's Guide to Manipulated Video," *Washington Post*, June 25, 2019, https://www.washingtonpost.com/politics/2019/06/25/introducing-fact-checkers-guide-manipulated-video/.
3. Eugene Kiely, D'Angelo Gore, and Robert Farley, "Republican Closing Ads: Immigration," FactCheck.org, November 2, 2018, https://www.factcheck.org/2018/11/republican-closing-ads-immigration/.
4. D'Angelo Gore, "Sen. Manchin, Often Votes with Trump," FactCheck.org, August 24, 2018, https://www.factcheck.org/2018/08/sen-manchin-often-votes-with-trump/.
5. Lori Robertson, "Democratic Closing Ads: Health Care and Taxes," FactCheck.org, November 2, 2018, https://www.factcheck.org/2018/11/democratic-closing-ads-health-care-and-taxes/.
6. "Seeing Is Believing: The Fact Checker's Guide to Manipulated Video," *Washington Post*, https://www.washingtonpost.com/graphics/2019/politics/fact-checker/manipulated-video-guide/?noredirect=on.
7. Julia Carrie Wong, "'It Might Work Too Well': The Dark Art of Political Advertising Online," *Guardian*, March 19, 2018, https://www.theguardian.com/technology/2018/mar/19/facebook-political-ads-social-media-history-online-democracy.
8. Eugene Kiely, D'Angelo Gore, and Robert Farley, "Republican Closing Ads: Immigration," FactCheck.org, November 2, 2018, https://www.factcheck.org/2018/11/republican-closing-ads-immigration/.
9. Eugene Kiely, "PAC Attack on Kelli Ward Badly Misfires," FactCheck.org, August 15, 2018, https://www.factcheck.org/2018/08/pac-attack-on-kelli-ward-badly-misfires/.

Credits

Fig 1.1: Wineburg, Wineburg, Sam and McGrew, Sarah and Breakstone, Joel and Ortega, Teresa, (2016), "Evaluating Information: The Cornerstone of Civic Online Reasoning," Stanford Digital Repository

Fig 1.2: Wineburg, Sam and McGrew, Sarah and Breakstone, Joel and Ortega, Teresa, (2016), "Evaluating Information: The Cornerstone of Civic Online Reasoning," Stanford Digital Repository

Fig 8.1: NASA figure adapted from Goddard Insti,Analysis.

Fig 8.2: Credit: Luthi, D., et al.. 2008; Etheridge, D.M., et al. 2010; Vostok ice core data/J.R. Petit wet al.; NOAA Mauna Loa CO2 record.)

Fig 8.8: Prominent exostosis projecting from the occipital squama more substantial and prevalent in young adult than older age groups, David Shahar & Mark G. L. Sayers, Scientific Reports volume 8, Article number: 3354 (2018)

Fig 8.9: Flora Teoh, Em manuel Vincent/Health Feedback, healthfeedback.org

Fig 8.10: Flora Teoh, Emmanuel Vincent/Health Feedback, healthfeedback.org

Fig 9.6: By permission of The Ridge Wallet

Index

Note: Figures are indicated by an *f*

A

AAP. *See* American Academy of Pediatrics
ABC News, bias rating for, 138
accuracy, 122
ACPeds. *See* American College of Pediatricians
ad hoc hypothesis, 234
ad hominem fallacy. *See* appeal to person fallacy
advertising. *See also* internet advertising; native advertisement; political advertising
   bias and, 137
   defined, 284
   facts behind, 284
   fallacies used in, 286
   how it works, 284–86
   identification used in, 290
   McManus on, 137
   misleading comparisons, 290–91
   as motivated reasoning, 284
   old school tricks in, 290–91
   online, 285
   reasonable skepticism about, 285–86
   slogans, 290
   suspicion, 285–86
   weasel words, 291
advocacy
   Atkins on, 129–30
   benefits of, 129
   bias and, 127–30
   downside of, 129–30
   opinion writing as, 129–30
affirming the antecedent, 43, 46
affirming the consequent
   hypothesis and, 223
   as invalid, 45, 46
after that, therefore because of that. *See* post hoc, ergo propter hoc
AI. *See* artificial intelligence
airplane travel example, 77
AllSides.com, 101
American Academy of Pediatrics (AAP)
   background about, 98–99, 98*f*
   fact-checkers view of, 100
   reading laterally and, 98–100, 98*f*
American College of Pediatricians (ACPeds)
   background about, 98–99, 99*f*
   fact-checkers view of, 100
   historians view of, 100
   reading laterally and, 98–99, 99*f*, 100
   students view of, 101
analogical induction, 48–49
analysis
   bias and, 127–30
   opinion compared with, 128
Anaximander, 244
anecdotes, 264
animal studies, 265
antecedent, 43, 46
anti-ICE ad, 293–94, 293*f*
antipathy, 72
appeal to common practice, 71
appeal to emotion fallacy
   defined, 161, 165
   forms, 162–63
   persuasion and, 162
appeal to ignorance fallacy
   burden of proof and, 160–61
   defined, 159, 165
   evidence and, 159–60
   irrelevant premises and, 159–61, 165
   negative claim and, 161
   nonexperts and, 194
appeal to person fallacy
   circumstances and, 154
   claims and, 153–54
   defined, 152, 165
   irrelevant premises and, 152–56
   personal attack, 154
   poisoning well and, 155–56
   responding to, 156
   stereotyping and, 176, 178
   Trump and, 152*f*, 153*f*, 155*f*
   tu quoque as, 154
   varieties, 154–56
   whataboutism as, 154–55
appeal to pity, 162
appeal to popularity
   fallacy of, 157–58, 165
   groupthink and, 71
appeal to tradition fallacy, 158–59, 165
apple polishing, 162
argument. *See also* conclusion; deductive argument; inductive argument; invalid argument; premises; valid argument
   appeal to popularity and, 157–58
   assessing long, 52–56
   begging the question fallacy, 166–67
   clarity and, 36
   conclusion and, 32, 53
   conditional, 43, 169
   critical thinking and, 30
   decision-point fallacy and, 169–70
   defined, 31
   discrimination example, 53–54
   dissection tips for, 36–37
   enumerative induction, 47–48
   explanation versus, 34
   faulty analogy fallacy, 173
   fluff and, 55
   forms of, 37
   hasty generalization fallacy and, 172
   how to win, 30
   indicator words and, 34–35
   inference and, 32
   logical structure of, 38
   online, 41
   opinion, unsupported, and, 55
   from outrage, 163
   with parts identified, 32
   patterns, 42–52
   persuasion versus, 37
   reasons and, 31–37
   slippery slope fallacy and, 170–72
   straw man fallacy and, 164–65
   structure, 37–42

argument. (continued)
  torture example, 55–56
  with trolls, 51
  two kinds, 28
  variations of, 35–36
  verbiage sans, 32–34
Aristotle, 241
artificial intelligence (AI), 112–14
Atkins, Larry, 129–30
authority. *See* fallacious appeal to authority
autism, 204
autonomy, 102
availability error
  airplane travel example, 77
  defined, 9
  environmental hazards and, 78
  hasty generalization as, 78
  as mental obstacle, 77–78

B

backfire effect, 82
background information
  claims and, 187–89
  defined, 187
  fallibility of, 188–89
  trust in, 187–88
Beauchamp, Tom L.
  on accuracy, 122
  on completeness, 122
  on fairness, 123–24
  on objectivity, 123
begging the question
  critical thinking and, 15
  fallacy, 166–67, 172
Behe, Michael, 248
belief
  alternative medicine and, 220
  appeal to popularity and, 157–58
  backfire effect and, 82
  background information and, 187–89
  coincidence influencing, 201–2
  conservatism and, 235–36
  contrary evidence denial and, 9
  critical thinking and, 5
  demagoguery and, 148
  about expertise, 186
  false consensus effect and, 80
  freedom and, 6
  morality and, 68
  prejudice and, 71

  reasons and, 5
  Russell on, 189
  self-interested thinking and, 67
  statement and, 29
  technology influencing, 10–11
  true, 5
  worldview and, 5
bias. *See also* commercial bias; confirmation bias; partisan bias
  accuracy and, 122
  advertising and, 137
  advocacy and, 127–30
  analysis and, 127–30
  Atkins on, 129–30
  checking your own, 105–6
  cognitive, 78–82
  completeness and, 122
  connotation and, 125–26
  context revealing, 125
  defined, 124
  against experts, 194
  of experts, 192–93
  fake news and, 8–9, 13, 94, 105–6
  financial gain and, 193
  inconsistency and, 134
  liberal and conservative, 130, 132–34
  MBFC and, 124, 137–40
  objectivity and, 122–27
  opinion and, 127–30
  opinion poll, 270
  pandering, 135–36
  ratings, 138–40
  Schiffer on, 132–33, 135
  sensationalism, 136
  skewed focus, 136–37
  social media and, 78–82
  sources accuracy and, 137–40
  source selection and, 124–25
  turned tables test revealing, 134
  value-laden words revealing, 126–27
bin Laden, Osama, 109, 109f
Bloodworth, Kirk, 200
Blum, Lawrence, 72
Border Patrol agents fake image, 110, 110f
Borg example, 69–70
bot
  defined, 7
  Dixson as, 11
Brandt, Mark, 177

Brooking, Emerson T.
  on bots, 11
  on Dixson, 10–11
  on homophily, 9
burden of proof, 160–61
Buscemi, Steven, 112, 112f
Bush, George W.
  false dilemma fallacy used by, 168
  gut knowing of, 18
  reality and, 133

C

capital punishment example, 74, 88–89
Carter, Jimmy, 153
causal confusions
  cause and effect, 204–5
  coincidence, 201–2
  dose-response relationship, 202
  factors, multiple, and, 200–201
  nonintervention studies and, 226
  personal experience and, 199–205
  post hoc, ergo propter hoc, 202–4
  relevant factor misidentification, 199–200
  temporal order, 202–4
celebrity endorsements, 290
Center for Information Technology and Society, 93
chocolate during pregnancy story, 261, 261f, 262
circular reasoning, 15
civil discourse, 10
claims
  appeal to person fallacy and, 153–54
  appeal to tradition fallacy and, 158–59
  background information and, 187–89
  conflicting, 187
  demagoguery and, 148
  experts disagreement of, 189–90
  face saving and, 67
  illegitimate reasons for accepting, 96–97
  negative, 161
  passion and, 68–69
  questions to ask for verifying, 102–3

reasonable skepticism about, 96–97
reasons and, 29–30
self-interested thinking undermining, 67
Clifford, W. K., 68
climate change
cold weather and, 259
conspiracy of scientists theory of, 255–56, 258
"Global Climate Change," 252
global mean surface temperature and, 251f
greenhouse gas emissions and, 251–52, 252f
human activity theory, 256–59
IPCC on, 250–52
natural cycle theory of, 253–55, 258
Nisbet on, 249–50
popular theories of, 253–58
prevention, 254
regional trends in, 252–53
sun warming theory of, 255, 258
TEST formula applied to, 249–59
Climate Science Special Report (CSSR), 250
Clinton, Hillary
Harris and, 95
Manchin and, 294
red herring used against, 163–64
Russian fake news and, 93
CNN, bias rating for, 138
cogent inductive argument, 42
cognitive bias, 78–82
coincidence
belief influenced by, 201–2
probability and, 206
Colbert, Stephen
ridicule by, 178
on truthiness, 12
Collins, Francis, 249
Commentary (magazine), 140
commercial bias
advertising and, 137
forms of, 135–37
interests conflict leading to, 135
pandering, 135–36
Schiffer on, 135
sensationalism, 136
skewed focus, 136–37
completeness, 122
composition fallacy, 150–51, 165
conclusion

arguments revealing, 32
begging the question fallacy and, 166–67
deductive argument, 38–39
defined, 31
discrimination example, 53–54
dissection tips for, 36–37
equivocation fallacy and, 157
finding long argument, 53
hasty generalization fallacy and, 172
indicator words and, 34–35
inductive argument, 39
torture example, 55–56
true versus false, 40–42
unstated, 36
conditional argument
explained, 43
false dilemma fallacy and, 169
confidence level, 271–72
"Confident Idiots" (Dunning), 81
confirmation bias
backfire effect and, 82
capital punishment example and, 88–89
confirming/disconfirming evidence and, 75–76
defined, 8–9
as mental obstacle, 74–76
motivated reasoning as, 76
Nichols on, 75
connotation
bias and, 125–26
defined, 125
dysphemisms and, 175–76
euphemisms and, 175–76
consequent. *See* affirming the consequent; denying the consequent
conservatism
belief and, 235–36
bias and, 130, 132–34
criteria of, 51, 234–37
criteria of adequacy and, 234–37
defined, 235
evolution versus creationism example, 245
explanation and, 51
intolerance and, 177
plausibility and, 236
Ptolemaic theory and, 241–42
consilience, 217
consistency
internal/external, 228

TEST formula and, 229
conspiracy theories
conspiracy of scientists theory, 255–56, 258
criteria of adequacy and, 238
as nonfalsifiable hypotheses, 238
science and, 220
simplicity refuting, 51–52, 238
constructive mental tendency, 198
constructive perception, 232–33
context, 125
contrary evidence denial
defined, 9
as mental obstacle, 73–74
Copernicus versus Ptolemy example
Aristotle and, 241
Copernican theory, 242–43
Ptolemy theory, 241–42
TEST formula applied to, 241–43
criteria of adequacy
conservatism, 234–37
conspiracy theories and, 238
constructive perception and, 232–33
evolution versus creationism example and, 247
fruitfulness, 231–32
human activity theory and, 259
inference to best explanation and, 229–37
natural cycle theory and, 258
objectivity and, 237
preliminary assessment and, 240
rules for applying, 237
scientific theories and, 229–37
scope, 232–33
simplicity, 233–34
testability, 229–31
TEST formula using, 241
critical thinking. *See specific topics*
CSSR. *See* Climate Science Special Report
Cureg, Edgardo, 55–56

D

Daily Kos (blog and forum), 138
Darwin, Charles, 244
The Death of Expertise (Nichols), 75
death penalty example, 74, 88–89
decision-point fallacy, 169–70, 172
deductive argument
affirming the antecedent, 43, 46

deductive argument (continued)
  affirming the consequent, 45, 46
  conclusion and, 38–39
  denying the antecedent, 45, 46
  denying the consequent, 43–44, 46, 222
  disjunctive syllogism, 46
  hypothetical syllogism, 44, 46
  inductive argument compared with, 42
  invalid, 38–39
  patterns, 43–46
  premises, 38–39
  reductio ad absurdum, 44–45
  sound, 40
  truth and, 38
  valid, 37–38
deepfakes
  Buscemi and Lawrence, 112, 112f
  dangers of, 113–14
  defined, 112
  face swapping, 112, 112f
  fake news and, 112–14
  of Obama, 112, 112f
  reading laterally to combat, 114
  technology driving, 112–13
  of Zuckerberg, 112, 113f
demagoguery, 148
democracy, fake news and, 92–93
Democrat
  partisan bias and, 13–14
  stereotyping of, 176–77
denotation, 125
denying contrary evidence. *See* contrary evidence denial
denying the antecedent, 45, 46
denying the consequent
  scientific method and, 222
  as valid, 43–44, 46
depression, 267–68
Diaz, Alan, 110, 110f
discrimination example, 53–54
disjunctive syllogism
  false dilemma fallacy and, 169
  as valid, 46
display ads, 288
division fallacy, 151–52, 165
Dixson, Angee, 10–11
doctors, 191
domino theory. *See* slippery slope fallacy
dose-response relationship, 202
double-blind study
  element missing in, 263
  scientific method of, 225

Drudge Report, bias rating for, 140
Dunning, David, 81
Dunning-Kruger effect
  avoiding, 82
  defined, 81
  expertise and, 81–82
  ignorance and, 80–81
  social media and, 80–82
dysphemisms, 175–76

E

The Economist, bias rating for, 138–39
education, 192
effectiviology.com, 156
Einstein, Albert, 231–32
emotion. *See also* appeal to emotion fallacy
  self-interested thinking and, 69
enumerative induction
  argument, 47–48
  opinion polls as, 47, 268–69
  sample and, 47–48, 272
epistemology
  defined, 14
  intuition and, 18
  post-truth and, 14–15
equivocation fallacy, 157, 165
ethics
  belief and, 68
  fake news and, 102
  of journalism, 122
euphemisms, 175–76
Evaluating Media Bias (Schiffer), 132–33, 135
evidence
  anecdotal, 220
  appeal to ignorance fallacy and, 159–60
  assessment, 239
  background information and, 187–89
  burden of proof, 160–61
  confirming and disconfirming, 75–76
  defined, 73
  demagoguery and, 148
  denial of contrary, 9, 73–74
  for human activity theory, 256–57
  for natural cycle theory, 253–54
evolution versus creationism example

  conservatism and, 245
  criteria of adequacy and, 247
  ID and, 248
  indirect confirmation and, 246
  novel predictions and, 245–46
  religion and science in, 247–49
  scope and, 246–47
  simplicity and, 246
  testability and, 244–45
  TEST formula used with, 243–49
expectation, 198–99
experience, 192. *See also* personal experience
experiment, double-blind study, 225
experts
  background information and, 187–89
  beliefs about, 186
  bias against, 194
  bias of, 192–93
  causal confusions influencing, 199–205
  celebrity and, 196
  claims disagreement among, 189–90
  constructive mental tendency and, 198
  critical thinking and, 193–94
  The Death of Expertise, 75
  defined, 186
  doctors as, 191
  Dunning-Kruger effect and, 81–82
  education and, 192
  expectation and, 198–99
  experience and, 192
  fallacious appeal to authority, 190–91
  issues beyond, 194
  judging, 191–96
  memory and, 198
  Nichols on, 81–82, 195
  nonexperts and, 187–91
  outside one's field, 190–91
  perceptual impairment and, 197–98
  personal experience and, 196–205
  predictions of, 195
  prerequisites for, 192
  professional accomplishments and, 192
  reputation among peers for, 192
explanation. *See also* inference to best explanation

Index

argument versus, 34
conservatism and, 51
criteria for, 50–51
defined, 34
simplicity and, 51–52
external consistency, 228
eyewitness testimony, 200

F

Facebook
  ads, 288, 288f
  appeal to popularity and, 158
  disguised sources example from, 104
  groupthink and, 70
  Hoax-Slayer.com and, 105
  political advertising, 297–98
  ProPublica and, 297–98
  Russian fake news and, 93
  Truth-O-Meter scale and, 174
face saving, 67
face swapping, 112, 112f
fact-checkers. See also Media Bias/Fact Check
  political advertising and, 293
  trustworthy, 105
  views of AAP and ACPeds, 100
FactCheck.org, 105
facts
  behind advertising, 284
  backfire effect and, 82
  nothing but, 123
  opinion contrasted with, 14, 131
  telling difference between opinion and, 131
fairness, 123–24
fake images
  Border Patrol agents, 110, 110f
  detecting, 111
  Guatemalan Caravan, 108, 108f
  Haiku Bird, 107, 107f
  history of, 106
  lion and zebra, 109–10, 109f
  McCain and bin Laden, 109, 109f
  obstacles to identifying, 106–7
  reasonable skepticism about, 107
  sexual slavery, 107–8, 107f
  Snopes.com debunking, 107–10, 107f, 108f, 109f, 110f
  technology and, 106
fake news
  availability error and, 9

bias and, 8–9, 13, 94, 105–6
checking your own bias and, 105–6
confirmation bias and, 8–9
contrary evidence denial and, 9
data collection and, 9–10
deepfakes, 112–14
defined, 7–8
democracy undermined by, 92–93
disguised sources, 104
ethics of sharing, 102
examples, 8
factories, 8
filter bubbles and, 10
Google and, 103–4
Harris, 95
hoaxes and, 94
homophily and, 9
within infosphere, 7–8
masterpiece, 95
opinion and, 94
partisan bias and, 13
Pizzagate incident, 93
polarization created by, 92
propaganda and, 94
psychological factors leading to, 8–10
questions to ask for revealing, 102–3
reading laterally to combat, 97–101
reasonable skepticism and, 96–97
Russian agents propagating, 93
satire and, 96
social media and, 8, 93–94
taxonomy of, 94–96
technology upholding, 10–11
telling real from, 96–106
Wikipedia and, 104–5
fallacies
  in advertising, 286
  appeal to emotion, 161–63, 165
  appeal to ignorance, 159–61, 165, 194
  appeal to person, 152–56, 165, 176
  appeal to popularity, 157–58, 165
  appeal to tradition, 158–59, 165
  begging the question, 166–67, 172
  categories of, 148–49
  composition, 150–51, 165
  decision-point, 169–70, 172
  defined, 148

division, 151–52, 165
equivocation, 157, 165
false dilemma, 168–69, 172
faulty analogy, 172, 173
gambler's fallacy, 206
genetic, 149–50, 165
hasty generalization fallacy, 172
irrelevant premises and, 148–65
poisoning well, 155–56
red herring, 163–64, 165
reminders about, 149
slippery slope, 170–72
straw man, 164–65, 176
tu quoque, 154
two wrongs make a right, 165–66
unacceptable premises and, 166–73
whataboutism, 154–55
fallacious appeal to authority
  celebrity and, 196
  defined, 190
  two forms of, 190–91
false
  conflicting claims and, 187
  expertise beliefs, 186
  illusion-of-truth effect and, 79–80
  premises, 40–42
  Truth-O-Meter scale and, 174
false consensus effect, 80
false dilemma fallacy
  conditional form of, 169
  defined, 172
  disjunctive form of, 169
  famous examples, 168–69
  headlines and, 169
Farid, Hany, 113–14
faulty analogy fallacy, 172, 173
filter bubbles, 10
Fox News, bias rating for, 140
freedom, 6
fruitful, 231–32

G

Gaetz, Matt, 295–96, 295f
gambler's fallacy, 206
genetic fallacy, 149–50, 165
geocentric model, 241–43
Gilovich, Thomas, 74
"Global Climate Change" (NASA), 252
global warming. See climate change

Goldwater, Barry, 292
Goleman, Daniel, 270
González, Elián, 110, 110f
Gonzalez, Emma, 296, 296f
Google
  appeal to popularity and, 158
  fake news and, 103–4
Graham, Lindsey, 109, 109f
greenhouse gas emissions, 251–52, 252f
groupthink
  Borg and, 69–70
  conformity and, 70
  critical thinking and, 69–73
  overcoming, 72–73
  prejudice and, 71
  racism from, 72
  social media and, 70
  subtypes, 71
  tribalism and, 71
Guatemalan Caravan fake image, 108, 108f
gut knowing, 18

H

Haiku Bird, 107, 107f
Harris, Cameron, 95
Harrison, Guy
  on Dunning-Kruger effect, 82
  on filter bubbles, 10
  on groupthink, 70
  on trolls, 51
hasty generalization
  defined, 78
  fallacy, 172
  sample size and, 47
Hawkins, John, 153
headlines
  false dilemma fallacy and, 169
  health news, 260–61, 261f, 262f
health news
  anecdotes and case studies, 264
  animal studies, 265
  depression and, 267–68
  getting science wrong in, 260–68
  headlines, 260–61, 261f, 262f
  hyping of, 261–63
  misunderstanding science in, 263–65
  nonintervention studies, 264–65
  single studies and, 263–64
  small studies and, 264

trustworthy sources in, 273
veracity of, 265–68, 266f, 267f
heliocentric model, 241–43
Hill, French, 293
hoaxes, 94
Hoax-Slayer.com, 105
homophily, 9
horns from phone use story, 260, 262–63, 263f
human activity theory
  of climate change, 256–59
  consensus among scientists on, 258
  criteria of adequacy and, 259
  evidence for, 256–57
  nonhuman causation and, 257–58
Huxley, Thomas Henry, 68
hypothesis
  acceptance or rejection of, 221, 223
  ad hoc, 234
  affirming or denying, 223–24
  affirming the consequent and, 223
  double-blind study and, 225
  implications derived for testing, 222
  modus tollens applied to, 222
  nonfalsifiable, 238
  nonintervention studies and, 226
  scientific method formulating, 221–22
  vitamin C theory and, 224–25
hypothetical syllogism, 44, 46

I

ID. *See* intelligent design
identification, in advertising, 290
ideology, science and, 218–19
ignorance, 80–81. *See also* appeal to ignorance fallacy
illusion-of-truth effect, 79–80
Immigration and Customs Enforcement, U.S. *See* anti-ICE ad
indicator words, arguments and, 34–35
inductive argument
  analogical induction, 48–49
  cogent, 42
  conclusion and, 39

deductive argument compared with, 42
enumerative induction, 47–48
examples, 39–40
hypothesis and, 221–22
inference to best explanation, 49–51
opinion polls as, 268–69
patterns, 46–50
premises, 39
strong and weak, 39
true versus false premises and, 42
inference, 32
inference to best explanation
  conservatism and, 234–37
  constructive perception and, 232–33
  criteria for, 50–51
  criteria of adequacy and, 229–37
  everyday use of, 227
  fruitfulness and, 231–32
  as inductive argument, 49–51
  objectivity and, 237
  rules for applying, 237
  scientific theories and, 227
  scope and, 232–33
  simplicity and, 51–52, 233–34
  testability and, 229–31
inferiorization, 72
information
  defined, 4–5
  into knowledge, 4–7
infosphere. *See also specific topics*
  competing narratives of, 7
  fake news within, 7–8
  hazards of, 7–11
  promises broken in, 4
innuendo
  persuasion and, 175
  stereotyping and, 176
innumeracy, probability and, 205–8
intelligent design (ID), 248
Intergovernmental Panel on Climate Change (IPCC), 250–52
internal consistency, 228
internet advertising
  below surface of, 286
  display ads, 288
  how it works, 287
  native ads, 288–89, 289f, 290f
  paid search ads, 287–88, 287f
  social media ads, 288, 288f
  Srinivasan on, 287
  types of, 287–88

intuition, 18
invalid argument
   affirming the consequent, 45, 46
   deductive, 38–39
   denying the antecedent, 45, 46
IPCC. *See* Intergovernmental Panel on Climate Change
irrelevant premises
   appeal to emotion fallacy, 161–63, 165
   appeal to ignorance fallacy, 159–61, 165
   appeal to person fallacy, 152–56
   appeal to popularity fallacy, 157–58, 165
   appeal to tradition fallacy, 158–59, 165
   composition fallacy, 150–51, 165
   defined, 148–49
   division fallacy, 151–52, 165
   equivocation fallacy, 157, 165
   fallacies with, 149–66
   genetic fallacy, 149–50, 165
   red herring fallacy, 163–64, 165
   straw man fallacy, 164–65
   two wrongs make a right fallacy, 165–66

J

Johnson, Lyndon B., 292
journalism
   advocacy, 129–30
   ethics of, 122
   objectivity in, 122–23

K

Kahneman, Daniel, 79
Kessler, Glenn, 293
Kitcher, Philip, 248
Klaidman, Stephen
   on accuracy, 122
   on completeness, 122
   on fairness, 123–24
   on objectivity, 123
knowledge
   defined, 5
   information turned into, 4–7
   science and, 219
Kruger. *See* Dunning-Kruger effect
Krugman, Paul, 128–29

Kullberg, Kelly Monroe, 104

L

Lawrence, Jennifer, 112, 112*f*
liberal
   bias, 130, 132–34
   intolerance and, 177
Liberal Speak (news/opinion website), 140
lies
   autonomy and, 102
   fake news and, 94
   truth compared with, 94
Like War (Singer & Brooking)
   on bots, 11
   on Dixson, 10–11
   on homophily, 9
line-drawing fallacy. *See* decision-point fallacy
lion and zebra fake image, 109–10, 109*f*
Loftus, Elizabeth F., 200
logic, 5, 38

M

Manchin, Joe, 294–95, 294*f*
Mara Salvatrucha (MS-13), 293
margin of error, 271–72
Matthews, Chris, 153
MBFC. *See* Media Bias/Fact Check
McCain, John
   fake image and, 109, 109*f*
   innuendo used against, 175
McManus, John
   on advertising, 137
   on conflicting interests, 135
   on objectivity, 123
McSally, Martha, 295, 295*f*
mean, 272
media. *See also specific topics*
   illiteracy, 16–19
   literacy, 7
Media Bias/Fact Check (MBFC)
   information selection and, 124
   political bias scale of, 138
   sources evaluated by, 137–40
   website of, 105
median, 272
Medicare lie ad, 295, 295*f*
medicine. *See* health news

memory
   accuracy of, 198
   eyewitness testimony and, 200
mental obstacles
   availability error, 77–78
   confirmation bias, 74–76
   contrary evidence denial, 73–74
   to critical thinking, 73–78
   evidence and, 73
   motivated reasoning, 76–77
mere exposure effect
   defined, 79
   Kahneman on, 79
   on social media, 78–79
misinformation, psychological factors leading to, 8–9
misleading comparisons, in advertising, 290–91
mode, 272
modus ponens. *See* affirming the antecedent
modus tollens. *See* denying the consequent
motivated reasoning
   advertising as, 284
   backfire effect and, 82
   as confirmation bias, 76
   defeating, 77
   defined, 76
   as mental obstacle, 76–77
   science and, 219
   social media and, 76–77
MS-13. *See* Mara Salvatrucha

N

NASA. *See* National Aeronautics and Space Administration
National Academy of Sciences, 256–57
National Aeronautics and Space Administration (NASA), 252, 254
native advertisement
   on internet, 288–89, 289*f*, 290*f*
   students and, 16–17, 17*f*
natural cycle theory
   of climate change, 253–55, 258
   criteria of adequacy and, 258
   evidence for, 253–54
   recent temperature surge and, 254–55
natural selection, 244
Navarro, Peter, 128

New York Post, bias rating for, 139
New York Times, bias rating for, 138
Nichols, Tom
  on confirmation bias, 75
  on Dunning-Kruger effect, 81
  on expertise, 81–82, 195
Nisbet, Matthew C., 249–50
nonexperts
  appeal to ignorance fallacy and, 194
  experts and, 187–91
nonfalsifiable hypotheses, 238
nonintervention studies
  methodology, 226
  problems with, 264–65
Novella, Steven, 82

O

Obama, Barack
  deepfake of, 112, 112*f*
  reality and, 133
objectivity
  Beauchamp and Klaidman on, 123
  bias and, 122–27
  defined, 124
  fairness and, 123–24
  in journalism, 122–23
  McManus on, 123
  scientific theory and, 237
observational study. *See* nonintervention studies
obstacles. *See also* mental obstacles
  to critical thinking, 65–82
  fake images, 106–7
Ocasio-Cortez, Alexandria, 296, 296*f*
Oliver, John, 260–61
online. *See also* social media
  argument, 41
  motivated reasoning, 76
On the Origin of Species (Darwin), 244
opinion
  advocacy journalism and, 129–30
  analysis compared with, 128
  bias and, 127–30
  fact contrasted with, 14, 131
  fake news and, 94
  Krugman example, 128–29
  telling difference between fact and, 131
  unsupported, 55

opinion polls
  bias, 270
  confidence level, 271–72
  enumerative induction and, 47, 268–69
  as inductive arguments, 268–69
  margin of error, 271–72
  mean, median, and mode, 272
  questions going wrong, 270
  restricted choices in, 270
  sampling in, 269–71
  scientific, 268–72
  self-selecting sample, 269–70
Otto, Shawn, 216–17

P

paid search ads, 287–88, 287*f*
pandering, 135–36
parallax, 243
pareidolia, 199
Park, Robert L., 220
Parscale, Brad, 297
partisan bias
  extremism encouraged by, 13–14
  liberal and conservative, 130, 132–34
  as racism, 13
  Schiffer on, 132–33, 135
  Taub on, 13
passion, 68–69
"Peace, Little Girl" ad, 292, 292*f*
peer pressure, 71
peer review, bypassing, 220
perceptual impairment, 197–98
personal attack, 154
personal experience
  causal confusions influencing, 199–205
  coincidence and, 201–2
  constructive mental tendency altering, 198
  defined, 196
  expectation and, 198–99
  experts and, 196–205
  eyewitness testimony and, 200
  memory and, 198
  pareidolia impacting, 199
  perceptual impairment and, 197–98
  problems related to, 197–205
  reason to doubt, 197

relevant factor misidentification and, 199–200
persuasion
  appeal to emotion fallacy and, 162
  argument versus, 37
  dysphemisms and, 175–76
  euphemisms and, 175–76
  innuendo and, 175
  machinations of, 37
  rhetorical definitions, 179
  ridicule and, 178–79
  stereotyping and, 176, 178
Pew Research Center test, 131
Pizzagate incident, 93
poisoning well fallacy, 155–56
political advertising
  challenges of, 292
  doctoring of video and, 296, 296*f*
  Facebook, 297–98
  fact-checkers and, 293
  false or misleading messages in, 293–95
  historical background of, 292, 292*f*
  Kessler on, 293
  Medicare lie ad, 295, 295*f*
  misrepresentation in, 295–96, 295*f*
  "Peace, Little Girl" ad, 292, 292*f*
  ProPublica and, 297–98
  spliced videos and, 296, 296*f*
  video manipulation in, 295–96
  voting record ad, 294–95, 294*f*
  "We Must Enforce the Law" ad, 293–94, 293*f*
politicians, post-truth employed by, 12
Politico, bias rating for, 139
politics, science and, 219
PolitiFact.com
  as trustworthy, 105
  Truth-O-Meter scale and, 174
population studies. *See* nonintervention studies
post hoc, ergo propter hoc (after that, therefore because of that), 202–4
post-truth
  defined, 12
  epistemology and, 14–15
  partisan bias and, 13–14
  politicians employing, 12
  truthiness and, 12
Potter, W. James, 125

prejudice, 71. *See also* racial profiling; racism; stereotype
premises. *See also* irrelevant premises; unacceptable premises
  arguments revealing, 32
  begging the question fallacy and, 166–67
  deductive argument, 38–39
  defined, 31
  discrimination example, 53–54
  dissection tips for, 36–37
  equivocation fallacy and, 157
  finding long argument, 53
  implicit, 36
  indicator words and, 34–35
  inductive argument, 39
  torture example, 55–56
  true versus false, 40–42
probability
  calculating, 206–8
  coincidence and, 206
  gambler's fallacy and, 206
  innumeracy and, 205–8
ProCon.org
  bias rating, 139
  as perspectives comparison site, 101
propaganda
  defined, 148
  fake news and, 94
ProPublica, 297–98
Ptolemy. *See* Copernicus versus Ptolemy example

R

racial profiling, 55–56
racism
  from groupthink, 72
  partisan bias as, 13
  racial insensitivity compared with, 72
  tribalism and, 71
random sampling, 269, 271
Ravel, Ann, 297
reading laterally
  AAP and, 98–100, 98f
  ACPeds and, 98–99, 99f, 100
  AllSides.com and, 101
  deepfakes and, 114
  defined, 97
  fake news combated by, 97–101
  results of, 101

vertical reading versus, 97–98
Real Clear Politics, bias rating for, 139
reality, 132–33
reasonable skepticism
  advertising and, 285–86
  fake images and, 107
  fake news and, 96–97
reasons. *See also* motivated reasoning
  arguments and, 31–37
  belief and, 5
  circular reasoning, 15
  claims and, 29–30, 96–97
  inference and, 32
  statement and, 31
red herring fallacy, 163–64, 165
reductio ad absurdum (reduction to absurdity), 44–45
relativity theory, 231–32
relevant factor misidentification, 199–200
reliability, hierarchy of, 207
religion, 247–49
replication, 225
Republican
  partisan bias and, 13–14
  stereotyping of, 177–78
retrograde motion, 242–43
Reuters, bias rating for, 139
rhetoric
  defined, 149
  dysphemisms and, 175–76
  euphemisms, 175–76
  innuendo and, 175
  persuaders and, 173–79
  ridicule and, 178–79
  stereotyping and, 176, 178
  Truth-O-Meter scale measuring, 174
rhetorical definitions, 179
ridicule, 178–79
Russell, Bertrand
  on belief, 189
  on opinion, 68

S

sample
  confidence level and, 271–72
  enumerative induction and, 47–48, 272
  margin of error and, 271–72
  opinion polls and, 269–71

random, 269, 271
  self-selecting, 269–70
satire, fake news and, 96
scare tactics, 162
Schiffer, Adam J.
  on commercial bias, 135
  on partisan bias, 132–33, 135
  on reality, 132–33
  on skewed focus, 136–37
school shooting example, 126
science
  anecdotal evidence and, 220
  anecdotes and, 264
  animal studies, 265
  case studies, 264
  chocolate during pregnancy story, 261, 261f, 262
  consilience in, 217
  depression and, 267–68
  detection limits and, 220
  double-blind study and, 263
  headlines, misleading, 260–61, 261f, 262f
  health news veracity, 265–68, 266f, 267f
  horns from phone use story, 260, 262–63, 263f
  hyping, 261–63, 263f
  ideology and, 218–19
  media mistakes, 260–68
  misunderstanding, 263–65
  motivated reasoning and, 219
  natural law and, 220
  nonintervention studies, 264–65
  opinion polls and, 268–72
  as political, 219
  replication, 263–64
  revolution in, 216–17
  as self correcting, 218
  single studies, 263–64
  small studies, 264
  technology and, 219
  trustworthy sources in, 273
  warning signs of bogus, 220
  what it is, 217–18
  what it is not, 218–19
scientific method
  double-blind study, 225
  hypothesis acceptance or rejection, 221, 223
  hypothesis formulation, 221–22
  implications or consequences derived in, 221, 222
  modus tollens applied to, 222
  nonintervention studies and, 226

scientific method (*continued*)
　problem or question posed in, 221
　replication and, 225
　steps, 221–23
　testing and, 221, 223
　vitamin C theory and, 224–25
scientific theories
　ad hoc hypothesis and, 234
　climate change example, 249–59
　conservatism and, 234–37
　consistency and, 228
　conspiracy of scientists theory, 255–56, 258
　conspiracy theories and, 238
　constructive perception and, 232–33
　Copernicus versus Ptolemy example, 241–43
　criteria, 228–37
　criteria of adequacy and, 229–37
　evolution versus creationism example, 243–49
　fruitfulness and, 231–32
　human activity theory, 256–59
　inference to best explanation and, 227
　judging, 226–38
　natural cycle theory, 253–55, 258
　objectivity and, 237
　scope and, 232–33
　simplicity and, 233–34
　sun warming theory, 255, 258
　telling good from bad, 238–59
　testability and, 229–31
　TEST formula for, 239–41
scope, 232–33
self-interested thinking
　claims undermined by, 67
　consequences of, 67
　critical thinking and, 66–69
　emotion and, 69
　face saving in, 67
　forms of, 67
　guidelines countering, 68
　overcoming, 67–68
　passion and, 68–69
　risk of, 66–67
self-selecting sample, 269–70
sensationalism, 136
sexual slavery fake image, 107–8, 107*f*
Shapiro, Ben, 22*f*
Silver, Nate, 195
simplicity

ad hoc hypothesis and, 234
conspiracy theories and, 51–52, 238
Copernican theory, 242–43
criteria of adequacy and, 233–34
defined, 51
evolution versus creationism example and, 246
explanation and, 51–52
inference to best explanation and, 51–52, 233–34
Singer, P. W.
　on bots, 11
　on Dixson, 10–11
　on homophily, 9
Sinnott-Armstrong, Walter, 30
Skewed (Atkins), 129–30
skewed focus, 136–37
slippery slope fallacy, 170–72
slogans, 290
Snopes.com
　disguised, hateful sources and, 104
　as fake image debunker, 107–10, 107*f*, 108*f*, 109*f*, 110*f*
　as trustworthy fact-checker, 105
social media. *See also* Facebook; Twitter
　ads, 288, 288*f*
　appeal to popularity and, 158
　brain on, 78–82
　cognitive biases prevalent on, 78–82
　data collection by, 9–10
　Dunning-Kruger effect and, 80–82
　fake news and, 8, 93–94
　false consensus effect on, 80
　filters and, 10
　groupthink and, 70
　health news veracity on, 265–68, 266*f*, 267*f*
　illusion-of-truth effect and, 79–80
　mere exposure effect on, 78–79
　motivated reasoning and, 76–77
　Russian fake news and, 93
　technology and, 10
sock puppet, 7
Socrates, 6
sources
　accuracy of, 124–25
　disguised, 104, 124–25
　health news trustworthy, 273
　left leaning, 138–39, 140

MBFC evaluation of, 137–40
reliability, hierarchy of, and, 207
right leaning, 139–40
science trustworthy, 273
selection of, 124–25
spliced videos, 296, 296*f*
Srinivasan, Dina, 287
Star Trek: The Next Generation (television series), 69–70
statement
　defined, 29
　premises and, 31
　reasons and, 31
stereotype
　defined, 71
　of Democrat, 176–77
　of Republican, 177–78
　straw man fallacy and, 176
Stoneman, Marjory, 153
straw man fallacy
　argument and, 164–65
　defined, 164, 165
　stereotyping and, 176
strong inductive argument, 39
students
　ACPeds and, 101
　media illiteracy of, 15–19
　native advertisement and, 16–17, 17*f*
　nuclear birth defects photo and, 17, 17*f*
Sunsea case example, 127
sun warming theory, 255, 258

T

Talking Points Memo (TMP), 138
Taub, Amanda, 13
technology
　belief influenced by, 10–11
　bots, 11
　deepfakes driven by, 112–13
　fake images and, 106
　fake news upheld by, 10–11
　filter bubbles, 10
　revolution in, 216–17
　science and, 219
testability, 229–31
TEST formula
　climate change example, 249–59
　Copernicus versus Ptolemy example, 241–43
　criteria of adequacy used in, 241

evidence assessment, 239
evolution versus creationism example, 243–49
for scientific theories, 239–41
theory statement and consistency check, 239
testing
double-blind study and, 225
scientific method and, 221, 223
Think Before You Like (Harrison), 10
TMP. *See* Talking Points Memo
torture example, 55–56
tribalism, 71
trolls, arguing with, 51
Trump, Donald
appeal to person fallacy and, 152f, 153f, 155f
Dixson and, 10–11
Facebook political advertising and, 297
Gaetz video and, 295–96, 295f
Harris and, 95
Krugman on, 128–29
Manchin and, 294–95, 294f
red herring used by, 163–64
ridicule of, 178
Russian fake news and, 93
spliced video misrepresenting, 296
Truth-O-Meter scale and, 174
trust
in background information, 187–88
fact-checkers and, 105
health news and, 273
reliability, hierarchy of, and, 207
truth. *See also* post-truth
appeal to popularity and, 158
conflicting claims and, 187
deductive argument and, 38
demagoguery and, 148
elements of, 122
evidence and, 73

illusion-of-truth effect, 79–80
lies compared with, 94
premises and, 40–42
reasonable skepticism about, 96–97
reliability, hierarchy of, and, 207
science and, 219
self-interested thinking undermining, 67
tribalism and, 71
truthiness, 12
Truth-O-Meter scale, 174
TruthOrFiction.com, 105
Tucker, Clarke, 293–94, 293f
tu quoque fallacy, 154
turned tables test, 134
Twain, Mark, 178
Twitter
ads, 288, 288f
appeal to popularity and, 158
argument and, 41
groupthink and, 70
screen grabs from, 61f, 62f
two wrongs make a right fallacy, 165–66

U

unacceptable premises
begging the question fallacy, 166–67, 172
decision-point fallacy, 169–70, 172
defined, 148–49
fallacies, 166–73
false dilemma fallacy, 168–69, 172
faulty analogy fallacy, 172, 173
hasty generalization fallacy, 172
slippery slope fallacy, 170–72

United Nations Population Fund (UNFPA), 108
United Press International (UPI), 139
USA Today, bias rating for, 138

V

vaccine, 204
valid argument
affirming the antecedent, 43, 46
deductive, 37–38
denying the consequent, 43–44, 46
disjunctive syllogism, 46
hypothetical syllogism, 44, 46
reductio ad absurdum, 44–45
video
Gaetz video, 295–96, 295f
political advertising manipulation of, 295–96
spliced, 296, 296f
vitamin C theory, 224–25
voting record ad, 294–95, 294f

W

weak inductive argument, 39
weasel words, 291
"We Must Enforce the Law" ad, 293–94, 293f
whataboutism fallacy, 154–55
Wikipedia, 104–5
Wilson, Edward O., 217
Woods, James, 24f
worldview, 5. *See also* belief

Z

Zuckerberg, Mark, 112, 113f